AF690225

Taxcafe.co.uk Tax Guides

How to Save Inheritance Tax

By Carl Bayley BSc FCA

Important Legal Notices:

Published by:
Taxcafe UK Limited
2.4 West Bridge Mill
Kirkcaldy KY1 1TE

Email address: team@taxcafe.co.uk

Twenty-second Edition, May 2026

ISBN 978-1-917392-12-9

Copyright
Copyright © Carl Bayley 2003-2026. All rights reserved.

All rights reserved. No part of this publication may be reproduced, stored in a retrieval system, or transmitted in any form or by any means electronic, mechanical, photocopying, recording or otherwise, without the prior permission in writing of Taxcafe UK Ltd, except in accordance with the provisions of the Copyright, Designs and Patents Act 1988 or under the terms of a licence issued by the Copyright Licensing Agency.

Warning: Any unauthorised reproduction or transmission of any part of this tax guide may result in criminal prosecution and a civil claim for damages.

Trademarks
Taxcafe® is a registered trademark of Taxcafe UK Limited. All other trademarks, names and logos in this tax guide may be trademarks of their respective owners.

Disclaimer
Before reading or relying on the content of this tax guide, please read the disclaimer.

Disclaimer

This guide is intended as general guidance only and does NOT constitute accountancy, tax, investment or other professional advice.

1. The author and Taxcafe UK Limited make no representations or warranties with respect to the accuracy or completeness of this publication and cannot accept any responsibility or liability for any loss or risk, personal or otherwise, which may arise, directly or indirectly, from reliance on information contained in this publication.

2. Please note that tax legislation, the law and practices of Government and regulatory authorities (e.g. HM Revenue & Customs) are constantly changing. We therefore recommend that for accountancy, tax, investment or other professional advice, you consult a suitably qualified accountant, tax adviser, financial adviser, or other professional adviser.

3. Please also note that your personal circumstances may vary from the general examples provided in this guide and your professional adviser will be able to provide specific advice based on your personal circumstances.

4. This guide covers UK taxation only and any references to 'tax' or 'taxation', unless the contrary is expressly stated, refer to UK taxation only. Please note that references to the 'UK' do not include the Channel Islands or the Isle of Man. Foreign tax implications are beyond the scope of this guide.

5. While, in an effort to be helpful, this tax guide may refer to general guidance on matters other than UK taxation, Taxcafe UK Limited and the author are not expert in these matters and do not accept any responsibility or liability for loss which may arise from reliance on such information contained in this guide.

6. All persons described in the examples in this guide are entirely fictional. Any similarities to actual persons, living or dead, or to fictional characters created by any other author, are entirely coincidental.

7. The views expressed in this publication are the author's own personal views and do not necessarily reflect the views of any organisation he may represent.

About the Author

Carl Bayley is the author of over twenty 'Plain English' tax guides designed specifically for the layperson and the non-specialist. His aim is to help families, landlords, and other business owners understand the taxes they face and make savings through sensible planning and by having the confidence to know what they can claim. Carl's speciality is his ability to take the weird, complex world of taxation and set it out in the kind of clear, straightforward language taxpayers can understand. As he often says, "My job is to translate 'tax' into English."

Carl enjoys his role as a tax author, as he explains, "Writing these guides gives me the opportunity to use the skills and knowledge learned over more than forty years in the tax profession for the benefit of a wider audience. The most satisfying part of my success as an author is the chance to give the average person the same standard of information as the 'big guys' at a price everyone can afford."

He takes the same approach when speaking on taxation, a role he frequently undertakes with great enthusiasm, including his highly acclaimed annual 'Budget Breakfast' for the Institute of Chartered Accountants. In addition to being a recognised author and speaker, Carl has spoken on taxation on radio and television, including the BBC's 'It's Your Money' programme and BBC Radio 2's Jeremy Vine Show.

Beginning his career as a Chartered Accountant in 1983 with one of the 'Big 4' accountancy firms, Carl qualified as a double prize-winner then began specialising in taxation. He worked for several major international firms until beginning the new millennium by launching his own practice, through which he provided advice on a wide variety of taxation issues, especially property taxation, inheritance tax, and tax planning for small and medium-sized businesses, for twenty years, before deciding to focus exclusively on his favourite role as author and presenter.

Carl is a former Chairman of the Tax Faculty of the Institute of Chartered Accountants in England and Wales, and was a member of the institute's governing Council between 2003 and 2023. He is also a former President of ICAEW Scotland and member of the ICAEW Board. He co-organised the annual Practical Tax Conference from 2002 to 2019.

Aside from his tax books, Carl is an avid creative writer. He published his third novel, *Journey of Souls*, in April 2026 (see *bayleytheauthor.com* for more information). When he isn't working, Carl takes on the equally taxing challenges of hill walking and horse riding: his Munro tally is 106 and, while he remains, at best, an intermediate level rider, his progress in the saddle is cantering along nicely. Carl lives in the Scottish Borders, where he enjoys spending time with his partner, Linda.

Dedication and Thanks

At its heart, this book is, of course, about relationships. It seems appropriate, therefore, for me to dedicate it to those who represent the most important relationships in my life.

For the Past,
To Diana, the memory of your love warms me still. Thank you for bringing me into the light and making it all possible. To Arthur, your wise words still come back to guide me; and to my loving grandmothers, Doris and Winifred. Between you, you left me with nothing I could spend, but everything I need.

To Sarah, still with us forever in our hearts, it was truly a privilege to know you. Also, to my beloved friends: Mac, William, Edward, Rusty, Dawson, Morgan, and the world's oldest puppy, Ollie: always in our hearts. Thank you for all those happy miles, I still miss you all.

For the Present,
To the lovely lady Linda, bless you, my princess, I'm so proud of you. Thank you for bringing the sunshine back into my life, for opening my ears, and putting the song back into my heart. I owe you more than you will ever know.

For the Future,
To James, a true twenty-first century gentleman and one of the nicest guys I have ever met. To Robert, the 'chip off the old block', who is both cursed and blessed to have inherited a lot of my character; luckily for him, there is a lot of his mother in him too! I am so very proud of you both, and I can only hope I, in turn, will leave each of you with everything you need.

Thanks are due to:

The Taxcafe team, past and present, especially Gordon: for their help in making these books more successful than I could ever have dreamed; my old friend and mentor, Peter Rayney: for his inspiration and for showing me tax and humour can mix; Rebecca, Paul, and David: for taking me into the fold at the Tax Faculty and their fantastic support at our Practical Tax Conference over many years; Gregor: for the 'brain-storming' sessions and those extraordinary ideas that spring from his lateral thinking; Jane Evans: for some useful practical insights; Jonathan Woodwards and Alan Sacks: for their helpful constructive comments.

And last, but far from least, thanks to Nick for giving me the push!

C.B., Roxburghshire, May 2026

Contents

Chapter 1. Introduction **1**
1.1 A Personal Note 1
1.2 There Are Two Certainties in Life 2
1.3 Guide Overview 4
1.4 Terminology, Definitions, and Scope 6
1.5 Why Worry? 8
1.6 A Guide to Effective Inheritance Tax Planning 9

Chapter 2. Inheritance Tax Principles **11**
2.1 Transfers of Value 11
2.2 Who Is Liable for Inheritance Tax? 12
2.3 Who Actually Pays the Tax? 13
2.4 How Much Tax Is Payable? 14
2.5 What Is Your Estate? 14
2.6 The Basic Calculation on Death 15
2.7 Making the Payment 16
2.8 Grossing Up 20
2.9 Collection of Tax 21
2.10 Loans and Other Liabilities 22
2.11 Granting and Waiving Loans 26
2.12 Quick Succession Relief 26
2.13 Simultaneous Deaths 27

Chapter 3. The Main Exemptions **28**
3.1 What Is an Exemption? 28
3.2 The Nil Rate Band (NRB) 28
3.3 The Spouse Exemption 30
3.4 The Residence Nil Rate Band (RNRB) 34
3.5 Gifts to Charities & Other Exempt Bodies 37
3.6 Charitable Legacies 37
3.7 Other Exemptions 40

Chapter 4. Lifetime Transfers **41**
4.1 Inheritance Tax on Lifetime Transfers 41
4.2 Chargeable Lifetime Transfers 41
4.3 Potentially Exempt Transfers (PETs) 43
4.4 Problems with PETs 44
4.5 Death within Seven Years 45
4.6 Relief for Reduction in Value 50
4.7 Timing and Evidence 51
4.8 Gifts with Reservation 52
4.9 Why Not Just Give It All Away? 55

Chapter 5. Lifetime Exemptions **56**
5.1 Absolute Exemption 56
5.2 The Annual and Small Gifts Exemptions 56
5.3 Gifts in Consideration of Marriage 57
5.4 Maintenance of Family 58
5.5 Normal Expenditure Out of Income 59

5.6 Other Exempt Transfers 62

Chapter 6. Inheritance Tax Planning for Married Persons **63**
6.1 Scope of this Chapter 63
6.2 The Transferable Nil Rate Band (TNRB) & Residence Nil Rate Band (RNRB) 63
6.3 Using the Residence Nil Rate Band on First Death 64
6.4 Nil Rate Band Transfers in Practice 66
6.5 Remarriage 67
6.6 Separation & Divorce 68
6.7 Inheritance Tax Planning for Married Couples 69
6.8 The Second Time Around 73
6.9 Using the Transferable Nil Rate Band 78
6.10 Will Trusts 80
6.11 The Widow's Loan Scheme 80
6.12 The Spouse Bridge 82
6.13 The Family Debt Scheme 84

Chapter 7. The Tax Benefits of Business Property **85**
7.1 Introduction 85
7.2 How Useful Is Business Property Relief? 86
7.3 Qualifying Businesses 87
7.4 Property Investment or Letting Businesses 88
7.5 Businesses Exploiting Land (and Buildings) 90
7.6 What Does Wholly or Mainly Mean in Practice? 93
7.7 Relevant Business Property 94
7.8 The 100% Relief Allowance (HPRA) 97
7.9 Valuing a Business 101
7.10 Sole Traders and Partnerships 101
7.11 Business Property Relief for Company Shares 103
7.12 Financing a Business 106
7.13 Deducting Liabilities: Unincorporated Businesses 109
7.14 Deduction of Liabilities for Company Owners 110
7.15 Borrowing to Invest in Your Business 112
7.16 Multiple Transfers 112
7.17 The Minimum Holding Period 113
7.18 Replacement Business Property 114
7.19 Extra Rules for Lifetime Transfers 114
7.20 How to Preserve Business Property Relief 116
7.21 Maximising Business Property Relief 120
7.22 Director's Loan Accounts 122
7.23 Sheltering Investments with Business Property Relief 123
7.24 Changing the Business to Save Inheritance Tax 124
7.25 Smaller Shareholdings 125
7.26 AIM Shares 125
7.27 Agricultural Property Relief (APR) 127
7.28 Protecting the Family Farm 129
7.29 Farmhouses as Inheritance Tax Shelters 136
7.30 Planning for Larger Business Owners 137
7.31 Restoring Unlimited 100% Relief 140

7.32 The Safety Net 141
7.33 Make Hay While the Sun Shines 141
7.34 Investment Syndicates 142

Chapter 8. Inheritance Tax Planning with Trusts 143
8.1 What Is a Trust? 143
8.2 What Types of Trust Are There? 143
8.3 Transfers into Trust 146
8.4 Charitable Trusts 147
8.5 Bare Trusts 147
8.6 Bereaved Minors' Trusts 147
8.7 Old Interest in Possession Trusts 148
8.8 Disabled Trusts 149
8.9 Immediate Post-Death Interests 149
8.10 Transitional Serial Interests 150
8.11 18 to 25 Trusts 150
8.12 Relevant Property Trusts 151
8.13 End of Trust Interests within Beneficiary's Estate 151
8.14 The Relevant Property Regime 152
8.15 Ten-Year Anniversary Charges 153
8.16 Exit Charges 155
8.17 Income Tax for Trusts 157
8.18 Stamp Taxes for Trusts 158

Chapter 9. More Advanced Planning with Trusts 159
9.1 The Relevant Property Trust Shelter 159
9.2 How Useful Is the Relevant Property Trust Shelter? 163
9.3 How to Avoid Anniversary and Exit Charges 164
9.4 How to Avoid Inheritance Tax *and* Capital Gains Tax at the Same Time 164
9.5 Investment Property Trusts 166
9.6 Passing Assets Tax-Free to Adult Children and Other Beneficiaries 168
9.7 Passing Assets Tax-Free to Minor Children 169
9.8 Putting Business Property into Trust 170
9.9 Discounted Gift Trusts 174
9.10 Loan Trusts 175

Chapter 10. Inherited Pension Funds 176
10.1 Paradise Lost 176
10.2 Pensions and Inheritance Tax (From April 2027) 177
10.3 Exemptions from Inheritance Tax 182
10.4 Who Inherits the Pension? 183
10.5 What Do They Inherit? 184
10.6 Death Benefits and Income Tax 185
10.7 The Lump Sum and Death Benefit Allowance (LSDBA) 187
10.8 Payments Subject to Income Tax 190
10.9 Succession Planning with Pensions 193
10.10 The Added Benefits of Inherited Drawdown 199
10.11 Investment Growth 203
10.12 Tactics and Limitations 204
10.13 Pensions for Company Owners 213

10.14	Bypass Trusts	216
10.15	Deaths Before 6th April 2027	217
Chapter 11. Practical Aspects of Inheritance Tax Planning		**219**
11.1	The Bigger Picture	219
11.2	Related Property	220
11.3	Jointly Held Property	221
11.4	Mortgages	224
11.5	Residential Care Fees	224
11.6	Legal Domicile	225
11.7	Wills, Intestacy, and Statutory Rights	225
11.8	Life Insurance	227
11.9	Lottery Syndicates	229
11.10	Minor Problems	229
11.11	Anti-Avoidance Measures	231
11.12	The Pre-Owned Assets Charge	232
11.13	Foreign Issues	234
Chapter 12. Interaction with Capital Gains Tax		**235**
12.1	A Quick Capital Gains Tax Update	235
12.2	The Uplift on Death	235
12.3	The Capital Gains Tax vs Inheritance Tax Dilemma	236
12.4	Gifts of Business Assets	236
12.5	Business Property Relief (BPR) and Business Asset Disposal Relief (BADR)	238
12.6	Transfers to Spouses or Civil Partners	246
12.7	Capital Gains Tax and the Family Home	247
12.8	Capital Gains Tax and Gifts with Reservation	248
12.9	Exempt Transfers	249
12.10	Other Assets	250
12.11	Capital Gains Tax and Trusts	251
Chapter 13. The Family Home		**253**
13.1	When Our Main Asset Becomes Our Main Liability	253
13.2	Move Out Then Give It Away	255
13.3	Sell Up or Re-mortgage	255
13.4	Sale at Market Value	256
13.5	The Widow's Loan Scheme & The Family Home	256
13.6	Leave a Share to the Children	257
13.7	Leave a Share to a Discretionary Trust	259
13.8	The Full Consideration Method	259
13.9	Co-Ownership	259
13.10	Downsizing	260
13.11	The Residence Nil Rate Band and Gifts with Reservation	262
Chapter 14. Family Investment Companies		**266**
14.1	Introduction to Family Investment Companies	266
14.2	Shell Companies and Loan Accounts	266
14.3	Optional Extras	270
14.4	Growth Shares	271

14.5 Pick and Mix 273
14.6 More Optional Extras 274

Chapter 15. Other Advanced Inheritance Tax Planning 276
15.1 Business Buy Back 276
15.2 The Double Dip 277
15.3 Money Box Companies 279
15.4 Corporate Debt 279
15.5 Long-Term UK Residence and Emigration 280
15.6 Excluded Property 281

Chapter 16. The Inheritance Tax Planning Timetable 283
16.1 It's Never Too Early to Start 283
16.2 Marriage 283
16.3 Becoming a Parent 283
16.4 Adult Children 283
16.5 Your First Grandchild 284
16.6 Grandchild's Eighth Birthday 284
16.7 Middle Age 284
16.8 Retirement 284
16.9 Losing a Parent 285
16.10 Still Together After All These Years 285
16.11 Losing a Spouse 285
16.12 Remarriage 286
16.13 Life Expectancy Over Seven Years 286
16.14 Life Expectancy Three to Seven Years 286
16.15 Life Expectancy Two to Three Years 287
16.16 Loss of Capacity 287
16.17 Deathbed Planning 287

Chapter 17. Planning After Death 292
17.1 Deeds of Variation 292
17.2 Disclaimers 293
17.3 Transfers Out of Trusts within Two Years 293
17.4 Post-Mortem Relief 294

Appendices
A Connected Persons 295
B Abbreviations Used 296

Chapter 1

Introduction

1.1 A PERSONAL NOTE

I'll make no bones about it. I find the concept of taxing people for dying morally repugnant. So, I have an especially strong desire to help people save Inheritance Tax (referred to as IHT from now onwards).

To be honest, I have always found this a difficult subject to write about: not because of the undoubted technical complexities – as a tax author, I am well and truly accustomed to that. No, I find this particular tax difficult to write about from an emotional perspective, because it is, inevitably, largely about death. My first introduction to the topic, as a young accountancy student, came within weeks of my own mother's death and that, perhaps, may be why I have always found the subject somewhat distressing.

Nonetheless, as a professional tax writer, I have always tackled this subject to the best of my abilities and strived to give readers the quality of information and guidance they deserve, just as in all my guides. I am confident I have succeeded in this aim and I believe the guide you have here is as comprehensive and detailed as anyone could wish for.

But to help me, and I hope you too, deal with the emotional aspects of the subject, I have always tried to inject some humour into the topic. Sometimes, I have wondered if this humour is really appropriate and whether, perhaps, I should re-write the guide to reflect a more serious tone. I have considered this approach but, in the end, I still believe in trying to put a smile on people's faces (including my own), even when tackling such an emotive issue. So, the humour, such that it is, remains. If I offend anyone, I sincerely apologise, but I hope most readers will simply smile at my efforts.

When it comes to tax, I firmly believe no-one should ever pay more than their fair share. Taxpayers have every right to undertake sensible planning measures to legitimately reduce, or delay, their tax bills: especially to protect their family.

That's what this guide is all about. And, whatever form your family takes, be it a traditional spouse and children, or be it a collection of people connected only by the fact you want to take care of them, I fervently hope this guide helps you protect it.

1.2 THERE ARE TWO CERTAINTIES IN LIFE

Generally speaking, I find the oldest sayings are the truest. One old saying is, 'There are two certainties in life: Death and Taxes.' The point where these two great 'certainties' meet is IHT, and it is through the medium of this tax the Government will aim to get its final pound of flesh from you, just as you have departed this life.

Most people spend their lifetime trying to accumulate a reasonable amount of wealth, to take care of themselves in old age and then pass any remaining surplus to their children. Much of the Government's fiscal policy is aimed at encouraging this behaviour.

It is somewhat unfair then, that without careful planning and a great deal of pre-emptive action, many families will ultimately face a huge IHT bill. Unchecked, this tax bill will rob your family of a significant proportion of their rightful inheritance: up to 40% of it, in fact. Most people are absolutely appalled at this prospect, which, of course, is where IHT planning comes in!

IHT, as we know it today, arrived in 1986, the brainchild of Margaret Thatcher and her then Chancellor, Nigel Lawson. The tax is actually little more than a re-branding of its predecessor, Capital Transfer Tax, which, in turn, had replaced the earlier and rather more draconian Estate Duty that, in its day, had played a major part in turning many of Britain's stately homes into amusement parks!

It is quite ironic that IHT should have such a long lineage because it is, of course, usually one's descendants who will suffer its effects.

The principal difference between IHT and its predecessors is the fact there is a general exemption for most lifetime transfers to other individuals. This is part of the reason behind accusations the Labour Party once made to an old Conservative Government that they had allowed IHT to become a voluntary tax, paid only by the unwary, ill-advised and unprepared taxpayer, while wealthier taxpayers took expensive professional advice and avoided the tax.

Certainly, there was, and still is, an element of truth in this accusation. In recent years, however, it has become increasingly difficult to avoid this hated grave-robber's tax, with a host of measures introduced by Governments of all persuasions designed to block many of the popular methods used by families attempting to plan for the inevitable.

Help seemed to be at hand in 2007 when the Conservatives proposed a massive increase in the nil rate band exemption to £1m. Although this never materialised, it did at least prompt the then Labour Government into making nil rate bands transferable between spouses. Suddenly, overnight, it seemed almost every married couple, civil partnership, widow, widower and surviving civil partner had effectively doubled their nil rate band.

Since then, however, things have taken a turn for the worse: as it seems all our politicians are happy to break their promises when it comes to IHT. Alistair Darling kicked off the era of broken promises in 2009 when he announced the planned increase in the nil rate band set for the following year would not go ahead. Worse still, he went on to announce a five-year freeze in the nil rate band at its 2009 level of £325,000.

Soon afterwards, the Conservatives became the senior partner in a Coalition Government. Sadly, their promised increase in the nil rate band was swiftly shelved and Labour's freeze adopted in its place. Since then, the freeze has been extended numerous times, through several changes of Government, with the most recent extension to this seemingly endless ice age being made by current Chancellor, Rachel Reeves, in her November 2025 Budget, when she announced yet another additional year's freeze, bringing it to a total of ***22 years!***

Incredibly, we are now stuck with the 2009 nil rate band of just £325,000 until at least 2031. Not since 1946 has it remained the same for so long.

Inflation has already severely eroded the value of the nil rate band and its real value will reduce even further between now and 2031. This will undo all the benefit of the transferable nil rate band regime introduced in 2007 (and then some!) And those who are single or divorced never had that benefit anyway.

Make no mistake about it: the freeze in the nil rate band is a significant tax-raising measure. As the value of the band decreases in real terms, the Government's IHT take is steadily increasing.

But, as if that wasn't enough, to add to the agony of this 22-year ice age, we are facing some fundamental changes to the IHT regime that are likely to have a significant, and devastating, impact on many bereaved families.

Firstly, from April 2026, the previously unlimited exemptions for qualifying business and agricultural property have been capped at just £2.5m (that may sound a lot, but it often isn't when land and property are involved). We'll look at the impact of this horrendous threat to UK businesses, including farms, in Chapter 7.

Then, perhaps worst of all, pension fund death benefits are to be subject to IHT from April 2027, robbing many families of a large proportion of their loved one's hard-earned savings. We'll look at the implications of this diabolical measure in Chapter 10.

It is, without doubt, a time of enormous change for IHT. Nonetheless, despite fears to the contrary, many of the tax's fundamental principles remain unaltered, and what seems likely to remain true for the foreseeable future is the fact it is the moderately wealthy members of society who suffer the greatest proportionate burden.

The problem for many people in the middle wealth bracket is they face a fundamental dilemma. On the one hand they have, on paper, sufficient wealth to leave their family with a substantial tax burden. On the other hand, they do not really have a great deal of disposable income, despite leading reasonably modest lifestyles. This means the simple expedient of just giving all their surplus wealth away is, in practical terms, simply not an option.

This all too common 'asset rich/cash poor' situation many people find themselves in is exacerbated by increases in property values over recent decades, which have pushed more and more people into the IHT bracket. Despite a desperately convoluted attempt by George Osborne at deluding us into thinking he'd fulfilled his 2007 promise property values are still the number one cause of most people's IHT burden. (Whether this will remain the case once pension funds are fully exposed to IHT after April 2027 remains to be seen!)

As ever, there remain two effective ways to avoid IHT: die poor, or plan ahead. Most of us find the first option somewhat unpalatable and also quite difficult to achieve without a remarkable sense of timing!

In the past, planning ahead was seen as the prerogative of the very wealthiest members of society, leaving the moderately wealthy to pick up the bill. However, my aim in this guide is to help put an end to this situation. If the Government is still prepared to allow IHT to be even partly 'voluntary', albeit to a far lesser extent than previously, then why should ***anyone*** volunteer?

Early and careful planning is the key to reducing the eventual IHT burden on your family and you don't need to be a millionaire to do it. Or to ***need*** to do it either, for that matter! Besides which, a great many people are surprised to discover when they add up all their assets they are, in fact, millionaires anyway: on paper, at least.

While some tax can still be saved through last-minute planning, a great deal more unnecessary tax can be avoided by planning for death and taxes throughout your lifetime. Read on and I will show you how.

1.3 GUIDE OVERVIEW

In this opening chapter, we start by taking a brief look at some background issues important to an understanding of the rest of the guide, including giving consideration to the future of IHT and what it may mean for you and your family.

Following that, in Chapter 2, we will cover some of the basics, including how the tax is calculated and who pays it. All of this comes under the general heading of 'know your enemy', because it is important to understand what you're up against before you start to make plans to combat it.

We then move on, in Chapter 3, to look at the main exemptions available at any time, both during your lifetime and on death; as well as those only available on death.

Chapters 4 and 5 look at the area of lifetime transfers, including the additional exemptions available and how to maximise them.

The first five chapters prepare us for Chapter 6, which is devoted to IHT planning for married couples, widows, and widowers (including civil partners). The changes introduced in 2007 fundamentally altered the IHT planning landscape for married couples. In many cases, something that was the best advice before is now the very last thing you should do!

Married couples therefore need to consider everything contained in the rest of this guide in the context of the guidance in Chapter 6. The chapter also analyses the position facing widows and widowers, with guidance on crucial tax-saving action that needs to be taken by the recently bereaved. Even those who are currently single or divorced will benefit from Chapter 6, as it includes guidance on the potential IHT benefits of marriage.

Chapter 7 covers the important areas of business property relief and agricultural property relief, among the most valuable pieces of equipment in our IHT planning armoury. While the changes applying from April 2026 mean these reliefs no longer provide an unlimited shelter from the scourge of IHT, they remain highly beneficial, providing massive tax saving opportunities.

We move into the realm of trusts in Chapters 8 and 9, where we will see what powerful tools these vehicles can be in the battle against IHT.

In Chapter 10 we look at pension savings. Planned changes mean that, from April 2027, these will no longer escape IHT, but that is only part of the story, and we will see how pensions can still be used to pass wealth to your heirs, or even further down the generations, tax efficiently.

Chapter 11 builds further on this all-important broader view by reminding us there is a bigger picture than merely saving IHT, and here we widen our sights to take in other aspects of estate preservation. This is reinforced in Chapter 12 with a look at the interaction between IHT and Capital Gains Tax.

In Chapter 13, we look at passing on the family home. Here we will take a detailed look at some of the practical implications of the residence nil rate band, as well as some of the other planning techniques available to shelter the family home from the Government's most despised form of taxation.

Chapter 14 focuses on the powerful long-term planning strategy of family investment companies, which has the potential to save landlords, other investors, business owners, and farmers millions of pounds in IHT.

After that, in Chapter 15, we look at some other more advanced planning techniques, including perhaps the most drastic of all: emigration. This area of IHT planning has recently undergone some fundamental changes, and we will look at what these mean.

Chapter 16 provides a whole life timetable for IHT planning, which puts everything we have learned into context and also reassures us, while it's never too early to start planning, it's never too late either!

Chapter 17 covers the planning a bereaved family can still carry out even after someone has died. While this is not the ideal time for truly effective IHT planning, it is surprising how much can still be achieved if the deceased's family acts quickly.

This extensive guide, fully updated for the drastic changes introduced over the last few years, and those coming in the years ahead, as well as the latest planning ideas available today, has something of value for everyone, and provides an indispensable tool in the battle against the Government's most despicable form of taxation.

1.4 TERMINOLOGY, DEFINITIONS, AND SCOPE

For the purposes of this guide, any references to being 'married' or being a 'married couple' include being in a registered civil partnership; any reference to an individual's 'spouse' includes their civil partner where relevant; and any reference to 'husbands' or 'wives' includes civil partners. Similarly, any reference to 'widows' or 'widowers' includes surviving civil partners.

For the avoidance of doubt, I would, in particular, point out the spouse exemption covered in Section 3.3, and the planning issues covered in Chapter 6, apply equally to civil partners. However, it remains important to remember that, for tax purposes, a 'spouse' does not include an unmarried partner, and only includes a legally married spouse or legally registered civil partner.

For IHT purposes, your 'child' includes your natural child, adopted child, or step-child. The rather old-fashioned IHT legislation also specifies that it includes an illegitimate child (as if that wasn't obvious!) An adopted child must be your legally adopted child. A step-child must be the natural or adopted child of your spouse, as defined above. The child of an unmarried partner does not count as your child unless they are also your natural or legally adopted child (hence, for IHT purposes, Soon-Yi Previn does not count as Woody Allen's daughter, as he never married Mia Farrow).

Whether someone is classed as your direct descendant (child, grandchild, great-grandchild, etc.) for IHT purposes generally follows the same principles. For the specific purposes of the residence nil rate band only, however, this definition is expanded to include certain other individuals, as explained in Section 3.4.

IHT, like many other UK taxes, is administered by reference to the UK tax year, i.e. the twelve-month period ending 5th April. Thus the 2026/27 tax year is the year ending 5th April 2027. References to the 'tax year' should be construed accordingly. Other periods are also important for IHT purposes and a reference to 'seven years' or 'more than two years', for example, means a strict period of calendar years rather than tax years.

Trust concepts and terminology are key to an understanding of IHT planning. As well as the various types of trust, we will encounter important concepts such as 'interest in possession' and 'life interest'. A full explanation of trust terminology is included in Chapter 8.

IHT law is the same throughout the UK, but there are many critical interactions with other aspects of the law, which may differ in the different nations of the UK. Unless stated to the contrary, references to general legal principles are based on English law.

In legal terms, the word 'property' has a wide application and can mean any form of asset, including cash. Sometimes though, when we talk about 'property' we mean land and buildings: legally termed 'real property'. In this guide, I will use the word in both its common meaning and its legal meaning, and leave the context to make it clear which I mean on each occasion.

Life expectancies quoted in this guide are as per the Office for National Statistics (ONS). Naturally, these take no account of personal circumstances.

Throughout the guide I have allowed myself a few abbreviations. Some of them, like 'UK', are in common usage. I will explain what the others mean the first time I use them and they are set out again in Appendix B for ease of reference. Large amounts of £1,000,000 or more may be abbreviated by use of the letter 'm'. For example, £2,500,000 may be written as '£2.5m'.

Ignorance is Bliss

For the sake of illustration, I am generally going to ignore the Capital Gains Tax (CGT) annual exemption (now just £3,000) and the dividend allowance (now just £500), as these have become too small to have any significant impact.

Which Annual Exemption?

Confusingly, from 2024/25 onwards, the annual CGT exemption and annual exemption for IHT are the same amount: £3,000. They are, however, two completely different exemptions, operating in completely different ways, for different taxes. Throughout this guide, unless expressly stated to the contrary, any mention of the annual exemption means the annual exemption for IHT, covered in Section 5.2.

Property Stamp Taxes

IHT planning often involves the transfer of UK property. This will sometimes lead to tax charges arising on the transfer in the form of some variation of Stamp Duty. The type of Duty arising will depend on which part of the UK the property is located in, as follows:

England:	Stamp Duty Land Tax (SDLT)
Scotland:	Land and Buildings Transaction Tax
Wales:	Land Transaction Tax
Northern Ireland:	Stamp Duty Land Tax (SDLT)

The rules applying under each form of duty are broadly similar. There are some variations in rates, however. Details of the rates applying to all UK property are included in the Taxcafe guide *How to Save Property Tax*. For the sake of simplicity, I will refer only to SDLT for the rest of this guide, but similar charges will arise on property in Scotland or Wales, except the duty will have a different name and will be charged at different rates.

Residence and Domicile

An individual's liability to IHT can be affected by their residence status: i.e. whether or not they are, or have previously been, UK resident, and for how long. We will look at this issue in Sections 2.2 and 15.5.

For deaths or transfers of value occurring before 6th April 2025, an individual's IHT liability could also be affected by their legal domicile (a concept similar to nationality). Even now, legal domicile remains important for a number of reasons, so we will look at this concept in Section 11.6.

Most people living in the UK are long-term UK residents and thus, as we shall see in Section 2.2, liable to IHT on their worldwide assets. Apart from Sections 2.2, 3.3, 15.5, and 15.6, and unless stated to the contrary, we will assume throughout this guide that both the individual and their spouse (if they have one) are long-term UK residents.

About the Examples

In preparing the examples I have assumed the UK tax regime will remain unchanged in the future except to the extent of any announcements already made at the time of publication. However, if there is one thing we can predict with any certainty, it is that change ***will*** occur. The reader must bear this in mind when reviewing the results of the examples.

1.5 WHY WORRY?

Of course, ***you*** won't actually have to pay the IHT on your own estate. Furthermore, for many people, everything can safely be left to their spouse free from IHT. And if you have no other dependants or potential beneficiaries, but just resent paying unnecessary tax, you can simply leave it all to charity.

But most people ***do*** have someone they care about. Usually they have children, other family, or friends who they want to see benefit from the assets they have built up in their lifetime, and they don't want to see the Government taking 40% of it away. Even if, in the first instance, you are leaving everything tax free to your surviving spouse, your accumulated wealth will eventually be hit by IHT if you don't plan ahead.

As we will see later, you need to take action ***now*** to safeguard your family's future prosperity. Alternatively, you may be the potential beneficiary yourself, trying to get an elderly relative to plan for the preservation of ***your*** inheritance. Either way, there is plenty to worry about!

But Am I Wealthy Enough to Worry?

Most people are quite surprised to discover just how much they are actually worth. How often have you heard someone say, "I'm worth more dead than alive?" Very often, especially as we get older, it's true (in pure financial terms only, of course).

This is basically because it takes an enormous amount of capital just to support one person. When that person dies, the capital that was previously tied up in supporting them is freed (after the Government gets its share!) Hence, although you may not feel particularly wealthy, you may still find you have a large potential IHT bill. You'd be amazed just how many 'paper millionaires' there are these days.

Example: *Rosemary is a divorcee with no children of her own: although she is very close to her sisters and their children. She owns an average-sized detached house, which her ex-husband transferred to her under the terms of their divorce settlement. The house is bigger than she needs, but she has fond memories of the many holidays her nephews and nieces spent there, so she is quite attached to it. She has been advised its current market value is £550,000.*

Rosemary is retired and lives off her savings and an investment portfolio she managed to accumulate after her divorce. Although these produce an annual income of only £20,000, their total value is approximately £430,000. She also has some jewellery, some silver, and a few antiques. Altogether, these are worth £15,000. Lastly, she has a small car, worth £5,000.

Nobody would call Rosemary rich by any stretch of the imagination. She's living off only £20,000 a year. But add it all up and you will find she is a millionaire. This means Rosemary's family has a potential IHT bill of £270,000!

You don't need to be nearly as 'wealthy' as Rosemary to have an IHT problem. Once your estate is worth over £325,000, you have a potential exposure to tax at 40% on the excess (subject to any transferable nil rate band: see Chapter 6; and any available residence nil rate band: Section 3.4). £325,000! What's that these days? A house, a car, some savings, and you're easily there! So, yes, generally speaking, if you can afford to buy this guide, there is a strong chance you are wealthy enough to worry about IHT!

1.6 A GUIDE TO EFFECTIVE INHERITANCE TAX PLANNING

All tax planning needs to be undertaken carefully and in full knowledge of the circumstances of the taxpayer's individual situation. This is probably never truer than in the case of IHT, where a detailed review of the individual's situation is vital.

In this guide, I have provided a detailed examination of current IHT law on the basis of our present understanding. However, it is important to understand that further changes or restrictions could be introduced at any time, and the precise meaning of some areas of law will only become apparent when tested in court: possibly many years from now.

I have highlighted some of the more popular planning techniques currently being used successfully by taxpayers wishing to protect their wealth from the scourge of IHT, or which are at least currently believed to work.

HM Revenue and Customs (HMRC) does, however, have very wide powers to enable it to closely examine any IHT planning technique and will do its utmost to overturn any planning strategy when the law permits it to. The associated operations rules and general anti-abuse rule covered in Section 11.11 are both particularly wide-ranging in this regard.

For these and many other reasons, the reader must bear in mind the general nature of this guide. Individual circumstances vary and the tax implications of an individual's actions will vary with them. It is always vital to get professional advice before undertaking any tax planning or other transactions that may have tax implications.

The Challenge

The great challenge with IHT planning is that much of the position will only be determined when an individual dies. Hence, since IHT law is constantly changing, no-one can be sure of having avoided this evil tax until they are safely tucked up in their grave!

For most people that will be many years from now, so there is plenty of time for the Government to move the goalposts. None of this means you shouldn't undertake IHT planning but it does mean, in addition to taking professional advice when putting your plans into effect, you should have a regular professional review to ensure your planning remains effective. Every IHT planning technique runs the risk of being undermined by changes in the law, which can happen at the stroke of a pen.

In fact, it may not even be IHT you are trying to avoid. In January 2020, an all-party parliamentary group on 'inheritance and intergenerational fairness' published a report calling for radical changes to the death tax regime, including replacing IHT with a Death Tax and lifetime Gift Tax.

Up to now, the Government has shown no interest in these proposals, although some of them may be adopted in future. Or a future Government may do something completely different; or simply carry on tinkering with the current regime, as every Government for the last forty years has done.

Personally, I think taxing death, or personal gifts between family members, is completely immoral and just plain wrong. If it was up to me, IHT would be abolished tomorrow. However, I'm sorry to say that looks unlikely in the foreseeable future.

As far as the current Labour Government is concerned, they certainly hit the ground running: pressing ahead with plans to abolish the privileges enjoyed by so-called 'Non-Doms' (Sections 15.5 and 15.6); capping the 100% relief for farms and other qualifying businesses (Chapter 7); subjecting pension savings to IHT (Chapter 10); and extending the nil rate band freeze to an astonishing 22 years!

That might be it for this Parliament, or they might just be warming up. We cannot predict exactly what further changes we may see beyond what we already know. But I am sure something will happen: politicians do love to mix things up. So, while death is certain, the tax regime you will face is not. Despite this, early and effective IHT planning is still the best way to protect your family, whatever the future may hold.

Chapter 2

Inheritance Tax Principles

2.1 TRANSFERS OF VALUE

"Inheritance Tax is payable on death. Everyone knows that, don't they?" Like so many things 'everyone knows' (like 'man will never fly' and 'an iceberg will never sink a ship'), this is **WRONG!**

What actually triggers IHT is not death but a 'transfer of value'. In principle, IHT is chargeable on any transfer of value made by any person at any time. Thankfully, however, there are a number of exemptions, and these ensure we don't have to pay the Government 40% every time we give the kids their pocket money.

The reasons we tend to think of IHT as applying mainly on death are three-fold:

i) On death, we are inevitably forced to transfer our entire wealth to others, thus causing, for most of us, the biggest transfer of value of our lives
ii) Most lifetime transfers to other individuals are exempt, or at least only become chargeable in the event of death within seven years
iii) The name of the tax implies (falsely) that it is only related to death

In fact, point (i) is reflected in the legislation, which deems an individual to have made a transfer of value equal to their entire total net wealth the moment before their death. So, technically, IHT isn't payable on death at all, but a moment before it instead!

In practice, though, despite these peculiar legal technicalities, by far the biggest part of the IHT the Government collects arises on the occasion of someone's death. Furthermore, most of the remainder arises due to attempts to offload some wealth before then.

So, while it isn't technically correct, it is reasonable to say that IHT is generally payable on death, but with the important proviso that other transfers of value made during an individual's lifetime can also be caught. (And, by the way, an iceberg ***can*** sink a ship.)

What is a Transfer of Value?

A transfer of value occurs whenever you dispose of something and, as a result, your total net wealth is reduced. Your total net wealth is referred to as your estate, and we will explore this concept further in Section 2.5.

What you are disposing of may be money or any other asset with monetary value. Furthermore, it is the reduction in your net wealth that generates the transfer of value, not necessarily the value of the asset disposed of. We will see an example of this a little later.

Any disposal of wealth by way of a transaction at arm's length between unconnected persons is not treated as a transfer of value. Hence, the most basic transactions in life, such as buying the weekly groceries, will not be classed as a transfer of value, even though your total net wealth is inevitably reduced. Furthermore, when dealing at arm's length with unconnected persons, merely striking a poor bargain will not be a transfer of value.

Even a transaction with a connected person (Appendix A) will still not give rise to any transfer of value if it is carried out in the same way as it would have been if it had been an arm's length transaction.

The Amount of the Transfer of Value

A transfer of value occurs whenever you make a disposal that is not at arm's length and, as a result, there is a reduction in your total net wealth (your estate). The simplest type of transfer of value is therefore a straightforward gift. If you give someone £10,000 in cash, that is a transfer of value of £10,000, if you give someone a painting worth £5,000, that is a transfer of value of £5,000.

A transfer of value also occurs when sales take place between connected persons at an undervalue, or an overvalue. If you sell your son a painting for £2,000 when it is, in fact, worth £10,000, that is a transfer of value of £8,000; if you buy a car from your daughter and pay her £5,000, when the car is worth only £1,000, that is a transfer of value of £4,000.

But what is important to remember is that it is the reduction in the value of your overall estate that gives rise to the transfer of value.

Example: *Bjorn has a set of six antique chairs worth £20,000. He gives his son, Benny, one of the chairs. The value of a single chair, which is not part of a complete set, is only £1,500.*

However, the transfer of value here is not the value of Benny's single chair. No, the transfer of value is the reduction in the value of Bjorn's estate. Previously, he had a set of chairs worth £20,000. After the gift to Benny, he has five chairs worth £1,500 each, a total of £7,500. Hence, the reduction in the value of Bjorn's estate, and thus the amount of the transfer of value, is £12,500.

2.2 WHO IS LIABLE FOR INHERITANCE TAX?

Any individual owning UK assets, including land and buildings situated in the UK, is subject to IHT on those assets. Long-term UK residents are additionally subject to IHT on any overseas assets. In other words, they are subject to IHT on their worldwide estate. This extends to former long-term UK residents for a number of years after they cease to be UK resident. In all cases, this is subject to the various exclusions, exemptions, and reliefs we will look at throughout this guide.

The rules that determine who is classed as a long-term UK resident for this purpose changed on 6th April 2025. Furthermore, prior to that date, other individuals with legal domicile in the UK (see Section 11.6) were also subject to IHT on their worldwide estate.

In Section 15.5, we will look at the rules that determine which individuals are subject to IHT on their worldwide estate from 6th April 2025 onwards. We will also look at the potential benefits of emigration. For details of the rules on which individuals were subject to IHT on their worldwide estate up to 5th April 2025, see the nineteenth edition of this guide.

For the remainder of this guide, unless stated to the contrary, we will assume individuals are subject to IHT on their worldwide estate. This is the position for the majority of people either currently living in the UK, or who have only recently left.

2.3 WHO ACTUALLY PAYS THE TAX?

Despite my comments in Section 2.1, most IHT does arise on death and, naturally, the deceased is not around to pick up the bill. So, who actually has to pay the tax?

Subject to the points below, the usual default position is the liability for IHT arising on death falls on the personal representatives, who must settle the tax out of the general assets of the deceased's estate. Where the deceased has left a valid Will, their executors are their personal representatives. In the case of a person dying intestate (without a valid Will), the person applying for a grant of representation (probate), or confirmation in Scotland, will be the personal representative. Where no personal representative has been appointed by the court within twelve months after the end of the month of death then the deceased's beneficiaries will be required to fulfil the obligations regarding payment of IHT, delivery of accounts, etc, which would normally fall on the personal representatives.

It is, however, possible for the Will to direct that a beneficiary should bear the tax on a legacy themselves. This can be useful to avoid the extra cost of 'grossing up' (see Section 2.8).

A beneficiary becoming entitled to a life interest in property under the terms of a Will must generally bear the tax arising on their legacy. For property already held in trust, but which is included in the deceased's estate for IHT purposes (as explained in Chapter 8), the tax may fall on the trustees or on another beneficiary of that trust, depending on the exact circumstances.

For the position where IHT is due on funds held within a pension scheme (rare at present, but expected to apply in many cases from April 2027), see Section 10.2.

Lifetime Transfers

The primary responsibility for any IHT arising immediately on lifetime transfers falls on the transferor. It is possible, however, to stipulate that the transferee should bear any IHT arising.

Additional IHT liabilities frequently arise when the transferor dies within seven years of a lifetime transfer. These liabilities usually fall on the transferee. IHT on lifetime transfers is examined in Chapter 4.

2.4 HOW MUCH TAX IS PAYABLE?

On death, IHT is levied, generally at one single rate of 40%, on the entire value of your estate, less certain exemptions. The most important exemptions are the nil rate band (NRB), which is £325,000 for deaths occurring between 6th April 2009 and 5th April 2031, the exemption for transfers to spouses (Section 3.3), and the residence nil rate band (RNRB) (Section 3.4).

Personal representatives of widows/widowers may be able to claim up to double the current NRB and RNRB where the first spouse to die did not fully utilise their NRB or RNRB. We will cover this subject in detail in Chapter 6.

Lifetime Transfers

Where a lifetime transfer gives rise to an immediate IHT charge, the rate applying is 20%, sometimes known as the lifetime rate. Extra tax will often become payable on lifetime transfers in the event of the transferor's subsequent death within seven years, and we will look at this in detail in Section 4.5.

Transfers made directly to spouses are usually tax free. Furthermore, the £325,000 NRB can be deducted from the total value of transfers made in the last seven years. As we shall see in Chapter 4, this is very important because it means tax-free transfers equivalent to the NRB can be made every seven years.

2.5 WHAT IS YOUR ESTATE?

Your estate means everything you own, including land and property, shares and securities, savings accounts, cash, antiques, jewellery, paintings, your car, your furniture, and anything else with any monetary value whatsoever.

Two things that can usually be excluded *at present*, are your pension savings and any life insurance proceeds, as these are generally held in trust on your behalf and do not fall into your estate. However, as announced in the October 2024 Budget, the Government is planning to bring pension savings within the scope of IHT from April 2027. We'll look at the impact of these despicable proposals in Chapter 10. Even at present, there are some pitfalls to watch out for, so we will take a detailed look at pensions in Chapter 10, and life insurance in Section 11.8.

Many people assume other tax-advantaged products, such as Individual Savings Accounts (ISAs) are exempt from IHT because they are supposedly tax-free. Unfortunately, this is not the case and ***ALL*** assets held directly in your own name have to be included in your estate, regardless of their treatment for Income Tax or CGT purposes.

Income arising up to the date of death must also be included (e.g. unpaid state pensions, annuities, salary, accrued bank interest, etc). Also included in the deceased's estate will be: the net value of assets held on their behalf in certain types of trust (Chapter 8); the value of any relevant gifts with reservation (Section 4.8); and the value of any assets they elect to have included in their estate (Section 11.12).

For the purposes of IHT, any non-exempt transfers of value made in the seven years prior to death will also effectively be brought back into the deceased's estate. Reduced IHT rates do, however, apply to transfers of value made at least three, but less than seven, years prior to death.

Any liabilities, such as your mortgage, overdrafts, bank loans, credit card bills, outstanding utility bills, etc, may generally be deducted; although restrictions may sometimes apply (see Section 2.10). You may even deduct outstanding Income Tax or CGT liabilities!

Reasonable funeral expenses may be deducted. What is reasonable depends on your standard of living. (In one extreme case, the expense of a private army providing a funeral honour guard was deemed reasonable.)

Sadly, the costs of obtaining UK probate and administering your UK estate may ***not*** be deducted; although the costs of obtaining foreign probate and realising the value of foreign assets (e.g. selling them) may be deducted up to a maximum of 5% of the value of those assets, where these are subject to UK IHT (see Section 2.2).

In summary, subject to a few adjustments, your estate is basically your total net worth: currently excluding pension savings (usually), but only until April 2027. All the property transferred on your death is subject to IHT in the same way, whether it transfers under the terms of your Will, by intestacy, survivorship (for jointly held property), or by any other means.

Many people take out insurance policies to cover outstanding liabilities, such as credit card bills or bank loans, if they should pass away unexpectedly. The result of this is these liabilities would not be deductible from the value of the estate as they were automatically settled on the taxpayer's death. It would be far better to make provision for such liabilities by other means (see Section 11.8) and thus ensure they are deducted from the value of your estate for IHT purposes. As we shall see in Section 2.10, it remains important the liability is actually settled out of the assets of the estate.

Household personal effects are generally overvalued, resulting in unnecessary overpayments of IHT. The valuations most people have on their personal effects (jewellery, antiques, silverware, etc) tend to be insurance valuations. However, the amount on which IHT is payable should only be the open market value of the assets and this is often considerably less.

2.6 THE BASIC CALCULATION ON DEATH

To illustrate the basic IHT calculation, let's look at a simple example:

Example: *Arthur has been careful with his money all his life. At the time of his death in December 2026, his estate amounts to £3m. Arthur has been divorced for many years and his Will leaves his entire estate to his son, Tony. Hence, there are no exemptions available, other than the NRB. (We will see why the RNRB is not available in this case in Section 3.4.) The first £325,000 of Arthur's estate is exempt from IHT, covered by the NRB. The remaining £2.675m is charged to IHT at 40%, giving rise to a charge of £1.07m!*

The tax is of course reduced (or even eliminated) where there is an exempt beneficiary such as the deceased's surviving spouse or a charity. These exemptions are explored further in Sections 3.3 and 3.5 respectively.

The example above is about as simple (and painful) as it gets. In other cases, there will be more than one beneficiary. This will not alter the total amount of IHT payable (unless any of them are an exempt beneficiary), but it may affect who ends up bearing the tax.

Example: *John dies with a total estate worth £1m. He leaves his nephew, Paul, a house worth £300,000 on condition he settles any tax arising. He leaves his elder son, George, £250,000 in cash, stating in his Will that this sum should be free of all taxes, and he leaves the remainder of his estate to his younger son, Richard.*

There are no exemptions available apart from the NRB. (By leaving his house to his nephew, John is unable to claim the RNRB: see Section 3.4. We will also assume there is no TNRB available: see Section 6.2.) Hence, the IHT arising is £1m – £325,000 = £675,000 x 40% = £270,000.

This amounts to 27% of the total value of the estate, so this is the effective rate applying in this case, sometimes known as the estate rate. As Paul has to settle the IHT on his bequest directly, he will pay IHT at the estate rate of 27% on the value of the house, giving him a liability of £81,000 (£300,000 x 27%).

As George's bequest is free of tax, John's personal representatives must pay the remaining £189,000 (£270,000 – £81,000). This means John's estate is effectively divided up as follows:

Paul:	*£300,000 (the value of the house)*
George:	*£250,000 (his tax-free legacy)*
Richard:	*£261,000 (£1m – £300,000 – £250,000 – £189,000)*
HMRC:	*£189,000 (with a further £81,000 payable by Paul)*

The £261,000 received by Richard after dealing with specific legacies and paying the IHT due is often referred to as the residue. In effect, as the recipient of the residue, Richard is suffering the IHT on both George's legacy and his own. In Section 2.8, we will see what happens when there is also an exempt beneficiary.

2.7 MAKING THE PAYMENT

IHT arising on death is normally due six months after the end of the month of death. Hence, in the case of Arthur, who died in December 2026, it will be due by 30th June 2027. The same payment date applies to all IHT arising on death; both on the deceased's estate and gifts made within the previous seven years (Section 4.5).

Personal representatives may sometimes have to pay the tax earlier, as the liability is triggered when they deliver their accounts for probate or confirmation purposes. From April 2024, however, personal representatives are able to obtain a 'grant on credit' without having to seek commercial loans first.

This means it is now possible to obtain probate without having to settle the deceased's IHT liability first.

Instalment Option

The personal representatives may elect to pay tax on certain assets in the deceased's estate in ten equal yearly instalments, commencing six months after the month of death. If any of the assets concerned are subsequently sold, the remaining unpaid IHT relating to that asset is payable immediately.

For deaths after 5th April 2026, the instalment option is available on *any* assets qualifying for business property relief (BPR) or agricultural property relief (APR) (see Chapter 7).

In other cases, including deaths at any time, the instalment option is available for the tax arising on:

- Land and buildings
- Certain shares and securities
- An unincorporated business (a sole trade or a share in a partnership)

For these existing rules, which also continue to apply where BPR/APR are not available, shares and securities must either have given the deceased control of the company, or be unquoted and:

a) At least 20% of all the IHT payable on the estate arises on assets qualifying for the instalment option;
b) Be shares worth more than £20,000 that comprise at least 10% of the nominal value of all the shares in the company or, in the case of ordinary shares, at least 10% of the nominal value of the ordinary shares in the company; or
c) HMRC is satisfied that payment of the tax in a single lump sum would cause undue hardship

See Section 7.7 for the meanings of 'control' and 'unquoted', which apply equally for these purposes.

Tax payable by trustees on the death of a beneficiary with an interest in possession in certain types of trust (see Section 8.2) may also be paid in instalments when it arises on the same types of assets.

Interest-Free Instalments

For deaths after 5th April 2026, instalments are interest free (provided paid on time) when the tax arises on *any* asset qualifying for BPR or APR.

In other cases, including deaths at any time, instalments are interest free (provided paid on time) when the tax arises on:

- Shares or securities in a company carrying on a qualifying business for the purposes of BPR (see Chapter 7)
- An unincorporated business (a sole trade or a share in a partnership)
- Land and buildings qualifying for APR (Section 7.27)

Where the tax arising qualifies for interest-free instalments but an instalment is paid late, interest is only charged from the due date for the instalment.

Interest Charges
Interest is generally charged on late payments. Subject to the exemptions covered above, it is also charged on payments made by instalments. The rate is currently a whopping 7.75% (since 6th April 2025 it has been set at 4% over the Bank of England base rate: at one point it was an outrageous 8.5%). This is the same as the rate used for most other major taxes: clearly, the Government has absolutely no sympathy for bereaved families suffering both financial turmoil and emotional distress!

At the current interest rate of 7.75%, the cost of paying a 40% IHT bill by instalments (if not covered by the interest exemptions above) is increased to a total effective rate of just under 54% (53.95% to be precise). For example, if an IHT bill of £400,000 would normally be due by 31st May 2026, but is instead paid by instalments, the payments, including interest (assuming it remains at the current rate), will be due as follows:

31 May 2026	£40,000	31 May 2031	£55,500
31 May 2027	£67,900	31 May 2032	£52,400
31 May 2028	£64,800	31 May 2033	£49,300
31 May 2029	£61,700	31 May 2034	£46,200
31 May 2030	£58,600	31 May 2035	£43,100
		Total	£539,500

When interest arises on either instalments or other late payments of IHT, there will be no Income Tax relief for it.

Financing the Inheritance Tax Bill
Where the personal representatives borrow money to settle the IHT arising on delivery of their accounts, they can claim Income Tax relief (against income arising within the deceased's estate) for interest arising on those borrowings over the next twelve months.

Otherwise, however, there is no provision for either the personal representatives or beneficiaries to claim Income Tax relief for interest on borrowings used to settle their IHT bills, as these are regarded as a personal liability.

There is a potential way around this problem if the beneficiary re-mortgages their home to pay the IHT bill. If they subsequently move out of their home and adopt it as a rental property, they will be eligible for Income Tax relief on the mortgage interest against their rental income. The beneficiary could then move into one of the inherited properties and adopt it as their new home.

Alternatively, the beneficiary may be able to obtain Income Tax relief by re-mortgaging one or more rental properties up to the level of their market value at the time of introduction into the rental business. Furthermore, now that it is possible to obtain probate under a grant on credit (as explained above), the best strategy may be to re-mortgage an inherited property, use this to pay the tax and then rent that property out. But if an inherited property is already a rental property, interest relief will only be available on borrowings against the property up to its value when it was first rented out by the deceased.

Interest relief for borrowings on residential rental property is now restricted to basic rate only for Income Tax purposes. Furthermore, while HMRC generally accepts that interest relief is due under the circumstances described above, some resistance does arise from time to time. If any problems arise over this issue, refer HMRC to Example 2 in BIM 45700 in their own manuals.

Subject to these issues, the techniques described above provide at least some relief for the cost of financing IHT bills: after all, relief at the basic rate of 20% is better than no relief at all. For a full discussion of interest relief on rental property, see the Taxcafe guide *How to Save Property Tax*.

If it becomes necessary to sell one or more inherited properties in order to pay IHT, there is one crumb of comfort in the fact there is unlikely to be much CGT to pay, as we shall see in Section 12.2.

Lifetime Transfers

Where IHT is payable on a lifetime transfer, it is due as follows:

- Gifts made between 6th April and 30th September: IHT is due on 30th April in the following year.
- Gifts made between 1st October and 5th April: IHT is due six months after the end of the month in which the gift is made.

From a pure cashflow point of view, the best day to make a chargeable gift is 6th April. (This has other benefits too, as we shall see in Section 5.2; although it does need to fit in with the rest of your planning.)

The instalment option covered above is available to transferees suffering IHT on the death of a transferor within seven years (Section 4.5). It is available for the same types of assets, except that, for deaths before 6th April 2026, or deaths at any time where the transferred assets do not qualify for BPR or APR, shares and securities must either have given the transferor control of the company, or be unquoted and fall under headings (b) or (c) above (heading (a) applies only to transfers on death).

The transferee must either still own the gifted assets at the date of the transferor's death (or the transferee's death, if earlier) or own qualifying replacement assets for the purposes of either BPR or APR (see Section 7.19). Shares or securities that were unquoted at the time of the transfer must also remain unquoted at the date of the transferor's death (or the transferee's death, if earlier).

Repayments

Where there is an overpayment of IHT, the current rate of interest applying to the repayment of the excess is just 2.75%. This scandalous differential in the rates of interest on under- and overpayments effectively means the Government is making an additional profit of 5% (7.75% less 2.75%) from the many bereaved families forced to make estimated IHT payments in an effort to meet the Government's deadlines!

2.8 GROSSING UP

The amount of IHT payable on a specific asset or bequest may be affected by whether it is paid by the personal representatives. This is due to the procedure known as grossing up. The rationale behind grossing up is that where the personal representatives are bearing the tax, this effectively represents an additional transfer of value.

However, grossing up can only apply to the IHT arising on death where there is also an exempt beneficiary (see Section 2.6). It is that exempt beneficiary, often the surviving spouse, who will ultimately suffer the impact of the grossing up.

Hence, we are ***only*** concerned with grossing up (on death) where there is a mixture of exempt and non-exempt beneficiaries and the personal representatives are bearing the IHT on one or more bequests to a non-exempt beneficiary.

The grossing up process is more complex where there are exemptions available. This will apply in the majority of cases, since the NRB is usually available for a start. However, for the sake of illustration, I will start with a scenario where there are no exemptions available, apart from the spouse exemption. This might occur, for example, where the deceased has made gifts in excess of the NRB within the last seven years (see Section 4.5).

Example: *In 2021, Winston made a gift of £400,000 to his son, Stuart. Sadly, Winston dies in March 2027. The total value of his estate is £2.75m. He has no TNRB entitlement and the RNRB will not be available due to tapering (see Section 3.4). Hence, in summary, the only exemption available is the spouse exemption.*

Winston leaves a property worth £160,000 to his nephew Pete on condition he settles any tax arising. He also leaves his daughter Julia the sum of £480,000 in cash, stating in his Will this sum should be free of all taxes. He leaves the remainder of his estate to his widow, Cynthia.

As Pete has to settle the IHT on his bequest directly, he will pay IHT at a straightforward rate of 40%, i.e. £64,000. The IHT on Julia's bequest will, however, be paid by Winston's personal representatives. This brings grossing up into play. In other words, Julia's bequest must be grossed up to account for the IHT being paid out of Winston's estate.

The grossing up factor is two-thirds. Hence, an additional two-thirds must be added to Julia's bequest, producing a grossed-up amount of £800,000 (£480,000 x 2/3 = £320,000 + £480,000 = £800,000). The IHT due on this bequest is £320,000 (£800,000 x 40%). As can readily be seen, this is equal to the amount of the grossing up, meaning the personal representatives can give the original sum of £480,000 to Julia free of any further tax liabilities.

In this example, it is Cynthia who effectively ends up bearing the tax on Julia's bequest since it reduces the amount remaining to be distributed to her. Furthermore, as the tax is paid by the personal representatives, it is increased from the £192,000 it would have been if Julia had paid it, to £320,000 instead. The rate of IHT on the bequest has effectively increased from 40% to 67%. If the family are in agreement, this outcome can be avoided by using a deed of variation (Section 17.1) to alter the terms of the Will so the beneficiary bears the tax, which is thus reduced back to 40%.

The two thirds rate of grossing up shown in the above example is very much the worst-case scenario. Where any exemptions are available, these are taken into account first, before applying grossing up, meaning the overall effective rate can be much reduced. To see how this applies in practice, let's return to the example with a couple of modifications.

Example Revisited: *On further investigation, it turns out Winston's gift to Stuart was actually made in 2019 (this is why it is so important to document gifts properly: see Section 4.3), so Winston's NRB is available after all. A later Will is also found in which Winston states his personal representatives should bear the tax on the property left to Pete. Hence, grossing up will now apply to both legacies.*

The total of Pete and Julia's legacies amounts to £640,000. From this, the personal representatives can deduct Winston's NRB of £325,000, leaving the sum of £315,000 subject to grossing up. As before, the grossing up factor is two thirds, producing a total IHT liability of £210,000 (£315,000 x 2/3). Winston's estate is therefore distributed as follows:

Pete:	*£160,000 (the value of the property)*
Julia:	*£480,000 (her tax-free legacy)*
Cynthia:	*£1,900,000 (£2.75m – £640,000 – £210,000)*
HMRC:	*£210,000*

If the personal representatives wish to pay the IHT on Pete's property by instalments (Section 2.7), this element can be calculated on a simple pro rata basis: £210,000 x £160,000/£640,000 = £52,500.

As before, it is Cynthia, the exempt beneficiary, who effectively ends up bearing the cost of the grossing up.

More Complexity

You may be wondering why I changed the example so the personal representatives were bearing the tax on Pete's legacy. This was done purely for the sake of illustration. Where, in addition to there being exemptions available, there is also a mixture of legacies on which the beneficiary is bearing their own tax, and legacies on which the personal representatives are bearing the tax, the grossing up calculations become extremely complex. Nonetheless, the principles remain that IHT being borne by the personal representatives must be grossed up to account for the additional transfer of value, and the exempt beneficiary ultimately suffers the consequences.

Grossing up can also apply to lifetime transfers, although a lower grossing up rate of one quarter applies. See Section 4.2 for further details.

2.9 COLLECTION OF TAX

As we saw in Section 2.3, liability for IHT may fall on any of: the transferor, transferee, the deceased's personal representatives, or the deceased's beneficiaries. Naturally, HMRC will, in the first instance, attempt to collect the tax from the correct party. But if they encounter difficulty collecting the tax, they will look to any other party to the relevant transfer of value.

Hence, in the case of IHT arising on death, if a beneficiary is required to pay their share of the tax under the terms of the deceased's Will, but is unable to do so, HMRC will collect it from the personal representatives out of the remaining assets of the estate. Furthermore, the tax may then have to be grossed up (see Section 2.8).

Conversely, a beneficiary who should have received a bequest free from IHT could end up having to bear part of the IHT arising when there are insufficient liquid funds left in the remaining estate.

Transferees should usually bear any extra tax arising when the transferor dies within seven years of making a gift (see Section 4.5) but this rule will also be overridden if HMRC finds it necessary.

Example: *In July 2024, George, a single man, gave his old friend Andrew £500,000 to help him out. Sadly, things continue to go from bad to worse for Andrew and, in 2026, he is declared bankrupt.*

In March 2027, George dies and the earlier gift to Andrew becomes chargeable to IHT. George had also made earlier chargeable transfers in excess of his NRB during the seven years prior to July 2024, so the gift to Andrew is fully exposed to IHT (see Section 4.5). As HMRC will be unable to collect the IHT due from Andrew, they will look to George's personal representatives to pay the tax out of the assets of the estate. Instead of the original £200,000 (at 40%), however, the IHT due on this gift will now be £333,333 (two-thirds: see Section 2.8).

In short, HMRC doesn't really care who pays the tax, as long as it is collected. This is why it will often make sense to take out term insurance to cover IHT costs arising in the event of an early death and we will look at this further in Section 11.8.

2.10 LOANS AND OTHER LIABILITIES

A number of restrictions apply to the deduction of liabilities for IHT purposes. In this section, I will cover the general principles and look at how they apply in a few practical scenarios. As we progress through the guide, I will also look at how the restrictions affect various IHT planning techniques. Note that, for the examples in this section, I am going to assume for the sake of illustration that neither the TNRB, nor RNRB apply.

Liabilities on Death

Subject to the restrictions discussed below, the general rule is that all the deceased's liabilities are deducted from the general assets of their estate. In particular, except as noted below, unsecured liabilities are not usually deducted from the value of assets eligible for payment of IHT by instalments (see Section 2.7). However, some liabilities are, in the first instance, specifically allocated as follows:

- Secured loans (e.g. mortgages) are allocated against the assets on which they are secured
- Business liabilities (see Sections 7.10 and 7.13) are allocated against the value of the relevant business
- Foreign debts are allocated against foreign property

Where the liabilities exceed the value of the relevant assets, the excess will again generally be deducted from the general assets of the estate. These allocations under general principles may be altered by the additional rules and restrictions discussed below.

Restrictions
Liabilities may generally only be deducted from the value of the deceased's estate where the liability is actually discharged (i.e. paid) out of the assets of the estate. The only exception to this rule arises where there is both a commercial reason for the non-payment of the liability; and the non-payment does not give rise to any tax advantage (or any such advantage that arises was not a main purpose behind the non-payment).

For there to be a valid commercial reason for the non-payment, it is necessary to show either that the liability was due to an unconnected party operating on an arms' length basis, or that an unconnected party operating on an arms' length basis would have accepted the non-payment.

As far as tax advantages arising out of the non-payment are concerned, this provision is very wide-ranging and generally covers any situation where any person enjoys any saving or deferral of any kind of tax. However, it only applies where the non-payment of the liability gives rise to a tax advantage: not simply because the liability itself creates a tax advantage.

Example 1: *Leona dies and leaves her house to her daughter Alexandra. The house is subject to a mortgage. The lender allows Alexandra to take over the mortgage so that it does not need to be repaid immediately. The lender is an unconnected party operating on an arms' length basis so, although the mortgage has not been repaid out of Leona's estate, it may still be deducted for IHT purposes.*

Example 2: *Gareth lends £20,000 to his father, Simon, on condition it be repaid on the later of Simon and his wife's deaths. Simon dies first. The loan is not repaid at that time. Allowing a loan to be repaid on the second of a couple's deaths is a normal commercial arrangement. Hence, although Gareth is a connected party, the non-payment of the loan at the time of Simon's death does not prevent the loan being deducted from the value of Simon's estate for IHT purposes.*

This example shows it is possible for a loan from a connected party to not be repaid immediately and still be deductible from the deceased's estate: provided the non-payment is permitted on a normal commercial basis.

It is, however, vital that the loan documentation is drawn up correctly. If, for example, the loan agreement merely stated 'the lender may *permit* the loan to be repaid on the second death' then an unconnected party operating on an arms' length basis would generally call for the loan to be repaid on the first death: unless the loan were secured (on the borrower's home or other property) and subject to interest at a commercial rate. (Such interest would give rise to Income Tax liabilities for the lender.)

In other cases, a liability is only likely to be deductible if:

- It is a secured loan on full commercial terms and one or more of the deceased's beneficiaries takes over the liability together with the asset on which the loan is secured,
- It is an arms' length commercial arrangement, which one or more of the deceased's beneficiaries takes over (e.g. a business overdraft), or
- It is repaid out of the assets of the deceased's estate

Paying Liabilities Out of the Estate

There are a number of ways in which liabilities may be paid out of the assets of the estate in order to qualify for deduction for IHT purposes.

Firstly, of course, the personal representatives can simply pay the liability out of cash held by the deceased or the proceeds of sale of the deceased's assets. There is no restriction where the cash or assets are themselves exempt (e.g. foreign bank accounts held by certain individuals: see Section 15.6).

Alternatively, the deceased's personal representatives could take out a new loan and use it to repay the liabilities. The new loan would need to be charged against the estate's assets. It would then need to be repaid by selling some of the assets of the estate before they are passed to the beneficiaries, or taken over by one or more of the beneficiaries inheriting those assets.

A new loan used to repay the deceased's liabilities could come from any source: including the deceased's beneficiaries.

Life Insurance & Pension Fund Death Benefits

If a life insurance policy has been written in trust so that it falls outside the deceased's estate (see Section 11.8), it is vital the proceeds are not used directly to settle the deceased's liabilities, as these would not have been paid out of the assets of the estate and would not be deductible. The same currently applies to most pension fund death benefits (see Section 10.15).

Life insurance proceeds or pension fund death benefits could, however, be paid out to one of the deceased's beneficiaries who could then lend those funds to the deceased's personal representatives to enable them to pay the deceased's liabilities.

Example 3: *Sharon dies leaving a house worth £800,000. She had a life insurance policy written in trust which yields £250,000 and she owed her son Jack £200,000: the total of a number of loans he made to her in her latter years.*

If Jack's loan is not repaid, it cannot be deducted from Sharon's estate and her IHT liability will be £190,000 (£800,000 – £325,000 = £475,000 x 40%). If the life insurance proceeds are paid directly to Jack to settle his loan then the loan will not have been settled out of the assets of Sharon's estate and her IHT liability will again be £190,000.

Instead, the life insurance proceeds are paid out to Sharon's sister, Kelly. Kelly then lends £200,000 to Sharon's estate. The loan is charged against Sharon's house. Sharon's personal representatives use the £200,000 borrowed from Kelly to repay Jack, meaning his loan can be deducted from Sharon's estate for IHT purposes. This reduces Sharon's IHT liability to £110,000 (£800,000 – £200,000 – £325,000 = £275,000 x 40%).

Sharon's house is then passed to Kelly subject to the £200,000 charge against it. Since the charge is in Kelly's name, she can then have it removed.

In theory, a similar strategy could be used where Jack was the sole beneficiary of both Sharon's estate and the life insurance policy. It would, however, be vital to ensure Jack's original loan was repaid by way of a new loan from him to the estate and not repaid directly out of the insurance proceeds. In such a case, a good lawyer who knew their way around all the necessary documentation would be essential!

Liabilities Incurred to Acquire Relievable Property, Etc

Certain types of business property, agricultural property, and woodlands are eligible for relief from IHT. We will look at these types of relievable property and the relevant reliefs in detail in Chapter 7.

Liabilities incurred to finance the acquisition, enhancement or maintenance of relievable property, must be taken to reduce the value attributed to that property (subject to the comments below regarding liabilities incurred before 6th April 2013).

A liability is deemed to have financed relievable property where it is used directly or indirectly for that purpose. Guidance issued by HMRC indicates they take a very broad view of what can be taken to have indirectly financed relievable property. An example of some of their thinking on this subject is included in Section 7.12 although, as ever, it must be emphasised HMRC guidance is not the law and it is for the courts to decide whether such a case would actually be caught in practice.

Liabilities incurred before 6th April 2013 are exempt from being attributed to relievable property and may generally be deducted from the general assets of the deceased's estate (subject to the other rules described in this section and the treatment of business liabilities discussed in Section 7.13).

However, where a liability incurred before 6th April 2013 is refinanced or varied on or after that date, it will be treated as a new liability and will then be caught by the rules discussed above.

This means replacing or varying loans or other liabilities incurred before 6th April 2013 that have been used, directly or indirectly, to finance business property, agricultural property, or woodlands, in any way, could lead to significant increases in your IHT liability.

I will look at the practical implications of the restriction on liabilities incurred to acquire relievable property in more detail in Chapter 7.

A similar restriction operates where liabilities are incurred to acquire excluded property. This generally means foreign property and certain other assets owned by individuals not subject to IHT on their worldwide estate: see Section 15.6.

Artificially Created Debts

No deduction is allowed for an artificially created debt where, in effect, the debtor themselves had originally provided the assets or funds that later gave rise to the debt. For example, if a father gifts money to his son and then borrows it back, there would be no deduction from the father's estate.

2.11 GRANTING AND WAIVING LOANS

HMRC's IHT manual states: 'The grant of an interest free loan repayable on demand is not a transfer of value (because the value of the loan is equal to the amount of it)' [IHTM 14317]. This opens up significant IHT planning opportunities and we will see several possible applications in this guide.

Nonetheless, the downside of granting a loan is that its value remains in the lender's estate and will continue to be subject to IHT on their death. In some cases it may, at some later stage, make sense for the individual granting the loan to subsequently waive the outstanding sum due. This will be a transfer of value but, if the loan was made to another individual, the waiver will be a potentially exempt transfer (Section 4.3), meaning the value of the loan should escape IHT if the lender survives at least seven years after making the waiver.

However, for legal reasons, the waiver of a loan is only effective if documented in a formal deed. While an individual can prepare their own deed, most people will tend to use a lawyer for this.

There are some alternatives to using a formal deed, but accepting a small, nominal sum in repayment of the loan will not suffice on its own. Accepting a nominal sum in full settlement where the loan is repaid early *is* effective, but this can only work where the loan had a fixed term.

Oddly, accepting anything other than money in settlement of a loan is also effective, regardless of what the lender accepts. You might accept an old television in settlement of a £1m loan and this would be effective in removing the value of the loan from your estate. But, to be frank, despite the additional cost involved, the safest method is to waive the loan under a formal deed.

2.12 QUICK SUCCESSION RELIEF

Quick succession relief provides some partial relief from IHT when a transferee dies within five years of receiving an earlier transfer on which IHT was paid, or on which IHT later becomes payable (remembering tax can arise up to seven years after the original transfer). The amount of relief is given by the formula: 'Percentage' x Original Tax x Net Transfer/Gross Transfer.

The 'Percentage' is 100% where the transferee dies no more than a year after the original transfer. It then reduces in steps of 20% the day after each anniversary of the original transfer until, after five years, the relief is no longer available.

Example: *In May 2024, Ewan died leaving a legacy of £1.2m to his daughter, Kirsty; and the rest of his estate to his widow. Kirsty bore the IHT arising, which amounted to £350,000, leaving her with a net sum of £850,000. Sadly, in December 2026, Kirsty is killed in a boating accident, and leaves her estate to her friend Shane. Kirsty's executors claim quick succession relief of: 60% x £350,000 x £850,000/£1.2m = £148,750.*

If we assume the value of Kirsty's estate is equal to the same net sum of £850,000, and the only other exemption or relief available is the NRB, the IHT payable by her executors will be £61,250 (£850,000 – £325,000 = £525,000 x 40% = £210,000 – £148,750 = £61,250).

Despite the relief, the same funds that originally flowed from Ewan have still suffered a total of £411,250 (£350,000 + £61,250) in IHT, equivalent to 47% of the amount in excess of the NRB.

Quick succession relief can also apply where either the first or second transfer (or both) was a lifetime transfer made within seven years of the transferor's death. It is not to be confused with taper relief (see Section 4.5), however, as the two reliefs operate independently of each other.

2.13 SIMULTANEOUS DEATHS

Where two or more individuals die simultaneously, or in circumstances where it is not possible to determine who died first, for legal purposes in England and Wales, the oldest person is deemed to have died first (then the next oldest, etc).

Where the older person has left any funds or other assets to the younger person in their Will then, for IHT purposes, those funds or assets are still taxed in the same way, regardless of the younger person's death. However, they are not included in the younger person's estate for IHT purposes, and hence are not taxed again due to their death.

One of the most important consequences of this principle is that, where a married couple die simultaneously and the elder spouse leaves some or all of their estate to the younger spouse in their Will, that part of their estate escapes IHT completely. This arises because those assets are covered by the spouse exemption on the elder spouse's death and are effectively ignored on the younger spouse's death.

This beneficial result (beneficial for IHT that is) does not arise if the elder spouse dies intestate (see Section 11.7 for details of what happens then) or if the elder spouse's Will contains a clause requiring the younger spouse to survive them by a specified period before becoming entitled to the assets.

In Scotland the position is different and the deaths are treated as having occurred at the same instant for all purposes. Neither person is treated as surviving the other and for legal and IHT purposes the assets pass as specified in the deceased's Wills or under the laws of intestacy, as appropriate (Section 11.7). The same generally applies in Northern Ireland, although there are exceptions. Which country's laws apply depends on the person's legal domicile at the date of death (see Section 11.6).

Chapter 3

The Main Exemptions

3.1 WHAT IS AN EXEMPTION?

IHT exemptions come in many different forms. Some are based on value, others on the relationship between the transferor and transferee, still others on the nature of the transferee alone, and some even on the circumstances of the transferor's demise.

Some exemptions have a general application, others apply only to lifetime transfers, and others only to transfers on death. In Chapter 5 we will look at IHT exemptions that apply only to lifetime transfers. In this chapter, we concentrate on exemptions that apply regardless of whether the gift or transfer is made during the transferor's lifetime or on death; or that apply only on death.

3.2 THE NIL RATE BAND (NRB)

The NRB is probably the most important exemption for the vast majority of people. As the name suggests, an IHT rate of nil is applied to the first part of your estate, which falls within this band.

The amount of NRB available depends on the date of death (or the date of transfer in the case of chargeable lifetime transfers: see Section 4.2). The current NRB applying to deaths or chargeable lifetime transfers between 6th April 2009 and 5th April 2031 is £325,000.

Any part of the NRB that was not used on the earlier death of the deceased's spouse may additionally be claimed. This means up to double the normal amount of NRB may be available on the death of a widow/widower. This has enormous implications for IHT planning for married persons and we will look at this subject in detail in Chapter 6.

Despite this, it remains important to note that each individual has their own NRB. I will come back to this point and explain its significance later.

Until 2009, the NRB was generally increased in line with inflation, based on the increase in the Retail Prices Index. However, in 2010, Labour Chancellor Alistair Darling announced a five-year freeze at its 2009/10 level of £325,000. This disgraceful departure from Gordon Brown's earlier promise to increase the band to £350,000 was later compounded by another despicable U-turn from George Osborne, who abandoned his party's plans to increase the NRB to £1m and extended Darling's five-year freeze to twelve!

In the March 2021 Budget, just as we were within weeks of finally coming to the end of Osborne's twelve-year freeze, Rishi Sunak extended the freeze by a further five years; Jeremy Hunt added another two years in his November 2022 Autumn Statement; Rachel Reeves, added yet another two years in her October 2024 Budget, and another year on top of that in her second Budget, in

November 2025, thus bringing this fiscal ice age up to its current expected duration of ***22 years!***

This generation-spanning freeze means we are stuck with the 2009 NRB of £325,000 until ***at least*** 5th April 2031.

Inflation for the period from September 2009 to September 2025 totalled almost 90%. This means, if Gordon Brown had kept his promise in 2010, and the NRB had then kept pace with retail price inflation thereafter, it should have been around £665,000 for 2026/27.

If we assume an annual inflation rate of, say, 3.5% over the next four years, by 2030/31 we would have expected the NRB to be around £765,000. That means the Government will be collecting an extra £176,000 from many bereaved families because of the freeze. In fact, as we shall see later in the guide, in some cases it will be a lot more.

The Impact of Property Prices
But that is just retail price inflation. The largest source of IHT, by value, comes from property (land and buildings). Hence, it is more appropriate to compare the NRB's lack of growth with house price inflation.

Even before the current 22-year freeze began in 2009, the NRB was already failing to keep pace with house price inflation, so let's go back a little further to see just how bad the situation really is.

Over the period from September 1996 to September 2025, average UK house prices increased by ***377%!*** Hence, if the NRB, which was £215,000 in 1997, had been increased, as seems most appropriate, in line with house price inflation, it should have stood at around £1,025,000 by now. Furthermore, if we assume house prices continue to grow at a relatively modest average rate of 5% per year, by 2030/31 we would have expected to see a NRB of about £1.25m.

That will leave many homeowners facing around £370,000 in extra IHT simply because of the Government's failure to keep pace with property prices. Admittedly, this reduces to around £300,000 where the RNRB is available but, as we shall see in Section 3.4, this will not always be the case. How's that for stealth tax!

The Future of the Nil Rate Band
To be frank, after so many broken promises, I have long since given up believing anything we are told about the future of the NRB. However, among the many contradictory announcements made by various Chancellors was a proposal that the NRB would be increased in line with the Consumer Prices Index (CPI) once the freeze comes to an end (if ever). The CPI is the Government's preferred inflation measure, as it is generally lower than the far more realistic Retail Prices Index (RPI), which is a much more accurate reflection of what we all see in the shops.

Historically, the CPI runs at around 1% to 1.5% less than the RPI. Hence, even when the current, seemingly endless, freeze finally comes to an end, using this lower index will severely slow the rate of increase in the NRB and lead to even greater shortfalls in the long-term when compared to house price inflation. And it is the long-term that matters when we look at IHT planning!

Predicting the future is always difficult, but it is something one has to do to some degree when engaged in long-term planning. Hence, for the remainder of this guide, unless stated to the contrary, any predictions about the NRB beyond 5th April 2031 will be based on the assumption that, after that date, it is increased annually in line with the CPI, and this lower inflation measure averages 2.5% per annum. Each year's increase, as calculated under this assumption, is also rounded up to the nearest £1,000. I have also applied the same principles to forecast increases in the RNRB from 2031/32 onwards.

However, I must emphasise, this assumption, and the consequent future NRBs and RNRBs used in some of the examples in this guide, is only my 'best guess' used purely for the sake of illustration.

3.3 THE SPOUSE EXEMPTION

Except as noted below, transfers of property made directly to your spouse are completely exempt from IHT. This covers both lifetime transfers and transfers on death. The exemption for transfers to a spouse opens up a wealth of planning opportunities, which we will return to in Chapter 6.

Transfers to a Spouse Who is Not a Long-Term UK Resident

The general exemption for transfers to a spouse usually operates without limit. However, in the case of transfers after 5th April 2025, from a long-term UK resident individual to a spouse who is not a long-term UK resident, the exemption is restricted.

For transfers before 6th April 2025, the same restriction applied where the transferor spouse was either domiciled or deemed domiciled in the UK and the transferee spouse was neither domiciled nor deemed domiciled in the UK.

See Section 15.5 for the definition of a long-term UK resident applying after 5th April 2025; see Section 11.6 regarding legal domicile; and see the twentieth edition of this guide for details of deemed domicile for tax purposes before 6th April 2025.

For the rest of this section, I will refer only to whether an individual is, or is not, a long-term UK resident. Note, however, that unless stated to the contrary, precisely the same rules apply for transfers made before 6th April 2025, except that whenever I refer to whether or not an individual is a long-term UK resident, this needs to be read as whether or not they were either domiciled or deemed domiciled in the UK.

It is possible to remove the restriction on the exemption for transfers to a spouse who is not a long-term UK resident if that spouse elects to 'opt in' and be treated as a long-term UK resident for IHT purposes. This election has both benefits and pitfalls, so it is worth taking professional advice first.

In the absence of any such election covering the time at which a transfer is made from a long-term UK resident individual to their spouse who is not a long-term UK resident, only a maximum of £325,000 may be covered by the spouse exemption. This limit is equal to the amount of the NRB, but is a separate exemption.

One single limit applies for the whole of the transferor's lifetime, even if they are divorced or widowed and later marry again. The limit applies on a cumulative basis, taking account of all transfers covered by the spouse exemption (including earlier transfers to a long-term UK resident spouse). Once the limit is exceeded, any further transfers to a spouse who is not a long-term UK resident, both during the transferor's lifetime and on death, will be treated like any other transfer to an individual other than their spouse. Prior to April 2013, the limit was £55,000.

Example: *In 2012, Henry, who is both UK domiciled and a long-term UK resident, gave £100,000 to his wife, Catherine. As she was domiciled in Spain, only the first £55,000 of the gift was covered by the spouse exemption, the remainder was a potentially exempt transfer (Section 4.3).*

In 2025, Henry divorced Catherine and married Anne. She is a long-term UK resident, so Henry can give her any amount and it will be covered by the spouse exemption. In the event, he gives her a total of £125,000 before her untimely death in 2027.

A grief-stricken Henry marries once again. His new wife, Jane, is not a long-term UK resident when Henry himself dies a short time later and leaves everything to her.

The remaining spouse exemption available to cover Jane's inheritance is just £145,000. This is because both the £55,000 covered by the exemption on the gift to Catherine in 2012, and all £125,000 of the gifts to Anne, must be deducted from the £325,000 limit.

Amounts not covered by the spouse exemption remain eligible for other exemptions in the same way as transfers to any other individual.

Many lifetime transfers between spouses will not be a capital transfer of value and would be exempted under one of the provisions covered in Sections 5.4 to 5.6. Where these provisions apply, there is no capital transfer of value and any payments do not need to be counted towards the spouse exemption limit.

For transfers on death in excess of the limit, the NRB is available in the usual way, meaning a long-term UK resident will often be able to leave up to £650,000 to a spouse who is not a long-term UK resident free from IHT where they have not previously used their spouse exemption. This does depend on whether they have any other beneficiaries and on whether they have made other chargeable transfers in the last seven years. In other words, once the spouse exemption has been exhausted, a spouse who is not a long-term UK resident is in the same position as any other beneficiary (unless they 'opt-in').

Where the transferor is alive, an 'opt in' election can be backdated by up to seven years prior to the date of the election, and is known as a 'lifetime election'. Where the transferor has died, the election can be backdated by up to seven years prior to the date of the transferor's death. The election must generally be made within two years of the date of death and is known as a 'death election'.

While 'opt in' elections can be backdated as described above, the couple must have been married on the relevant date. For elections to be effective from a date after 5th April 2025, the transferor must have been a long-term UK resident on that date, and the transferee must not have been a long-term UK resident. For elections to be effective from a date before 6th April 2025, the transferor must have had legal domicile in the UK (and not merely deemed UK domicile). The transferee must have had legal domicile abroad, but it does not matter if they had deemed domicile in the UK on the relevant date. The election does not affect an individual's legal domicile, it is only relevant for IHT purposes.

These changes mean some transferee spouses who were previously unable to make an 'opt in' election are now able to do so (since 6th April 2025): for example, where the transferor spouse is non-UK domiciled, but has been UK resident for many years.

An 'opt in' election is irrevocable and, unless it lapses (see below), continues to deem the electing spouse to be a long-term UK resident for the rest of their life (and on their death). Where a spouse elected to be treated as UK domiciled any time before 6th April 2025, they are automatically treated as a long-term UK resident thereafter. An election can, however, lapse under certain circumstances, as follows:

- Elections made before 30th October 2024: after four consecutive years of non-UK residence
- Elections made after 29th October 2024, but applying from a date before 6th April 2025: after ten consecutive years of non-UK residence
- Lifetime elections applying from a date after 5th April 2025: after ten consecutive years of non-UK residence

A death election applying from a date after 5th April 2025 cannot lapse. Hence, if making a death election, it will generally be wise to backdate it to a date before 6th April 2025 if possible.

Alternatively, for potential transferees where this would not be possible (e.g. where the couple only married after 5th April 2025, or the transferor did not have legal domicile in the UK), it may make sense to make a lifetime election while the transferor is still alive.

Where an election made before 30th October 2024 lapses, it remains possible for the electing spouse to be a long-term UK resident in their own right (Section 15.5) and this will take precedence.

There is no requirement for an electing spouse to be UK resident when an election is made, or on the date it is effective from. However, the period of non-UK residence required for an election to lapse can only commence at the beginning of a subsequent tax year after the election is made.

There is no restriction on transfers in the opposite direction: *from* a spouse who is not a long-term UK resident *to* a long-term UK resident spouse. Why would there be: such transfers may eventually increase the tax haul. Beware, however, transfers made by an individual who is either non-UK resident or has legal domicile abroad may have foreign tax implications!

Other Exceptions to the Spouse Exemption

The general exemption for transfers between spouses is also restricted in a few other circumstances. The exemption may be lost where the transfer: only takes effect after the expiry of another third party's interest, or after the expiry of some other period of time; is dependent on a condition that is not satisfied within twelve months; or is made as consideration for the transfer of a reversionary interest in some other property.

It is nonetheless acceptable to have a condition in your Will that your spouse must survive you by a certain period before becoming absolutely entitled to an asset. Some people do this in order to ensure assets pass directly to their ultimate intended beneficiaries under these circumstances. Such a condition may, however, backfire in the event of you and your spouse dying together: as assets that could otherwise have escaped IHT will be exposed to tax (see Section 2.13).

Transfers into Trust for the Benefit of a Spouse

The spouse exemption does not generally apply to a transfer into trust during the donor's lifetime. Transfers on death that confer an 'immediate post-death interest' (Section 8.9) on a surviving spouse are eligible for the spouse exemption.

What is a Spouse?

For IHT purposes, a spouse must be your legally married husband or wife, or your legally registered civil partner. Beyond that, a spouse is not specifically defined in tax legislation but, for IHT purposes, HMRC takes the view that the exemption continues to apply to any transfer between persons who are still legally married at the time of that transfer. Unlike CGT, the IHT exemption for transfers between spouses continues to apply to separated couples right up until the granting of a decree absolute (see Section 12.6 for details of the spouse exemption for CGT purposes).

Hence, transfers between spouses on separation or as part of divorce proceedings will be covered by the exemption if made before the granting of a decree absolute. See also Section 5.6 regarding another potential exemption that may apply under these circumstances.

Generally speaking, a couple who are legally married under the laws of another country will similarly be recognised as legally married for tax purposes in the UK. This will even include polygamous marriages when they are legally valid in the taxpayer's country of origin. In such cases, the spouse exemption limit discussed above must be applied to the cumulative value of transfers made to all the transferor's spouses.

The spouse exemption applies only to married couples. There is no exemption for transfers to common-law partners! If you intend leaving most of your estate to a common-law partner, try to get married before you die. Deathbed marriages have been known to save ***millions*** of pounds in IHT and it is one planning device that is almost impossible for HMRC to overturn. It worked for Ken Dodd, after all!

3.4 THE RESIDENCE NIL RATE BAND (RNRB)

The RNRB provides an additional exemption on qualifying residential property. It operates in addition to the 'normal' NRB but is only available on death. Where the RNRB applies, it takes priority over the NRB (i.e. it is used first). For deaths occurring between 6th April 2020 and 5th April 2031, the maximum RNRB available to a single individual is £175,000. Like the NRB, it has been frozen until 2031. (See Section 3.2 regarding forecast future RNRBs beyond 2031 used in the examples in this guide.)

Qualifying Property

In order to qualify for the RNRB exemption, a property must have been the deceased's private residence at some point during their ownership. Generally, the property will also need to be in their estate at the time of their death (i.e. still owned by them), except that:

- Property included in their estate under the gifts with reservation rules (Section 4.8) may qualify. (It must have been gifted to one or more qualifying individuals, as described below.)
- The downsizing provisions allow the exemption to be claimed where a former qualifying residence has been sold after 7th July 2015. This covers both cases where the deceased no longer owns a qualifying residence at the time of death, and other cases where using these provisions yields additional relief. We will look at these provisions in detail in Section 13.10.

If an individual owns more than one qualifying property when they die, their personal representatives may elect which property the exemption applies to.

Where an individual resides in job-related accommodation, a property they had acquired with the intention of adopting as their private residence may qualify for the exemption. See the Taxcafe guide *How to Save Property Tax* for further details regarding job-related accommodation.

Closely Inherited (Qualifying Individuals)

Subject to the exceptions noted above, the RNRB exemption only applies where the property is passed, on death, to one or more qualifying individuals, as follows:

- Direct descendants (children, grandchildren, etc: see further below)
- Spouses of direct descendants
- Widows/widowers of direct descendants who have never remarried (up to the time of the deceased's death)

The deceased's direct descendants for the purposes of the RNRB are determined using an expanded definition of an individual's children. In addition to the usual definition in Section 1.4, the following are also counted as an individual's child for this purpose:

- Any person who has previously been the individual's step-child at any time
- Foster children of the individual
- Any person for whom the individual was appointed (or treated by law as having been appointed) as a legal guardian at any time before that person was 18 years old

So, if your son's ex-wife's adopted daughter fosters a little boy and, when that boy grows up, he is appointed as a sixteen-year-old orphan's legal guardian, then that orphan may qualify as your direct descendant for the purposes of the RNRB. On the other hand, your unmarried partner's children don't qualify, unless they're your children too.

Generally, the property must pass directly to one or more qualifying individuals in order to qualify. However, the property may also qualify where it is passed to a trust for the benefit of one or more qualifying individuals. Only certain types of trust qualify for this purpose, as detailed in Section 8.3.

For simplicity, for the rest of this guide, I will generally only refer to direct descendants for the purposes of the RNRB. But please bear in mind that, in practice, all the people described above are qualifying individuals for the purposes of this exemption.

Using the Residence Nil Rate Band: A Simple Example
Nicki divorced her husband many years before her death in 2026. She leaves her estate, worth £600,000, to her daughter. Nicki's estate includes her former home, which is worth £250,000 at the time of her death. The RNRB exempts £175,000 of the value of Nicki's former home. This reduces her taxable estate to £425,000 before deduction of her main NRB of £325,000, which reduces it to £100,000. The IHT payable on Nicki's estate at 40% is thus £40,000.

Mortgages and Loans
Any mortgages or other loans secured over a property generally have to be taken into account when allocating the RNRB. For example, where a property worth £250,000 is passed to the deceased's son, but the property was subject to an outstanding mortgage of £180,000 at the time of the deceased's death, the exemption will be limited to just £70,000: as this is the net equity value falling into the deceased's estate.

Exceptions may arise, however, where the outstanding mortgage or loan must be allocated to a different asset, or is not deductible from the estate at all: see Section 2.10 for further details of scenarios where this may arise.

Tapering
The RNRB is withdrawn from estates worth in excess of £2m. This withdrawal is at the rate of £1 for every £2 by which the estate exceeds this threshold, which has been frozen at its current level until 5th April 2031 (for the sake of illustration, I have also assumed no increase in this threshold in later years throughout this guide).

Example: *Ollie has an estate valued at £2.1m at the time of his death in January 2027. This exceeds the threshold by £100,000, so his available RNRB is reduced by £50,000, from £175,000 to £125,000.*

The withdrawal of the RNRB means it may effectively be lost if the deceased's estate exceeds £2.35m. This effective threshold may be as high as £2.7m where the deceased is a widow/widower, for the reasons explained below.

The value of the deceased's estate for the purpose of tapering is as detailed in Section 2.5. The estate is valued before deducting any reliefs: so even qualifying business property and assets the deceased is leaving to their spouse will be counted in full. Transfers of value prior to death are ***not*** included for the purpose of tapering, however. We will look at the planning implications of this in Section 16.17.

In many cases, the tapering rules mean there is an effective marginal IHT rate of ***60%*** on the value of the estate falling into the bracket from £2m to £2.35m; or up to £2.7m in the case of many widows/widowers. This potentially makes planning measures to reduce the amount of the estate within this bracket one and a half times as valuable (e.g. reducing the estate by £10,000 could save up to £6,000 in IHT).

Unused Exemption Passing to Spouse

Like the main NRB, any unused proportion of the RNRB passes to the deceased's spouse. This is not automatic, however: the additional transferred RNRB must subsequently be claimed by the spouse's personal representatives when that spouse also dies.

Tapering applies to the amount that may be transferred. Hence, for example, in Ollie's case above, only 71.43% (£125,000/£175,000) of his RNRB would transfer to his spouse if he did not use it himself.

Where a married individual died before the RNRB was introduced in April 2017, their entire RNRB is deemed unused and transfers to their widow/widower. This transfer also remains subject to tapering where the deceased spouse's estate was worth in excess of £2m.

Put simply, this means all widows/widowers whose late spouse died before 6th April 2017, with an estate worth not more than £2m, are entitled to double the normal amount of RNRB (hence, they are entitled to up to £350,000 at the rates applying until at least 5th April 2031).

For deaths after 5th April 2017, the fact the RNRB is used first, in priority to the NRB, means the amount of TNRB arising may sometimes be enhanced. We will look at some of the planning issues regarding transfers of unused NRBs and RNRBs to widows/widowers in Chapter 6. In both cases, it is important to remember it is the unused ***proportion*** that transfers, not the unused ***amount***. See also Section 6.3 for guidance on using the RNRB on the first spouse's death where the couple's combined estate exceeds £2m.

3.5 GIFTS TO CHARITIES & OTHER EXEMPT BODIES

Generally, gifts to UK-registered charities are exempt from IHT. This covers both lifetime gifts and legacies left to charities on death. For lifetime gifts made before 26th November 2025 and legacies on a death before 6th April 2026, the exemption extended to gifts to a charitable trust. From those dates onwards, however, the legacy or gift must generally go directly to the charity (subject to an exception for interest in possession trusts already in existence before 26th November 2025: see Section 8.13).

For gifts and legacies before 1st April 2024, the exemption also applied to charitable organisations based anywhere in the European Union, Iceland, or Norway. Charitable organisations outside the UK had to have been accepted as a qualifying organisation by HMRC by 14th March 2023.

It is easy enough to ensure lifetime gifts are made directly to UK-registered charities but, following the recent changes, it is also essential for individuals to review their Wills to ensure any charitable legacies still qualify for the exemption: especially if they are hoping to benefit from the additional relief in Section 3.6.

Community Amateur Sports Clubs (CASCs): If you're more interested in sport than charity, registered CASCs are treated the same as UK-registered charities for all IHT purposes, including the exemption outlined above and the relief described in Section 3.6.

Gifts to Housing Associations: Transfers of value attributable to land in the UK and made to registered social landlords are exempt from IHT.

Gifts for National Purposes: Gifts to institutions such as the British Museum or any of the other bodies listed in section IHTM11224 of HMRC's manuals are exempt from IHT.

Gifts to Political Parties: Gifts to qualifying political parties are exempt from IHT. Funny that, isn't it? To qualify, the party must either have had at least two members elected to the House of Commons, or have received no fewer than 150,000 votes in total and had one member elected to the House of Commons, at the last general election.

3.6 CHARITABLE LEGACIES

Charitable legacies are exempt from IHT: provided the legacy meets the criteria examined in Section 3.5. An additional relief also applies where the deceased leaves 10% or more of a component of their estate to charity (or a registered CASC: for the rest of this section, we'll take it as read that any mention of charity also includes CASCs). There are three components of the deceased's estate for this purpose:

i) The survivorship component: property passing by survivorship (e.g. a share in a property held as joint tenants: Section 11.3)

ii) The settled property component: property held in an interest in possession trust that is deemed to form part of the deceased's estate (see Section 8.2)

iii) The general component: the rest of the estate, but excluding any property deemed to form part of the estate under the gift with reservation rules (Section 4.8)

For deaths after 5th April 2027, it is expected that pension death benefits will need to be included in the general component, although this is not yet entirely clear.

Where 10% or more of the net value of a component is left to charity, the rate of IHT charged on that component is reduced to 36%. The net value of a component for this purpose is the value of that component after deducting the appropriate proportion of the deceased's NRB and any other applicable IHT exemptions and reliefs (but still including the amount left to charity).

To simplify matters, let's look at an example where there is only one component: the general component.

Example: *Carter, a divorced man, dies in May 2026 leaving an estate valued at £1m. He leaves £67,500 to the local dog and cat home (a registered charity) and everything else to his niece, Megan. Deducting the NRB of £325,000 from his estate leaves Carter with a net estate chargeable to IHT of £675,000. He has given 10% of this amount to charity, so the IHT rate on Megan's inheritance is reduced to 36%.*

After deducting the charitable legacy (which is exempt), and the NRB, the chargeable estate amounts to £607,500, so the IHT payable at 36% is £218,700. Megan will therefore inherit a net sum of £713,800 (£1m – £67,500 – £218,700).

If Carter had not left anything to charity, the IHT bill would have been £270,000 and Megan would have received a net sum of £730,000. The relief does not leave the non-charitable beneficiary better off than they would have been without the charitable legacy, so it is not worth contemplating such a legacy just to save IHT. But, if you are already planning to leave a sizeable amount to charity, it is certainly worth checking whether you will meet the 10% threshold.

If, in our example above, Carter had left £60,000 to charity, his chargeable estate would have amounted to £615,000 (£1m – £60,000 – £325,000), giving rise to an IHT bill, at 40%, of £246,000. Megan's net inheritance would then have been just £694,000 (£1m – £60,000 –£246,000). Hence, increasing the charitable legacy by £7,500 would actually leave her £19,800 better off overall!

Planning Issues

For many years, it was thought it was not possible for charitable legacies to be 'topped up' to the required 10% threshold by way of a deed of variation (Section 17.1). Recent changes suggest HMRC may now allow this, although, being a cautious man, I would prefer not to rely on it. There are also a number of practical difficulties with deeds of variation, so my suggestion would generally be to make the appropriate provisions in your Will. As no-one can be sure exactly how much their net estate will be, this requires a formula-based approach to ensure the correct result.

As we saw in our example, however, there is no point making charitable legacies just to save IHT: your main beneficiaries will suffer an overall cost equal to at least 24% of the legacy, even after taking account of the relief.

But, as we also saw, where charitable legacies are already planned, there may be an overall saving for your main beneficiaries if you can top up those legacies so they reach the 10% threshold. The question is: when does a top up become worthwhile?

The answer is your main beneficiaries will generally be better off if you top up your charitable legacies to the 10% threshold when you would otherwise have left charitable legacies equal to more than 4% of your net estate. For example, in Carter's case, he had a net estate of £675,000, so Megan would benefit from an increase in his charitable legacies to the 10% threshold if he had already planned to give more than £27,000 to charity anyway.

Finally, remember, a legacy only counts as a charitable legacy for the purposes of this relief where it meets the criteria for the charity exemption outlined in Section 3.5.

Multiple Components

Each of the three components described above may potentially qualify for the relief in their own right, although it is perhaps unlikely in the case of the survivorship component.

Where one component qualifies, the relief can also be claimed on either or both of the other components and/or any assets deemed to be included in the estate due to the gift with reservation rules: provided the 10% threshold is met for the combined value of all the elements included in the claim.

Example: *Ozzy is unmarried and has no children of his own. In the last seven years of his life, he made gifts totalling £400,000: hence there are no exemptions available on his death.*

Ozzy leaves an estate deemed to be valued at a total of £2.5m, which includes a house subject to a gift with reservation worth £800,000, and assets in an old interest in possession trust set up by his mother in 2003 worth a total of £500,000. The general component of his estate thus amounts to £1.2m.

Scenario 1: *Let's say under the terms of the interest in possession trust, half the assets of the trust pass to charity on Ozzy's death. This amounts to £250,000, or 10% of the entire value of Ozzy's estate. His executors can therefore pay IHT at the reduced rate of 36% on the whole chargeable value of Ozzy's estate (which will amount to £2.25m in this case).*

Scenario 2: *The assets of the trust pass to Ozzy's cousin on his death. If Ozzy leaves at least £120,000 to charity, the reduced rate will apply to the general component of his estate. If he increases this to £170,000, his executors could also claim the reduced rate on the trust assets; increasing the charitable legacy to £200,000 would mean the reduced rate could be claimed on either the trust assets or the house subject to a gift with reservation; increasing it to £250,000 would mean the reduced rate can be claimed on Ozzy's entire estate.*

Many other scenarios are possible: but it gets complicated!

For simplicity, I only referred to Ozzy's executors in the example. In practice, claims to pay the reduced rate in such scenarios would require joint elections by all those responsible, potentially including trustees of interest in possession trusts and recipients of property subject to a gift with reservation, or passing by survivorship.

3.7 OTHER EXEMPTIONS

National Heritage Property: Have you ever wondered why so many stately homes are open to the public? Well, just like the bricked-up windows in Georgian houses and the roofless buildings we used to see back in the 1970s, it's all because of tax. IHT arising on transfers of national heritage property can be deferred when the owners give an undertaking to conserve and protect the property. They also need to provide reasonable access to the public. The conditions to be satisfied to claim this exemption are somewhat complex, including, in most cases, the need for the property to be pre-eminent for its national, scientific, historic, or artistic interest.

Death on Active Service: There is a complete exemption from IHT arising on the death of a person from wound, accident, or disease contracted while on active military service. A certificate issued by the Ministry of Defence is required to support a claim. The exemption extends to emergency service personnel killed in the line of duty, or whose death is accelerated due to injuries sustained in the line of duty; and to aid workers dying under similar circumstances, or due to a disease contracted while providing aid. Serving and former police officers or service personnel who are targeted (e.g. by terrorists) because of their status are also covered by the exemption.

Medals and Awards: The value of medals and certain other awards is exempt from IHT when these have never been purchased for consideration in money or money's worth. Hence, the exemption only applies to the original recipient and their subsequent heirs.

Chapter 4

Lifetime Transfers

4.1 INHERITANCE TAX ON LIFETIME TRANSFERS

In Section 2.1, we established what triggers IHT is not death, but a transfer of value. Despite this, few transfers made during an individual's lifetime actually give rise to an immediate IHT liability. The reason for this seemingly contradictory position is the fact lifetime transfers to another individual are treated as potentially exempt transfers (PETs): free of IHT after seven years.

We will return to this concept in Section 4.3 because it remains important to realise 'potentially exempt' also means 'potentially taxable' and many lifetime transfers are therefore still potentially subject to IHT.

4.2 CHARGEABLE LIFETIME TRANSFERS

As explained in Section 4.1, many lifetime transfers are potentially exempt. However, lifetime transfers of value by an individual to a company, or most types of trust *will* be chargeable (i.e. taxable) lifetime transfers (with the exception of transfers to a disabled trust, a bare trust, or, before 26th November 2025, a charitable trust).

Some readers unfamiliar with the nature of trusts may not feel this is much of a problem until I tell you many insurance premiums represent a transfer of value into trust (although most are exempt, as we will see).

Chargeable lifetime transfers may be *immediately* chargeable to IHT, depending on the cumulative value of such transfers made by the transferor within the last seven years. The main incidence of chargeable lifetime transfers arises on transfers into trust, which we will be covering extensively throughout the rest of the guide, particularly Chapters 8 and 9. We will look at transfers into companies, and how to avoid any immediate IHT charges on them, in Chapter 14.

The amount of the chargeable transfer is arrived at by deducting any available exemptions (Chapters 3 and 5) from the transfer of value. The amount on which IHT is actually chargeable is then the lower of the amount of the chargeable transfer, or the sum derived as follows:

Other chargeable transfers within the last seven years	X
PLUS	
This chargeable transfer	X
LESS	
Nil rate band	(X)

Only one NRB may be deducted when calculating the IHT on a chargeable lifetime transfer. The TNRB (see Section 6.2) applies only on death.

IHT on lifetime transfers is charged at half death rates, i.e. 20%. Where other chargeable transfers made in the last seven years already equal or exceed the amount of the NRB, the tax due on the current chargeable transfer is simply a straight 20%.

Example *(I will ignore all exemptions and reliefs, other than the NRB): Two years ago, Elvis gifted investments worth £50,000 into a discretionary trust, giving rise to a chargeable transfer. No IHT was payable at the time, as this was well within his NRB. Elvis now gifts his former home, Graceland, worth £375,000, into a discretionary trust (for the purpose of this example, it doesn't matter whether this is the same trust), on condition the trust settles any IHT arising. The trust's IHT liability is calculated as follows:*

Previous chargeable transfers within last seven years	*£50,000*
Plus this chargeable transfer	*£375,000*
Equals cumulative chargeable transfers	*£425,000*
Less nil rate band	*(£325,000)*
Amount chargeable	*£100,000*
IHT payable at lifetime rate (20%)	*£20,000*

Alternative Scenario with Grossing Up
If Elvis had settled the IHT himself, it would have been subject to grossing up:

Amount chargeable, as before	*£100,000*
Grossing up factor – one quarter	*£25,000*
Grossed up amount	*£125,000*
IHT payable at lifetime rate (20%)	*£25,000*

In this example, Graceland was Elvis's ***former*** home. This is an important point since, as we will see later, it is more difficult to make an IHT-effective transfer of your current home.

If Elvis were married, he could have avoided any IHT on his gift of Graceland by first transferring it into joint names with his spouse before they both jointly gifted it to the discretionary trust. Each of them would have made a chargeable transfer of only £187,500. Even after taking his previous chargeable transfer into account, Elvis would then be covered by his NRB.

Elvis's spouse would also be covered by their NRB as long as they had not made other chargeable transfers within the last seven years in excess of £137,500. (Elvis's spouse must be under no obligation to make the subsequent transfer to the ultimate intended recipient.)

Avoiding Grossing Up
In the above example, we looked at the position where the IHT is paid by the transferee (the trust), as well as where it is paid by the transferor (Elvis).

More tax is generally payable where the transferor is settling the liability. This is because the transferor is deemed to be making a gift not only of the original asset transferred, but also of the tax arising. This, in turn, is because the transfer of value is calculated by reference to the reduction in value of the transferor's overall estate and the payment of the IHT arising naturally increases the amount of that reduction.

The bad news is, in the absence of any evidence to the contrary, the transferor is assumed to be liable for any IHT. Hence, if care is not exercised, you may find the value of any gifts you make turns out to be 25% more than you expected. The way to avoid this is to draw up a memorandum that stipulates the transferee is to pay any IHT arising.

4.3 POTENTIALLY EXEMPT TRANSFERS (PETS)

Lifetime transfers made by an individual to another individual, a bare trust, or a disabled trust, are generally PETs, which fall out of the IHT net after seven years. Transfers made *by* a trust are subject to different rules and we will explore these in Chapter 8.

Exceptions: The following transfers will not be treated as PETs:

- Transfers covered by the spouse exemption (these are fully exempt, except as noted in Section 3.3)
- Transfers covered by another general or lifetime exemption (see Chapters 3 and 5). This will usually be of no practical consequence unless the transferor dies within seven years of making the transfer
- Any transfer that does not result in an increase in the value of the transferee's estate (see further in Section 4.4)
- Transfers of value caused by alterations to share capital, loan capital, or other rights in most private companies
- A transfer of value to a disabled trust that does not consist of a transfer of property into the trust (see further in Section 4.4)

What Do We Mean By 'Potentially Exempt'?

Put simply, these transfers are *potentially* exempt because all the transferor has to do is survive seven years after making the transfer for it to become fully exempt and completely free of any IHT liability (subject to the gifts with reservation rules: see Section 4.8).

In the meantime, the transfer is treated as if it is exempt (i.e. no IHT is due) and only becomes chargeable if the transferor dies within seven years of the date the transfer was made. If the transferor is still alive at the beginning of the seventh anniversary of the transfer, full exemption is achieved.

Example: *On 4th August 2019, Chuck gave £1m to his little brother, Richard. Sadly, on 10th August 2026, Chuck is electrocuted while playing his electric guitar in a rainstorm. The gift to Richard was a PET and, since Chuck survived the requisite seven years (just!), this sum is exempt from IHT on Chuck's death.*

If Chuck had died a week earlier, IHT would have been payable on his gift to Richard (see further in Section 4.5). Hence, it is essential to have the documentary evidence to prove the gift took place when it did. See also Section 4.7 regarding the timing of gifts made by cheque.

4.4 PROBLEMS WITH PETS

One little known, but potentially important, point about PETs is there must be an increase in the value of the transferee's estate in order for the transfer to qualify. Furthermore, where the transferee is a disabled trust, there must be an actual gift of property into the trust.

Any transfers that do not qualify as PETs as a result of failing to meet these requirements will be chargeable lifetime transfers, unless some other exemption is available.

Transfers that do not increase the transferee's estate might include:

i) A grandparent paying their grandchild's school fees. The grandchild, while receiving an indirect benefit, does not enjoy any increase in the value of their estate.
ii) Paying an insurance premium on a policy held for someone else's benefit. The value of the policy remains the same before and after payment of the premium, so there is no increase in the value of the transferee's estate.
iii) A parent paying the maintenance costs for their adult child's house. The value of the house may not necessarily be increased through routine maintenance, so neither is the child's estate.

Each of these payments might be exempt under the normal expenditure out of income exemption (Section 5.5). It only matters that they are not PETs when they are not already exempt under that exemption, or one of the other exemptions we will examine in Chapter 5.

Nevertheless, in IHT planning, it is important to understand the status of every transfer of value. Remember that chargeable lifetime transfers must effectively be accumulated over a seven-year period and IHT charges will result if the cumulative total exceeds the NRB.

Hence, a transfer made today, which turns out to be a chargeable lifetime transfer instead of a PET, could cause additional IHT charges to arise at any time over the next seven years, even if the transferor survives throughout this period.

Looking after your PETS

In the first situation outlined above, the grandparent could avoid the problem by giving the necessary funds to cover the school fees to the child's parent, who would then pay the school fees themselves.

Alternatively, the parent could contract to pay the school fees, with the result that the payment by the grandparent gives rise to an increase in the value of the parent's estate, thus meaning a PET has taken place. The key point is that the grandparent should not contract directly with the school unless they can be certain the normal expenditure out of income exemption will apply.

The second situation above is perhaps the one most likely to be covered by the normal expenditure out of income exemption. In other cases, the position might be rectified by giving the money to pay the premium to the beneficiary, who then pays it themselves, although this does depend on who the policyholder is and whether the policy is held in trust. We will return to the subject of insurance premiums in Section 11.8.

The position in the third situation is perhaps arguable. In a case like this, there is a PET to the extent the value of the child's house is increased as a result of the work paid for by the parent. The remainder of the parent's expenditure, however, represents a chargeable lifetime transfer (unless covered by another exemption).

Example: *Joe's daughter, Sam, would like to have her house completely redecorated. Joe offers to get the work done at his own expense. He contracts for a decorator to do the work, which is then carried out at a cost of £20,000. Joe has therefore made a transfer of value of £20,000.*

Before the redecoration work, Sam's house was worth £300,000. Immediately after the work, it is worth £308,000. Joe has made a PET of £8,000 (the increase in the value of Sam's house). The remaining spending of £12,000 will be a chargeable lifetime transfer (unless covered by other exemptions).

Joe could have prevented any chargeable lifetime transfer very easily by simply giving all the money for the work to Sam and leaving her to contract for the work and pay the bill herself. Alternatively, if Sam had contracted for the work herself and was therefore liable for the decorator's bill, Joe could settle that bill and this would also be a PET as Sam's estate increases when her liability is settled. Either way, it is sensible for Sam to contract for the work!

If Joe were contractually liable for the work on Sam's house, but he gave Sam the money to pay the bill and she settled it, this could result in further PETs of £20,000 both from Joe to Sam and from Sam to Joe, as well as the transfers already described in the example above. If *either* of them died within seven years, this could result in additional IHT liabilities.

The requirements for a transfer to qualify as a PET where the transferee is a trust are even more restrictive. If Sam's house was held by a disabled trust for her benefit, the only way for Joe to fund the redecoration work as a PET would be for him to give the trust £20,000. The trustees could then contract and pay for the work.

If Joe settled the decorating bill, this would be a chargeable transfer regardless of who had contracted for the work. Settling a debt on behalf of a disabled trust will not qualify as a PET.

4.5 DEATH WITHIN SEVEN YEARS

For CGT purposes, death is often a good tax-planning strategy. The same cannot be said of IHT. Both chargeable lifetime transfers and PETs made in the seven-year period prior to death are effectively brought back into the deceased's estate for IHT purposes. This applies whether any IHT was payable at the time of the original transfer or not.

Subject to the tapering provisions set out below, IHT becomes payable at the death rate (40%) on transfers made within the seven years prior to the transferor's death. Any IHT paid on the original transfer may be deducted, so that just the excess arises on death.

The additional IHT liabilities arising are usually the responsibility of the transferees. In other words, the situation may be like this: "I'm very sorry to hear about your father, son, but do you remember that gift of £10,000 he gave you two years ago? Well, I'm afraid you're going to have to pay some tax on it." Now do you see why I call it an 'immoral and evil tax'?

The best way to avoid unwanted liabilities falling on transferees in the event of your death within seven years is to record your intention to bear any tax arising in a memorandum at the time of the gift. Alternatively, you can make a specific bequest in your Will in respect of the IHT falling on the transferee.

To avoid doubt, it is probably best to do both. There are two problems with both of these approaches, however. Firstly, the payment of IHT arising at the time of your death from out of your estate will itself represent another transfer of value and hence grossing up at full death rates may apply (see Section 2.8).

Secondly, the primary responsibility for any IHT arising on death remains with the transferee. If there are insufficient funds remaining in your estate to cover the tax, the transferee will still have to foot the bill. In practice, it often makes more sense for the transferee to take out term insurance on the life of the transferor in order to cover any potential IHT arising on the latter's death.

Conversely, the transferor will often be concerned to ensure any IHT arising on earlier gifts does not come out of his or her estate and thus reduce the value of the net estate passing to their primary beneficiaries.

In theory, of course, the IHT arising on transfers made in the last seven years of the transferor's life should be paid by the transferees. However, as we saw in Section 2.9, HMRC is more concerned with collecting the tax than with who gets hurt. To put matters (reasonably) beyond doubt, it is therefore wise to use a memorandum specifying the transferee's responsibility for any IHT arising. Sadly, even this will not help if the transferee simply cannot pay.

Tapering

Fortunately, there is some relief when death occurs at least three, but less than seven, years after the lifetime transfer. In these cases, the rate of IHT arising on death is tapered as follows:

No. of years after transfer before death occurs:	**Proportion of 40% Death Rate payable**
Less than 3	100% (= IHT @ 40%)
At least 3, less than 4	80% (= IHT @ 32%)
At least 4, less than 5	60% (= IHT @ 24%)
At least 5, less than 6	40% (= IHT @ 16%)
At least 6, less than 7	20% (= IHT @ 8%)

Thanks to the tapering provisions, IHT savings may start to arise once the transferor has survived three years. Hence, even if you don't think Great Aunt Maude stands any chance of lasting seven years, it may still be worth looking at getting her to make some gifts.

The reductions in the amount of IHT payable apply from the date of the relevant anniversary. The savings only relate to the lifetime gifts made by the deceased. Tapering has no effect on the amount of IHT payable on the estate itself. Tapering can therefore only produce a saving where the deceased has made lifetime gifts in excess of the NRB.

In the case of chargeable lifetime transfers (Section 4.2), the tapering provisions could result in the final IHT liability on death being less than the amount already paid. Unfortunately, this simply means no further IHT is due; it does not result in any repayment.

In calculating the IHT due on each transfer made within the seven years prior to death, any chargeable transfers in the seven years before *that* transfer must be taken into account. For this reason, chargeable lifetime transfers made up to fourteen years previously may continue to have an impact on the IHT arising on the transferor's death.

The calculation of the tax arising on transfers made within the seven years prior to death is almost a repeat of the calculation we saw in Section 4.2 for a chargeable lifetime transfer, except that:

- The full death rate (40%) is used
- Tapering relief (as set out above) is applied
- The NRB available at the date of death is used in the calculations, rather than the NRB applying at the time of the transfer
- Any unused NRB on the earlier death of the deceased's spouse is also available (see Section 6.2 for further details)
- PETs made in the seven years prior to death must be brought into the calculation

Example *(I will again ignore any exemptions and reliefs, except the NRB): Roy is a lifelong bachelor and a kind, generous, rich old man. Sadly, despite the fact his nurses handle him with care, he dies on 6th December 2026. Roy made no chargeable transfers prior to 2016 but, in the last decade of his life, he made the following gifts:*

- *On 10th December 2016, he gave £200,000 in cash to the Wilbury Discretionary Trust*
- *On 1st December 2019, he gave £50,000 in cash to his nephew George*
- *On 13th January 2020, he gave another £145,000 in cash to the Wilbury Discretionary Trust. He paid £5,000 in IHT at that time (grossing up applied)*
- *On 8th May 2022, he gave his friend Jeff some shares in the Electric Light Company Inc. At that time, the shares were worth £50,000*
- *On 7th December 2023, he gave his friend Tom some shares in Heartbreakers.com plc, which were worth £80,000 at that time*
- *On 24th August 2024, he gave his friend Bob £100,000 in cash*

The IHT payable by each transferee on Roy's death is as follows:

The Wilbury Discretionary Trust (First Gift): *Roy's first gift to the trust in December 2016 was made more than seven years prior to his death. This gift itself will therefore not be subject to IHT on his death. However, because gifts to discretionary trusts are chargeable transfers, it will have an impact on other gifts made in the following seven years.*

George: *Roy's gift to George was a PET made more than seven years prior to his death. On the seventh anniversary of that gift, 1st December 2026, it became fully exempt and hence can now be completely ignored for the purposes of calculating the IHT arising on Roy's death.*

The Wilbury Discretionary Trust (Second Gift): *Due to grossing up, Roy's second gift to the trust in January 2020 was deemed to have been £150,000. As this gift was within the last seven years of Roy's life, it is effectively pulled back into his estate for the purposes of his IHT calculation. Furthermore, in calculating the IHT now due on this gift, we must also take account of his previous gift to the trust, as that first gift was a chargeable transfer made within the seven-year period prior to the second gift.*

The gift to George in December 2019 can be ignored as this has become fully exempt. The cumulative total of chargeable lifetime transfers made by Roy up to the time of the second gift to the trust was therefore £350,000. After deducting the NRB of £325,000, there remains a chargeable sum of £25,000.

As the gift took place more than six, but less than seven, years before Roy's death, IHT is chargeable at 20% of the death rate, i.e. 8%. Hence the IHT charge arising on Roy's death is £2,000. As this is less than the IHT already paid by Roy at the time of the gift (£5,000), no further IHT is payable.

Jeff: *Roy's gift of shares to Jeff in May 2022 was a PET. Unfortunately, as Roy has died within seven years of making that gift, it has now become a chargeable transfer. Both of the gifts to the Wilbury Discretionary Trust took place within the seven-year period prior to the gift to Jeff, so the cumulative value of chargeable transfers at this point is £350,000, meaning the NRB has been fully exhausted and the gift to Jeff is fully chargeable to IHT.*

However, since the gift took place more than four, but less than five, years before Roy's death, IHT is only chargeable at 60% of the death rate, i.e. 24%. Jeff therefore has an IHT liability of £12,000 (£50,000 x 24%).

Tom: *Tom is going to be heartbroken. His gift took place just one day short of three years before Roy's death. IHT is therefore payable at the full death rate, 40%. Furthermore, the total cumulative value of chargeable transfers within the previous seven years amounts to £400,000, made up as follows:*

First gift to Wilbury Discretionary Trust	*£200,000*
Second gift to Wilbury Discretionary Trust	*£150,000*
Gift to Jeff	*£50,000*
Total	*£400,000*

Both gifts to the Wilbury Discretionary Trust are included as they both took place within the seven-year period prior to the gift to Tom. The gift to Jeff is also included, as it has now become a chargeable transfer due to Roy's death within seven years. Tom therefore has an IHT liability of £32,000 (40% x £80,000).

Bob: *This gift took place within the last three years of Roy's life, so there is no tapering of the IHT liability. The cumulative value of chargeable transfers within the seven years prior to this gift is £280,000, made up as follows:*

Second gift to Wilbury Discretionary Trust	*£150,000*
Gift to Jeff	*£50,000*
Gift to Tom	*£80,000*
Total	*£280,000*

The first gift to the Wilbury Discretionary Trust is not included as it took place more than seven years before the gift to Bob. Adding Bob's own gift to the above figure gives a total of £380,000. From this, we are able to deduct the NRB of £325,000, leaving Bob with a chargeable transfer of £55,000. Bob's IHT liability is therefore £22,000 (40% x £55,000).

The total value of chargeable transfers in the last seven years of Roy's life amounts to £380,000. His NRB is therefore already exhausted before we even begin to look at his estate.

A point to note is that the oldest gift in our example, made almost ten years before Roy's death, had a major impact on the recipients of later gifts, despite the fact it was made before the critical seven-year period.

It is also interesting to note the oldest gift within the seven-year period did not give rise to any more IHT for the recipients of that gift. This will often be the case for chargeable lifetime transfers made more than five years prior to the transferor's death. This position may be altered, however, where there are significant amounts of PETs made within seven years of the transferor's death, but prior to the chargeable transfer in question.

As we saw in the example, these two earlier gifts used up Roy's NRB, which had a major impact on some of the later transferees. This was particularly unfortunate for Tom, since a mere four days' delay to his gift would have meant the first gift to the Wilbury Discretionary Trust would have been made more than seven years previously. Tom's gift would then have been completely covered by the NRB.

Where practical, it may make sense to leave a seven-year gap after making a large chargeable lifetime transfer before making further chargeable transfers or PETs. Naturally, of course, delaying your gifts carries other conflicting risks, which you will need to weigh up. However, a delay of just four days in order to bring the NRB back into play would surely make sense!

By the time of Bob's gift in 2024, part of the NRB was available once more, thus giving him a lower IHT bill on a larger gift. This ably demonstrates that, with careful planning, **the NRB is available not just once a lifetime, but once every seven years!**

While none of us knows exactly when we have seven years left to go, it is also worth bearing in mind that gifts in the last seven years of your life will be dealt with chronologically when you die.

Although kind old Roy cannot really be blamed for the final outcome in the example, things might have turned out fairer if he had made some of the smaller gifts first.

A Final Observation

As discussed in Section 3.2, the NRB had originally been due to increase to £350,000 in 2010 but was, instead, frozen at its 2009/10 level of £325,000. By 2026/27, the NRB should perhaps be something like £665,000 (even if only increased in line with retail price inflation), £340,000 more than it actually is. At first glance, one might think this freeze could only cost a maximum of £136,000 (£340,000 x 40%) in extra IHT on the occasion of one person's death. Think again!

In our example above, the freeze in the NRB has effectively cost Jeff £12,000, Tom £32,000, Bob £22,000, and will also cost Roy's estate an extra £114,000: a total of £180,000. In fact, the freeze in the NRB could cost some bereaved families up to £544,000 in extra tax in 2026/27; and perhaps as much as £704,000 by 2030/31.

4.6 RELIEF FOR REDUCTION IN VALUE

Where IHT becomes payable on the transferor's death within seven years of making a lifetime transfer of property that has subsequently reduced in value, the transferee may claim relief from IHT in respect of that reduction in value. To claim relief, the following conditions must be satisfied:

i) The property transferred must not be tangible moveable property with a predictable useful life not exceeding fifty years (e.g. a car, or other machinery), and
ii) Either:
    a) At the time of the transferor's death the property is still held by the transferee or their spouse, or
    b) The property has been sold by the transferee or their spouse by way of a sale at arm's length to an unconnected person

When such a claim is made, the IHT on that transfer is calculated by substituting the property's market value at the relevant date for its value at the date of the transfer. Where the property is still held by the transferee or their spouse at the date of the transferor's death, the relevant date is the date of death. Where the property has been sold in an arm's length transaction with an unconnected party, the relevant date is the date of the sale.

The amount of relief given is the reduction in value of the transferred asset itself, without taking account of other assets that may have affected the amount of the transfer of value (see Sections 2.1 and 11.2).

The relief cannot be used to obtain any repayment of IHT that arose immediately on a chargeable lifetime transfer (see Section 4.2); it applies only to the tax arising on the donor's death.

The IHT on any other transfers and on the deceased's estate is unaffected. This is because the value of the transferred property is reduced only for the purposes of this relief and not for the purposes of calculating cumulative chargeable transfers in any seven-year period.

Example: *At the time of Roy's death, Jeff still holds the shares in the Electric Light Company Inc. that Roy gave to him when they were worth £50,000. Unfortunately, they are now worth only £30,000. Nonetheless, Jeff is pleased to discover he can reduce his IHT bill to just £7,200 (£30,000 x 24%: see Section 4.5).*

Tom is also very excited at the prospect of a relief claim under these provisions as his shares in Heartbreakers.com plc fell rapidly in value after Roy gave them to him and Tom eventually sold them for just £1,000.

According to Tom's calculations, he should therefore be able to reduce his IHT bill to just £400 (£1,000 x 40%). However, it transpires that Tom sold the Heartbreakers.com plc shares to his son. This was not an arm's length sale to an unconnected party and Tom's IHT bill remains £32,000 (see Section 4.5). Heartbroken again!

The IHT liabilities for Roy's personal representatives and Bob are unaffected by Jeff's claim. (Nor would they be affected by Tom's claim if it had been valid.)

It does not matter whether Tom sold his shares to his son at market value. Because he and his son are connected, Tom loses his ability to claim relief for his shares' reduction in value. He therefore ends up with some shares that are virtually worthless and an IHT liability of £32,000.

A transferee holding property that was transferred to them less than seven years ago, and which has reduced in value since then, would be wise to avoid making any transfers of that property other than a sale at arm's length to an unconnected person, or a transfer to their spouse.

4.7 TIMING AND EVIDENCE

A gift made by cheque is deemed to be made when the cheque is cleared by the transferor's bank. This will inevitably cause a slight delay to the date the gift is deemed to take place. While the delay may be slight, it could have disastrous consequences.

If the cheque clears after the transferor's death, for example, it will no longer be regarded as a lifetime gift and will form part of the transferor's estate on death. This will mean none of the lifetime exemptions can apply, including the annual exemption and small gifts exemption.

For the sake of certainty, it may often be worth incurring the additional cost of putting the cheque through same day clearing. Alternatively, where the transferor has access to online or telephone banking facilities, it might be more efficient for them to make their gifts by way of electronic transfer. While the point has not yet arisen in a suitable court case, it would seem logical to assume gifts made by way of electronic transfer will be treated as having been made when the funds are deducted from the transferor's account. While this will undoubtedly speed up the process, it will remain vital to prepare suitable documentation to evidence the gift. HMRC will try very hard to get assets back into the deceased's estate in order to increase the amount of IHT payable.

To prevent questions like, "How do we know this money wasn't just a loan; can you prove she didn't expect you to repay it?" or, "Yes, we know your parents gave you the house, but what about the contents; there's nothing to prove they gave them to you," it is vital that gifts are evidenced. Furthermore, it is important the documentary evidence of the gifts is specific about exactly what is being gifted.

4.8 GIFTS WITH RESERVATION

To give something away so that it is no longer part of your estate for IHT purposes, you need to completely deprive yourself of that asset and any enjoyment of it. Any purported gifts where you retain a beneficial interest in the gifted asset are ineffective for IHT purposes and are effectively treated as still being part of your estate.

For example, if you 'give' a painting to your son but keep it in your house then you are still enjoying that asset and it remains part of your estate for IHT purposes.

These types of transfer are known as gifts with reservation. This is a particular problem when looking at the family home and we will return to this subject in Chapter 13.

Broadly speaking, a gift with reservation occurs whenever:

i) The transferee does not obtain genuine possession and enjoyment of the gifted asset,
ii) The transferor is not excluded from enjoyment of the gifted asset, or
iii) The transferor has some form of contractual right over the gifted asset

We have already seen an example of (i): the gifted painting being kept in the transferor's house. An example of (ii) would be to give a holiday cottage to your daughter, which you then use for a month each year. An example of (iii) would be to grant yourself a lease over your own property then transfer the freehold to your children.

Although you have to be excluded from the enjoyment of a gifted asset, there is a little leeway. If you give your son a painting, which he keeps in his house, there is no need to wear a blindfold every time you visit.

The strict rule is that the transferor must be virtually excluded from the enjoyment of the asset. Mere incidental enjoyment of a gifted asset when making a short visit to the transferee is permitted. Hence, if you give your daughter a house and visit her for dinner once every six months, you will not usually have a problem. If, on the other hand, you stay at the house every second weekend, there could be a gift with reservation.

The gift with reservation rules apply to property if the transferor is in occupation. HMRC's guidance suggests this requires an element of control and exclusion: for example, the ability to access the property freely, or store items there. Use of a property that fulfils these criteria will amount to occupation, even if only occasional, thus leading to a gift with reservation.

Thankfully, one group of gifts that would otherwise almost always fall foul of the gift with reservation rules are generally exempted from these provisions: gifts covered by the spouse exemption (Section 3.3).

Unforeseen Changes in Circumstances

In the case of a property that a transferor has gifted to a relative, there will not be a gift with reservation if the transferor is forced to move back into that property due to an unforeseen change in circumstances whereby he or she is unable to care for themselves due to ill health, old age, or infirmity.

This, for example, may cover the situation where a person has transferred a property to their son or daughter and some years later has to move into the property so their family can care for them.

The move back into the property must be for the provision of reasonable care and maintenance by the transferee, who must also be a relative. You can't just move back in because you'd like to see a bit more of the grandchildren. This change must also be unforeseen. If you are already ill when you make the gift, the gift with reservation rules will still apply.

What's So Bad about Gifts with Reservation?

Plenty! Firstly, although the gift is ineffective when it comes to excluding the gifted asset from your estate, it is nevertheless still a transfer of value and could give rise to an IHT charge if you die within seven years, or even an immediate charge in the case of a transfer into trust (see Section 4.2).

Some relief is given to prevent a double charge, but it does not entirely eliminate the problem. Where the transferor dies within seven years of making a gift with reservation, two IHT calculations must be prepared. In the first calculation, IHT is calculated as if the transfer had never taken place and the transferor still owned the gifted asset at the date of death. A second calculation must then be prepared on the basis the transfer *did* take place.

The bad news is the calculation that produces the greater amount of IHT is then used. In other words, the tax payable is the *greater* of the amount payable on the transfer *or* the amount payable on the asset deemed to still be in your estate on death!

Generally, where the gifted asset is increasing in value, we would expect the greater tax to arise by including the asset in the estate on death. The overall effect of this is to render the gift ineffective for IHT purposes. However, in some cases, the second calculation will produce the greater tax, meaning the transfer has actually cost your family more. We will see an example of one way this might arise in Section 13.11. In short, a gift with reservation where that reservation still applies at the time of the donor's death is at best ineffective and at worst may even increase the total IHT due.

Another problem is the fact the gifted asset will also be included in the transferee's estate, thus giving rise to a possible double charge. Additionally, while the gift is ineffective for IHT purposes, it will still be a disposal for CGT purposes. This means CGT liabilities could arise on the gift. Furthermore, the transferee may not be entitled to the same reliefs as the transferor would have been if they had retained the asset. We will explore the potential impact of this further in Chapter 12.

Reservation Reliefs

Assets treated as still being part of your estate on death under the gifts with reservation rules remain eligible for a number of important reliefs, including the RNRB (Section 3.4), business property relief (Chapter 7), and agricultural property relief (Section 7.27). We will take a look at the position where the RNRB applies to a gift with reservation of the family home in Section 13.11.

What Happens If the Reservation Ends?

If the reservation ends during the transferor's lifetime, a new transfer is deemed to take place. For example, if a mother gave a house to her two sons in 2006, but continued to live in it until 2026, there would be a deemed transfer of the house in 2026. This time the transfer *is* effective for IHT purposes. It is treated as a PET, so it will not cause any immediate IHT charges, but it does give rise to a few problems.

The main problem, of course, is that the transferor will have to survive at least seven years after the reservation ends before the transferred asset is exempt from IHT. Furthermore, the value of the deemed transfer will be the asset's value at the date the reservation ends, not the date of the original transfer.

Deemed transfers on cessation of a reservation are ineligible for a number of reliefs, including the RNRB and annual exemption (Section 5.2).

If the transferor dies within seven years of the cessation of a reservation, the property subject to the reservation will effectively fall into the deceased's estate. Hence, the mother in our example would need to live until at least 2033 for her transfer of the house in 2006 to be exempt from IHT. If she should pass away before then, the value of the house when she moved out in 2026 will effectively be brought back into her estate. However, since there has now been an IHT-effective lifetime transfer (albeit in 2026 rather than 2006), the RNRB will not be available to exempt any of the house's value.

Where both the original transfer and the deemed transfer on cessation of the reservation take place within the seven years prior to the transferor's death, it will again be necessary to prepare two IHT calculations: one including the original transfer and one including the deemed transfer. Once again, the calculation producing the greater amount of tax will be used. The RNRB will not be available to exempt any of the transferred asset's value in either calculation under these circumstances.

4.9 WHY NOT JUST GIVE IT ALL AWAY?

After reading Section 4.3, you may have been thinking that avoiding IHT is simple. All you need to do is give everything away to your family and survive seven years. Well, yes, in theory, in the right circumstances, simply giving your property away during your lifetime can be an effective way to avoid IHT.

Certainly, there is no problem with giving away whatever parts of your estate you can afford to. Just remember to make sure the gifts are PETs and then take good care of yourself for seven years. (Or take out some term insurance to cover the IHT risk: see Section 11.8.)

Unfortunately, however, in practice, there are a few catches. Firstly, as we have already seen, any gifts where you retain a beneficial interest are treated as still being part of your estate. Secondly, even where a transfer appears to avoid the gifts with reservation rules, there may be an Income Tax benefit-in-kind charge applying if the transferor continues to enjoy the use of the asset. This charge may also apply to any future use by the donor of an asset purchased with gifted funds (see Section 11.12).

Thirdly, when gifting assets other than cash, you may be exposed to CGT. Most lifetime gifts are treated like a sale at current market value for CGT purposes. (Here there is no problem with the family home, as it is generally exempt from CGT under private residence relief: this issue is fully explained in the Taxcafe guide *How to Save Property Tax*.)

Lastly, in practice, you cannot simply give all your assets away because you will need something to live off for the rest of your life. This may include the need to pay care home fees at some point in the future: an issue we will discuss further in Section 11.5.

So, it's fine if you're happy to spend the rest of your days in a monastery or nunnery, or live off your last £325,000 (for at least seven years) but, in reality, very few people would be happy to follow such a drastic course of action. Hence, at this point, we need to start looking at what exemptions and reliefs are available and how you can use them to best effect.

Chapter 5

Lifetime Exemptions

5.1 ABSOLUTE EXEMPTION

There are a number of exemptions available to cover lifetime transfers. These are absolute exemptions, not dependent on whether you survive for any particular period.

Transfers covered by these exemptions would be free from IHT even if you were to pass away the very next day, or even on the way home from the lawyer's office. (Don't laugh: I know of one sad, but true, case where the taxpayer was knocked down by a bus outside the lawyer's office!)

These exemptions therefore provide useful IHT planning tools under the right circumstances. Sadly though, the monetary values of the exemptions covered in Sections 5.2 and 5.3 have remained the same since 1981 and 1975 respectively. These values are long overdue for an increase, since retail price inflation alone should have increased them around six-fold by now!

5.2 THE ANNUAL AND SMALL GIFTS EXEMPTIONS

The first £3,000 of any transfers of value, which are not otherwise exempt, that each individual makes in each tax year, are exempt from IHT. Married couples have an annual exemption of £3,000 each. If the annual exemption is not used one year, it may be carried forward and can be used in the next tax year if that following year's annual exemption is fully exhausted.

The annual exemption may not be very large, but it is important to bear it in mind when undertaking IHT planning. Making best use of the exemption is a matter of timing. The ability to carry it forward one year gives you a second chance, but the use of the annual exemption should nevertheless be reviewed at least every other year. A couple who manage to make effective use of the annual exemption in the final few years of their lives will save around £20,000 in IHT.

According to HMRC, the taxpayer's annual exemption must be applied on a strictly chronological basis. In their view, the exemption must be utilised against any PETs taking place before chargeable lifetime transfers made later in the same tax year. This could have some unfortunate consequences.

Example: *Brian gives £6,000 to his brother Carl on 6th April 2026. This (according to HMRC) uses up Brian's annual exemptions for 2025/26 and 2026/27, despite being a PET. On 10th April 2026, Brian gives £331,000 to the Wilson Phillips Discretionary Trust for the benefit of his many nephews and nieces. After deducting the NRB of £325,000, the remaining £6,000 must be grossed up at the rate of one quarter, giving Brian an IHT bill of £1,500. If, instead, Brian had made his gifts in the opposite order, his annual exemptions would have been deducted from his chargeable transfer, leaving £325,000, which would be covered by his NRB, leaving no IHT to pay.*

HMRC's interpretation on this point is based entirely on a flaw in the drafting of the IHT law. What Parliament actually intended was for the annual exemption to be used first against any chargeable lifetime transfers, with any excess remaining available to cover PETs if they subsequently became chargeable on the transferor's death.

This difference in interpretation will affect not only those making large chargeable lifetime transfers in excess of the NRB, like Brian in the example above, but also the transferees calculating their own IHT bill in the event of the transferor's death within seven years. In the latter case there will be winners and losers but, in the former, only HMRC can be the winner!

In practice, I would always advocate planning your affairs on the basis of HMRC's interpretation wherever possible. Chargeable lifetime transfers should therefore be made earlier in the tax year than PETs whenever possible.

But, if you find you are already in a position where their interpretation is putting you at a disadvantage, you should argue for the law to be applied as it was quite clearly intended by Parliament: an argument frequently used by HMRC, so why shouldn't the taxpayer argue the same!

Transfers made on the same day are treated as simultaneous. Any available annual exemption is divided between the same-day transfers in proportion to their value.

The Small Gifts Exemption
There is also a general exemption for outright gifts of up to £250 to any one person each tax year. This exemption applies to any number of such small gifts to separate persons each year. It can only apply to straightforward gifts to other individuals and cannot apply to transfers into trust. A married couple may each use this exemption separately in their own right.

The small gifts exemption only covers gifts *up to* £250. Unlike the annual exemption, it does not cover the first part of a larger gift. Hence, a gift of £251 is not covered by this exemption at all. Note also that the exemption has to cover all gifts to the same person in the whole tax year.

The small gifts exemption cannot be used in conjunction with the annual exemption. In other words, it is not possible to exempt gifts totalling £3,250 to the same person by using both exemptions together.

5.3 GIFTS IN CONSIDERATION OF MARRIAGE

It's an expensive business when the kids get married, but it does provide an additional opportunity for some IHT planning. Gifts made in consideration of marriage are exempt from IHT up to the following limits:

- Parents: £5,000
- Grandparents, Great-Grandparents, etc: £2,500
- One party to the marriage to the other: £2,500
- Other donors: £1,000

All these limits apply on an individual basis and the relationships referred to must be to one of the parties to the marriage. Hence, for example, the groom could receive £5,000 from each of his parents, £2,500 from each of his grandparents, and £1,000 from each of his aunts and uncles; while the bride could receive the same from her family.

Alternatively, the bride's family could make their gifts to the groom or the groom's family could make their gifts to the bride. And all the same applies where there are two grooms or two brides.

Additionally, within the same exemption (and within the same overriding limits set out above), gifts could be made to a trust for the benefit of:

i) One or both of the parties to the marriage
ii) Children of either or both parties to the marriage
iii) Future spouses of children of either or both parties to the marriage
iv) A future spouse of either party to the marriage
v) Children of any subsequent spouse of either party to this marriage and future spouses of those children

This all sounds terribly complicated, but it means the marriage provides an opportunity to put money into trust for both living and unborn children of either or both parties without giving rise to a chargeable lifetime transfer.

To fall within the exemption gifts must be made on or shortly before the marriage and must be fully effective when the marriage takes place. For example, 'I give you my property at Valotte on condition you marry my daughter.'

Where the gifts exceed the limits shown above, the excess may be covered by the annual exemption, if available. Otherwise, the excess will be treated like any other lifetime transfer, as explained in Chapter 4.

All of the above applies equally to same sex marriages and registered civil partnerships. See Section 1.4 for the definition of who counts as your child, grandchild, etc, for the purpose of this exemption.

5.4 MAINTENANCE OF FAMILY

Anything you do for the maintenance of your family (as defined below) is exempted from being a transfer of value for IHT purposes. Just as well since otherwise, every time you bought the weekly groceries you would be at risk of causing an IHT liability! This covers expenditure for the maintenance of your spouse, plus expenditure for the maintenance, education, or training of:

- Your child (see Section 1.4), who was either under 18 or still in full-time education or training on the key date.
- Any other child who:
  a) is not in the care of a parent and was under 18 on the key date, or
  b) has been in your care for a substantial period and was still in full time education or training on the key date.

The 'key date' in each case is the last 5th April prior to the time of the relevant expenditure.

One major absentee from this list is your unmarried partner and hence, technically, any expenditure for the maintenance of a common-law co-habiting partner could be a transfer of value. Thankfully, however, such expenditure will generally be covered by the normal expenditure out of income exemption (Section 5.5), or the exemption for transfers not intended to confer a gratuitous benefit (Section 5.6): since most transfers of value in an unmarried couple are simply domestic cost-sharing arrangements.

Even so, this might still present a problem in a few cases, as a large part of a co-habiting partner's expenditure in the last seven years of their life could potentially be subject to IHT (sugar daddies and cougars beware!) Furthermore, since much of this maintenance expenditure will not increase the value of the transferee's estate, it might even be considered a chargeable lifetime transfer!

The maintenance of family exemption also extends to expenditure that represents a reasonable provision for the care or maintenance of a dependent relative. A dependent relative for this purpose is your widowed, separated, or divorced mother or mother-in-law (by concession, an unmarried mother may also be included, as long as she is genuinely financially dependent on you); or any other relative of yours or your spouse's who is incapacitated by old age or infirmity, as a consequence of which they are unable to maintain themselves.

HMRC should, for example, accept that renting a property for your elderly and financially dependent relative to live in represents reasonable provision for their maintenance. They will not, however, accept buying a property for them and transferring it into their name to give them added security, as being reasonable care or maintenance.

This exemption is useful when an individual pre-deceases one of their parents, or where someone is providing care or maintenance for a disabled relative, such as a sibling or adult child.

5.5 NORMAL EXPENDITURE OUT OF INCOME

Lifetime transfers are exempt to the extent that: i) They are part of the normal, habitual, or typical, expenditure of the transferor; ii) Taking one year with another, they are made out of income (i.e. not out of capital); and iii) the transferor is left with sufficient net income to maintain his or her usual standard of living.

This is an extremely useful exemption, since there is no financial limit to the amount that can be covered if the transferor can afford it. However, it must be said that, since the expenditure has to come out of income, the exemption, while extremely useful, cannot be used to reduce the capital value of your estate exposed to IHT. In other words, it's a case of preventing things from getting any worse, rather than making them any better.

The amount of gifts or other expenditure involved does not need to be exactly the same every year, as long as it is part of a regular pattern. All of the following might potentially be covered if they meet the above tests:

- Giving your son £10,000 every year
- Giving your daughter a sum of money every year, which you increase annually in line with retail price inflation (or use the consumer price index if, like the Government, you don't feel so generous)
- Paying your granddaughter's school fees
- Giving your nephew all your dividend income every year
- Buying your brother a new car every three years
- Passing all the income you receive from a trust each year over to your elderly father
- Paying a monthly life insurance premium on a policy in favour of your daughter

Maintaining Your Usual Standard of Living

It is generally accepted this test is met if the transferor is left with sufficient income to maintain their usual standard of living ***on average***. For this purpose, it is generally understood HMRC is willing to consider the position over a three-year period (for example, surplus income remaining from 2026/27 might be used to fund exempt gifts made in 2027/28 or 2028/29, provided these are normal, habitual expenditure).

It has also been suggested that HMRC does not generally question the validity of gifts out of income if they do not, in total, exceed one third of the transferor's net annual after-tax income. Nevertheless, I imagine they would still scrutinise any case where they had reason to think otherwise!

In some circumstances, the transferor might reasonably gift a greater proportion of their income and still maintain their usual standard of living, e.g. a very wealthy person with a very frugal lifestyle. I have, however, met the 'chicken and egg' situation where HMRC has argued the transferor's modest standard of living arose ***because*** of the expenditure in question. To avoid this argument, there will clearly need to be some surplus income remaining most years, on average.

HMRC regards income for the purposes of this exemption as net, after-tax income. Furthermore, not everything that is treated as income for Income Tax purposes will be regarded as income for the purposes of the exemption (another example of HMRC having their cake and eating it!)

There are, for example, cases where the proceeds of company share sales are treated as income for Income Tax purposes. This often occurs as a result of specific statutory provisions relating to employee shares. The underlying nature of this deemed income would, however, remain capital, and hence this would not be income that could be relied upon for the purposes of the normal expenditure out of income exemption.

For a self-employed transferor, income for the purposes of the exemption would generally be based on the results shown in their business accounts. Hence, income will be arrived at after deducting items such as business entertaining or, for those using traditional accruals basis accounting, depreciation: even though these are not allowed for Income Tax purposes. Nonetheless, the full Income Tax charge will still need to be deducted from the accounts income in order to arrive at the net after-tax income available for the purposes of the exemption.

Tax exempt income such as dividends and interest within an ISA, or attendance allowance payments, may be included as income for this purpose. However, items that form an effective income stream, but which are actually capital in nature, cannot generally be counted. This includes the annual tax-free 5% withdrawal from an investment bond; loan repayments received from family investment companies (Chapter 14) or loan trusts (Section 9.10); payments from a discounted gift trust (Section 9.9); and other director's loan account repayments (Section 7.22).

Habitual Gifts

Establishing a gift as part of your normal, habitual expenditure is a question of fact. The matter will be determined by looking at the particular facts of each individual case and considering the behaviour of the transferor over a number of years.

HMRC will usually consider expenditure to have become normal, or habitual, when it has been made three times, with the intention of continuing to make further similar payments. It is, however, possible to establish a gift has become part of your normal, habitual expenditure even if you should die after only one such gift. This is because the exemption will still apply if it can be shown it was the transferor's intention to make the gift regularly on a habitual basis.

A contractual commitment to make regular payments will usually be accepted as evidence of an intention to make the expenditure part of the transferor's normal pattern of expenditure. In the absence of such a commitment, some other documentary evidence of the transferor's intentions is advisable.

Establishing an intention to make a gift on a habitual basis will require some evidence to prove it. For example, if you intend paying your niece's school fees on a regular basis, it would be wise to write a letter to the school confirming this. If you should then unfortunately pass away soon after paying the first set of fees, the letter will confirm this payment was intended to be normal habitual expenditure and thus exempt from IHT (as long as the other requirements set out above are also met).

Another good way to establish an intention to make a gift on a habitual basis is to set up a standing order. This shows a clear intention to make a series of gifts. (See Section 16.16 for another reason standing orders may be a good idea.)

To be covered by this exemption, the relevant gifts or expenditure must also be maintained on a regular basis. Hence, you must keep making your habitual gifts every year (or such other period as is your habit). Unlike the annual exemption, there is no scope for carrying this exemption forward!

The Danger of Irrelevance

Where the gifts concerned are made directly to another individual, this all only becomes relevant when the transferor has died within seven years since, otherwise, the gifts will be PETs in any case (see Section 4.3). Unfortunately, what this means in practice is the true status of these transfers is generally not established until after the transferor's death, leaving a great deal of uncertainty for their beneficiaries. It is vital, therefore, to maintain records of your normal expenditure out of income throughout your lifetime, to assist your executors in establishing the correct position when dealing with your estate after your death.

5.6 OTHER EXEMPT TRANSFERS

There is a general exemption for a transfer that is not intended to confer a gratuitous benefit on the transferee. An important example of such a transfer is one made as part of a divorce or separation agreement. Recent changes to the CGT rules for transfers made by separated or divorcing spouses give rise to even greater opportunities to benefit from this exemption: we will look at these in more detail in Sections 6.6 and 12.6.

Settlements between common-law partners might also be covered under this exemption, as well as simple transactions, such as friends sharing the cost of a holiday or restaurant bill.

Transfers of value made for the purposes of a trade, and thus allowable for Income Tax, are exempt from IHT. This covers paying your employees' wages, for example; including employees who are also family members, provided they genuinely earn those wages.

There is also an exemption for payments securing pension or other retirement benefits for an employee who is not otherwise connected with the transferor, or the widow, widower, or dependants of such an employee. Payments securing pension benefits for family members are not covered by this exemption (but could be covered by other exemptions).

Chapter 6

IHT Planning for Married Persons

6.1 SCOPE OF THIS CHAPTER

In this chapter, we are going to take a detailed look at the IHT planning opportunities available as a consequence of marriage. We will cover people who are married now, widows/widowers, and those contemplating marriage in the future.

Everything that applies to married people applies equally to civil partners and everything that applies to a widow/widower applies equally to a surviving civil partner. Unless expressly stated to the contrary, it is assumed throughout this chapter that both spouses are subject to IHT on their worldwide estate (see Section 2.2).

6.2 THE TRANSFERABLE NIL RATE BAND (TNRB) & RESIDENCE NIL RATE BAND (RNRB)

Any proportion of the NRB that is unused on a married person's death is transferable to their spouse. In simple terms, this means all widows/widowers are potentially entitled to a double NRB. Furthermore, since we all have the potential to become a widow/widower one day, this means we all have the potential to double our NRB. As we will see in Section 6.7, this has turned a great deal of IHT planning on its head!

The TNRB must be claimed by the widow/widower's personal representatives within two years of the widow/widower's death. No claim is necessary on the first spouse's death and it does not matter how long ago the first spouse died.

Furthermore, it does not matter whether the first spouse actually had any assets at the time of their death. Even if they died penniless, their widow/widower can still claim a TNRB.

It is the ***proportion*** of the NRB unused on the first death that transfers, not the amount. This means the widow/widower benefits from any increase in the NRB since their spouse's death.

In the simplest case where none of the NRB was used on the first spouse's death the widow/widower will be entitled to a double NRB. For widows/widowers dying between 6th April 2009 and 5th April 2031, this amounts to £650,000 (regardless of when the first spouse died). Where some of the first spouse's NRB was used, the amount transferred to the survivor will be reduced.

Example: *Lee died on 1st September 2002 when the NRB was £250,000. She left a legacy of £100,000 to her son Peter and her remaining estate to her husband Lenny. 60% of Lee's NRB was unused (£150,000/£250,000) and transfers to Lenny.*

Lenny dies in January 2027 and is entitled to his own NRB plus a further 60% transferred from Lee. His total NRB is thus:

Own NRB:	*£325,000*
NRB transferred from Lee (£325,000 x 60%):	*£195,000*
Total NRB available	*£520,000*

In later chapters, I will sometimes refer to this total NRB (£520,000 in Lenny's case) as the individual's 'NRB/TNRB'. Similar principles apply to the transfer of a spouse's RNRB, although this is subject to the tapering provisions explained in Section 3.4. Further details on the amount available are included in Sections 3.4 and 13.10.

Example Continued: *As Lee died in 2002, she would not have used any of her RNRB. If her estate was worth no more than £2m at the time of her death, her entire RNRB will therefore transfer to Lenny, giving him a total RNRB at the time of his death in January 2027 of £350,000: made up of his own RNRB of £175,000 and Lee's unused RNRB of £175,000.*

Combining his RNRB of £350,000 with his enhanced NRB of £520,000 (see above) gives Lenny a total potential exemption of £870,000. He will, however, have to meet the rules outlined in Section 3.4 in order to benefit from the RNRB element of this exemption.

6.3 USING THE RESIDENCE NIL RATE BAND ON FIRST DEATH

As explained in Section 3.4, tapering provisions apply to reduce the amount of RNRB available on the death of an individual with an estate worth in excess of £2m. Hence, where a married couple's ***combined*** net assets exceed £2m, it may be worth ensuring the RNRB is utilised on the first spouse's death since, otherwise, it will be reduced or eliminated through the tapering that applies on the second death.

Where a married couple's combined net assets exceed £4m, there are also potential savings to be made by keeping one spouse's estate to no more than £2m. In that way, the poorer spouse will retain their full RNRB entitlement.

To use that entitlement, it may also be necessary to leave some property qualifying for the RNRB directly to a direct descendant on the poorer spouse's death. For this reason, it would generally be preferable for the poorer spouse to be the one with the shorter life expectancy, although this may require a little negotiation among the family!

In the case of smaller combined estates worth less than £2m, there may be other reasons why it is wise to use the RNRB on the first spouse's death in preference to using any, or more, of their NRB.

As we know, both the NRB and RNRB are frozen at their current levels until at least 5th April 2031. Thereafter, we would expect both bands to increase at approximately the same rate in future years. Hence, for married persons dying after 5th April 2020, preserving either part of the TNRB or an equivalent amount of the RNRB for transfer to their widow/widower can be expected to have broadly the same value in future.

However, the RNRB has a quite restricted application whereas the TNRB is generally available against any assets in the widow/widower's estate and is not tapered away for more valuable estates. Since the TNRB is far more flexible, it will therefore generally make sense to use the RNRB on the first spouse's death in preference to the NRB, wherever possible.

As we saw in Section 3.4, the RNRB is used in priority to the NRB where both are applicable to the same legacy, but sometimes the use of the RNRB will depend on what assets are being inherited, and by whom.

Example: *David dies intestate (see Section 11.7) but had always said he would like to leave either his Cornish cottage or an equivalent amount in cash to his daughter, Angie, and the remainder of his estate to his wife, Iman.*

The family are about to enter a deed of variation to put his wishes into effect and are uncertain whether to pass the Cornish cottage, worth £140,000, to Angie, or to give her the equivalent sum in cash. The cottage is eligible for the RNRB, so if this goes directly to Angie, only 20% of David's RNRB (£35,000/£175,000) will remain unused and will transfer to Iman. Alternatively, if Angie takes £140,000 in cash, this will use up part of David's NRB, leaving only 56.9% (£185,000/£325,000) to transfer to Iman.

Iman dies many years later, when the NRB stands at £412,000 and the RNRB is £223,000. She leaves an estate worth £2m, which includes one property eligible for the RNRB: Starman House, worth £330,000. Neither she nor David ever owned a private residence worth more than this, so the downsizing provisions (Section 13.10) are not relevant.

Scenario 1: Angie took the cottage; Iman leaves her Starman House: *Iman has a full TNRB entitlement, plus her own RNRB and 20% transferred from David. This gives her a total exemption of £1,091,600 (£412,000 x 2 + £223,000 + £223,000 x 20%). Her chargeable estate is thus reduced to £908,400, giving her an IHT bill of £363,360.*

Scenario 2: Angie took the cash; Iman leaves her Starman House: *Iman is entitled to her own NRB plus a further 56.9% transferred from David. She has a potential entitlement to both her own RNRB and David's. These would total £446,000. However, Starman House is only worth £330,000, so that is as much RNRB as she is able to claim. Hence, Iman's total exemption is only £976,428 (£412,000 + £412,000 x 56.9% + £330,000). Her chargeable estate is thus £1,023,572, giving her an IHT bill of £409,429.*

As we can see, if Angie had taken cash on David's death, rather than using the RNRB by taking the cottage, this would ultimately cost Iman an additional £46,069 (£409,429 – £363,360). This is effectively the cost of the RNRB's rather restrictive nature when compared with the TNRB.

That cost would be the same if Iman left Starman House to any other qualifying individual (see Section 3.4), but what if she wanted to leave it to someone else?

Scenario 3: Angie took the cottage; Iman's sister inherits Starman House: *Iman has a full TNRB entitlement, but cannot claim any RNRB. Her total exemption is £824,000 (£412,000 x 2), giving her a chargeable estate of £1.176m and an IHT bill of £470,400.*

Scenario 4: Angie took the cash; Iman's sister inherits Starman House: *Iman is entitled to her own NRB plus a further 56.9% transferred from David. She cannot claim any RNRB. Her total exemption is just £646,428 (£412,000 + £412,000 x 56.9%), giving her a chargeable estate of £1,353,572 and an IHT bill of £541,429.*

This time, the decision to allow Angie to take cash on David's death will ultimately cost Iman an additional £71,029 (£541,429 – £470,400).

In summary, it may often make sense to 'cash in' the RNRB on the first death, including cases where the surviving spouse may have an estate worth more than £2m on their death; may not own any private residence worth at least twice the RNRB; or may not wish, or not be able, to leave their private residence to a direct descendant.

6.4 NIL RATE BAND TRANSFERS IN PRACTICE

Applying the TNRB system in practice is fraught with problems. The first spouse may have died many years ago with an estate that was clearly nowhere near the amount of the NRB. No-one will have given much thought to IHT at that time since it was clearly irrelevant. Now, many years later, we will be faced with the prospect of attempting to ascertain how much of the NRB was used at that time. The first question is 'how much was the NRB?' Here, at least, HMRC has been helpful and has published the NRBs going back to 1914:
www.gov.uk/government/publications/rates-and-allowances-inheritance-tax-thresholds-and-interest-rates

Where the first spouse died before 1986, they will have been subject to a different tax regime, but the previous equivalent of the NRB is used for the purposes of calculating the TNRB. However, there is a problem for widows/widowers whose spouse died before March 1975. Under Estate Duty, there was no general exemption for transfers to spouses. For deaths between 21st March 1972 and 12th March 1975 there was a limited exemption of £15,000. Prior to that, there was no spouse exemption at all. Hence, where the first spouse died before 13th March 1975, there may be little or no TNRB available, even if the first spouse's entire estate passed to their widow/widower.

There will, of course, be some straightforward cases where the first spouse did not use any of their NRB, including cases where that first spouse:

- Died after 12th March 1975 and left their entire estate to their widow/widower,
- Left their entire estate to their widow/widower except for a private residence that was fully exempted by the RNRB (Section 3.4),
- Left everything to charity,
- Had nothing of any financial value, or
- Died on active service (see Section 3.7)

Remember, however, the first spouse may have used some of their NRB if they:

- Made transfers of value in the last 7 years of their life (Section 4.5),
- Made any gifts with reservation (Section 4.8), or
- Elected to include an asset in their estate in order to prevent an Income Tax charge (Section 11.12)

Example: *When Pete died in March 2006, he left everything to his civil partner, Roger. However, Pete had also given £96,250 to his friend Keith in 2002. The gift to Keith in 2002 became chargeable on Pete's death. This was not important at the time as Pete left his entire estate to his civil partner, but it meant Pete used £96,250, or 35% (£96,250/£275,000), of his NRB. Only 65% of Pete's NRB therefore transfers to Roger, or £211,250 at current rates.*

The impact of even small gifts and legacies made by the first spouse could be quite significant. For married couples who are both still alive, it is therefore vital to keep accurate records of all transfers that take place.

6.5 REMARRIAGE

It is, of course, not unusual for a widow/widower to remarry. Furthermore, some people (particularly widows) go on to outlive two or more spouses. Sadly, however, a widow/widower can only be entitled to a maximum of one TNRB regardless of how many spouses they bury.

Example: *In 1987, Liz married Eddie. He died in 1995 leaving Liz his entire estate. She remarried in 1998, to Richard, who died in 2001 and also left her his entire estate. Although Liz has survived two husbands, neither of whom used any of their NRB, she is only entitled to one TNRB. Liz herself dies in March 2027. Her personal representatives may therefore claim a NRB of £650,000, comprising her own NRB plus one TNRB.*

A widow/widower whose spouse used part of their NRB may, however, continue to accumulate further TNRB through remarriage until such point as they have accumulated a total of one additional NRB.

Example: *Kurt died in 1991 when the NRB was £140,000, leaving a legacy of £70,000 to his cousin Dave and the remainder of his estate to his wife, Courtney. Courtney is thus entitled to a TNRB of 50% from Kurt.*

In 1998, Courtney remarried to Michael. Sadly, in August 2026, Michael died, leaving a house worth £260,000 to his sister Kylie and the rest of his estate to Courtney. Kylie's legacy used up 80% of Michael's NRB so, this time, Courtney is only entitled to a TNRB of 20%.

Courtney can, however, add her two TNRBs together to give her a total 70% of TNRB. If she should die before 6th April 2031, her personal representatives could therefore claim a TNRB of £227,500 (£325,000 x 70%) in addition to her own NRB of £325,000.

If Courtney were to remarry again and subsequently be widowed a third time, she would be entitled to claim any unused NRB on the death of her third spouse up to a maximum of 30% (to bring her up to a total of one TNRB).

Courtney is an interesting case on the whole but, unlike Courtney, many widows/widowers already have the maximum TNRB when they remarry. We will look at the IHT planning consequences in Section 6.8.

Taking the Residence Nil Rate Band into Account

Similar principles apply to ensure a widow/widower who remarries can only ever be entitled to a maximum of one additional RNRB. Those who outlive more than one spouse will again be able to accumulate additional proportionate amounts of RNRB until they reach an additional 100%.

At first glance, one might expect someone like Courtney, in our example above, to already be entitled to a full additional RNRB, since her first husband died before the exemption became available. However, it is important to remember, if his estate was worth in excess of £2m at the time of his death, tapering would apply and the proportion of RNRB passing to Courtney would be reduced (see Section 3.4 for details).

6.6 SEPARATION & DIVORCE

As we saw in Section 3.3, for the purposes of the spouse exemption, a couple continue to be regarded as married for IHT purposes throughout any period of separation and right up until the granting of a decree absolute. As far as we know, it is reasonable to assume the same definition of marriage can be used in applying the TNRB system.

In other words, even if the couple were separated at the time of the first spouse's death, it appears the surviving spouse will still be entitled to claim any unused proportion of the first spouse's NRB or RNRB. This could save their family up to £200,000 at current rates.

However, the practical difficulty facing the surviving spouse will be ascertaining how much of the first spouse's NRB and RNRB is available to claim. This will make any tax planning more difficult. In some cases, where the couple have been separated for many years, the survivor may not even know their spouse has died!

One thing they will know, if they can at least ascertain that their late spouse died before 6th April 2017 with an estate not exceeding £2m, they will definitely be entitled to a full transferrable RNRB.

Divorce

Divorce was always a costly business! Now, there is a further cost: the loss of the TNRBs. If the IHT definition of married continues to apply as set out in Section 3.3, a separated couple will both continue to have the potential to claim any part of their estranged spouse's NRB or RNRB that is unused on that spouse's death.

If the couple divorce, the TNRBs will no longer be available to either of them. Hence, for IHT purposes, it may sometimes make sense for separated couples to stay married. If your ex is not that well off when they die, you may benefit!

In many cases, it is the couple's children who will ultimately benefit from any TNRB or RNRB, which provides even more incentive to stay married. If you do decide to divorce, however, there are some useful IHT planning opportunities available.

Inheritance Tax Planning on Separation and Divorce
As we saw in Section 5.6, transfers not intended to confer a gratuitous benefit are exempt from IHT. This provides the opportunity to put property into trust as part of a formal, legal divorce or separation agreement without creating a chargeable lifetime transfer. Not only is this probably preferable from a practical perspective (e.g. the ex-spouse's interest can be terminated in the event of their re-marrying), it also means the property will not fall into the ex-spouse's estate and can later pass to the children without a 40% charge on the ex-spouse's death.

While the property can pass into the trust free from IHT under this exemption, anniversary and exit charges may still apply (see Chapter 8). Nevertheless, on balance, the technique will often be beneficial overall.

Note that exemption from IHT does not necessarily mean a transfer of property is exempt from other taxes. In particular, it is not possible to hold over capital gains arising on a transfer into a trust for the benefit of your own minor children (see Section 9.4). However, a new exemption for transfers on divorce or separation made after April 2023 means a transfer of the whole or a part share in the former marital home may be exempt from CGT under these circumstances: see Section 12.6 for details.

6.7 INHERITANCE TAX PLANNING FOR MARRIED COUPLES

When the TNRB was introduced in 2007, it completely changed the IHT planning landscape for married couples. Before then, the first step was to ensure the first spouse to die would use their NRB effectively. Now, in most cases, this is no longer necessary, as any unused NRB will transfer to the surviving spouse. In fact, there is a case for saying the best planning now is to ensure none of the NRB is used on the first spouse's death.

The important point to remember is the surviving spouse is able to claim whatever ***proportion*** of the NRB is unused on the first spouse's death. The ***amount*** of that claim will depend on the amount of the NRB at the time of the widow/widower's death. This means some former IHT planning techniques may sometimes have a disadvantageous effect.

Example: *John and Dee were a married couple. Many years ago, they took professional advice on their IHT position. Following this, they amended their Wills to implement a 'widow's loan scheme' (Section 6.11) when the first of them died. The effect of the scheme was to ensure the first one to die would use their NRB. The survivor would then be able to deduct an amount equal to that NRB from their estate. This was good planning at the time since, as things stood, this was likely to save John and Dee's family over £100,000 in IHT.*

John died in 2005 when the NRB was £275,000 and the widow's loan scheme was put into action. A sum of £275,000 was left to a discretionary trust. Dee inherited the remainder of John's estate and, following one of the mechanisms explained in Section 6.11, was left owing a sum of £275,000 to the trust.

At this point everything seemed fine. Dee still had her own NRB and would also be able to deduct her debt of £275,000 from her estate. In effect, to begin with, this was the same as having a TNRB.

However, once the actual TNRB system was introduced in 2007, Dee was put at a disadvantage. While the NRB went on to be increased to £325,000, the value of her debt to the discretionary trust remained just £275,000. Already the obsolete planning implemented in 2005 is going to cost her family an extra £20,000 in IHT (£50,000 x 40%), but things may get even worse.

Dee lives on for many years, through many changes of Government and much political manoeuvring and eventually dies when the NRB is £1.5m. On her death, Dee's NRB and her debt to the discretionary trust add up to £1.775m of effective exemption (provided the debt is settled out of the assets of her estate: see Section 2.10).

If John had not implemented the widow's loan scheme, however, his NRB would have been unused and would have transferred to Dee. On Dee's death, her personal representatives would have been able to claim a TNRB of £1.5m in addition to her NRB, giving her estate total effective IHT exemption of £3m.

In this example, the earlier planning has resulted in £1.225m worth of lost exemption for Dee's family, costing up to £490,000 in extra IHT (at today's rates). The reason for this is the fact the NRB increased by £1.225m during the period between John and Dee's deaths.

This gives us the general principle that a married couple's family will lose out to the extent of:

- The proportion of the NRB used on the first spouse's death TIMES
- The increase in the NRB between the first spouse's death and the second spouse's death TIMES
- The rate of IHT at the time of the second spouse's death

What Does This Mean for IHT Planning for Married Couples?

Using any of the NRB on the first spouse's death may potentially have a detrimental effect on the second spouse's death. The first spouse may use part of their NRB through any of the following:

- Legacies to anyone other than their spouse or one of the exempt bodies in Section 3.5
- Chargeable lifetime transfers in the last seven years of their life
- PETs in the last seven years of their life
- Gifts with reservation (Section 4.8)
- An election to include an asset in their estate in order to prevent an Income Tax charge (Section 11.12)

Any of the above put a married person's NRB in jeopardy. This means any lifetime transfer by a married person not covered by one of the absolute exemptions in Chapter 5 carries an element of risk and may have a detrimental effect on their spouse's IHT position. This is particularly relevant to PETs, as well as chargeable lifetime transfers covered by the transferor's NRB (see Chapter 4 for further details).

Example: *In January 2021, Richard gave his son Zak a gift of £65,000. This was a PET as Richard had already used up any other available exemptions. Sadly, Richard dies in March 2027 and leaves his entire estate to his wife Barbara. The earlier gift to Zak becomes chargeable and uses up 20% of Richard's NRB. This means Barbara receives a TNRB of only 80%. Whatever the NRB may be when Barbara dies, she will lose out on 20% of it because of Richard's gift to Zak.*

At this point, it is tempting to suggest married people should avoid making any lifetime transfers not covered by an immediate exemption. This is not the case: it only means such transfers carry a degree of risk that they might actually make the position worse.

On the other hand, lifetime transfers by married people will often be beneficial, such as when the transferor survives at least seven years; the transferor's spouse already has a TNRB from a previous marriage (see Section 6.5); or the assets grow in value faster than the NRB.

Example Revisited: *Let us suppose the gift from Richard to Zak in our previous example comprised quoted shares worth £65,000. Let's also suppose these shares increase in value at an average compound rate of 5% per year until Barbara's death in early 2041. This means Zak's shares will be worth £172,500 at the time of Barbara's death.*

If the shares had not been transferred to Zak, they would still have been in Barbara's estate and would thus increase her IHT liability. Instead, the gift to Zak means the shares are not in Barbara's estate, but she loses 20% of the TNRB. Hence, if the NRB for 2040/41 is less than £862,500 (£862,500 x 20% = £172,500), the family will be better off overall because of Richard's original gift to Zak.

Let's say the NRB for 2040/41 is £423,000 (using our forecast method in Section 3.2). This means Richard's gift of the shares now worth £172,500 results in Barbara losing £84,600 of her TNRB (£423,000 x 20%), but the family will be £35,160 better off (£172,500 – £84,600 = £87,900 x 40%).

It may be worthwhile for a married person to use part of their NRB on the transfer of funds or assets that will grow in value faster than the rate at which the NRB increases.

Following this principle in practice may be difficult, as it involves a good deal of 'crystal ball gazing'. Will a future Government increase the NRB significantly at some stage? Will the current freeze be extended for even longer? Will we be stuck with simple inflationary increases for many years after 2031? No-one can say.

For a lifetime transfer, there is the added bonus that any growth in the value of the transferred asset up to the point of the transferor's death is effectively free of any IHT cost. In our example, for instance, it was the value of the shares when they were transferred in 2021 that was used to calculate the restriction in

Barbara's TNRB, not their value at the date of Richard's death (which may have been around £87,000 at our forecast growth rate).

Furthermore, the freeze in the NRB until 2031 provides the transferred asset with a significant head start. At an annual growth rate around 5%, assets transferred now could be worth 25% to 30% more before we even begin to see any increase in the NRB.

Planning on the First Death

At this point, it seems reasonable to say most married couples will be better off if they **do not** use any of the planning techniques previously designed to utilise the first spouse's NRB without actually passing any wealth to other beneficiaries at that time.

We saw an example of the detrimental effect such planning could have in John and Dee's case above. The planning techniques in Sections 6.9 to 6.11 are therefore no longer beneficial for most married couples.

The position may differ where one or both of the couple have remarried following the death of a previous spouse. We will look at planning for these couples in Section 6.8. It is for the benefit of these couples that the techniques in Sections 6.9 to 6.11 are still included in this guide.

Those couples aside, any other married couple should generally avoid using any scheme that simply uses up the first spouse's NRB without actually passing any assets or funds to other beneficiaries.

What is less certain is whether it is worth using the first spouse's NRB on genuine legacies to other family members. Here we must go back to the principle set out above, i.e. such legacies may be worthwhile if they consist of funds or assets that will grow faster than the rate at which the NRB increases.

In the case of a legacy, however, the proportion of TNRB lost will be based on the value of the relevant asset at the date of the first spouse's death. This means the growth rate must be greater than in the case of a lifetime transfer before the legacy is worthwhile for IHT purposes.

Remember also that the reduction in the surviving spouse's TNRB caused by a legacy to another beneficiary is permanent. A gift of the same asset from the surviving spouse to another person would instead be a PET and would be exempt if that spouse survives another seven years.

In many cases, therefore, and especially where the survivor still has a long life expectancy, it may be preferable to avoid legacies to other beneficiaries. Subject to the comments below, the family will often achieve a better overall result if the surviving spouse makes lifetime transfers instead.

Passing on Wealth Tax Efficiently

Of course, it's all very well me telling you not to give your children (or other beneficiaries) anything unless they are going to invest it at better rates of growth than the NRB, but what if they need money now, or you simply want to help them out?

In most cases, you will probably give them money during your lifetime and this will be a PET. As we know, this will lead to a reduction in the TNRB if the person making the PET dies within seven years.

You will therefore reduce the risk of a reduction in the TNRB if the spouse with the longer life expectancy makes the PET. This is not foolproof, but it improves your chances.

Remember, you can pass wealth to your spouse first free from any IHT risk and they can then make the PET if they choose to do so. However, you cannot make it a pre-condition of a gift to your spouse that they will pass that gift on to another person. If any such condition existed, the first gift is ignored and you will be treated as having made the gift directly to the ultimate recipient, meaning you will have made the PET.

Alternatively, you may wish to pass some wealth to someone other than your spouse when you die. As we have already discussed, a direct legacy has the drawback of causing a permanent reduction in the amount of TNRB that can ultimately be claimed against your spouse's estate.

You may therefore wish to consider passing the wealth to your spouse and leaving it in their hands to decide what to do. This would enable the surviving spouse to make appropriate gifts as PETs. If the survivor lives another seven years, these will be exempt from IHT and the full TNRB will be available against the rest of their estate.

As with a lifetime transfer, it is imperative there is no prior agreement that your spouse will pass the assets or funds to another person. You ***must*** leave the decision entirely in their hands. This point is crucial, and is explored in Section 6.12, where we will also see it is often wise for the surviving spouse to wait at least two years and a day after the first spouse's death before making any transfers of assets or funds inherited from their late spouse.

Another way you can help your children (or anyone else) without putting your spouse's TNRB at risk is to make loans instead of gifts. A loan does not represent a transfer of value, so there is no impact on your NRB if you should die within seven years: although, of course, the value of the loan remains in your estate.

The loan can be unsecured and interest free, but it is wise to document it. If it should later turn out that you are the surviving spouse, you can, if you wish, simply waive the debt, thus turning the loan into a gift at that stage (but see Section 2.11 regarding legal requirements for waiving a debt). As long as you survive seven years after the waiver, the value of the original loan will escape IHT on your death.

6.8 THE SECOND TIME AROUND

Where one or both of a married couple have remarried following the death of an earlier spouse, the position may be different to that outlined in the previous section. This is because one or both of them may already have a TNRB entitlement.

If, however, the whole of the previous spouse's NRB was used on their death then the current married couple will be in the same position as a 'first time' couple and should go back to Section 6.7 for guidance on their IHT planning position.

This, for example, may apply to someone like Dee (the first example in Section 6.7) and any future spouse she may have. As you may recall, Dee's late husband carried out some IHT planning which, while it made sense at the time, has proved disadvantageous. This will be a common scenario for individuals widowed before October 2007 who subsequently remarry.

Existing Transferable Nil Rate Band Entitlement

Leaving such cases to one side, let's now focus on those who already have some entitlement to a TNRB. As explained in Section 6.5, a widow/widower cannot claim more than one additional NRB. This, in turn, means we are back in the position where some or all of the NRB of the first spouse in the current couple to die will effectively go to waste unless we undertake some appropriate planning. Let me explain this further with an example.

Example: *When George died a few years ago, he left a sum equal to half the NRB to his son Ravi and the rest of his estate to his wife, Patti. Patti is therefore already entitled to claim an additional 50% TNRB, or £162,500 at current rates. Patti is now married to Eric (who has never married before). At the moment, Eric and Patti's Wills both leave everything to each other.*

If Patti dies first, her NRB will go unused and will transfer to Eric. The additional half NRB that transferred from George to Patti will go to waste. If Eric dies first, his NRB will go unused and will be available to transfer to Patti. However, as Patti already has half a TNRB, she will only be able to claim half of Eric's unused NRB and the other half will go to waste. Either way, whether Eric or Patti dies first, half a NRB will go to waste!

As we can see, where one of a couple already has an entitlement to part of a previous spouse's unused NRB, that entitlement will go to waste if the couple do not plan effectively. Where the previous spouse's NRB was completely unused, that whole NRB may potentially go to waste. At current rates, that amounts to £130,000 worth of wasted tax relief.

Whatever amount of TNRB is already available, the current couple will achieve the best result by ensuring the same proportion of NRB is used on the first of their deaths. We will look at how this can be done in the next few sections.

Double Second-Timers

Where both of the current couple already have some entitlement to a TNRB, the amount potentially going to waste on the first death will be the sum of their existing entitlements. Preserving both existing entitlements in this case will necessitate the first spouse to die using all their existing TNRB plus all or part of their own NRB.

Example: *Buddy died some years ago and used 25% of his NRB. His widow, Holly, later remarried to Waylon, who was a widower himself. Waylon's previous wife Jenny had used 60% of her NRB when she died. As things stand, Holly is entitled to a 75% TNRB and Waylon is entitled to a 40% TNRB. The couple's existing entitlements total 115% and this is how much will go to waste without effective planning.*

Holly and Waylon therefore both draw up Wills to put a widow's loan scheme into effect on their death that will utilise 115% of the value of the NRB at that time. (I am assuming each of them has enough wealth to do this.)

If Holly dies first, the widow's loan scheme will use up all her existing TNRB entitlement, plus 40% of her own NRB, leaving a further 60% TNRB entitlement to transfer to Waylon. If Waylon dies first, the widow's loan scheme will use up all his existing TNRB entitlement, plus 75% of his own NRB, leaving a further 25% TNRB entitlement to transfer to Holly. Either way, the survivor will end up with a full TNRB entitlement and none of the couple's existing entitlement will have gone to waste.

In the case of a couple who both have an existing entitlement to a full TNRB, the amount of additional relief that can be preserved in this way will be equal to double the NRB. At current rates, this amounts to £260,000 worth of tax relief.

Before we look at how to use an existing TNRB entitlement effectively, it is worth pausing to consider whether we think it is worth the effort. Most married couples now only have a potential exposure to IHT when their combined total wealth exceeds £650,000. In some cases, where there is a suitable qualifying property and the couple intend to leave it, or its eventual sale proceeds, to their children, the potential exposure will only be on wealth in excess of £1m (due to the RNRB: see Section 3.4).

The planning we are now considering is designed to increase the point at which the couple's IHT exposure begins to an even greater level, often as much as £975,000, or even £1.3m: *PLUS* whatever further exemption they can achieve with the RNRB. Whether this is worthwhile depends on how large an estate you anticipate the second spouse having at the time of their death.

The Second Time Around and the Residence Nil Rate Band

Like the main NRB, a widow/widower can only accumulate one additional RNRB. Hence, where any part of the RNRB was unused on a previous spouse's death, there is a danger the transferred RNRB may go to waste when one of the current, second time around couple dies. Among other cases, this will apply whenever one of the couple had a previous spouse who died before 6th April 2017 with an estate worth less than £2.2m.

However, there is less scope for planning with the RNRB as it is only of any use if a property, or proceeds from the sale of a property, is left to a direct descendant. This may not always be possible, meaning there is no waste of relief if the surplus RNRB is not used.

Furthermore, even with a transferred RNRB from a previous spouse, the RNRB cannot be available when an individual dies with an estate worth £2.7m or more, and will be restricted whenever an estate is worth more than £2m. Nonetheless, despite these restrictions, there will be cases where using some of the RNRB on the first death in the current, second time around couple may be beneficial.

Example: *Marvin's first wife Mary died in 2015 leaving only a half share in their home, worth £250,000 at the time, which passed to him. As a result, Marvin is already entitled to a transferred RNRB, giving him a current entitlement of £350,000. Marvin is now married to Kim. If one of them dies without using any of their RNRB, the RNRB that transferred from Mary will go to waste.*

Instead, when Marvin dies in 2026, he leaves the property, now worth £350,000, to Kim and her daughter Tammi equally as joint owners. The half share left to Kim is covered by the spouse exemption, the half share left to Tammi is covered by Marvin's RNRB, but still leaves £175,000 to transfer to Kim, so that she now has the maximum entitlement of £350,000.

By leaving a half share to his step-daughter, Tammi, Marvin has ensured none of the RNRB that transferred to him from his first wife has gone to waste. At current rates, this could ultimately save up to £70,000 IHT (£175,000 x 40%), although this depends on the size of Kim's estate at the time of her death (it would generally need to be at least £1m to get the full saving), and on whether she is able to utilise her full RNRB entitlement: the downsizing provisions (Section 13.10) may help in this respect in a case like this.

In this example, Marvin would also have a full TNRB entitlement from his first wife, so it would make sense to also undertake additional planning to utilise one NRB on his death. Not only will this save up to a further £130,000 (£325,000 x 40%), it will also reduce the risk that Kim's estate will exceed £2m leading to a loss of some of her RNRB.

If it is likely that Kim's estate will exceed £2m it may, in fact, be better for Marvin to leave the property to Tammi alone, thus using all of his RNRB at this stage. This does, however, mean Kim will not benefit from any future increase in the RNRB in respect of the proportion that might otherwise have transferred to her from Marvin. Nonetheless, if her estate is much more than £2m, this could still be the better option.

Example Continued: *Kim dies in late 2035, leaving her entire estate to Tammi. The NRB is now £371,000, and the RNRB is £200,000. Marvin's former home is now worth £600,000. Kim also owns another property worth £500,000 that she has occupied as her main residence since Marvin's death, plus other assets with a total net value of £1.5m (after taking account of the planning implemented to use a NRB on Marvin's death).*

Let's compare the position under two scenarios: a) where Marvin left Kim a half share in his former home; and b) where Marvin left his former home to Tammi alone.

	Half Share to Kim	***Tammi Alone***
Marvin's former home	*£300,000*	-
Kim's new home	*£500,000*	*£500,000*
Other assets	*£1,500,000*	*£1,500,000*
Kim's Estate	*£2,300,000*	*£2,000,000*
Nil rate band (Kim's own)	*(£371,000)*	*(£371,000)*
Nil rate band (from Marvin)	*(£371,000)*	*(£371,000)*
Residence nil rate band (own)	*(£200,000)*	*(£200,000)*
Residence nil rate band (Marvin's)	*(£50,000)**	-
Chargeable estate	*£1,308,000*	*£1,058,000*
Inheritance Tax @ 40%	*£523,200*	*£423,200*

* *Because Kim's estate exceeds £2m, Marvin's RNRB has been tapered away by £150,000 (£300,000/2), reducing it to £50,000.*

In either case, Tammi, the ultimate beneficiary ends up with all the same assets but, by using all of Marvin's RNRB entitlement on his death, she benefits from a further £100,000 saving in IHT.

It's also worth pointing out that, if Marvin had simply left his former home to Kim alone and thus not used any of his RNRB, Kim's estate would have been worth £2.6m, her RNRB entitlement would have been tapered down to just £100,000 (2 x £200,000 – £600,000/2), and her IHT liability would have been £703,200 (£2.6m – 2 x £371,000 – £100,000 = £1.758m x 40%). By leaving his former home to Tammi instead of Kim, Marvin would thus have ultimately engineered a total IHT saving of £270,000 (£703,200 – £423,200).

And that's on top of the £130,000 saved by using a NRB on his death utilising one of the methods covered in Sections 6.9 to 6.11. In fact, that additional planning will have saved a total of £170,000 since, without it, Kim would have had no RNRB left at all.

So, what's going on here is that this second time around couple have saved a total of at least £440,000 by planning carefully on the first death. (As we will see in the next section, this planning can often be implemented within two years after death.)

Note, while Tammi was Kim's daughter in the example, Marvin's RNRB could have been used by passing property to any combination of his, Mary's, or Kim's direct descendants. Kim's RNRB (including any part transferred from Marvin) could have been used by passing property to any combination of her or Marvin's direct descendants.

While the property was conveniently worth the right amount to use Marvin's RNRB, in practice it's possible to fix the value left to a direct descendant by putting the property into joint ownership as tenants in common (Section 11.3). For example, if Marvin's former home had been worth £437,500 at the time of his death, he could have used half his RNRB entitlement (£175,000) by leaving a 40% share to Tammi; or used all his RNRB entitlement (£350,000) by leaving her an 80% share. In either case, the remainder could be left to Kim and thus be covered by the spouse exemption. Alternatively, where Kim's estate is expected to exceed £2m, all of the property could be left to Tammi as part of the planning to use Marvin's existing TNRB entitlement.

We'll look at another example of the potential benefits of using the RNRB on the first spouse's death in a second time around couple in the next section. See also Chapter 13 for more on the benefits of leaving a half share in the family home to children, and Section 11.3 regarding further potential benefits of holding property jointly (which I have ignored in this section).

6.9 USING THE TRANSFERABLE NIL RATE BAND

As explained in the previous section, many 'second time around' couples will benefit from using all or part of the first spouse's NRB plus, in some cases, their existing entitlement to a TNRB. The amount of additional relief generated in this way may be up to double the NRB, producing savings of up to £260,000 at current rates.

Example: *Thomas died in March 2027, leaving his net estate worth £3m to his brother, Arthur (who is also Thomas's executor). Thomas was a widower who had survived two wives: Alice who died in 2005, without using any of her NRB, and Doris, who died in November 2026.*

After claiming the TNRB to which Thomas was entitled, as well as Thomas's own NRB, Arthur is left to bear IHT at 40% on £2.35m (£3m – 2 x £325,000), i.e. £940,000.

However, within Thomas's estate there was a property worth £650,000 that he had inherited from his second wife, Doris. Doris herself had been entitled to a TNRB as a result of a previous marriage to Tony, who had died some years ago without using any of his NRB.

Since Doris left the property to her husband and it was exempt anyway, both her NRB and her TNRB (from Tony) were never used. What Doris should have done was leave her property to Arthur. No IHT would have been payable on her death, as her property was covered by her NRB and TNRB entitlement.

But when Thomas died later, his estate would have been worth £650,000 less, i.e. £2.35m. After deducting Thomas's NRB and TNRB entitlement, Arthur would have had to pay IHT at 40% on just £1.7m. Arthur's IHT bill would thus have been £680,000, giving him a saving of £260,000. In effect, Arthur would have benefited from four NRBs instead of just two!

The non-spousal legacy (e.g. the one from Doris to Arthur in the example) doesn't need to be one specific property. It could be a whole group of assets, or simply worded as a legacy equal to the appropriate multiple of the NRB to be paid out of the general assets of the estate.

This strategy is pretty simple to follow when, like Thomas and Doris above, there are plenty of assets around. The problem for some second time around married couples is they can't afford to simply give their children, or other beneficiaries, up to £650,000 when one of them dies. The surviving spouse will need to retain sufficient assets to support them for the rest of their life including, in most cases, the family home. Fortunately, as we shall see in the sections that follow, there are some planning strategies available to deal with this dilemma.

Too Much of a Good Thing?

When including a non-spousal legacy or any other technique designed to use all or part of your NRB, in your Will, it is best not to word the legacy as a specific sum. What you may wish to do instead is draft your Will so it includes a legacy equal to the appropriate proportion of whatever the NRB happens to be at the time of your death. That way, the amount of the legacy will automatically adjust in line with the NRB (when the happy day ***finally*** comes that the NRB starts to increase again!) This may have some practical drawbacks, however. If a future Government were to drastically increase the value of the NRB, this strategy could cause some practical problems for your family. 'What's the problem,' you say: after all, you can just amend your Will if that happens. Probably, yes, and if you keep the situation under review you will be able to do this. But what happens if you no longer have legal capacity (see Section 16.16) at that time? To guard against this possibility, you may also wish to place a cap on the maximum value of the legacy.

What about the Residence Nil Rate Band?

You will also need to factor the RNRB into your planning. It is likely that anyone with an existing TNRB entitlement will also have an entitlement to their former spouse's RNRB: although this will not always be the case, for the reasons we explored in Sections 3.4 and 6.3. Nonetheless, where one or both of the current spouses have an existing entitlement to a previous deceased spouse's unused RNRB, this may provide scope for some further savings.

Example Revisited: *Let's take the same facts as before, except we will say Arthur was Thomas's son rather than his brother, and the property Doris initially left to Thomas was worth £1m and was a qualifying property for RNRB purposes. Let us also say Doris, Alice, and Tony each died with estates worth less than £2m.*

None of this would alter Arthur's IHT bill of £940,000 if Doris had left her entire estate to Thomas. However, if Doris had left her property worth £1m to Arthur (instead of Thomas), it would have been fully exempted by her own NRB, her TNRB (from Tony), her RNRB and the RNRB transferred from Tony (£325,000 x 2 + £175,000 x 2 = £1m).

Thomas's estate would now be worth £2m, meaning he would be entitled to his own RNRB and the one transferred to him from his first wife, Alice. If his estate included a qualifying property worth at least £350,000, or the sale proceeds from such a property (see Sections 3.4 and 13.10), this would provide a further exemption of £350,000, leaving him exposed to IHT on just £1m (£2m – £325,000 x 2 – £350,000) and giving Arthur an IHT liability of just £400,000.

In conclusion, a non-spousal legacy on the first death in a second time around couple could produce savings of up to £540,000!

If Only We'd Known About This Before!
Don't despair if you think you've left it too late. Any of the methods described in this guide that are available to utilise a TNRB or a former spouse's RNRB can be put in place through a deed of variation made within two years of the relevant spouse's death. See Section 17.1 for further details.

Estate Equalisation
One thing you cannot do, however, even with a deed of variation, is put money into the hands of the deceased. For a second time around married couple with some existing TNRB entitlement, it is therefore important to ensure both spouses have sufficient net assets in their own right to utilise the appropriate proportion of the NRB (plus the RNRB where appropriate).

6.10 WILL TRUSTS

One method for using an existing TNRB is to set up a discretionary trust through your Will (see Chapter 8 for an explanation of discretionary trusts).

Assets with a value equal to the appropriate proportion of the NRB (which will otherwise go to waste: see Section 6.8), are left to the trust. The surviving spouse will be one of the beneficiaries of the trust and, in practice, can retain all the benefits of ownership of the assets within the trust. This can be achieved by ensuring the trustees exercise their discretion in such a way that the surviving spouse receives the income from, and enjoyment of, the assets.

There is, however, a danger HMRC may attack this type of discretionary trust on the basis it is really a de facto interest in possession trust. This would mean the trust constituted an 'immediate post-death interest' (see Section 8.9). This, in turn, would mean the assets of the trust remain in the surviving spouse's estate for IHT purposes, thus rendering this planning void.

Nevertheless, this type of Will trust should still work where the trust is genuinely discretionary in nature. This would necessitate avoiding the usual letter of instruction to the trustees stating the surviving spouse is to receive all income from the trust. It would also be wise to ensure other beneficiaries did, indeed, receive some trust income.

This method cannot be used to utilise a transferred RNRB. It is also generally unsuitable for IHT planning with the family home, although we will see some variations that may be suitable in Chapter 13.

Some standard 'off the shelf' Will trusts give rise to an interest in possession and are thus of no use for this type of planning. This can even apply to standard Will trusts provided by some quite reputable organisations. As usual, this just goes to show there is no substitute for taking proper professional advice.

6.11 THE WIDOW'S LOAN SCHEME

Another method for utilising an existing TNRB is to leave a specific legacy of a sum equal to the appropriate proportion of the NRB (see Section 6.8) to a discretionary trust in your Will and the remainder of your estate (or most of it) to your spouse. Your spouse would be a beneficiary of the trust, together with other family members (usually).

There are a number of variations to this method but, in essence, the basic principle is that all (or most) of the deceased's assets are passed to the surviving spouse who therefore ends up owing a sum equal to the appropriate proportion of the NRB to the trust.

The charge scheme is one such variation and, unlike the simple Will Trust (Section 6.10), it is well suited to IHT planning with the family home. Under this scheme, the trust initially takes possession of the deceased's share of the family home and then takes a charge over it for a sum equal to the required proportion of the NRB. The deceased's share of the property is then passed to the surviving spouse subject to the charge.

When the surviving spouse subsequently dies, the amount of this charge is deductible from their estate (subject to the points below regarding payment of the debt), thus effectively providing relief for the TNRB that would otherwise have gone to waste (see Section 6.8).

Some experts suggest that where the charge scheme is being used, the surviving spouse should not be an executor of the deceased's estate. It is not absolutely clear if this would actually be a problem, but it is wise to play it safe in these matters.

The so-called debt scheme is a simpler variation of the widow's loan scheme, but has some technical problems that can lead to difficulties if the main bread-winner turns out to be the survivor.

Another variation that appears to avoid such technical problems is to leave the appropriate proportion of the NRB to a discretionary trust and leave the remainder of your estate to an interest in possession trust for the benefit of your spouse, rather than to your spouse directly. As explained in Section 8.9, the interest in possession trust is entitled to the spouse exemption, but will be left owing the appropriate sum (which you need in order to utilise the existing TNRB) to the discretionary trust.

Once again, the debt due to the discretionary trust will be deductible from the surviving spouse's estate on their subsequent death (subject to the points below regarding payment of the debt).

There is a school of thought that it may be necessary for the discretionary trust to charge interest on the loan to make the widow's loan scheme effective. Although some interest charged could be passed back to the surviving spouse (as a trust beneficiary), this would still lead to an Income Tax cost (see Section 8.17).

Payment of the Debt

In most cases, it is essential that the debt due to the discretionary trust is repaid out of the assets of the surviving spouse's estate (see Section 2.10). Where an interest in possession trust is used (as described above) the debt will need to be repaid from the assets of that trust.

In many cases, this will be easy to achieve by simply selling some or all of the assets of the estate (or the interest in possession trust, as the case may be) and making a suitable cash payment to the discretionary trust. In other cases, one of the alternative techniques outlined in Section 2.10 may be used instead.

As discussed in Section 2.10, there may also be cases where the debt is structured on a sufficiently commercial basis that it can be left outstanding. This would generally require, as a bare minimum, that:

- The loan is subject to interest at a commercial rate
- The interest is actually paid to the discretionary trust (see Section 8.17 regarding the Income Tax consequences of this)
- The loan is secured
- The loan is taken over by a person or persons who do not pose a greater risk than an arms' length lender would be willing to accept

Whichever variation is followed, the widow's loan scheme cannot be used to utilise a transferred RNRB. It's a complex scheme, so professional advice is essential. Despite its name though, it works equally well for a widower.

6.12 THE SPOUSE BRIDGE

A spouse with a longer life expectancy can be used as a 'bridge' to transfer assets to children or other beneficiaries. Assets are transferred to the spouse either during lifetime or on death and this transfer is exempt from IHT (subject to the points in Section 3.3). The spouse can then transfer the assets to the children as a PET (Section 4.3) and, as long as the spouse survives for seven years after that transfer, IHT is avoided.

In theory, any spouse will do for this strategy, including an estranged spouse who the transferor has not yet divorced, or a spouse who is not a parent of the children who are ultimately supposed to benefit.

Example: *Tremela divorced her ex-husband many years ago and has single-handedly raised her daughter Alisha and built up a large portfolio of investment properties. Tragically, Tremela has found out she has only a short time to live and wishes to leave everything she owns to Alisha, who is now a young adult.*

Tremela has been friends with Brian for many years and now decides to marry him. When Tremela dies a short time later, she leaves £325,000 to Alisha but leaves the rest of her estate to Brian. No IHT is due as everything is covered by either the NRB or the spouse exemption. Brian can then give Alisha all the property received from Tremela and, as long as he survives seven years, IHT will be avoided.

To date, HMRC has not had any success in challenging the validity of a marriage, but there are still a few potential problems with this strategy. Firstly, PETs of anything other than cash may give rise to CGT liabilities. However, transfers of recently inherited assets should not usually give rise to significant CGT liabilities due to the 'uplift on death' (Section 12.2).

Secondly, where there is an informal request asking the beneficiary under a Will to transfer inherited property to another person and the beneficiary does indeed make the transfer within two years of the deceased's death, the transfer is treated as a direct transfer from the deceased to that other person.

This particular provision can be side-stepped by either making a lifetime transfer to the spouse (but see further below) or by the spouse waiting two years and a day after the deceased's death before passing the assets to the ultimate recipient. While the latter approach may mean suffering some CGT on the capital growth in the assets' values, this cost is likely to be considerably less than the IHT at risk.

Thirdly and perhaps more importantly, there is the question of whether the transferee spouse will behave as the transferor hopes. They cannot be forced to pass the assets to the children, or the initial transfer will be ignored.

Preliminary transfers to a spouse are a perfectly good way to avoid or reduce IHT liabilities, as long as there is no obligation on the transferee spouse to make the subsequent transfer to the ultimate recipient. If, however, the arrangement for the second transfer is already in place, the initial transfer to the spouse would be disregarded and the position would revert to that given by a single transfer direct from the transferor spouse to the ultimate recipient.

A similar method that might be used to pass assets to a minor child is set out in Section 9.7.

Further Hazards for Lifetime Transfers to Spouses

Where the initial transfer to the spouse is a lifetime transfer then, even with no fixed arrangements for the assets to be passed to the children, there is still some risk HMRC might invoke the associated operations rules (Section 11.11).

That initial transfer would then again be ignored, resulting in the loss of the spouse exemption. How anyone could do this in the face of such a terrible tragedy as Tremela's premature death escapes me, but that is the nature of IHT!

In the more usual case of a married couple still living together at the time of the initial transfer, this risk is greatly reduced, as HMRC does not usually attack arrangements between married couples still living together.

In the case of a separated couple, or a marriage of convenience like Tremela and Brian, the risk of such an attack is greater, but may possibly be avoided if the transferee retains the assets for a few years before passing them to the ultimate recipient.

Finally, it is important to remember a lifetime transfer to a spouse means foregoing the uplift on death for CGT purposes (Section 12.2), so it will often be inappropriate for investment property and other appreciating assets. Also, separated spouses only enjoy the blanket CGT exemption for all transfers between them for a limited period: see Section 12.6.

6.13 THE FAMILY DEBT SCHEME

A sale of an investment asset to your spouse can be used as a means to reduce the value of your estate for IHT purposes without increasing the value of theirs to the same extent.

The asset, such as an investment property, is sold to the spouse for any price up to its full market value. Although the transfer is not a gift, the sale still represents a transfer between spouses and is exempt from both IHT and CGT.

Some form of Stamp Duty will be payable in many cases, however, and the rates involved can be quite prohibitive (see the Taxcafe guide *How to Save Property Tax*). Nonetheless, SDLT can be avoided on residential property sold to a spouse for a consideration not exceeding £125,000. In the case of non-residential property, there is no SDLT due where the consideration does not exceed £150,000. If you sell shares to your spouse, Stamp Duty will be payable at the rate of 0.5%.

The sale consideration is left outstanding as a loan; or an 'IOU' if you like. The vendor spouse then gives the IOU to their children or other intended beneficiaries. This is a PET, meaning the value of the IOU will be exempt from IHT if the vendor spouse survives seven years. This provides the reduction in the vendor spouse's estate since they no longer hold either the original asset or the IOU.

On the purchasing spouse's death, the value of the IOU will be deducted from their estate: ***provided*** the sum due under the IOU is actually paid out of the assets of their estate (see Section 2.10). This will cancel out some or all of the value of the transferred property. The debt does not fall foul of the artificially created debt rules (Section 2.10) since there is an actual sale of property from one spouse to the other.

This method is generally used for investment assets not qualifying for business or agricultural property relief (Chapter 7), including rental property. However, the restrictions now applying to these reliefs mean it could also be useful for business or agricultural property in some cases, and we will take a closer look at this in Section 7.31.

Chapter 7

The Tax Benefits of Business Property

7.1 INTRODUCTION

Where the appropriate conditions are satisfied, relief is available on the transfer of relevant business or agricultural property. The two reliefs are known, quite appropriately, as 'business property relief' and 'agricultural property relief'. For the rest of this guide, to save a little space, we will refer to them as BPR and APR respectively.

As a result of BPR and APR, it is possible to pass on many small family businesses free from IHT. Care must be exercised, however, as there are a great many pitfalls awaiting the unwary. In particular, property rental businesses very rarely qualify for relief and other businesses where the use of land or buildings by customers is one of the main elements are also at risk. We will look at this issue further in Sections 7.4 and 7.5 and some ways to potentially resolve the problem in Sections 7.6 and 7.23.

Another major problem is caused by the rules relating to deduction of liabilities (Section 2.10). These rules create a whole extra set of problems for business owners looking to pass their business to the next generation. In some cases, these rules may effectively wipe out the benefit of the relief: we will see an example in Section 7.12.

The reliefs for business and agricultural property apply, in principle, to both lifetime transfers and transfers on death, although, as we shall see in Section 7.19, there are extra conditions to be met in the case of lifetime transfers.

Prior to 6th April 2026, unlimited relief at 100% was available in many cases, meaning the transfer of the business or agricultural property could escape IHT altogether, regardless of the value of the business. Sadly, the current Labour Government has now capped 100% relief at £2.5m. This cap, known as the '100% relief allowance' applies to the total combined amount of relief claimed by any individual under both BPR and APR. I will be discussing this new allowance a lot in the rest of this guide so, to save a little space, we will refer to it as the 'HPRA' from now on.

Widows/widowers may also claim any proportion of the HPRA unused by their late spouse, meaning many will have a total HPRA of £5m.

For claims in excess of the HPRA, relief is now given at just 50%, thus creating an effective IHT rate of 20% on value in excess of £2.5m in many family businesses, including farms (or £5m in the case of most widows/widowers).

The 50% rate already applied in some cases before 6th April 2026, and has now been further extended. We will take a closer look at the current rules, the old rules, and the impact of the recent changes in Sections 7.7 and 7.8.

Where relief is given at 50%, it is given before applying other exemptions, such as the annual exemption or the NRB. This effectively doubles the value of these other exemptions.

Example: *Cliff has an industrial building worth £662,000 on which BPR is available at the rate of 50%. He wishes to transfer the building to the Marvin-Welch Discretionary Trust. This will be Cliff's first chargeable lifetime transfer. After BPR at 50%, the chargeable transfer is reduced to £331,000. Cliff's annual exemptions for the current and previous years are still available. Deducting these (at £3,000 each) leaves a chargeable transfer of £325,000, which is covered by Cliff's NRB.*

There is a risk IHT liabilities could arise if Cliff dies within seven years of making this transfer. We will return to the subject of BPR on lifetime transfers in Section 7.19. BPR and APR also apply to the anniversary and exit charges for trusts: see Section 9.8 for further details.

7.2 HOW USEFUL IS BUSINESS PROPERTY RELIEF?

BPR is available on transfers of business property that meet each of the following three conditions:

- The business is a qualifying business (see Sections 7.3 to 7.6),
- The asset itself is relevant business property (see Section 7.7), and
- The asset has been owned by the transferor for the relevant minimum period (see Section 7.17)

There is no requirement for the business to be located in the UK (but see Section 7.27 regarding agricultural property).

There is no limit to the amount of BPR a taxpayer can claim where the qualifying conditions are met: although, from 6th April 2026, 100% relief is restricted to the HPRA (Section 7.8) and any excess attracts relief at just 50%.

Despite the restriction in 100% relief, major savings are still available to those who maximise the value of assets qualifying for BPR within their estate. We will return to this important area of IHT planning in Section 7.21.

But BPR isn't just for those with an existing business. The relief provides a useful mechanism to give IHT-exempt funds to family and friends, as we shall see in Section 7.25. There are even investments that may qualify for at least some relief, as we shall see in Sections 7.26 and 7.34. Furthermore, it generally takes just two years for assets to qualify for BPR, which is much better than the seven-year period needed for a PET to achieve full exemption.

Sadly, however, it is all too easy to lose BPR by failing to meet the qualifying conditions at the appropriate time. There are some particularly nasty pitfalls to watch out for with BPR. In fact, not only is the relief very easy to lose, but this also has a tendency to happen at the point in life when IHT planning is becoming most important.

There is also the problem that some quite normal commercial structures will leave the business owner with BPR at just 50% on their most valuable asset when they could so easily have had 100% (on the first £2.5m or £5m, at least).

Furthermore, the rules on liabilities incurred to finance relievable property (Section 7.12) mean some business owners will enjoy little or no benefit from BPR. Worst of all, refinancing an existing loan could lead to the loss of relief in some cases (see Section 7.12).

Given the importance of this relief and the ease with which it can be lost, we will now take a long, detailed look at the relevant qualifying conditions. Some of this gets quite technical, but it is important for anyone wanting to benefit from one of the most powerful weapons in the battle against IHT.

7.3 QUALIFYING BUSINESSES

For this purpose, any business is a qualifying business as long as it is being carried on with a view to profit and does not consist wholly or mainly of dealing in securities, stocks or shares, or land and buildings, nor of making or holding investments (except for the holding company of a trading group).

This may not initially sound too restrictive but, as we shall see, the definition of what constitutes making or holding investments can be a great deal broader than what one might normally think, especially in the case of land and buildings.

Despite this, Lloyd's underwriters generally qualify for at least some BPR and the businesses of market makers or discount houses on the Stock Exchange also generally qualify. As in many fields of taxation, special rules apply.

What is a Business?

Case law suggests a business exists where at least some of the following six tests apply. Namely, the activity being undertaken:

- Is a serious undertaking earnestly pursued, or a serious occupation
- Is an occupation or function actively pursued with reasonable or recognisable continuity
- Has a measure of substance, measured by the value of supplies made
- Is conducted in a regular manner on sound and recognised business principles
- Is predominantly concerned with making supplies to consumers
- Involves the supply of goods or services of a kind which, subject to differences in detail, are commonly made by those who seek to profit by them

Where some or all of the above tests are satisfied, the activity will constitute a business and will generally qualify for BPR unless it falls under one of the exclusions outlined above. However, even though it may be accepted a business exists, the intention to make a profit remains essential. The profit motive requirement means businesses like stud farms or the business activities of artists or authors may sometimes be ineligible for the relief.

Preparing a credible business plan would provide valuable supporting evidence that you had a reasonable expectation of making a profit. A documented annual review will also be useful, as the profit expectation test must be met at the time of the eventual transfer. However, a business plan will not help if it clearly bears no resemblance to your actual behaviour.

7.4 PROPERTY INVESTMENT OR LETTING BUSINESSES

Unfortunately, as so often seems to be the case in UK taxation, property investment or letting businesses are generally not accepted by HMRC as qualifying businesses for the purpose of BPR. The HMRC view is that holding investment property and collecting rent does not constitute a business for BPR purposes (although this does not seem to stop them collecting tax on income generated by this 'non-business' activity!)

Sadly, HMRC's view is supported by the fact it was specifically stated the letting of land would not qualify for BPR during the parliamentary debates when the relevant rules were first enacted.

Doubtless, those of you with property letting businesses will think this is unfair. This is certainly what the executor of a certain Mrs Burkinyoung thought in 1995 when he made a claim for BPR on the furnished flats Mrs Burkinyoung had been letting. Unfortunately, when the case got to court, the judge decided otherwise, holding that Mrs Burkinyoung's properties were only investments and did not constitute a business for IHT purposes.

It also turns out it would not have helped the Burkinyoung family if the late Mrs Burkinyoung had instead been letting out commercial property. In another case, BPR was denied where the deceased's business consisted of letting out small industrial units. Once again, the judge held that the lettings amounted to the mere holding of investments.

That same judge and others (in later cases) went on to say the provision of property maintenance, security services, heating, or cleaning as part of the terms of the lease would still not be sufficient, in their opinion, to create a qualifying business. The judges thought these services were merely incidental to the holding of investments, even though they acknowledged such services would constitute a qualifying business if provided independently of the letting business. Separating out ancillary services into a separate business may therefore provide landlords with scope to get BPR on at least part of their business.

You may think, perhaps, the reason the cases referred to above were lost could be that the letting businesses concerned were too small. Sadly, this is not the case since, in yet another case, a company letting out more than a hundred properties was still not regarded as having a qualifying business.

Furnished Holiday Lets

I don't know where they get these judges from, or why they persist in regarding property letting as an easy and passive way to make a living (have they heard of the Renters' Rights Act?) Nevertheless, as the law stands, it appears the only type of rental properties that might occasionally attract BPR are furnished holiday lets.

The rules for BPR on furnished holiday lets are very restrictive and far from clear. They are dependent on case law rather than any statutory definition: although that does at least mean BPR is unaffected by the abolition of the furnished holiday letting regime for Income Tax and CGT purposes in April 2025.

Historically, the view generally taken was that furnished holiday lets might be accepted as a business for BPR purposes when the lettings were predominantly short-term (e.g. a week or fortnight) and the owner was substantially involved with the holidaymakers' activities. However, following a spate of cases that went against the taxpayer, it now seems the courts are willing to support HMRC's view that furnished holiday lets will not generally qualify for BPR, even when significant services are provided to tenants.

Nonetheless, there is room for some hope as the taxpayer was successful in one case: although it seems the bar has been set very high when it comes to what constitutes being substantially involved with holidaymakers' activities.

The successful case concerned the late Mrs Graham and her daughter, who provided guests at their self-catering holiday flats with the use of a solar-heated outdoor pool, extensive well-maintained gardens, a sauna, games room, laundry, barbecue area, and guest lounge with books.

All these facilities were regularly maintained. A golf buggy and bicycles could also be hired and each flat was supplied with fresh flowers, homemade food and drink, bed linen, towels, toiletries, and cleaning materials. Furthermore, guests were provided with a welcome pack and refreshments on arrival and the property owners were on hand to help take in shopping, organise birthday and other celebrations and advise on local activities.

There was no doubt this was a business (even HMRC accepted that), but the question in court was whether it was a business of 'making or holding investments' or whether this was outweighed by other components such as the services provided and the onsite facilities.

The taxpayer won in this case but, like me, you are probably shocked there was ever any doubt over the issue. You will be even more shocked to hear that, when the judge gave his decision, he stated this "was an exceptional case which does, ***just***, fall on the non-investment side of the line."

"Just!" It beggars belief, but there it is. The courts seem to think you need to lavish the level of personal care given by Louise Graham (the deceased's daughter) before a furnished holiday let can qualify for BPR.

So, it seems a very high level of involvement with holidaymakers is required before a furnished holiday let might qualify for BPR. Services provided to tenants will need to be far beyond the normal level where landlords merely provide maintenance and cleaning services. Significant additional facilities will need to be provided. In the vast majority of cases you simply have to accept the relief will not be available and plan accordingly.

In the rare cases where you are able to turn the property into something more like a holiday park (as Louise Graham did), you might succeed, but it will be far from certain. (See Section 7.32 for a good way of testing the position.)

In Conclusion
Investment property is highly unlikely to qualify for BPR. You will usually need to be using property in a qualifying trading business. A few furnished holiday lets may qualify, but this will be quite rare.

7.5 BUSINESSES EXPLOITING LAND (AND BUILDINGS)

A great many businesses involve the 'exploitation of land'. This is a legal term to cover any situation where the use, by customers, of land or buildings is a vital component of the business.

Before everyone panics, let me first reassure you I am not talking about businesses where the customer merely enters the land or buildings in order to be provided with goods or services. Hence, retail businesses, restaurants, cafes, health professionals, and most other trading businesses are unaffected. The problem only arises where the customer has some form of right to use the land or buildings themselves. In these cases, HMRC will often attempt to argue the business consists merely of the holding of an investment.

The best defence against this argument is to show the provision of services or sale of goods is essential to the business. The customer must want the goods or services provided rather than the use of land or buildings alone. Many taxpayers have failed in BPR claims where the services provided were merely ancillary to the use of land or buildings rather than being core to the customers' needs.

There is a key distinction between land or buildings held as an investment that will generate income in its own right, as opposed to land or buildings that are an essential component integral to some other business activity. HMRC has a tendency to regard all businesses that involve the use of land or buildings by customers as being investment businesses, but this is not always the case.

Let's take a look at how the exploitation of land argument has been interpreted in some specific types of business.

Hotels: Hotels do not usually fall foul of the 'making or holding investments' rule and hence generally qualify for BPR. There may, however, be problems for hostels, guest-houses, or hotels with long-term residents.

Serviced Offices: Generally speaking, serviced offices do not qualify for BPR as the services provided are regarded as merely ancillary to the rental of the offices. In one case, the office tenants were provided with meeting rooms, receptionist, restaurant, gallery area, gym, hair salon, and social events: and yet the court ***still*** denied BPR on the basis that what the tenants really wanted was office space and the additional services supplied were merely incidental. (Note that, as explained in Section 7.4, if ancillary services were provided by a separate business then ***that*** business might qualify for BPR.)

Property Development: While dealing in land and buildings does not qualify for BPR, a property development business will qualify and both the business's own trading premises (and other assets) and the land and buildings held as trading stock will be covered by the relief.

Livery Businesses: In another case, HMRC tried to deny BPR for a livery business, arguing that, if similar accommodation and services were provided to humans rather than horses, the business would be regarded as akin to a furnished holiday let and thus merely the holding of an investment (see Section 7.4 regarding BPR for furnished holiday lets).

Luckily this rather peculiar analogy did not convince the judge: perhaps partly because it is difficult to envisage the owner of a furnished holiday let worming their guests, or checking them for lameness and bloating.

The late owner's son (her executor) argued that a livery business was more akin to a children's nursery than a furnished holiday let, since the owner was responsible for the animals' health and wellbeing. In the end, the judge accepted the business offered significantly more than the right to occupy a parcel of land and hence BPR was allowed.

Stately Homes: Stately homes open to the public may be covered by BPR. In one case, a claim for BPR was upheld by the court when just 78% of the property was open to the public. Despite the fact that 22% of the property was closed to the public, the whole property qualified as it had to be viewed as a single asset and, furthermore, the entire exterior was important to the paying public's enjoyment of the property.

The implication is that any building, of which more than 50% is used for the public's enjoyment, as part of a commercial enterprise, might qualify for BPR. This would surely also extend to private museums and other similar enterprises, as long as the profit motive (see Section 7.3) is present. (All is not lost where less than 50% of the property is used for business purposes, as we shall see in Section 7.10.)

Sporting, Shooting, and Fishing: These are generally regarded as qualifying trading activities, although as with everything, this will depend on the facts of each individual case.

Caravan Parks: Caravan parks have occupied a lot of the courts' attention when it comes to BPR. To date, there have been five major cases on the subject. So far, the score is HMRC 3 - Taxpayers 2. In essence, the taxpayers lost the cases where the majority of income came from site fees or pitch fees (basically a form of rent) but won the cases where the majority of income came from the provision of other services or sale of caravans.

Most recently, the long and tortuous case of *George & Loochin (Stedman's Executors)* was eventually decided in favour of the deceased's executors when it reached the Court of Appeal. This case concerned a caravan park where a major proportion of the business income comprised site fees for the storage of caravans and mobile homes. However, the saving grace for this caravan park was the fact that 72% of those fees were absorbed by overheads, mainly the upkeep of common parts of the park.

Nevertheless, HMRC still argued the site fees represented income from the exploitation of land and the caravan park business was thus tantamount to the mere holding of an investment.

Thankfully, the judge in the Court of Appeal stated the holding of property as an investment was only one component of the business and did not prevent it from qualifying for BPR. He found it difficult to see why an active family business of this kind should be excluded from BPR just because a necessary component of the business was the holding of land.

This last judgement tells us a few things:

- An 'active' business should qualify for BPR
- Caravan parks are very much a borderline case, as they are partly concerned with the exploitation of land
- You get a better quality of judge in the Court of Appeal

But seriously, any business that involves some element of exploitation of land runs a risk of not qualifying for BPR.

General Guidelines

The key to obtaining BPR is to ensure the majority of the business income comes from the provision of services and not from the mere exploitation of land. We will look further at the question of what constitutes the majority of the business income in the next section.

Life Interests in Land

The cases where difficulty arises due to the exploitation of land argument involve taxpayers who actually own that land. Naturally, this means their estate is extremely valuable, which is why the BPR claim is so important.

It has been established, however, that a taxpayer who only held a life interest in land could not be held to have a business that consisted of making or holding investments. That taxpayer's business therefore qualified for BPR, which was very useful since, as we shall see in Chapter 8, there are some cases where the underlying assets in which the deceased had a life interest have to be included in their estate.

This provides a possible method for ensuring a business that could potentially fall foul of the exploitation of land problem will qualify for BPR. The drawback is that BPR is only given at the rate of 50% where the transferor had a life interest in the property rather than absolute ownership (see Section 7.7).

Nonetheless, despite this drawback, BPR may sometimes be maximised by splitting the ownership of the business from the ownership of the underlying land, and placing the land in a life interest trust. This should enable the owner to claim 100% relief on the business (up to their available HPRA) and 50% relief on the land, when there may have been no relief at all if they had owned the underlying land outright.

Example: *Tom owns a caravan park in South Wales. On his death, he leaves the park business to his wife Joan and the land on which the park is set to a life interest trust with Joan as the beneficiary. Tom's NRB is unused and therefore transfers to Joan (see Section 6.2).*

On Joan's subsequent death in March 2027, her executors claim 100% BPR on the park business, worth £750,000, and 50% BPR on the park land, worth £1.3m. After BPR, the chargeable value of the land is reduced to £650,000 and this is covered by Joan's NRB plus the TNRB received from Tom, leaving no IHT to pay.

If Joan owned both the park business and park land outright, she might not have been eligible for any BPR. The IHT arising on the park would then have been at least £560,000 (£750,000 + £1.3m – £650,000 = £1.4m x 40%).

The drawback to this technique is it may mean 50% relief on the value of the underlying land has been sacrificed if, in fact, the business would have qualified for BPR anyway. For more valuable businesses worth at least £5m (excluding the underlying land), this drawback has now been eliminated, due to the HPRA, but it remains an issue for the majority of small businesses.

A better approach may therefore be to only put the structure described above into place via a deed of variation after a BPR claim on the first spouse's death has already failed. See Section 7.32 for a way to safely test the position on the first spouse's death.

The method described above is based on an old case that was only won in the Court of Appeal on a 2-1 majority. It is therefore possible this decision could be overturned one day!

7.6 WHAT DOES WHOLLY OR MAINLY MEAN IN PRACTICE?

As stated in Section 7.3, a business will not qualify for BPR if it consists wholly or mainly of dealing in securities, stocks or shares, or land and buildings, or making or holding investments. Naturally, however, it follows that, while it cannot consist wholly or mainly of these activities, it can still consist partly of them.

Quite simply, 'wholly or mainly' means 'at least 50%'. "50% of what?" I hear you ask. Case law has sometimes, though not exclusively, interpreted the 50% test as relating to net profits. To be on the safe side, however, I would suggest trying to ensure the business consists of qualifying activities to the extent these account for over 50% of each of the following:

- Turnover (i.e. sales)
- Gross profit
- Net profit
- Proprietor's time
- Employees' time
- Assets employed in the business (although, as we have seen already, land employed in the business may be regarded in a number of ways)

Hybrid Businesses
It is important to remember what is required for BPR purposes is that the business consists wholly or mainly of qualifying business activities. If the wholly or mainly test is met then the whole business will qualify, including those parts that are not themselves qualifying activities. This has important IHT planning implications as it means BPR may be available in respect of an investment business component that represents a minority element of a qualifying business.

Example: *Ray and Dave run a property business, Kink Properties, in partnership together. Kink Properties derives around 75% of its income from property development and the remainder from property letting. While HMRC would argue that part of the business amounts to the non-qualifying activity of holding investments, the main part, property development, represents a qualifying activity. Kink Properties therefore qualifies for BPR. Furthermore, the whole business qualifies, including the investment properties.*

To get relief on the whole value of the business, it is important to ensure all the assets held by the business are actually used in the business. A completely unrelated quoted shareholding, for example, might be regarded as a non-business asset and would thus be ineligible for relief.

There is an important distinction between business assets used in a non-qualifying part of the business (like Ray and Dave's investment properties), which do attract relief, and assets that are not business assets at all (like those unrelated quoted shares), which are excluded from relief. Assets excluded from relief are known as excepted assets and we will return to this concept again in Section 7.10.

7.7 RELEVANT BUSINESS PROPERTY

In broad terms, a sole trader business, partnership share, or shares in a private company, qualify for BPR at 100% up to the amount of the business owner's available HPRA (usually either £2.5m; or £5m for widows/widowers: see further in Section 7.8). In each case, the business entity must be carrying on a qualifying business.

For both deaths and lifetime transfers after 5th April 2026, any amount in excess of the business owner's available HPRA attracts relief at just 50%.

For deaths before 6th April 2026, and lifetime transfers before 30th October 2024, these assets qualified for unlimited 100% relief. See Section 7.8 regarding lifetime transfers between 30th October 2024 and 5th April 2026.

None of this alters the fundamental principles regarding the treatment of lifetime transfers (Chapter 4), including the fact that transfers to another individual (PETs) will generally be exempt from IHT if the transferor survives seven years.

Let's Get Technical
In technical terms, the assets listed at (i) to (iii) below qualify for BPR at 100% up to the amount of the taxpayer's available HPRA, and at 50% on any excess.

For deaths before 6th April 2026, and lifetime transfers before 30th October 2024, these assets attracted unlimited relief at 100%.

i) An interest in a qualifying unincorporated business (i.e. a sole trade or profession, or share in a partnership)
ii) Unquoted shares in a company carrying on a qualifying business that are *not* traded on any stock exchange
iii) Unquoted securities (e.g. loan stock) in a company carrying on a qualifying business that are *not* traded on any stock exchange and which, either alone, or together with other unquoted shares or securities, give the transferor control of the company

Other types of property qualify for relief at 50% (regardless of value), and do not use up the taxpayer's HPRA:

iv) Quoted shares or securities in a company carrying on a qualifying business that, either alone, or together with other quoted shares or securities, give the transferor control of that company
v) Assets held personally by the transferor but used wholly or mainly for the purposes of a qualifying business carried on by a company under the transferor's control, or a partnership in which the transferor is a partner (or was prior to death in the case of transfers on death)
vi) Assets held in an interest in possession trust on behalf of the transferor and used wholly or mainly for the purpose of a business under the transferor's control or a business carried on by a partnership in which the transferor was a partner. (This applies only to interests in possession deemed to form part of the transferor's estate for IHT purposes: see Chapter 8)
vii) Shares in a company carrying on a qualifying business that are traded on the Alternative Investment Market (AIM), or any other stock exchange, but which are nonetheless classed as unquoted (see below)
viii) Unquoted securities in a company carrying on a qualifying business that are traded on AIM, or any other stock exchange, and which, either alone, or together with other unquoted shares or securities, give the transferor control of the company

For deaths before 6th April 2026, and lifetime transfers before 30th October 2024, assets under (vii) and (viii) attracted unlimited relief at 100%. See Section 7.8 regarding lifetime transfers between 30th October 2024 and 5th April 2026.

For BPR purposes, 'unquoted' means not listed on a recognised stock exchange. In general, any stock exchange recognised by the laws of the country in which it is situated will usually be a recognised stock exchange and shares listed there will be treated as quoted.

Shares traded on AIM are not listed, and are thus regarded as unquoted. Similarly, shares traded on any stock market that is not a listed market of a recognised stock exchange are also regarded as unquoted. In both cases, these shares now fall under heading (vii) above and may attract BPR at 50%, having previously been eligible for unlimited relief at 100%.

Similar principles apply to determine whether securities fall under heading (viii) above.

For guidance on recognised stock exchanges and 'listed' markets, see: https://www.gov.uk/government/publications/designated-recognised-stock-exchanges-section-1005-income-tax-act-2007

Despite the technical definition of 'unquoted', for the rest of this guide, unless stated to the contrary, any reference to unquoted shares, private company shares, or shares in an unquoted company, means shares that are not traded on any stock market. Hence, provided the company is carrying on a qualifying business, the shares fall under heading (ii) above, and may qualify for BPR at 100% (up to the amount of HPRA available).

Most shares in small or medium-sized private companies carrying on a qualifying business qualify for BPR under heading (ii), and hence the issue of control is not important for the shares themselves. However, control is essential in the case of shares, securities, or other assets falling under any of headings (iii) to (vi), or (viii).

Furthermore, an important point to note about headings (iii), (iv), and (viii) is that it is only shares or securities that actually contribute to the transferor's control of the company that qualify for BPR. For example, a shareholder who controls a quoted company by means of voting ordinary shares will not be entitled to BPR on non-voting preference shares in the same company. It also follows that very few securities (loan stock, etc.) will qualify for BPR.

Control is generally taken to mean the transferor is able to control over 50% of the voting powers on all questions affecting the company as a whole. A transferor holding 50% of the voting shares plus the right to a casting vote will also have control. In deciding whether the transferor can control the requisite proportion of voting power, we can include: shares held by their spouse; shares transferred by them or their spouse to a charity, or other exempt body, after 15th April 1976 and still held by the transferee body at any time within the last five years; and shares treated as part of their estate or their spouse's estate (e.g. some types of interest in possession: see Chapter 8).

Control need only exist immediately before the relevant transfer. The availability of BPR is unaffected by whether control is lost as a result of the transfer in question: although, of course, subsequent transfers may be affected.

When planning a transfer of shares that may result in a loss of control of the company, it may therefore make sense to make other transfers first, such as smaller transfers of shares or securities falling under headings (iii), (iv), or (viii), or transfers of property used in the company's business falling under headings (v) or (vi).

A company held 50/50 by two individuals is not under the control of either individual. Hence, unless those individuals are a married couple, this means there can be no relief for any property under headings (v) or (vi). Subject to commercial requirements, it may therefore make sense to make a slight change to the company shareholdings so that one of the individuals has control and will be eligible for relief.

Since it is quite rare for securities to qualify for BPR, I will generally ignore them for the remainder of this chapter. However, readers should bear in mind that securities can qualify if they meet the criteria set out above: they will then be subject to the same considerations as apply for qualifying shares, as discussed throughout this chapter.

A partnership includes a Limited Liability Partnership (LLP). Members' capital accounts in a partnership carrying on a qualifying business will qualify for BPR but members' loan accounts do not. This is a particular problem for LLPs.

7.8 THE 100% RELIEF ALLOWANCE (HPRA)

In this section, we are going to look at how the HPRA, introduced on 6th April 2026 operates. We'll look at some additional planning issues relating to the allowance later, in Sections 7.28 to 7.31.

The HPRA has initially been set at £2.5m, and frozen at its current level (like the NRB and RNRB) until at least 5th April 2031. Any unused HPRA on the death of a married person transfers to their spouse: we'll take a closer look at how this works later.

The HPRA limits the total combined amount of both BPR and APR at 100% that a taxpayer may claim. Where a taxpayer makes relevant transfers of value (see below) in excess of their HPRA, the rate of relief drops to 50% on the excess, thus creating an effective IHT rate of 20% (40% x 50%).

For example, a business worth £10m could thus potentially give rise to an IHT bill of £1.5m (£10m – £2.5m = £7.5m x 20%): although this assumes no other reliefs are available.

While this is an atrocious assault on both farmers and other business owners, from a planning perspective it is worth remembering BPR and APR continue to provide an effective IHT *saving* of 20% on amounts in excess of £2.5m.

A separate 'trust HPRA' applies to trusts: see Section 9.8 for details.

Relevant Transfers of Value

The HPRA applies to the following transfers of assets eligible for BPR or APR at 100% (see Sections 7.7 and 7.27):

- Transfers on a death after 5th April 2026
- Chargeable lifetime transfers after 5th April 2026*
- Chargeable lifetime transfers between 30th October 2024 and 5th April 2026 where the transferor dies after 5th April 2026 but within seven years**
- PETs after 29th October 2024 where the transferor dies after 5th April 2026 but within seven years**

* Chargeable lifetime transfers after 5th April 2026 use up the HPRA (or part of it) for a period of seven years

** These transfers only use up the allowance if BPR or APR at 100% is available at the time of the transferor's death (see Section 7.19)

Claims restricted to 50% relief do not use up the allowance. This includes lifetime transfers of shares or securities listed on AIM after 29th October 2024 and lifetime transfers of other assets falling under headings (vii) or (viii) in Section 7.7 after 5th April 2026.

The 100% Relief Allowance in Practice

Let's look at a couple of examples to show how the £2.5m HPRA works in practice. For the moment, we will look at cases where there is no additional allowance available from a deceased spouse (we'll look at that later).

Example 1: *Frank, who has been divorced for many years, dies in October 2026, leaving the shares in his unquoted trading company, Artanis Ltd, worth £4m, to his daughter, Nancy. He also leaves her his home and a few other assets worth a total of £325,000, which use up his NRB (his estate is too large for him to be entitled to the RNRB).*

Frank's executors can claim BPR of:

£2.5m @ 100%	*£2,500,000*
£1.5m @ 50%	*£750,000*
Total	*£3,250,000*

This leaves £750,000 chargeable to IHT at 40%, leaving Nancy lumbered with a bill of £300,000.

If Frank had died before 6th April 2026, there would have been no IHT to pay, but now Nancy has to find £300,000. She has inherited other assets worth £325,000, but among them is Frank's home. Perhaps it's her home now, meaning she can't really sell it and may have very little in the way of liquid assets to fund her IHT bill.

So, Nancy may have to look to Artanis Ltd to provide the funds she needs. She can apply to pay the IHT in ten yearly instalments and, as the shares qualified for BPR, she will not suffer the extortionate interest charges arising in many other cases (see Section 2.7).

Let's say Nancy already takes enough salary and dividends out of the company to make her a higher rate taxpayer. That means any further dividends will suffer Income Tax at 35.75% or more. So, to get the £300,000 she needs over a ten-year period, she will need to take extra dividends totalling at least £466,926 (after paying Income Tax of £166,926, this will leave her with the £300,000 she needs). If the company is paying CT (Corporation Tax) at the main rate of 25% (this seems likely given its value), it will take pre-tax profits of £622,568 to fund dividends of £466,926 (which must be paid out of after-tax profits).

In effect, the 2.5m cap on 100% BPR has led to an overall cost of £622,568 on the value of the business in excess of that cap (£1.5m in this case). Hence, in a case like this, the effective overall rate of tax on qualifying business property in excess of £2.5m is not 20%, but ***at least 41.5%!***

Furthermore, a sum equal to ***around 16%*** of the company's value will have to be utilised paying IHT instead of being available to invest in the business: how's that for your growth agenda, Rachel?

See the Taxcafe guide *Salary versus Dividends* for detailed guidance on how company owners can extract funds from their company most tax efficiently.

Example 2: *In 2025, Neneh gave 25% of the shares in her unquoted trading company, Manchild Ltd, to her daughter, Mabel. These shares were worth £600,000 at the time of the gift, but the consequent reduction in the value of Neneh's estate, and hence the transfer of value (Section 2.1), was £1.5m.*

Sadly, Neneh, who was unmarried, died at seven seconds past midnight on 6th April 2026, leaving her entire estate, worth £3.8m, to Mabel. This consists of:

Remaining shares in Manchild Ltd	*£3,000,000*
AIM shares	*£100,000*
Family home	*£550,000*
Other assets	*£150,000*

The lifetime gift to Mabel uses up £1.5m of Neneh's HPRA, leaving just £1m. Neneh's executors, Eagle Eye & Co, therefore claim BPR as follows:

Manchild Ltd	
First £1m @ 100%	*£1,000,000*
Remaining £2m @ 50%	*£1,000,000*
AIM shares	
£100,000 @ 50%	*£50,000*
Total	*£2,050,000*

This reduces Neneh's chargeable estate to £1.75m (£3.8m – £2.05m). However, her NRB of £325,000 is available in full as the lifetime gift to Mabel is fully relieved by BPR at 100%. This reduces Neneh's chargeable estate to £1,425,000, leaving Eagle Eye & Co to cough up £570,000 in IHT (at 40%).

Once again, it will be difficult for the executors to pay the IHT bill, and Mabel will either need to sell the family home or extract additional funds from Manchild Ltd (see Example 1 above for the effective cost arising).

If Neneh had died just one day earlier (eight seconds earlier, in fact), her executors would have been able to claim BPR of £3.1m (the total value of her remaining shares in Manchild Ltd plus her AIM shares). After her NRB, this would have left just £375,000 exposed to IHT (£3.8m – £3.1m – £325,000), giving rise to a bill, at 40%, of £150,000. This could have been settled from liquid assets, without the need to sell the family home or extract additional funds from Manchild Ltd.

So, in this case, the cap on 100% BPR has cost Mabel (the beneficiary) an extra £420,000, and put her mother's business in jeopardy.

As an aside, it's worth noting that, if Neneh had given Mabel enough shares in Manchild Ltd (as a lifetime transfer) to reduce her estate to £2m or less, this would have yielded an indirect saving of £70,000 (£175,000 x 40%) because Neneh's RNRB would then have been available.

Widows and Widowers

Every individual has a HPRA, whether they own any business or agricultural property or not. When a married person dies, any unused allowance transfers to their widow/widower. Where they died before 6th April 2026, the whole allowance is deemed unused and transfers to the surviving spouse. As with the NRB, it is the unused proportion of the allowance that transfers, not the amount.

The upshot of all this is that most widows/widowers will have a HPRA of £5m. So, if, in Example 1 above, Frank had been a widower, Nancy would have had no IHT to pay. Similarly, the IHT on Neneh's estate would have been drastically reduced:

Example 2 Revisited: *The facts are the same as before, except it transpires that Neneh was, in fact, a widow: her estranged husband, Youssou, died penniless many years ago. Her HPRA is therefore £5m, and the IHT on her estate is calculated as follows:*

Remaining shares in Manchild Ltd	*£3,000,000*
BPR @ 100%	*(£3,000,000)*
AIM shares	*£100,000*
BPR @ 50%	*(£50,000)*
Family home	*£550,000*
Other assets	*£150,000*
Nil rate band	*(£325,000)*
TNRB (from Youssou)	*(£325,000)*
Chargeable estate	*£100,000*

This leaves Mabel with just £40,000 to pay in IHT. Her mother's long-forgotten marriage has saved her £530,000!

In this revised scenario, if Neneh had made a big enough lifetime transfer of shares in Manchild Ltd to reduce her estate to £2.5m or less, she would have had at least £100,000 of her RNRB available and this would have wiped out Mabel's IHT bill altogether.

The transfer of unused HPRA to a widow/widower works in a similar way to the TNRB (as detailed in Chapter 6), in that:

- It is the unused proportion that transfers, not the amount, so the widow/widower will benefit from future increases in the allowance (if they *ever come!*)
- Additional amounts of HPRA can be accumulated if you outlive two or more spouses, but

- Only a maximum of one additional transferred allowance can be accumulated (hence, at current rates, the maximum total HPRA for a widow/widower is £5m)

7.9 VALUING A BUSINESS

Valuing an unincorporated business (a sole trade or partnership), or an unquoted company, is a notoriously difficult exercise. In theory, the market value of a business is the price that a willing buyer and willing seller would agree upon when dealing with each other at arms' length. That's all very well, but unless there is an actual deal on the table at the relevant time, it's all completely hypothetical.

So, it's horrifying to realise this totally hypothetical exercise will now determine how big a financial burden the family of many small or medium-sized business owners will be forced to bear after their death.

The problem is not entirely new as the value of a business can also impact the deductibility of liabilities (Section 7.12) and whether the RNRB is available (Section 3.4). There are also a number of other issues to be taken into account, as explained in Sections 7.10 and 7.11. Nonetheless, before 6th April 2026, in many cases, it was possible to just assume the business would be fully exempted by BPR without having to be too concerned about its value. Now, that will often no longer be the case.

Valuing a business is a specialist skill and I am not going to attempt to explain it in this guide. If you want a value you can rely on for planning purposes, or even just so you can understand the burden that will fall on your family, professional advice is essential. Any valuations quoted in this guide are for the purposes of illustration only.

In particular, it is important to note the value of a successful, profitable business is usually more than the sum of its parts (i.e. more than the total of its net assets). This is because of the additional, often invisible asset: goodwill.

Furthermore, the values appearing in the business accounts prepared for Income Tax or CT purposes, or to impress the bank, are not always relevant. Land and buildings may have appreciated considerably, the value given for other assets will be the product of the business's accounting policy and may be far removed from actual market value. Accounting standards may require assets to be recognised when, in fact, they are only leased. Goodwill does not generally appear in the accounts at all, but may be extremely valuable.

In short, when it comes to the value of a business for IHT purposes, a professional valuation is generally going to be required: what a tragedy it is that the Government has chosen to place the burden of this further cost on bereaved families, as well as the additional tax arising. The only people celebrating are the valuers!

7.10 SOLE TRADERS AND PARTNERSHIPS

Subject to the points in Section 7.9, the value of an unincorporated business is made up of the total value of all the assets of the business, including goodwill, less any business liabilities. The assets and liabilities of the business are all those items a purchaser would take into account in order to ascertain a value for the whole business.

Business liabilities (like trade creditors, for example) need to be deducted in arriving at the value of the business. Loans and other liabilities are not usually deducted in arriving at the value of the business, but generally need to be deducted for the purposes of a BPR claim. We will look at the distinction between these two types of liabilities in Section 7.13.

Money owed to a transferor by their own business cannot be included as an additional asset in a BPR claim.

Non-business property on which business loans are secured cannot be included as part of the value of the business. However, loans and other liabilities incurred to purchase or finance the business may need to be deducted from the value of the business for the purposes of the BPR claim. Again, we will look at these in more detail in Section 7.13.

The value of a partnership share will often be affected by the terms of the partnership agreement: we will look at this issue further in Section 7.20.

Excepted Assets

The general rule is that BPR is not available on the value of an asset which has neither been used wholly or mainly for business purposes for the period of two years prior to the transfer, or the period since acquisition, if less; nor is required for the future use of the business.

In the case of property falling under heading (v) in Section 7.7, however, the rule is revised so that, in order to qualify for BPR, the asset in question must have either been used for the purpose of the business of the partnership or company throughout the two years prior to the transfer; or have replaced a similar previous asset (see Section 7.18) and the two assets taken together were used in the relevant business for a combined total of at least two years within the five-year period prior to the transfer.

Remember, as discussed in Section 7.6, the asset only needs to be used in the business. In the case of a hybrid business qualifying under the wholly or mainly rule, the asset might be used in a non-qualifying component of the business and could still qualify for BPR.

Buildings with Partial Business Use

In Section 7.5, we saw that a building used at least 50% for business purposes would qualify for BPR as a result of the wholly or mainly rule. In many cases, however, a smaller proportion of a building may be used for business purposes. Examples might include a dentist, doctor or vet using part of their home for an office, waiting room and surgery; or a shopkeeper using the ground floor of their three-storey house as shop premises.

In cases like this, a BPR claim may be made in respect of the business portion of the property, provided this portion is used exclusively for business purposes. This applies to claims under headings (i), (v) or (vi) in Section 7.7.

Note that, while exclusive business use of part of your home could save IHT, it could also lead to a CGT liability if you dispose of the property during your lifetime (see the Taxcafe guide *How to Save Property Tax*). Furthermore, exclusive business use may not save any IHT if the property is to be left to a direct descendant and would be covered by the RNRB otherwise (Section 3.4).

7.11 BUSINESS PROPERTY RELIEF FOR COMPANY SHARES

Valuing unquoted company shares is a highly complex subject worthy of an entire book in its own right. To begin with, for shareholdings of less than 100%, it is not simply a case of valuing the company as a whole and taking the appropriate proportion. Different shareholdings will have different values: generally speaking, the smaller the percentage owned by an individual, the lower the value per share. We will look at that later, but first let's focus on valuing the company itself and working out how much BPR can be claimed.

To value the company, it is necessary to take account of goodwill and all the company's liabilities. There is no distinction here between business liabilities and other liabilities such as loans. The company's tax liabilities will also need to be taken into account (this may sometimes include the potential tax arising if it were to sell its assets at current market value: although this depends on the valuation method used).

In Section 7.7, we examined the conditions to be satisfied before shares in a company may qualify for BPR. However, just because the shares qualify in principle, this does not necessarily mean the whole value of those shares qualifies.

In order to calculate the available BPR, it will be necessary to take into account any excepted assets held by the company. The definition of excepted assets for this purpose is the same as the general definition given in Section 7.10 (not the revised one for transfers under heading (v)).

To establish what *proportion* of a company's value is based on excepted assets, we continue to follow the principles outlined in the previous section regarding the valuation of a business. In other words, the company's total value is derived after taking account of *all* its liabilities but, for the purposes of working out any restriction in BPR due to excepted assets, we only take account of *business* liabilities.

Example: *Tommy owns all the share capital in Pinball Ltd, a trading company operating amusement arcades. The company has total assets, including goodwill, valued at £1.2m, net of business liabilities. However, this includes £300,000 in cash held in a deposit account, which is surplus to the company's business requirements and not used in its trade. 25% (£300,000/£1.2m) of the company's value is therefore deemed to be attributable to a non-business asset (the surplus cash).*

In addition to its business liabilities, Pinball Ltd has a £50,000 CT liability and an interest-free loan of £350,000 from the company's founder. These liabilities reduce the value of the company to £800,000, but the £300,000 of surplus cash still represents just 25% of the total value of its net business assets (£1.2m).

Tommy's shares are thus worth £800,000, but he can claim BPR of £600,000 (£800,000 less 25%).

If Tommy did not own all the shares in the company, his shares would have a lower value, but his BPR claim would continue to be restricted by 25%.

It's worth pointing out that if the company used all its surplus cash to pay off most of its interest-free loan, there would be no restriction in Tommy's BPR. However, as the loan is interest free, Tommy may not wish to do this (I'm assuming that Tommy is not the loan creditor in this case).

Cash on Deposit

Just because a company has cash on deposit does not necessarily make that cash an excepted asset. The question is whether that cash is surplus to the company's business requirements. In a case like Pinball Ltd, it will often be possible to argue at least some of the cash is required for working capital. Exactly how much will depend on the circumstances of each case.

Cash held by a company for a specific identifiable business purpose may also be included as a business asset.

Example: *Johnny owns San Quentin Ltd, a company he originally formed to own and operate a nightclub, 'Ring of Fire'. In August 2026, San Quentin Ltd sells Ring of Fire for £1m. The company keeps the money on deposit because Johnny is actively looking for a new nightclub San Quentin Ltd can buy. Sadly, however, Johnny dies before the company can buy the new nightclub.*

Johnny leaves his San Quentin Ltd shares to his son, Sue. Thankfully, full BPR is available on the shares because the cash held on deposit was earmarked for a specific business purpose.

This example is based on a real case (but with different names: especially the boy named Sue), which the taxpayer's executors won. In another case, however, a similar claim was denied when the executors claimed surplus funds were being held pending a suitable business opportunity. The court felt this was too vague and cash on deposit could only be counted as a business asset when it was required for a palpable business purpose. Hence, in Johnny's case, if he had decided he'd had enough of the nightclub business and was looking for another investment opportunity, BPR would have been denied.

The key to maintaining full BPR on shares in a company holding surplus cash is to have an identifiable business requirement for that cash. This should be documented in business plans, cashflow projections, directors' board minutes, etc. It is also worth noting the same surplus cash would not generally qualify for BPR when held personally. Hence, it may make sense to retain business sale proceeds within a company when intending to reinvest them (this generally has other tax benefits too).

Other Investments
Other short-term investments held by the company might be eligible for inclusion as business assets if the rationale discussed above can be established. Alternatively, as we saw in Section 7.6, the company may have a hybrid business, and the investments might therefore be business assets in their own right.

HMRC accepts the holding of investments by a company may often be part of its normal business activities, although they will still attack cases where they perceive the company is simply being used as a repository for non-business assets in order to artificially increase the amount of BPR available.

Shareholdings Less than 100%
Very often, the value of unquoted shares held by an individual is dependent on what proportion of the company they own. A controlling (over 50%) shareholding in a private company might be worth £5,000 per share, for example, while a small minority holding in the same company might be worth just £600 per share. These changes in proportionate value can have major implications for transfers of value that result in the transferor's shareholding falling into a lower value category.

Example: *Mick owns a thousand ordinary shares in Fleetwood Ltd out of the company's total issued share capital of 10,000 shares. There is only one class of shares. It has been established that shareholdings of 10% or more (but less than 25%) can be valued at £2,000 per share but holdings of less than 10% are worth only £600 per share. Hence, Mick's shareholding is valued at £2m (1,000 x £2,000).*

Mick decides to give one share to his daughter, Stevie. This reduces the value of his remaining holding of 999 shares to £599,400 (999 x £600). The gift to Stevie is therefore treated as a transfer of value of £1,400,600 (£2m - £599,400), despite the fact her share is worth just £600.

This preposterous result could be absolutely disastrous for Stevie. If Mick should die within three years of making this gift, Stevie could face an IHT bill of up to £560,240 (assuming BPR is not available: see Section 7.8 for the consequences if it is). All for a share worth just £600: clearly, there are times when you ***should*** *look a gift horse in the mouth!*

Valuing unquoted company shares is a highly complex matter, but it is perhaps worth pointing out the requirements of company law relating to shareholders' resolutions effectively create some key thresholds where increases in share values can be expected to apply. These thresholds are: 10%; 25%; 50%; over 50%; over 75%; over 90%; and 100%.

Financing the Company
Loans and other liabilities incurred by a shareholder in order to purchase company shares, or to finance the company in some other way, may need to be deducted from the value of the borrower's shares when claiming BPR. We will

look at this issue in more detail in Section 7.14; as well as the position where a shareholder lends funds to their own company.

7.12 FINANCING A BUSINESS

As explained in Section 2.10, liabilities incurred to finance the acquisition, enhancement or maintenance of qualifying business property, must be deducted from the value of that property for BPR purposes.

Liabilities incurred before April 2013 are exempt (see further below) but, since then, these rules have meant it is not possible to obtain additional BPR simply by borrowing funds to purchase qualifying business property.

Sadly, these rules effectively also deny relief for many genuine business investments financed with debt, but that doesn't mean such investments are not beneficial in the long run, as we'll discuss in Section 7.15.

We'll take a closer look at the application of these rules to unincorporated businesses (sole traders and partnerships) in Section 7.13, and company shares in Section 7.14. But first, in this section, let's examine some of the principles that apply equally to all forms of qualifying business property.

Example: *In 2016, Amy (who is single) borrowed £600,000 by remortgaging her house and used the money to buy a trading business, 'The Wine House'. In March 2027, Amy dies. She leaves her house to her sister, Adele and she leaves The Wine House to her brother, Pete. By this point, her house is worth £1m and The Wine House is worth £800,000. Amy's Will specifies both beneficiaries are to bear the tax arising on their legacies.*

The Wine House is eligible for BPR, so it can be passed to Pete without any IHT liability. However, the deemed value of The Wine House for BPR purposes is only £200,000, as Amy's mortgage must be deducted from its actual value of £800,000.

Amy's executors arrange for her house to be transferred to Adele subject to the existing mortgage (this satisfies the requirement for a commercial reason for non-repayment: see Section 2.10). Adele therefore acquires a house with equity of just £400,000 (£1m – £600,000). However, she will be liable for IHT on the full £1m value of the house (less Amy's NRB) because the mortgage has been set against the value of The Wine House.

This gives Adele an IHT liability of £270,000 (£1m – £325,000 = £675,000 x 40%), which amounts to 67.5% of the value of her inheritance!

These rules create an incredibly unfair result. The IHT due on Amy's house falls on Adele, but she is denied any relief for the mortgage she has taken over. She ends up facing liabilities totalling £870,000 by inheriting a house worth only £1m. Meanwhile, Pete obtains a business worth £800,000 free from any liabilities at all!

Business owners who have borrowed to finance their business may wish to consider adjustments to legacies to prevent such unfair results. Amy could have left an additional £240,000 to Adele and specified this was to be charged against the assets of The Wine House. This would have compensated Adele for being denied relief for the mortgage on Amy's house.

In addition to the unfairness seen above, these rules could also lead to the collapse of many businesses.

Example: *In 2018, Dusty borrowed £850,000 by mortgaging her house and invested it in her business. Over the next few years, she borrowed further sums by way of personal loans, credit cards, etc, in order to fund her business.*

In March 2027, Dusty, who has never married, dies and leaves her entire estate to her brother, Tom. At this point, her house is worth £1.2m and the other debts she incurred to fund her business total £400,000.

Tom will be denied any relief for the mortgage over Dusty's house or the other debts she incurred to fund her business, so he will be left with an IHT bill of £350,000 (£1.2m – £325,000 = £875,000 x 40%). Leaving the business to one side for the moment, Tom has inherited a house worth £1.2m but faces total debts of £1.6m (the mortgage of £850,000, other debts of £400,000, and IHT of £350,000).

Hence, even if Tom were to sell Dusty's house, he would still face liabilities of £400,000 (more after taking sale costs into account). If Tom had no significant assets of his own, this would have to be funded from Dusty's business meaning that, in all likelihood, Tom would be unable to continue trading.

The amount of BPR Dusty receives is drastically reduced. If her business had been worth, say, £1.5m, she would have received BPR of just £250,000 (£1.5m less £850,000 mortgage less £400,000 of other liabilities).

Business Property with Lower Value than Liabilities

In the last example, I assumed Dusty's business had a value in excess of the liabilities she incurred to fund it (£1.25m). Where the value of the business property is less than the outstanding liabilities incurred to finance it, the excess liabilities may be deducted from the remainder of the owner's estate.

Example Revisited: *Let's take the same facts as above, but assume Dusty's business is worth just £800,000 at the time of her death. The liabilities incurred to finance her business total £1.25m, but it will now only be necessary to set £800,000 of these against the value of the business. This leaves £450,000 that can be set against the remainder of her estate, reducing Tom's IHT bill to £170,000 (£1.2m – £450,000 – £325,000 = £425,000 x 40%).*

In this revised example, Dusty receives no BPR at all: since the value of her business for this purpose is reduced to nil.

I assumed throughout both versions of the example that Dusty's liabilities are eligible to be deducted from her estate (see Section 2.10). For the sake of illustration, I also assumed in both of the above examples that the outstanding balances on the mortgages and other debts were unchanged. In practice, the outstanding balances at the date of the business owner's death (or date of transfer in the case of a lifetime transfer) should be used rather than the original amounts borrowed.

Inherited or Transferred Liabilities
Where a beneficiary takes over a liability secured on an inherited or transferred asset, the treatment of the liability in their estate, or on any lifetime transfers *they* make, is unaffected by the treatment applied to the transferor. Hence, in the examples in this section, the mortgages taken over by Adele and Tom would be fully deductible from their estates if they were to die while these liabilities were still outstanding.

Indirect Financing
Liabilities used, either directly or *indirectly*, to purchase, enhance, or maintain, qualifying business property must be deducted from the value of that property for BPR purposes. In this context, HMRC takes a very broad view of what is meant by 'indirectly'.

Example: *Ella owns a house worth £1.5m and has savings and investments totalling £1.2m. In 2026, she sells her investments and invests the proceeds, together with her savings, in shares in an unquoted trading company. (I have ignored CGT on the sale of her investments for the sake of illustration, but in practice this needs to be taken into account.)*

A short time later, Ella mortgages her house for £1m. She gives £600,000 to her grandchildren and uses the remaining £400,000 to replace some of her savings: to assist in funding her mortgage and provide her with a bit of a cushion.

According to HMRC's guidance, Ella should be treated as having used £400,000 of her mortgage to indirectly finance the purchase of her unquoted shares, restricting her BPR to £800,000 (£1.2m – £400,000). Their logic is that she could have achieved substantially the same result by investing just £800,000 of her savings in the shares and taking out a mortgage of £600,000 to provide funds to give to her grandchildren.

As always, HMRC's guidance is not the law, but it can often be persuasive and, until the matter is actually tested in court, it would be wise to operate on the basis their interpretation is correct. In other words, it may be sensible for someone in Ella's position to restrict their investment to the amount they can actually afford without taking on any additional borrowing.

Liabilities Incurred Before April 2013
Liabilities incurred before 6th April 2013 are exempt from the above rules. However, any variation in the terms of such a liability will make it a new liability for these purposes and will mean it must be deducted from the value of the relevant qualifying business property.

This could have disastrous consequences, and it is vital to understand, in addition to refinancing those existing liabilities, those same consequences may arise in the event of other, less significant, variations in the terms of the liability, such as: changes to the term (period) of a loan; changes in the security; a change from fixed interest to variable interest, or vice versa; or additional advances on the same loan account.

Put another way, an old debt used to finance business property has effectively become a valuable asset, worth up to 40% of the outstanding balance. If possible, it is therefore sensible to take professional advice before doing anything that might amount to a variation in the terms of the debt. Simple changes in the interest rate on a loan should not cause any problems, however: provided such changes are within the original terms of the loan.

For more information on the consequences of refinancing, or varying the terms of a liability incurred before 6th April 2013, see the twentieth edition of this guide. For the rest of this edition, unless stated to the contrary, we will assume any liabilities used to acquire, enhance, or maintain qualifying business property were incurred *after* April 2013.

7.13 DEDUCTING LIABILITIES: UNINCORPORATED BUSINESSES

As explained in Section 7.10, business liabilities must be deducted in arriving at the value of an unincorporated business. Loans and other liabilities incurred to finance the business will generally also need to be deducted from the amount of BPR available. To see what this means in practice, let's look at a typical business.

Example: *Duffy has her own business with qualifying business assets worth a total of £2m. She also has the following liabilities:*

Trade creditors	*£200,000*
Business overdraft	*£20,000*
Long-term business loan	*£300,000*
HP (hire purchase) liability on own car	*£10,000*
HP liability on employees' cars	*£25,000*
Income Tax on business profits	*£30,000*
Mortgage on her home	*£500,000*
Loan from her brother Warwick	*£250,000*

The trade creditors are a business liability and must therefore be deducted from the value of the business. In most cases, a business overdraft is an integral part of the business, meaning it would usually need to be taken into account in order to ascertain a value for the business and is therefore a business liability. There will be some cases where this does not apply, but we will assume the overdraft is a business liability in this case.

The long-term business loan is not classed as a business liability. This is because a purchaser looking to buy the business would not usually take over the loan. However, under the rules outlined in Section 7.12, the loan will generally need to be deducted from the value of the business for BPR purposes.

It is questionable whether Duffy's car is an asset of the business. While she may use it for business purposes, a purchaser looking to buy the business is unlikely to want her car. Hence, as the car is not a business asset, the HP liability on it does not need to be deducted from the value of the business.

The employees' cars are assets of the business: they will (most likely) transfer with the employees who are, in turn, an integral part of the business. Hence, the HP liabilities are business liabilities and must be deducted from the value of the business.

Duffy's Income Tax bill is a personal liability. It does not matter that it has arisen on business profits; it will not need to be deducted from the value of her business.

Duffy's mortgage will only need to be deducted from the value of her business if it has been used in any way, directly or indirectly, to finance her business. In this case, we will assume the mortgage has been used to finance Duffy's business.

Duffy borrowed the money from her brother in 2020 and used it to purchase some business assets and reduce her business overdraft. This loan will therefore need to be deducted from the value of Duffy's business for BPR purposes.

Duffy dies in December 2026. The following liabilities must be deducted from the value of her business for BPR purposes:

Trade creditors	*£200,000*
Business overdraft	*£20,000*
Business loan	*£300,000*
HP liability on employees' cars	*£25,000*
Mortgage	*£500,000*
Loan from Warwick	*£250,000*
Total:	*£1,295,000*

Duffy's BPR will be reduced to just £705,000 (£2m – £1,295,000). Her family's IHT bill will be increased by £420,000 because the business loan, mortgage, and loan from Warwick cannot be deducted from the general assets of her estate (£300,000 + £500,000 + £250,000 = £1.05m x 40% = £420,000).

7.14 DEDUCTION OF LIABILITIES FOR COMPANY OWNERS

As explained in Section 7.11, when calculating the value of shares qualifying for BPR, all the company's liabilities need to be taken into account. The owner of the shares will generally also need to deduct any liabilities used to directly or indirectly finance their shareholding, or maintain or enhance its value.

Example Part 1: *Robbie owns all the shares in a trading company, Old Swinger Ltd. We will assume the value of the company before taking account of any liabilities is £2m (in practice, valuing company shares is a much more complex process than this). The company also has the following liabilities:*

Trade creditors	*£200,000*
Business overdraft	*£20,000*
Long-term business loan	*£300,000*
HP liability on Robbie's car	*£10,000*
HP liability on employees' cars	*£25,000*
Corporation Tax due	*£30,000*
Loan from Robbie's brother Mark	*£250,000*
Total:	*£835,000*

All these items are company liabilities and must therefore be taken into account in establishing the value of the company and Robbie's shares. In this case, we will assume it is appropriate to simply deduct them from the value described above, leaving a net value for Robbie's shares of £1.165m (£2m – £835,000).

(I am assuming Robbie's car is a company asset. If it was his own private car then neither the car nor the HP liability on it would be taken into account.)

In 2015, Robbie mortgaged his house for £500,000 in order to buy his shares in Old Swinger Ltd. This liability must therefore be deducted from the value of his shares for BPR purposes, leaving him able to claim just £665,000.

The rules regarding deduction of liabilities generally have less impact on company owners than other business owners, since all company liabilities have to be deducted in any case. However, company owners remain vulnerable to the perils of varying existing loans taken out outside the company before 6th April 2013 (see Section 7.12).

Example Part 2: *Robbie re-mortgages his house for £800,000 and uses the new loan to both pay off his old mortgage and lend £300,000 to Old Swinger Ltd to enable the company to repay its long-term business loan. All other facts, as per Part 1, remain the same at the time of his death in December 2026.*

The value of Robbie's shares remains unaltered (£1.165m). The company has paid off its long-term loan but has simply replaced this liability with another: the debt due to Robbie. However, Robbie's estate now includes the £300,000 debt due from Old Swinger Ltd as an additional asset. This asset is not eligible for BPR (see below).

Any part of his new mortgage used directly or indirectly to finance the purchase of his shares or enhance their value must be deducted for BPR purposes and can't be deducted from the general assets of his estate. The £500,000 used to repay the original mortgage has been used indirectly to finance Robbie's shares and is thus caught by these rules. This sum must therefore be deducted from the value of Robbie's shares, reducing his BPR to £665,000, as before.

The £300,000 Robbie loaned to the company did not enhance the value of his shares, which was the same before and after he made the loan. Hence this part of his new mortgage can be deducted from the general assets of his estate. However, as the loan has become an additional chargeable asset in its own right, there is no overall IHT saving.

Loans to Your Own Company

In Part 2 of the example, we saw the impact of lending money to your own company. From the company's perspective, the borrowed funds will enhance its value but this will be matched by the liability due to you. Hence, there is no overall impact on the company's value.

You will have a new asset: the debt due to you from the company. This will need to be included in your estate. A debt due to you from your own company, often known as a director's loan account, is a separate asset in its own right and is highly unlikely to attract BPR. The treatment of director's loan accounts is examined further in Section 7.22.

In summary, lending money to your own company will not generally provide you with any additional BPR and will not immediately save any IHT. Naturally, there are many good reasons why you might lend money to your company and we will revisit this topic in Section 7.15.

Rights Issues
In Section 7.21, we will look at the potential benefits of rights issues for increasing the amount of BPR available to a company owner. In that section, it is assumed the company owner has substantial private wealth available to fund the rights issue. Funding the rights issue by way of borrowings will not work so well, however.

Example Part 3: *The facts are the same as in Part 2 above except that, instead of lending £300,000 to the company, Robbie subscribes for additional shares by way of a rights issue. The value of the company has now increased to £1.465m (£1.165m + £300,000) because there is no debt due to Robbie to match the liability that has been paid off.*

Robbie will not have acquired any additional asset: he will only have enhanced the value of his existing shareholding. As a result of this, however, the entire £800,000 of Robbie's new mortgage must now be deducted from the value of his shares for BPR purposes because it has all been used, directly or indirectly, to finance the purchase of his shares, or enhance their value. The end result is his BPR is again reduced to £665,000 (£1,465,000 – £800,000), the same as in both Parts 1 and 2 above.

7.15 BORROWING TO INVEST IN YOUR BUSINESS

The examples in Sections 7.12 to 7.14 demonstrate the fact that borrowings used to finance your business, by any means, will not give rise to any immediate IHT savings.

Naturally, however, financing your business will usually have other benefits and it is hoped the value of your business will increase as a result. This may lead to some indirect IHT savings as future growth in your business's value will be sheltered by BPR (or at least partly sheltered), whereas future growth in funds or investments held privately outside the business would be fully exposed to IHT.

In other words, the real benefit lies in making sensible commercial investments through the medium of a qualifying trading business and thus increasing your BPR as you grow your business (provided such investments do not endanger the business's trading status: see Section 7.6).

7.16 MULTIPLE TRANSFERS

Over the past few sections, we have seen how liabilities incurred to finance qualifying business property must generally be deducted from the value of that property. This applies to any chargeable transfer, including:

- Transfers on death
- Chargeable lifetime transfers (see Section 4.2)

- PETs becoming chargeable on the transferor's death within seven years (see Section 4.5)
- Trust anniversary and exit charges (Sections 8.15 and 8.16)

Once a liability has been taken into account on one chargeable transfer, it cannot be taken into account again on another transfer made by the same transferor (except where the earlier 'transfer' was a trust anniversary charge). Remember, however, that a PET only becomes a chargeable transfer if the transferor dies within seven years.

Example: *Woody mortgages his house for £1m and uses the money to purchase shares in a trading company, Movenelo Ltd. In 2026, Woody gives his shares in Movenelo Ltd to his elder daughter, Bev: this is a PET. In 2033, Woody dies, leaving his remaining estate to his younger daughter, Kelly.*

If Woody died within seven years of his gift to Bev, that gift will have become a chargeable transfer and his mortgage will have to be taken into account for BPR purposes. Kelly will then be denied any relief for the mortgage.

If, on the other hand, Woody was still alive on the seventh anniversary of his gift to Bev, that gift will have become fully exempt. Kelly will then be entitled to claim a deduction in respect of Woody's £1m mortgage, saving her £400,000 in IHT.

I have assumed in this example that Woody's mortgage will meet the necessary conditions for a deduction, as explained in Section 2.10.

In summary, where liabilities have been incurred to purchase, enhance, or maintain qualifying business property, full relief for those liabilities can be restored by making a PET of the relevant business property and then surviving seven years.

7.17 THE MINIMUM HOLDING PERIOD

To qualify for BPR, the relevant property must generally have been owned by the transferor for a minimum of two years prior to the transfer.

There is an exception to this requirement where the property replaced other qualifying property (see Section 7.18) and both assets taken together had been owned by the transferor for at least two years out of the five-year period preceding the transfer. This effectively provides a form of rollover relief for business assets for IHT purposes.

The minimum ownership period requirement is also ignored on the second of two successive transfers of the same property within two years where:

i) the earlier transfer qualified for BPR,
ii) the second transfer would otherwise qualify for BPR, and
iii) at least one of the two transfers occurred on death

When a widow/widower inherits business property, their ownership period for the purpose of BPR includes the ownership period of their deceased spouse. However, a transferor spouse's previous ownership period is ***not*** included in the case of a lifetime transfer (although the general rule above will often apply where the transferee dies soon after the transfer).

7.18 REPLACEMENT BUSINESS PROPERTY

The replacement of relevant business property by other relevant business property has been referred to a few times in the preceding sections. Broadly, this means on a disposal of the original business property, the same value was reinvested in new qualifying business property.

The replacement business property does not need to be in the same kind of business as the original business property, nor does it need to be the same type of property. For example, an individual could sell unquoted shares in an engineering company and reinvest the proceeds in a partnership share in a hotel business.

Provided all the other necessary rules are met, BPR may still be available even when more than one replacement has taken place. Hence, in the preceding sections, where I refer to 'the two assets taken together', this could also apply to three or more assets, each of which replaced their predecessor.

Where a taxpayer relies on a replacement to qualify for BPR, the amount of relief available is generally restricted to the amount that would have been available had the replacement not taken place. For the purposes of this rule, however, the formation, alteration or dissolution of a partnership; or the acquisition of a business by a company controlled by the former owner of that business; are disregarded.

7.19 EXTRA RULES FOR LIFETIME TRANSFERS

Where BPR applied on a lifetime transfer and the transferor dies within seven years, some extra conditions must be satisfied for BPR to also apply at the time of the transferor's death. The conditions are: i) The transferee must continue to own the original transferred assets throughout the period from the original transfer to the relevant date (see below); and ii) the original transferred assets must continue to be relevant business property for BPR purposes on the relevant date.

Where the transferee retains only part of the original asset at the relevant date, BPR continues to apply to that part, as long as condition (ii) is satisfied.

See also Section 7.8 regarding the application of the HPRA where the original transfer took place after 29th October 2024. Note: it is the transferor's allowance that is relevant here, not the transferee's.

The Relevant Date and the Relevant Period

For the purpose of the rules described in this section, the relevant date is the date of the transferor's death or, if earlier, the transferee's death. The relevant period is the period from the original transfer to the relevant date. Of course, the relevant date and relevant period are only relevant if the transferor dies within seven years of the original transfer.

The conditions set out above mean it's generally necessary for the assets to be qualifying business property in the transferee's hands at the time of the earlier of the transferor or transferee's death. This doesn't apply if the original assets were shares that were either already quoted at the time of the original transfer, or remained unquoted throughout the relevant period.

Where a transferee has a minority holding of unquoted shares, these will cease to be relevant business property if the company obtains a quotation. This could result in an IHT bill (or an increased bill in some cases) if the transferor dies within seven years of the original transfer.

The technical definition of 'unquoted' given in Section 7.7 applies for the purpose of these rules, so it includes shares traded on AIM or another stock market, but not 'listed' on a recognised stock exchange.

Replacement Assets
The transferee may retain their BPR entitlement if they dispose of the original assets and acquire replacement assets (as defined in Section 7.18). Qualifying agricultural property (Section 7.27) also qualifies as a replacement asset for these purposes. The following further conditions must be met:

a) The replacement assets must be acquired within three years of the transferee's disposal of the original assets
b) Both the transferee's sale of the original assets and their acquisition of replacement assets must take place on arm's length terms
c) The whole consideration received on the sale of the original transferred assets must be expended acquiring the replacement assets
d) The transferee must own the replacement assets at the relevant date unless the transferor dies first and within the allowed period (see below)
e) Apart from the allowed period, either the original transferred assets or the replacement assets must be owned by the transferee throughout the relevant period
f) The replacement assets must be relevant business property in the transferee's hands at the relevant date (except as noted below)

The Allowed Period
The three-year period under condition (a) begins when the transferee enters a binding contract to sell the original assets. Fortunately, it is only necessary for them to enter a binding contract to acquire the replacement assets within the requisite period: completion can take place later if necessary. (There's more on binding contracts coming up in Section 7.20.)

This three-year period, known as the 'allowed period', can extend after the transferor's death, so the replacement may sometimes take place after the transferor dies. For these purposes, condition (f) is amended so that the replacement assets need to be relevant business property when the transferee acquires them.

The legislation seems to suggest only one replacement is allowed under these circumstances, unlike other replacements (Section 7.18).

What all this means is, if you receive qualifying business property in a gift from someone else, you may find yourself with an IHT bill (or an increased IHT bill) if you sell that property within seven years. However, if you can wait at least four years before selling the gifted property, you will have the opportunity to restore your BPR by acquiring replacement business property if your benefactor should pass away unexpectedly.

Gifts with Reservation

A lifetime transfer of qualifying business property could still be a gift with reservation (Section 4.8). This would mean the property effectively remained in the transferor's estate and IHT would be payable if the property did not qualify for BPR at the time of their death (or more IHT in some cases).

In particular, excessive salary payments to the transferor could make the transfer a gift with reservation: i.e. excessive salary paid to the transferor following the transfer of a business, partnership share, or shares in a company. The same would apply to other benefits provided in excess of a normal commercial level, including excessive pension contributions.

Lifetime Transfers Becoming Chargeable on Death

If the transferee loses the BPR on a transferred asset, as explained above, then IHT will be payable if the transferor dies within seven years. Additional IHT may also be payable on a transferor's death when some or all of the value of the transferred asset only qualifies for BPR at 50%. In both cases, other available reliefs, such as the annual exemption, may be taken into account.

Where the original transfer was a chargeable lifetime transfer (e.g. to a trust), only that transferee will be affected by any loss of BPR. Where the original transfer was a PET, the whole of the transferor's estate must be recalculated on the basis set out in Section 4.5.

7.20 HOW TO PRESERVE BUSINESS PROPERTY RELIEF

For anyone with a qualifying business, BPR is incredibly valuable. Admittedly, its value in some cases has reduced since 6th April 2026, but it is still tremendously valuable. The trouble is you need to qualify for the relief at the moment a transfer takes place. That moment may be death in many cases and this carries some inherent problems.

Firstly, it is generally pretty unpredictable when this will be. Secondly, it may be some time after you cease to be interested in running a business. Most people will want to retire at some point and, unfortunately, this will often result in the loss of their BPR.

Selling Up

Generally speaking, from a tax perspective, the last thing anyone should do is sell a business qualifying for BPR. For a business worth no more than £2.5m (or £5m for most widows/widowers), on the day before the sale, the business would have been completely covered by BPR and available to pass on to their family free of IHT. The day after the sale, the proceeds would be completely exposed to IHT, resulting in the loss of up to 40%.

The IHT exposure on sale proceeds is on top of any CGT that arose on the sale. As we shall see in Chapter 12, CGT could generally be avoided if the family sold the business shortly after the original owner's death.

The position for more valuable businesses, worth in excess of the HPRA, will vary. A lot depends on how much CGT would arise on a sale and what the business owner intends to do with the sale proceeds. But let's look at an example where no IHT planning is carried out after the sale.

Example: *Eddie owns an unquoted trading company, Cochran Ltd. Eddie has spent his life building the company up from scratch and has never had time for a spouse or children, although he does have nieces and nephews he cares about and eventually intends to leave his estate to them.*

The deductible base cost of the company for CGT purposes is negligible and Eddie's NRB will be used up on other assets. He has had an offer from a French company, Aznavour S.A., to buy Cochran Ltd for £10m, and is unsure whether to sell up or keep going. His accountant prepares this basic comparison:

	Keep Going	***Sell Up***
Shares/sale proceeds	*£10m*	*£10m*
*CGT at 18% on first £1m**	-	*£0.18m*
CGT at 24% on remainder	-	*£2.16m*
Net value in estate	***£10m***	***£7.66m***
BPR at 100% on first £2.5m	*£2.5m*	-
BPR at 50% on remainder	*£3.75m*	-
Chargeable estate	***£3.75m***	***£7.66m***
IHT at 40%	***£1.5m***	***£3.064m***

** Assuming business asset disposal relief is available (see Section 12.5)*

If Eddie keeps going, his family will inherit a company worth £10m and an IHT bill of £1.5m, giving them a net inheritance of £8.5m. Furthermore, they will be able to pay the IHT bill over ten years without incurring interest charges (Section 2.7). If Eddie sells up, his family will inherit a net sum of £4.596m (£7.66m – £3.064m).

In this case, in the absence of any IHT planning after the sale, the family would be over ***£3.9m worse off*** if the business owner sells up (£8.5m – £4.596m = £3.904m). Even if Eddie gave his net sale proceeds to his family and then survived seven years, his family would still be £840,000 worse off (£8.5m – £7.66m).

For even more valuable businesses, the effect of both the HPRA and business asset disposal relief begins to diminish. If we ignore them altogether, we see that retaining the business will leave the owner's beneficiaries with at least 80% of the business's value; selling the business will usually leave them with just 45.6% (100% less 24% CGT = 76% less 40% IHT). This assumes little or no base cost for the business. That's not uncommon for business founders, but we'll look at other situations in Chapter 12.

For the moment then, despite the restriction on 100% relief from 6th April 2026, our general conclusion remains that it is generally better, from a tax point of view, to keep a business qualifying for BPR and not to sell up.

In practice, unfortunately, and much to HMRC's delight, it will sometimes be necessary to sell the business before the owner's death. A large proportion of a business's value can sometimes be lost when its proprietor dies. After all, it is better to let HMRC take 40% of a great deal than to deny them a share of very little.

Ideally, business succession planning is something that should be looked at much earlier on, when the original proprietor is still hale and hearty and looking forward to a well-deserved retirement. If a deathbed sale situation does arise, however, one way to avoid the pitfalls described above would be to sell the business in exchange for unquoted shares in a trading company. BPR entitlement would then be preserved and CGT can also generally be avoided.

Sale Contracts: A Major Pitfall

As soon as you have a binding contract for sale, you are, for IHT purposes, no longer regarded as owning the asset being sold. Instead, you are regarded as owning a right to the sale proceeds. That right is generally not a qualifying asset for BPR purposes. Hence, at one stroke of a pen, you can lose your BPR and substantially increase your family's IHT bill in the event of your death.

Example Continued: *Eddie decides to accept Aznavour S.A.'s offer. He flies to Paris, takes the Metro to Aznavour S.A.'s offices and signs a binding contract to sell his company. Leaving the office, Eddie looks the wrong way crossing the street and steps in front of a bus. Total tax bill: £5.404m!*

(That's CGT of £2.34m and IHT of £3.064m: see above.)

This example is based on a true story and readily demonstrates the ease with which BPR can be lost and the dire consequences that may result. An entrepreneur like Eddie might have been intending to reinvest his sale proceeds in a new business venture and hence might have regained the protection of BPR within a few weeks by virtue of the replacement property rules (Section 7.18). Perhaps Eddie should have considered taking out insurance to cover the increased IHT risk during this short interval!

When an individual who has sold a qualifying business within the last three years gets a little more warning of their demise, the replacement property rules might provide an answer. The protection of BPR can generally be maintained if the taxpayer reinvests all the sale proceeds from qualifying business property into new qualifying business property within three years.

A contract for sale will not result in a loss of BPR if it is: a) for the sale of an unincorporated business to a company that is to carry on that business where the purchase consideration is wholly or mainly shares or securities in that company; or b) for the sale of shares or securities in a company for the purposes of reconstruction or amalgamation. Once the sale is completed, however, BPR will only be available on the new shares or securities held by the original business owner if these new assets qualify in their own right.

Liquidation and Winding Up

BPR is lost on a company's shares if the company is in liquidation or being wound up. There is an exception to this, however, if the winding up is being carried out as part of a scheme of corporate reconstruction or amalgamation (e.g. a company reorganisation or merger of two companies).

Retirement

BPR is lost as soon as a partner retires from a qualifying partnership business. Any capital the retired partner leaves in the business is simply regarded as a loan and is ineligible for BPR. One way to avoid this problem is for the partner to continue in partnership, but with a very small profit share. (Remaining in partnership has commercial implications, which should also be considered.)

When a sole trader retires there is no business so there can be no BPR. The answer here may be to take on a partner and then, at a later date, to semi-retire: i.e. reduce to a small profit share in the manner described above.

An individual owning qualifying shares in a trading company can happily retire without any loss of BPR as their position depends on their shareholding and not on whether they actually participate in the company's business. Incorporating the business prior to retirement may therefore sometimes be a good way to preserve BPR.

Buy-Out Clauses on Death: A BIG NO-NO!

It is common practice for business partners to enter into an agreement whereby their executors will sell their partnership share to the surviving partners in the event of their death.

Similar agreements are also often used by shareholder/directors of unquoted companies whereby their executors sell their shares back to the company, or to their fellow directors, in the event of their death.

While these agreements make a good deal of commercial sense, from a BPR perspective they represent a disaster waiting to happen. This is because, at the moment of death, a binding sale contract will come into force and the estate will not hold relevant business property but, as we saw above, will instead hold a non-qualifying right to sale proceeds. To avoid this problem, it is essential to avoid any sort of agreement that may form a binding contract on the death of a partner or director.

Cross Options

A better alternative is to use non-coterminous cross options. In other words, the business partners should enter into an agreement whereby, in the event of a partner's death, their executors will have an option to sell the deceased's partnership share and the surviving partners will have an option to buy it.

Similarly, private company directors would enter into an agreement whereby, in the event of a director's death, their executors will have an option to sell the deceased's shares in the company and either the company itself or the surviving directors will have an option to buy them.

To be on the safe side, it is wise to ensure the options are non-coterminous. Broadly, this means the option to purchase and the option to sell may only be exercised at different times. (E.g. the deceased's executors must exercise the option to sell within thirty days of the deceased's death and the surviving business partners, or directors, must exercise the option to purchase more than thirty, but less than sixty days after the deceased's death.)

HMRC has specifically confirmed this approach is acceptable in the case of a business partnership and there is no reason to suppose the same principles would not be equally valid in the case of unquoted company shares.

Using cross options will therefore preserve any BPR entitlement while also satisfying the original commercial objective of allowing the deceased's share of a business to be bought out.

Other Approaches for Partnerships

HMRC has confirmed the following methods for dealing with a deceased partner's share of a business will preserve any BPR entitlement available:

- Partnership ceases on death, partnership assets to be realised and deceased partner's estate receives appropriate share of proceeds
- Partnership continues and deceased's estate represents the deceased
- Partnership share falls into deceased's estate with surviving partners having an option to purchase at either a valuation or an agreed formula-based price
- The deceased's partnership share accrues to the surviving partners but the deceased's estate is entitled to payment at either a valuation or an agreed formula-based price
- Cross options (as explained above), which must be exercised within a set period following the partner's death

7.21 MAXIMISING BUSINESS PROPERTY RELIEF

Where an individual owns and controls a qualifying trading company, the entire value of that company could benefit from BPR, albeit that amounts in excess of the HPRA now only qualify for 50% relief. Nonetheless, as that individual nears the end of their life, it may make sense to maximise the value of the company.

Assets held personally by the individual and used in the company's business only qualify for 50% BPR, regardless of value. For smaller companies, where the value of the company without those assets is less than the owner's available HPRA, it might again make sense to transfer the assets into the company.

Example: *Taylor is a wealthy widow whose husband died many years ago. Among her many assets is her unquoted trading company, Swiftie Ltd, which is currently worth £2m. This value takes account of the fact the company owes £250,000 for the purchase of new equipment and has a bank loan of £750,000. Taylor also owns a* *property worth £1.6m, which is used by the company. If Taylor were to die with things as they stand, her personal representatives would be able to claim BPR as follows:*

Swiftie Ltd: £2m @ 100%	*£2,000,000*
Property: £1.6m @ 50%	*£800,000*
TOTAL	*£2,800,000*

Realising she isn't immortal after all, Taylor decides to undertake some IHT planning. First, she transfers the property into the company. She is able to avoid CGT on this transfer by using a holdover relief election. SDLT is, however, payable on the market value of the property. In this case, the SDLT amounts to £69,500.

Taylor then uses £1,069,500 out of her substantial private wealth to subscribe for further new shares in Swiftie Ltd. This enables the company to pay off the bank loan, the debt for the new equipment and the SDLT on the property transfer. Swiftie Ltd will now be worth £4.6m and, after just two years, the whole of this value will be covered by 100% BPR (as a widow, Taylor has a HPRA of £5m).

The overall value of Taylor's estate will be virtually unchanged except for the £69,500 paid in SDLT. However, this simple piece of planning will save her family £747,800 in IHT!

The transfer of the property will provide an immediate IHT saving, but it will take two years for Taylor's new shares in Swiftie Ltd to qualify for BPR. This delay can, however, be easily avoided. New shares issued by way of a rights issue are treated as part of the original shareholding for the purposes of BPR.

Hence, a new investment into an existing qualifying trading company, which is structured as a rights issue, will be eligible for BPR immediately.

Although the transfer of the property in the above example can be carried out free of CGT, there may be other important tax consequences if the company subsequently sells the property. The potential advantages or disadvantages of holding business premises through a company are covered in depth in the Taxcafe guide *Putting it Through the Company.*

The IHT planning undertaken by Taylor worked because her company was in debt and was using the property in its business. If, on the other hand, she had injected so much capital into the company that it had a surplus in excess of its usual trading requirements, there would have been a restriction on her BPR under the excepted assets rules (see Section 7.11). If the surplus were large enough, the company might even fail the wholly or mainly test (Section 7.6) and cease to qualify for BPR altogether (well, haters gonna hate, eh?)

For larger companies, already worth more than the owner's available HPRA, a transfer of assets used in the company's business, but held personally by the company owner, will not yield any IHT saving. Furthermore, in the case of property, the transfer will often lead to a significant, and unnecessary, SDLT cost.

7.22 DIRECTOR'S LOAN ACCOUNTS

Most small company owners have a director's loan account with their company. This account represents money due to them from their company (a credit balance) or money they owe to their company (a debit balance).

Director's loan accounts can arise in several ways, including cash injected into the company by the director, cash withdrawn, or an accumulation of non-cash transactions such as unpaid salary, dividends, or rent. The IHT impact of a director's loan account depends on whether we are looking at a credit balance or a debit balance.

Credit Balances

A debt due to you from your own company is a completely separate asset to your company shares. Furthermore, it is highly unlikely this asset will qualify for BPR. As explained in Section 7.7, it is only debts in the form of securities that actually contribute to your control of the company that qualify for BPR.

A credit balance on a director's loan account can, however, readily be converted into a qualifying asset for BPR purposes simply by issuing new shares to yourself in place of the balance on your loan account. If this is done by way of a rights issue then, as explained in Section 7.21, the new shares are treated as part of the original shareholding for the purposes of BPR and may therefore qualify for relief immediately.

There is also the problem that, as a separate asset, your director's loan account may pass to a different beneficiary on your death. This may cause a few practical difficulties in some cases, and may not be what you would ideally like to happen, so it will be sensible to make a specific provision to deal with your director's loan account in your Will.

Alternatively, a director's loan account may sometimes be a useful way to provide your spouse, or another beneficiary, with a source of tax-free income. For example, you could leave company shares qualifying for BPR to one of your children, but leave your director's loan account to your spouse.

Future company profits could then be used to repay the director's loan account, giving your spouse an effective source of tax-free income. This is a tax efficient structure but is probably only suitable where the surviving family members are happy to co-operate.

A director's loan account has other advantages during your lifetime, when it is probably preferable to investing in additional shares. As with many things, there are different factors to weigh up and it is perhaps only as you grow older that you might wish to convert your director's loan account into shares. For some of the lifetime benefits of a director's loan account, see the Taxcafe guides *Putting it Through the Company* or *Using a Property Company to Save Tax.*

Debit Balances

A debt due from you to your own company will enhance your company's value provided the debt is recoverable (i.e. you have sufficient private assets to repay the debt). Relatively small balances that have arisen through normal everyday transactions should not affect the company's status for BPR purposes. However, large balances may effectively become investment assets in the company's hands, and could either be excepted assets (see Section 7.10), or may even threaten the company's qualifying status under the wholly or mainly test (Section 7.6).

As with any other liability, the director's loan account will need to be repaid out of the assets of your estate in order to be deductible on your death.

Debit balances on director's loan accounts may have CT consequences for the company, as well as personal tax consequences for the director. See the Taxcafe guide *Salary versus Dividends* for further details.

7.23 SHELTERING INVESTMENTS WITH BUSINESS PROPERTY RELIEF

BPR on company shares may be reduced, or possibly lost altogether, if a non-trading asset, such as an investment property or quoted share portfolio, were transferred into the company. Such a transfer may also give rise to CGT liabilities, plus SDLT in the case of a property.

However, as we have already seen, there would nevertheless remain the possibility of arguing a hybrid business, qualifying under the wholly or mainly principle (Section 7.6) existed, so that the investment property or quoted share portfolio might be sheltered from IHT within the trading company (or at least partially sheltered since 6th April 2026). But how far can we take this?

If investments are simply being dumped into a trading company, HMRC is unlikely to accept the hybrid business argument and, as we saw in Section 7.6, may argue the company is being used as a repository for non-business assets.

The important distinction to remember is that investments can only be sheltered within a trading company qualifying for BPR if they form part of the company's business. A random cobbled together collection of non-trading investments will not be good enough.

The best way to make use of the trading company shelter would therefore be to build an investment arm to the company's business over several years. It would be vital to ensure this part of the business remained comfortably less than 50% of the company's overall business, bearing in mind the various possible tests set out in Section 7.6.

To maintain full BPR entitlement on the company's shares, its investment business arm would need to be an integral part of the company's overall business and it is important to reflect this in the company's records, including management accounts, directors' board minutes, cashflow projections, etc.

Example: *Madge is an even wealthier woman than Taylor (Section 7.21) and, as well as substantial private assets, owns a trading company, Ciccone Ltd, currently worth £10m. Madge now begins to make some quoted investments within the company. She runs the entire enterprise as a single business, ensuring management* *accounts, directors' board minutes and other company documentation all reflect the fact the investment arm is an integral part of Ciccone Ltd's business.*

A few years later, the total value of the company is £20m, including £7.5m worth of investments and trading assets worth £12.5m. By building the investment portfolio within Ciccone Ltd instead of privately, Madge has therefore reduced her IHT exposure by £1.5m (£7.5m at an effective saving of 20%).

A similar approach could also be taken to shelter investments from IHT within a trading partnership. It would be difficult for a sole trader to achieve the same result, however, as HMRC would view them as having two businesses: one qualifying for BPR and one not. Nevertheless, this problem might perhaps be overcome if the investments were an integral part of the same business.

One good way to argue that investments are an integral part of any business is to make investments in companies operating in the same industry. These investments will provide the investor with valuable information on their competitors, including access to their competitors' shareholders' meetings, and there is therefore a strong argument this can be regarded as an integral part of the business.

Under the wholly or mainly test for BPR purposes, a company could still qualify with just under 50% of its activities being non-trading activities. However, for the purposes of a number of CGT reliefs, including business asset disposal relief and holdover relief on a gift of shares, the company may lose its trading status if just 20% of its activities are non-trading activities. This could have significant adverse consequences. Loss of business asset disposal relief could result in extra CGT of up to £60,000 per shareholder. We will look at holdover relief in Chapter 12.

Historically, the criteria to be used for the 20% test had been expected to follow broadly the same principles as we saw in Section 7.6 for the wholly or mainly test. However, recent case law has given us better guidance on this issue and we will look at this in Section 12.4.

If making investments via a trading company, it is important to ensure the company's Memorandum and Articles of Association permit this activity. Any activity not so permitted is strictly illegal and thus cannot be regarded as part of the company's business.

7.24 CHANGING THE BUSINESS TO SAVE INHERITANCE TAX

It is worth bearing in mind that a business only needs to qualify for BPR throughout the two-year period before the transfer. Hence, the business owner could build up a valuable non-qualifying business over many years and then change it into a qualifying business later. If the owner survives at least two years after the change, they can make substantial IHT savings.

Example: *Steve has built up an unquoted property investment company, Tyler Properties Ltd, over many years. He is now an 80-year-old widower and, in early 2026, he retires: his daughter Liv takes over the running of the company. Steve continues to own the company and Liv is paid a salary.*

Liv immediately begins to change the company's business to one of property development. This process is completed by March 2027. Sadly, in May 2029, Steve dies and leaves Tyler Properties Ltd to Liv. As the company had carried on a qualifying trading activity for the previous two years, the shares left to Liv are eligible for BPR: the first £5m of their value will effectively be exempt, any excess will suffer IHT at an effective rate of just 20%.

The change in the company's business activity may give rise to some additional CT costs. However, where the change takes place gradually, over a number of years, these should not be too severe.

Remember also that the change in activity does not need to be absolute, as it is only necessary for the company to pass the wholly or mainly test (Section 7.6) during the two years prior to the transfer.

Steve would also have been able to claim BPR on a lifetime transfer of his shares any time after the company had been carrying on a qualifying business for two years. However, Liv would then need to continue the qualifying business for up to another seven years in order to retain BPR (see Section 7.19). This could also lead to a CGT liability for Steve on the share transfer if the company still held investment assets at that time, and it would mean Liv missed out on the CGT uplift on death (Section 12.2) in respect of the shares.

7.25 SMALLER SHAREHOLDINGS

Any shareholding in an unquoted trading company qualifies for 100% BPR up to the amount of the HPRA (usually £2.5m, but often £5m for widows/widowers). The problem is when one considers the generally volatile nature of unquoted shares, combined with the minimum two-year holding period, putting your wealth into these types of assets just to save IHT is a pretty risky business. Nevertheless, under the right circumstances, it is certainly something to consider. Let's look at an example.

Example: *Noel wins a substantial sum on the National Lottery. "Great," his brother Liam says, "how 'bout helpin' me out with me business then?" Noel agrees to give Liam £250,000 to help get his new business started. However, if Noel simply gives Liam the money, this will be a PET and if Noel dies within seven years, it will have to be brought back into his estate.*

So, what Noel does instead is to subscribe for shares in Liam's company, Wonderwall Ltd. After just two years, the shares will qualify for BPR and Noel can then give them to Liam free from IHT (subject to the points in Section 7.19, and assuming they aren't worth more than £2.5m by then).

7.26 AIM SHARES

Until recently, shares traded on the Alternative Investment Market (AIM) were eligible for 100% BPR. Sadly, however, the rate of relief on all qualifying AIM shares (regardless of value) has now been reduced to 50%.

Nonetheless, AIM shares still provide an effective IHT saving of 20%, so they could still have a place in IHT planning for some people. Furthermore, for some estates, it may remain possible to avoid IHT altogether by investing in AIM shares.

Example: *Ariana is a widow with full entitlement to her late husband's TNRB and RNRB, giving her potential exemptions totalling £1m. She owns a house worth £500,000, which she intends to leave to her children, Ron and Dee, and savings totalling £800,000. Her total estate is thus £1.3m, giving her an IHT exposure of £120,000 (£1.3m – £1m = £300,000 x 40% = £120,000).*

Ariana invests £600,000 out of her savings in AIM shares. When she dies more than two years later, the AIM shares are eligible for BPR at 50%, meaning her chargeable estate is reduced to £1m and no IHT is due.

While Ariana has avoided IHT completely, her saving is only 20% of the amount invested in the AIM shares. Or, looked at another way, the change that came into effect in April 2026 means she has had to invest twice as much. Whether a 20% saving is enough to compensate for the commercial risks involved in such an investment may perhaps be questionable.

There's no denying the fact that AIM shares generally carry more risk than larger companies with a full stock market quotation. Furthermore, due to the relatively low level of trading, it can sometimes be difficult to sell AIM shares at a fair price.

However, the risk is substantially reduced if you invest in a portfolio of shares, and there are financial products available to enable you to do this, with professional fund managers choosing your AIM investments for you. The fund managers will monitor the performance of your investments and make changes to the portfolio to protect your investment and your BPR. Such changes can usually be made without any loss of BPR due to the replacement property rules (Section 7.18).

Better still, you can eliminate the risk altogether by investing in a protected IHT service with a built-in life insurance policy. If your investment has fallen in value when you die, the life policy will pay out the shortfall. The life policy itself can be made tax-efficient by being written into trust (see Section 11.8). All you need do is survive the requisite two years.

Naturally, a scheme like this does not come cheap and the fund managers' charges can be quite expensive. Furthermore, the life insurance premiums will typically absorb any income from the investment: and you will still have to pay Income Tax on dividends paid by the AIM companies in your portfolio.

So, whether this is all worthwhile for an ultimate saving of just 20% is perhaps debatable. Nonetheless, there are some points in favour of AIM shares. Firstly, while the saving will only be 20%, an investor just needs to survive two years to achieve this saving: that's a lot quicker than the seven years needed for a PET to escape IHT, or for many other planning methods to achieve their full potential.

Furthermore, anyone investing the proceeds from the sale of other qualifying business property within the last three years could obtain BPR immediately, thus exempting half their investment from IHT even if they die shortly afterwards.

And it's worth remembering an investment in AIM shares is not locked away permanently. If your circumstances change and you need to realise some of those funds, which are no longer surplus to requirements after all, you can simply sell some of your AIM portfolio. This makes an AIM portfolio attractive to anyone who wishes to save IHT without actually giving any of their money away. The portfolio provides a means to protect some of your wealth from the full impact of IHT when you are unsure whether you can genuinely afford to live without it.

On the other hand, in view of the costs inherent in a protected AIM portfolio investment and the fact it will only produce a 20% saving at best, a wealthy person with funds that are definitely surplus to requirements and a life expectancy of over seven years might do better to simply give that surplus away and take out term life insurance to cover the risk of a premature death.

While AIM shares are eligible for BPR in principle, it remains important that the companies in which you invest are carrying on qualifying businesses (Sections 7.3 to 7.6). If your AIM shares get a full listing, your BPR will be lost (unless you control the company). Having said that, if this does happen, you will probably have made a nice profit, so it wouldn't be all bad would it? Alternatively, you could sell the AIM shares before they are listed and reinvest the proceeds in replacement business property any time within the next three years, thus retaining your BPR.

Capital gains and dividends received on AIM shares are subject to CGT and Income Tax respectively in the normal way. There are no special reliefs applying to AIM shares for these taxes. (You could hold AIM shares via an ISA to avoid these problems, although this may not be the best use of your ISA allowance.)

7.27 AGRICULTURAL PROPERTY RELIEF (APR)

If there is one group of people who truly exemplify the 'asset rich/cash poor' dilemma that is the cause of so much misery when it comes to IHT, it must be farmers: which is why APR is so important, and why Rachel Reeves' attack on it is so disgraceful.

APR applies in a broadly similar way to BPR. The following types of property may be covered:

i) Agricultural land or pasture
ii) Buildings used for the intensive rearing of livestock or fish
iii) Stud farms
iv) Farmhouses, cottages, and other farm buildings
v) Woodlands

Property under (iv) or (v) must generally be occupied on a basis ancillary to property also occupied under (i), (ii), or (iii); although buildings used to grow indoor crops, such as mushrooms, may qualify in their own right without the need for any additional agricultural land.

For transfers of value (on death or otherwise) after 5th April 2024, the relief only applies to agricultural land in the UK. Previously, it also applied to agricultural land anywhere in the European Economic Area (EEA), the Channel Islands, or the Isle of Man. Land outside the UK actively farmed by the transferor for at least two years may still qualify for BPR: as this relief has no geographical limitations. However, BPR will not generally cover most of the value of the farmhouse.

To qualify for APR, the land or buildings must either have been:

a) Occupied (i.e. used) by the transferor for agricultural purposes for a period of at least two years prior to the date of transfer, or
b) Owned by the transferor and used for agricultural purposes (by anyone) for at least seven years prior to the date of transfer

Occupation by a partnership is treated as occupation by the partners. Occupation by a company controlled by the transferor is treated as occupation by the transferor: it is important to note only shares or securities that give the transferor control of the company qualify for APR.

APR is given at rates of 50% or 100%, depending on the exact circumstances of the transfer and subject to the usual raft of provisions designed to prevent abuse. Where the relief is available at 100%, this is now subject to the HPRA (Section 7.8), with the excess relieved at just 50%. Generally speaking the HPRA is £5m for most widows/widowers, and £2.5m for other individuals.

For example, for a farm worth £6m *not* owned by a widow/widower, the total relief would be £4.25m (£2.5m + £3.5m x 50%), leaving £1.75m of the farm's value exposed to IHT (subject to other reliefs such as the NRB and the spouse exemption).

The HPRA applies to total claims for 100% relief under both APR and BPR combined. Where both APR and BPR are claimed, the allowance must be divided in proportion to the amounts eligible for 100% relief. For example, where an individual with a HPRA of £2.5m has property eligible for APR worth £1m and property eligible for BPR worth £3m, the relief available will be:

APR: £625,000 (£2.5m x 1/4) at 100%; £375,000 at 50%: total £812,500
BPR: £1.875m (£2.5m x 3/4) at 100%; £1.125m at 50%: total £2,437,500

The total relief is £3.25m in this case. You may be wondering why it matters how this is allocated between APR and BPR: until you look at the next section when we focus on farmhouses (which mainly only qualify for APR in most cases).

It is essential that agricultural activities are being carried out on the land at the time of the transfer. Furthermore, APR is restricted to the agricultural value of the land or property: i.e. its value if subject to a condition it must remain in agricultural use. Any excess value may be eligible for BPR in some cases. Where the transferor is actively farming the land themselves, this will usually qualify as a trading activity for BPR purposes.

Solar farms, wind farms, and similar activities do not count as agricultural use and hence will not qualify for APR. Land used in these activities may qualify for BPR, depending on the circumstances, but not if the owner is simply renting the land to someone else.

A separate IHT deferral relief is available for woodlands that do not qualify for APR. Again, this is restricted to the UK only from 6th April 2024, but was previously available to woodlands in the EEA.

In better news, from 6th April 2025, APR has been extended to land in the UK managed under an environmental agreement with a qualifying Government body, or other approved responsible body.

The rules set out in Sections 7.12 to 7.16 apply equally to liabilities incurred to finance agricultural property, woodlands, or (where appropriate) shares in companies carrying on these activities.

7.28 PROTECTING THE FAMILY FARM

In this section, we are going to look at protecting the family farm from the scourge of IHT (at least as best we can). We will be focussing here on working farms (even if the owner has retired). For farms and farmland held as an investment, including surplus land rented to other farms, see Sections 7.29 and 7.34.

In many cases, a significant proportion of the farm's value lies in the farmhouse and, due to a complex interplay between various different reliefs, this is where things can get rather complicated. As a short, introductory overview, however, (and subject to the more detailed points below) we can say that:

- A farmhouse occupied by a retired farmer is effectively the same as any other family home (see Chapter 13)
- A farmhouse occupied by a working farmer enjoys some protection under APR: although this is not necessarily complete, in many cases the shortfall can be covered by other reliefs
- A married couple, widow, or widower with a total estate not exceeding £2m, including a farmhouse and other assets (excluding the rest of the farm) worth no more than £1m in total, will generally enjoy complete exemption from IHT if they leave the farmhouse to their children (or other direct descendants)
- A married couple, widow, or widower with a farm worth no more than £5m (excluding the farmhouse) and a farmhouse and other assets worth no more than £650,000 in total, will generally enjoy complete exemption from IHT
- An unmarried or divorced individual with a total estate not exceeding £2m, including a farmhouse and other assets (excluding the rest of the farm) worth no more than £500,000 in total, will generally enjoy complete exemption from IHT if they leave the farmhouse to their children (or other direct descendants)

- A working farmer who is unmarried or divorced, with a farm worth no more than £2.5m (including the agricultural use value of the farmhouse) will enjoy complete exemption from IHT if the market value of the farmhouse less its agricultural use value, plus any other assets the farmer owns totals no more than £325,000 (e.g. total value of the farm is £2.5m, market value of the farmhouse is £200,000 more than its agricultural use value, other assets do not exceed £125,000)

This is not an exhaustive list of all the cases where it may be possible to achieve complete exemption but, for the others, we need to take a more detailed look at that complex interplay.

For a genuine, working farmer, the farmhouse is also the family home. That means it could be eligible for the RNRB (Section 3.4). It is also generally exempt from CGT, unless any part of the house is used exclusively for business purposes (Section 12.7). But, ensuring the farmhouse is covered by APR will often remain important, especially since the RNRB will not be available to:

- Widows/widowers with an estate worth £2.7m or more
- Other individuals with an estate worth £2.35m or more
- Any farmer who will not, or cannot, leave the farmhouse to direct descendants

Furthermore, many farmhouses will be worth well in excess of the available RNRB meaning, without APR, some of the house's value could be exposed to IHT, even when it is eligible for the RNRB.

On the other hand, APR can only cover the agricultural use value of the farmhouse, which will often be considerably less than its market value. Furthermore, if the farm is worth more than £2.5m (or £5m for most widows/widowers), the rate of APR on the excess drops to 50%. Hence, the RNRB may be needed to plug the gap.

(Remember, the RNRB is only withdrawn where an individual's estate exceeds £2m at the date of death, whereas lifetime transfers can use up the HPRA: hence it is possible for the rate of APR available on a farmhouse to drop to 50%, but the RNRB to still be available.)

In an ideal world, therefore, it would be best if the farmhouse were eligible for both the RNRB *and* APR. The world is seldom ideal, however.

The RNRB could exempt up to £175,000 of the value of the farmhouse (350,000 for widows/widowers) but usually only if it is left to direct descendants on death (see below regarding gifts with reservation, however).

APR is only available if the farmhouse is occupied by the person with day-to-day responsibility for running the farm throughout the two years prior to the relevant transfer; or seven years where occupied by someone other than the owner for all or part of that time. In the latter case, the transferor or their spouse must generally also have owned the property for at least seven years.

This leaves many elderly farmers wishing, or needing, to retire, with a dilemma. The only way to ensure the farmhouse remains eligible for both the RNRB and APR may be to retain ownership, but move out so their successors can move in and run the farm from the house.

This may not always be practical, however, as the retired farmer will need somewhere else to live. Even if they are able to buy another property, they will face extortionate SDLT charges (including a 5% surcharge), and will only be able to claim the RNRB on one of their properties.

If, alternatively, the retired farmer retains the farmhouse and remains in occupation for the rest of their life, the house will be eligible for the RNRB, but not APR.

Widows, Widowers, and Married Couples

Generally speaking, unless they divorce, one of a married couple will eventually become a widow or widower. So, unless you're expecting to divorce (in which case, see below), the tax planning strategies for married couples are broadly the same as for widows/widowers.

Fortunately, for many widows/widowers and hence, by implication, many married farmers, the complex interplay between the different potential reliefs is not usually a problem for active working farms if:

- Any other assets excluding the farm are not worth more than £650,000; those assets plus the farmhouse are not worth more than £1m in total; and the whole estate, including the rest of the farm, is not more than £2m, or
- The farmhouse and any other assets excluding the farm are not worth more than £650,000 in total, and the rest of the farm is not worth more than £5m

Note that 'other assets' includes not just things you might expect, like savings, investments, and rental property, but also furniture and antiques, including any in the farmhouse. From 6th April 2027, it will also include pension funds.

This assumes the whole value of the farm (excluding the farmhouse) is covered by either APR or BPR (this assumption continues to apply for the rest of this section). The first scenario also assumes the farmhouse will be left to one or more direct descendants.

In these scenarios, the retired farmer can usually safely remain in occupation of the farmhouse without creating any IHT exposure. Furthermore, holding onto the farm until death will mean their beneficiaries benefit from the CGT uplift on death (Section 12.2).

In other cases, the best strategy may be for the retiring farmer to move out of the farmhouse, so their successors can move in and run the farm from the house, thus generally preserving APR on the property's agricultural use value (AUV). This will protect the retiring farmer's estate from IHT if they are a widow/widower and:

- Any other assets excluding the farm are not worth more than £650,000; those assets plus the farmhouse, less its AUV, do not amount to more than £1m in total; and the whole estate, including the rest of the farm and the farmhouse's total market value, is not more than £2m;
- The farmhouse, less its AUV, and any other assets excluding the farm do not amount to more than £650,000 in total, and the whole farm, including the farmhouse's AUV only, is not worth more than £5m; or
- The farmhouse (full market value) and any other assets excluding the farm do not amount to more than £650,000 in total, and the rest of the farm, excluding the farmhouse, is not worth more than £5m plus the farmhouse's AUV*

* This addition may seem odd but, in this scenario, part of the retired farmer's NRB, equal to the farmhouse's AUV, is available to use on the farm. That AUV can effectively be used twice, since any value in excess of the HPRA still gets a 50% reduction under APR.

The first scenario again assumes the farmhouse is left to one or more direct descendants. Up to now, I have also assumed there isn't another qualifying private residence. Another such private residence may alter the position in some cases: but only for the better.

Where none of the above scenarios apply, it may make sense to take things a step further and transfer ownership of the farmhouse to the retiring farmer's successors. As discussed earlier, this can usually be done free of CGT and, while the uplift on death will be lost, as long as the successors adopt the farmhouse as their main residence, they should be exempt from CGT on all or most of any capital gain arising on a future disposal of the property.

Even when the transferor does not survive seven years, their estate will generally escape IHT if they are a widow/widower and:

- Any assets they hold, excluding the farm and a private residence, plus the market value of the farmhouse at the date of transfer, less its AUV at that date, does not amount to more than £650,000 in total; that same total plus the value of the excluded private residence does not amount to more than £1m; and their whole estate at death, including the farm, but not the farmhouse, is not more than £2m;
- Any assets they hold, excluding the farm, plus the market value of the farmhouse at the date of transfer, less its AUV at that date, does not amount to more than £650,000 in total; and the AUV of the farmhouse at the date of transfer, plus the value of the rest of the farm at date of death does not exceed £5m; or
- Any assets they hold, excluding the farm, plus the full market value of the farmhouse at the date of transfer, does not amount to more than £650,000 in total; and the value of the rest of the farm at date of death does not exceed £5m plus the AUV of the farmhouse at the date of transfer

I have assumed that the private residence referred to under the first scenario is left to a direct descendant. Where there is no such private residence, this scenario does not apply. The same assumption/condition applies to the first scenario below.

If the farmer *does* survive seven years after transferring the farmhouse, their estate will generally escape IHT if they are a widow/widower and:

- Any assets they hold, excluding the farm and a private residence, do not amount to more than £650,000 in total; that same total plus the value of the excluded private residence does not amount to more than £1m; and their whole estate at death, including the farm, but not the farmhouse, is not more than £2m; or
- Any assets they hold, excluding the farm, do not amount to more than £650,000 in total; and the value of the farm, excluding the farmhouse, at date of death does not exceed £5m

I have assumed throughout this analysis that the retired farmer doesn't make any other transfers of value in the last seven years of their life. If they do, these effectively have to be included in the assets held at the time of their death for the purpose of each scenario (but not for the purposes of the £2m threshold where the RNRB is withdrawn). I have also assumed they had owned the farm for at least seven years at the time of their death, and I have ignored any possible increases in the NRB, RNRB, or HPRA after 2031 (we live in hope!)

Where none of the above scenarios apply, there may be some IHT exposure on the farm. However, it's worth noting that for every £1 of the farmer's NRB/TNRB not used elsewhere, an additional £2 over and above the HPRA can effectively be exempted from IHT where 50% APR (or BPR) is available.

For example, let's say a widow retires, but remains in occupation of the farmhouse until she dies, at which point the house is worth £450,000. If she has no other assets, this means £200,000 of her NRB is available to cover the farm. Hence, in this case, a farm worth up to £5.4m (excluding the farmhouse) would be exempt from IHT.

For more valuable farms, whose value exceeds the point where the NRB/TNRB and HPRA are all exhausted, further lifetime planning may be called for. We'll take a closer look at this type of planning below (albeit with the lower values applicable to unmarried or divorced farmers), and in Section 12.5.

Unmarried or Divorced Farmers

The position is less favourable for unmarried or divorced farmers. In effect, all the amounts given in our scenarios for widows/widowers above have to be halved: except the £2m threshold where the RNRB is withdrawn.

This means there will be an IHT exposure on the farm much more often and, in many cases, a detailed review will be necessary to determine the best course of action when the farmer retires.

Example: *Dolly is a divorcee who has been actively managing the family farm since her ex-husband, Kenny, an inveterate gambler, walked out on her many years ago, leaving her with four hungry children and a crop in the fields. Dolly is now in her* *seventies: things are getting a bit much for her, and she's looking to retire and pass the running of the farm over to her son, Garth. (For the avoidance of doubt, in case it isn't obvious, she has owned the farm for well over seven years.)*

The total value of the farm is £4.1m, including the farmhouse, which is worth £600,000, but has an agricultural use value of just £350,000. Dolly also has some savings and investments totalling £200,000.

Option 1: *Dolly retires, but continues to own and occupy the farmhouse until she dies. She will not be able to claim APR on the house, and her estate, totalling £4.3m, is too large for her to be eligible for the RNRB.*

The rest of the farm is worth £3.5m, so Dolly will be able to claim APR of £3m (£2.5m + £1m x 50%), plus her NRB, reducing her chargeable estate to £975,000 (£4.3m – £3m – £325,000), and leaving her with an IHT bill of £390,000.

Option 2: *Dolly moves out of the farmhouse, but continues to own it; Garth moves in and takes over the running of the farm. She purchases a local cottage to live in, which costs £180,000, plus £10,100 in SDLT (the 5% surcharge applies because she still owns the farmhouse).*

Dolly will now be able to claim APR on the agricultural use value of the farmhouse, so her claim increases to £3.175m (£2.5m + £1.35m x 50%), reducing her chargeable estate to £789,900 (£4.3m – £3.175m – £10,100 – £325,000), and leaving her with an IHT bill of £315,960. The total tax cost of this option is thus £326,060 (£315,960 + £10,100).

Option 3: *Dolly gives the farmhouse to Garth, then purchases the local cottage and moves out. Provided she owns no other residential properties at the end of the day of purchase (including any located on the farm), she will only pay SDLT of £1,100 this time.*

If Dolly dies within seven years, the gift to Garth will use up £350,000 of her HPRA (the agricultural use value of the farmhouse), leaving just £2.15m; and £250,000 of her NRB, leaving just £75,000.

Her APR claim on the rest of the farm, worth £3.5m, will now be £2.825m (£2.15m + £1.35m x 50%). Her estate is worth a total of £3,698,900, and her chargeable estate will be reduced to £798,900 (£3,698,900 – £2.825m – £75,000), giving her an IHT bill of £319,560, and a total tax cost of £320,660 (£319,560 + £1,100).

If Dolly survives seven years after the gift to Garth, it will be exempt and will not use up any of her HPRA or NRB. Her APR claim on the rest of the farm will then be £3m (as per Option 1). Her chargeable estate will be reduced to £373,900 (£3,698,900 – £3m – £325,000), giving her an IHT bill of £149,560, and a total tax cost of £150,660 (£149,560 + £1,100).

Option 4: *Dolly continues to own and occupy the farmhouse, but gives the rest of the farm to Garth. She leaves the farmhouse to him when she dies.*

If Dolly dies within seven years, the gift of the farm will attract APR of £3m (as per Option 1) and use up her NRB, leaving a chargeable lifetime transfer of £175,000. This will give rise to an IHT liability of between £14,000 and £70,000, depending how long Dolly survives after gifting the farm. Her estate will now be worth £800,000. She will be able to claim a RNRB of £175,000, reducing it to £625,000 and giving rise to an IHT bill of £250,000. The total tax cost is thus between £264,000 and £320,000.

If Dolly survives seven years after giving away the farm, both her NRB and RNRB will be deductible from her estate, reducing it to £300,000 and giving her an IHT bill of £120,000. The only practical way to improve on that would probably be to follow the co-ownership strategy in Section 13.9, as anything else is unlikely to leave Dolly with enough to live on.

Summarising the Example

The example shows the potential planning options to be considered when the value of a farm exceeds the available HPRA. In this case, the retiring farmer faced an IHT bill of £390,000 if they continued to occupy the farmhouse (Option 1).

Moving out of the farmhouse yielded a saving of £63,940 (Option 2). Giving the farmhouse away, and then moving out, increased that saving slightly (by £5,400), even if the retiring farmer died within seven years. More importantly, however, gifting the farmhouse led to the possibility of significantly increasing the saving, to £239,340, if the retiring farmer survived seven years (Option 3).

Alternatively, gifting the rest of the farm, instead of the farmhouse, led to a saving of between £70,000 and £126,000 if the retiring farmer died within seven years. That saving increased to £270,000 if they survived seven years (Option 4). But this option has the significant drawback that the CGT uplift on death is lost on the rest of the farm. In Section 12.5, we will take a detailed look at when, and how much, this will impact on the family.

I ruled out an Option 5, where Dolly gives away the entire farm, including the farmhouse, as this would probably not leave her with enough to live on, especially given that, from 6th April 2027, those 'savings and investments' I referred to would have to include pension savings.

Further Points on Farmhouses

Where a farmhouse is given away as a lifetime gift, not only will the RNRB not be available on the farmhouse (unless there is a gift with reservation) but, since there was no actual sale of the property, the downsizing provisions (Section 13.10) cannot apply. Hence, unless the transferor buys another property, they will not be able to utilise any available RNRB. Even if another residence is purchased, the RNRB will be limited to the value of that new property, which may often be less than the amount available. Furthermore, that new property, or the proceeds of its sale, will need to be left to direct descendants to qualify for the RNRB.

Having said all that, none of this matters if the farmer dies with a total estate worth £2.7m or more (for widows/widowers), or £2.35m (for other individuals).

To retain APR on the AUV of a farmhouse, it is generally only necessary for the person, or persons, who are taking over the running of the farm to move into the house. Provided the owner and their successors have run the farm from the house for at least seven years between them when the owner dies, APR will usually still be available. Nonetheless, while an actual transfer isn't necessary from a tax perspective, the successors will often want this for practical reasons, including, most importantly, to provide them with some security.

For a larger farmhouse, it may be possible for the original owner to remain in occupation after the successors have moved in. However, this may still result in a restriction in APR, as the farm would not be used exclusively by the person responsible for the running of the farm.

Occupation following a lifetime transfer would be a gift with reservation (see Sections 4.8 and 13.11). If the original owner were to die within seven years, there would effectively be two calculations, one with APR on the lifetime transfer and one with the RNRB available on death. The calculation producing the higher tax charge would then be used. So, it would be APR *or* RNRB, but not both, and HMRC gets to choose which!

One way to avoid a gift with reservation may be to follow the technique in Section 13.9, but there would still be a restriction in APR.

Separating the title to the farmhouse from the title to the adjoining farmland may be disadvantageous for SDLT purposes in the event of a sale or transfer to a company (see the Taxcafe guide *How to Save Property Tax*).

Temporary or Extended Absences

A problem frequently faced by elderly farmers is that they need to move out of the farmhouse for medical reasons, or because they need care.

If the absence is only temporary, this should not affect the APR available on the farmhouse. For example, if a farmer suffered a heart attack or a stroke and was taken into hospital for a month, but then recovered and was able to return home and resume running the farm, there would be no impact on their APR. Similarly, if they died after a short period of hospitalisation, there would again be no impact on their APR.

If, however, the farmer made only a partial recovery and was not able to resume running the farm, APR would be lost unless the farmer's successor or successors moved into the farmhouse fairly soon after this became apparent.

Where a farmer needs to be taken into care and this is likely to be permanent, it will again be necessary for their successor or successors to move into the farmhouse in order to retain APR on the property.

7.29 FARMHOUSES AS INHERITANCE TAX SHELTERS

If you ever discuss IHT in your local pub or golf club, some bright spark is bound to tell you they have avoided IHT by buying a farm. For a start, the mere fact they are around to make this bar room boast means they have not actually avoided IHT yet. More specifically, the problem with a lot of so-called farmhouses is they are really just a country house with some farmland nearby. This alone is not enough to secure APR.

A normal size farmhouse occupied by a working farmer is indeed eligible for APR, but it is essential the house is of an appropriate character, and occupied for the purposes of farming throughout the relevant period (see Section 7.27). A farm owner with only limited involvement in the day-to-day running of the farm does not occupy their home for the purpose of farming. So, simply buying a farmhouse isn't necessarily enough to claim APR.

Of course, the fact the farmhouse doesn't qualify does not necessarily preclude the rest of the farm from qualifying, so our bar room braggart may not be entirely wrong, but this will generally only be a small comfort, as the majority of the value will usually be in the house.

Alternatively, you could perhaps buy a farm and install a farm manager in the house (which must be of an appropriate character). But, unless you use a company to buy the farm, you would need to maintain this arrangement for at least seven years. Using a company could cut this down to two years, as long as you control the company (see Section 7.7). Either way, even after the requisite period, APR would only cover the house's agricultural value: its value if sold subject to a covenant requiring it to remain in agricultural use. In some cases, there will be a substantial difference between this and the house's open market value and the excess will not be eligible for APR. Whether any of the excess is eligible for BPR will depend on the circumstances of the case.

Remember also that APR is now restricted (Section 7.8). All in all, unless you are genuinely interested in investing in farms, there are easier ways to shelter your wealth from IHT.

7.30 PLANNING FOR LARGER BUSINESS OWNERS

Despite the introduction of the HPRA, individuals holding agricultural or business property qualifying for 100% relief generally continue to enjoy complete exemption from IHT on that property up to a value of £2.5m. Most widows/widowers enjoy exemption on up to £5m.

That's enough for many business owners, but those with more valuable businesses may wish to undertake some planning to protect their business. And remember, it's not the current value of the business that matters, it's the value when the ultimate transfer takes place, whether on death or otherwise.

Married business owners can, of course, generally leave everything, including their business, to their spouse free from IHT. That spouse will then be a widow/widower, who will generally enjoy £5m worth of complete exemption on qualifying business or agricultural property. But even that may not always be enough.

Furthermore, not everyone wants to leave their business to their spouse, and not everyone is married.

Lifetime Transfers
For a business worth over £2.5m (£5m for widows/widowers, or anyone intending to leave their business to their spouse), it may be possible to protect the business from IHT by passing the excess value to the owner's ultimate intended beneficiaries as a lifetime transfer.

Example: *Jolene is an unmarried business owner. Her unquoted trading company is worth £4m and she intends to leave it to her daughter, Tammy. As things stand, Jolene's BPR will amount to £3.25m (£2.5m + £1.5m x 50%), leaving £750,000 exposed to IHT and leaving Tammy with the burden of a £300,000 IHT bill.*

Instead, Jolene passes £1.5m worth of shares to Tammy now. If Jolene dies within seven years, this lifetime transfer uses up £1.5m of her HPRA, leaving just £1m to cover the remaining shares she still holds when she dies. Hence, if the value of the business is static, there is no saving.

If Jolene survives seven years, the lifetime transfer to Tammy is exempt. Jolene's HPRA will then cover her remaining shareholding, leaving no IHT to pay.

In practice '£1.5m worth of shares' should actually mean sufficient shares to reduce the value of Jolene's shareholding by £1.5m, as this is the correct way to calculate the transfer of value (see Sections 2.1 and 7.11). While this distinction is important, and must be followed in practice, we will assume, for the rest of this section, that shares can be valued on a pro rata basis.

This simple example assumes no change in value for the shares. In reality, a successful business will grow in value, although the rate will vary from one business to another, and from one year to another. On the other hand, some businesses will fall in value.

Most business owners hope their business will grow in value, especially if they intend to leave it to their family. This growth should be factored into your planning. It will also mean lifetime transfers of part of a business worth in excess of the HPRA will start to save some tax immediately.

Example Revisited: *Let's take the same facts as before, but assume Jolene's company is growing in value at a rate of 10% per year (compound). To cater for this growth, Jolene gives Tammy a 50% stake in the company, currently worth £2m. The saving produced, based on the number of years Jolene survives after making the gift can be summarised as follows:*

Years Survived	***Company Value***	***IHT Arising***	***IHT if No Transfer***	***Saving***
1	*£4,400,000*	*£340,000*	*£380,000*	*£40,000*
2	*£4,840,000*	*£384,000*	*£468,000*	*£84,000*
3	*£5,324,000*	*£432,400*	*£564,800*	*£132,400*
4	*£5,856,400*	*£485,640*	*£671,280*	*£185,640*
5	*£6,442,040*	*£544,204*	*£788,408*	*£244,204*
6	*£7,086,244*	*£608,624*	*£917,249*	*£308,624*
7	*£7,794,868*	*£279,487*	*£1,058,974*	*£779,487*

These figures are based on the assumption the HPRA remains £2.5m. After seven years, Jolene's HPRA is available once more. If she's comfortable with the idea, she could consider gifting further shares to Tammy at this stage, in order to make additional savings.

One downside to lifetime transfers is they mean foregoing the uplift on death for CGT purposes (Section 12.2), so it will generally make sense for the original owner to hang on to £2.5m worth of business assets (or £5m for a widow, widower, a couple owning the business jointly, or a married individual intending to leave the business to their spouse).

Aside from this point, CGT should not usually be a problem, as most such transfers will qualify for holdover relief. Nonetheless, we will look at the interaction between CGT and IHT on qualifying business assets in more depth in Section 12.5.

It is also worth bearing in mind that each individual needs to own their share of a business for at least two years to qualify for business asset disposal relief (Section 12.5): hence transfers may be a bad idea if there is a possibility of a sale in the near future.

There are, of course, other issues to be considered too, including maintaining sufficient right to income and retaining control over the business (although a trust will usually fix this). We will look at putting business or agricultural property into trust in Section 9.8.

Business Owners with Few Other Assets

For a business owner with significant private wealth, any business or agricultural property worth in excess of the HPRA will suffer IHT at an effective rate of 20%. For those with few non-business assets, however, a business worth in excess of the HPRA may still escape IHT. For example, an unmarried individual whose only other assets, net of non-business liabilities (see below), are worth just £125,000, could leave a business worth £2.9m free from IHT (BPR would amount to £2.5m + £400,000 x 50% = £2.7m, leaving £200,000, which would be covered by the individual's NRB).

In short, for every £1 of NRB that is not used on other assets, an extra £2 of business or agricultural property in excess of the HPRA can be sheltered. Note, however, that, from 6th April 2027, 'other assets' will include pension savings.

In some cases, it may be possible to increase the amount of unused NRB by making sufficient lifetime transfers to reduce the value of the individual's estate to no more than £2m, thus enabling them to claim the RNRB where appropriate (Section 3.4).

Example: *Dylan is a widower. He owns a business worth £6m, a house worth £750,000 and nothing else. He intends to leave everything to his daughter, Joni. As things stand, he will be entitled to a NRB/TNRB of £650,000 and BPR of £5.5m, leaving a chargeable estate of £600,000 and lumbering Joni with an IHT bill of £240,000.*

Dylan discovers he is terminally ill. He transfers his business to Joni immediately. When he dies a short time later, this transfer uses up his HPRA and £500,000 of his NRB/TNRB (leaving £150,000). However, it also means he is able to claim a RNRB of £350,000, reducing his chargeable estate to £250,000 (£750,000 – £150,000 – £350,000). This reduces Joni's IHT burden to £100,000, saving her £140,000.

The cost of this £140,000 saving is, of course, that Joni will miss out on the CGT uplift on death. That cost could have been reduced without impacting the IHT saving if Dylan had held onto a share of the business worth £1.25m, giving him an estate worth £2m at the time of his death.

Non-business liabilities deductible from the general assets of the estate do not generally include any loans or other liabilities used to fund the business (see Sections 2.10 and 7.12).

7.31 RESTORING UNLIMITED 100% RELIEF FOR BUSINESS OR AGRICULTURAL PROPERTY

Another option for married business owners with valuable businesses may be to look at a variation of the family debt scheme (Section 6.13).

Example: *Janis owns all the shares in her unquoted trading company, Big Brother Ltd, which is worth £10m. She sells 75% of the shares (worth £7.5m) to her husband, Seth, in exchange for an IOU for £5m. She gifts the IOU to the couple's children.*

Assuming Janis survives seven years, the gift of the IOU, as a PET, will be exempt from IHT. If she leaves her remaining Big Brother Ltd shares (worth £2.5m) to her children on her death, they will be fully covered by BPR.

When Seth dies, the IOU will be deducted from the value of his shareholding (assuming the debt is settled out of the assets of his estate: Section 2.10). This leaves only £2.5m of the shareholding originally sold to him by Janis, which will be fully covered by BPR.

Following this method, IHT can be avoided altogether on the shares, regardless of which order the couple die in, as long as: Janis survives at least seven years; and Seth's debt is settled out of the assets of his estate.

If Janis is the first to die, she could, alternatively, leave her shares to Seth. He would then have a HPRA of £5m and the end result would be the same. If Seth dies first, however, he needs to leave his shares to the children (and/or a discretionary trust if preferred) in order to get relief for the IOU.

If Janis hadn't taken any action, up to £2.5m could have been exposed to IHT, so the scheme has ***saved up to £1m*** in IHT.

The sale of the shares to Seth will be free of CGT (as it is a transfer between spouses) but will cost £25,000 in Stamp Duty (£5m x 0.5%). That will, of course, ultimately save another £10,000 (£25,000 x 40%) in IHT.

So, all in all, for a couple who do not wish to make lifetime transfers to their children (or other beneficiaries), the scheme may have saved up to £1.01m in

IHT at a cost of just £25,000. Plus, the uplift on death will have been preserved on the shares, potentially saving the children a great deal of CGT in the future too.

This method could effectively restore all the benefits of the former unlimited 100% exemption for qualifying business property at an ultimate net cost of just 0.3%, but there's a catch. The IOU has to be settled out of the assets of the transferee's estate on their death. There are many ways of doing this (see Section 2.10) but, in effect, in the above example, the family would somehow need to find £5m. Having said that, they do have assets worth at least £10m they can borrow against, so there must surely be a way?

So far, we've looked at a sale of shares. A sale of property (land and buildings) would be rather more costly in terms of SDLT, unless the transferor and their spouse are going into (or already in) partnership: in that case, the sale would be exempt from SDLT.

Lastly, it's worth mentioning the scheme should, in principle, work equally well for agricultural property.

7.32 THE SAFETY NET

Despite the new restrictions to BPR and APR, they remain extremely valuable reliefs. Given the numerous, highly complex conditions that must be satisfied to obtain BPR or APR, however, the matter will often be in doubt when the business owner dies.

If the owner simply leaves the business or agricultural property to their surviving spouse, the matter will still not be resolved as this transfer will usually be exempt anyway. However, if the deceased left the property to a discretionary trust in their Will, HMRC would need to examine the case and, hopefully, the matter will soon be resolved. But how does this help?

If BPR or APR is denied, there should be time to appoint the assets to the surviving spouse free from IHT (see Section 17.3). The tax is at least deferred and the family will know where they stand. Furthermore, the survivor may have time to correct whatever defects were in the property, so there is a better chance of claiming relief on their subsequent death.

If it turns out BPR or APR *is* available on the first death, there is an opportunity to do some further planning, as outlined in Sections 7.33 and 15.2.

7.33 MAKE HAY WHILE THE SUN SHINES

For businesses worth no more than £2.5m, there is a strong argument to suggest it would be wise to pass the business directly to the deceased's children, or other younger beneficiaries, rather than risk any possibility that BPR or APR may be lost before their surviving spouse or partner dies.

BPR or APR could be lost during the surviving spouse or partner's lifetime due to either a further change in legislation, or a change in the nature of the business. In the case of a family business, the fear of losing the relief may place unwelcome constraints on the business. By passing the business directly to the next generation, such constraints are effectively removed (although the problem will of course eventually return).

This approach will not suit every family, of course, and most people will want to be sure their spouse or partner is financially secure before they are happy to pass the family business straight to their children.

As we saw in Section 7.28, for those who literally are making hay, i.e. running the family farm, it is often a good idea to pass the farmhouse directly to the children on the first spouse's death since APR may subsequently be lost if the surviving spouse is unable to run the farm on their own.

Furthermore, for all types of business, passing the business directly to the children (or other beneficiaries) on the first death may help ensure the widow/widower's estate does not exceed £2m on the second death, thus preventing the loss of their RNRB due to tapering (Section 3.4).

7.34 INVESTMENT SYNDICATES

For those with spare cash, farming syndicate arrangements are available to provide IHT shelters for investments from as little as £10,000. Similar arrangements provide opportunities to invest in solar farms, wind farms, or other asset-backed trading businesses qualifying for BPR.

These syndicates could provide greater benefits than AIM shares (Section 7.26) as, depending how they are structured, they may continue to provide relief at 100% on up to £5m. Furthermore, they are often seen as less risky than AIM shares, as much of their value is derived from underlying assets (usually land).

As with any other assets qualifying for BPR or APR, it is important the investments are not directly or indirectly funded through borrowings, as this will render them ineffective for IHT purposes.

Chapter 8

IHT Planning With Trusts

8.1 WHAT IS A TRUST?

In its simplest form, a trust is an arrangement under which someone is given legal title to an asset and trusted to hold that asset on behalf of one or more beneficiaries. Trusts have a long and honourable history as a well-established mechanism for protecting the vulnerable, such as widows, orphans, or disabled people. They originated in the twelfth century when crusaders would entrust their assets to another person before setting off for the Holy Land.

Some definitions:
Trustee: The person trusted to hold the asset
Beneficiary: The person on whose behalf the asset is held
Settlor: The person who transferred the asset into the trust
Absolutely: When assets finally leave the trust and become property of the ultimate beneficiary, we say the beneficiary holds those assets 'absolutely'
Testator: A deceased person who left a valid Will (which may have been used to set up a trust)

Very often, the settlor will also be a trustee. Legally, there is nothing to prevent the settlor from being a beneficiary, although this usually renders the trust ineffective for IHT planning purposes, and can also give rise to unwanted CGT liabilities.

In legal parlance (and within tax legislation), the act of putting assets or funds into a trust is referred to as a settlement. When a trust is created, this is also referred to as a settlement. The assets held within the trust are known as settled property. Every time new assets or funds are put into the trust a new item of settled property is created. Each item of settled property has its own separate identity for IHT purposes. This is especially important when there are changes to the IHT treatment of trusts, as there were in 2006, when some fundamental changes with far-reaching consequences were made. It will often make a critical difference whether property was settled before or after the change. Naturally, when planning for the future, we are only concerned with the current regime and any potential future changes. Nonetheless, as we shall see later, many people will still be affected by the earlier rules.

8.2 WHAT TYPES OF TRUST ARE THERE?

In essence, there are really only two types of trust: interest in possession trusts and discretionary trusts. The distinction revolves entirely around whether any beneficiary is entitled to enjoy an interest in possession in settled property, and this is a crucial factor in determining how the trust will be treated.

For IHT purposes, it is necessary to further sub-divide the two main types into a number of other categories, each subject to different rules. We'll look at these categories later, but first let's focus on the two main types.

Interest in Possession Trusts
Whenever a specific individual is beneficially entitled, for a specified period, to the income from, or to otherwise enjoy, an asset within a trust, that person has an interest in possession. Where more than one person is to share the income or enjoyment of the assets for a specified period, this is also an interest in possession. The income may be shared in any proportion specified in the trust deed. If, however, the trustees have discretion over the income paid to the beneficiaries, this would make the trust a discretionary trust.

Example: *Nicole transfers several rental properties into the All Saints Trust. Under the terms of the trust, the rental profits must be paid to the beneficiaries as follows:*

- *Half to Nicole's sister, Natalie*
- *The first £10,000 of the remainder to her friend, Melanie*
- *The remaining balance to her niece, Shaznay*

Each beneficiary's interest is an interest in possession because each of them receives a specific defined amount under the terms of the trust deed not dependent on the discretion of the trustees.

All other things being equal, an interest in possession trust is generally to be preferred whenever possible as it enjoys a more beneficial Income Tax regime than a discretionary trust. See Section 8.17 for further details.

Life Interests: Where a beneficiary is entitled to an interest in possession for the remainder of their life, we refer to this as a life interest (sometimes known as a liferent). A trust subject to a life interest is often referred to as a life interest trust. Generally, the IHT treatment of a life interest trust is exactly the same as any other interest in possession trust.

The Remainder: The remainder is a term used to describe a right to assets that comes into force after an interest in possession ends. The most common example is when a person leaves a life interest in property to their spouse with the remainder to their children. This means on the spouse's death the property passes absolutely to the children.

Reversion to Settlor: It is possible to create an interest in possession trust where the remainder interest reverts to the original settlor. This, in itself, does not invoke the gift with reservation rules (Section 4.8) as long as the settlor is excluded from benefit during the period the interest in possession exists (in practice, the settlor's spouse would usually also need to be excluded).

Discretionary Trusts
A discretionary trust is basically any trust, or part thereof, where no person is entitled to an interest in possession. The trustees have discretion to decide who to allow the enjoyment of the trust's assets, who to pay the income of the trust to, and how much. There is usually a defined class of beneficiaries from whom the trustees can choose, such as 'all my grandchildren', for example. It is possible for a discretionary trust to have just one beneficiary, as long as there is a theoretical possibility of there being at least one other additional beneficiary at some time and the trustees have discretion over whether, and when, to pay out income.

Hybrid Trusts
A single trust may hold settled property subject to an interest in possession while other property is held on discretionary trust. For IHT purposes, each item of settled property is treated according to the rules relating to that particular item of property. Hence, we may sometimes get a hybrid trust subject to different rules on its different parts. Looked at another way, a trust may be regarded as an envelope containing any number of different items and types of settled property.

For the sake of simplicity, we will generally assume in this guide that each trust has only one type of settled property. Always remember, however, that IHT law applies to each item of settled property in its own right.

The Trust Hierarchy
For IHT purposes, the two main types of trust must be sub-divided into a number of different categories. These make up what I call 'the trust hierarchy'. Every trust will be categorised as the highest type within the hierarchy for which it qualifies. For example, a trust that qualifies as an immediate post death interest (ranked sixth in the hierarchy) cannot be an 18 to 25 trust (ranked eighth) even if it would otherwise qualify. The trust hierarchy is as follows:

1. **Charitable Trusts**
2. **Bare Trusts**
3. **Bereaved Minors' Trusts**
4. **Pre-22/3/2006 Interest in Possession Trusts**
5. **Disabled Trusts**
6. **Immediate Post-Death Interests**
7. **Transitional Serial Interests**
8. **18 to 25 Trusts**
9. **Relevant Property Trusts**

Discretionary trusts and post-22/3/2006 interest in possession trusts not falling into any other category will both be relevant property trusts.

As we shall see in the sections that follow, several categories of trust must be created immediately on the settlor's death. However, in Chapter 17, we will see both deeds of variation and distributions from most trusts made within two years of the settlor's death will be treated as if they had occurred immediately on death. Hence, in practice, most trusts that need to be set up immediately on death can usually be set up within the following two years.

Inheritance Tax Regimes for Trusts
In essence, there are three IHT regimes for trusts. The various categories of trust fall into these regimes, as follows:

Relevant Property:
Discretionary Trusts (Note 1)
Post-22/3/2006 Interest in Possession Trusts (Note 2)
18 to 25 Trusts (Note 3)

In Beneficiary's Estate:

Pre-22/3/2006 Interest in Possession Trusts
Disabled Trusts
Immediate Post-Death Interests
Transitional Serial Interests
Bare Trusts

Exempt:

Bereaved Minors' Trusts
18 to 25 Trusts (Note 3)
Charitable Trusts

Notes

1. Unless qualifying under another category.
2. An interest in possession created after 21st March 2006 that does not qualify under any other category will fall into the relevant property regime. This will occur in the case of most lifetime transfers into trust, or new interests in possession coming into force on termination of a previous interest.
3. 18 to 25 trusts are effectively exempt until the beneficiary attains the age of 18 and then fall into the relevant property regime thereafter.

Where settled property falls into the relevant property regime, it is subject to IHT charges in its own right, as detailed in Sections 8.14 to 8.16. Such settled property is referred to as relevant property for IHT purposes.

Most other categories of settled property are treated as if they belong to the beneficiary and are included in the beneficiary's estate for IHT purposes, as explained in Section 2.5.

The scope of the third regime, exempt trusts, was severely curtailed by Gordon Brown in 2006 but, as the name implies, it provides complete exemption from IHT for certain types of trust, including charitable trusts.

8.3 TRANSFERS INTO TRUST

Transfers into trust on the transferor's death are generally chargeable to IHT in the same way whatever type of trust is involved. The regimes described in the previous section determine how the settled property is treated later; they do not usually alter the amount of IHT arising on the transferor's death.

The only exception to this is the fact the spouse exemption applies to an immediate post-death interest for a surviving spouse (Section 8.9). For deaths before 6th April 2026, there was also an exception for transfers into a charitable trust but, as explained in Section 3.5, this no longer applies (this does not alter the treatment of the trust itself, it just means that, on a death after 5th April 2026, the transfer into the trust is subject to IHT).

In all other cases, transfers into trust arising on death form part of the estate in the normal way and will be subject to IHT as usual.

Transfers on Death and the Residence Nil Rate Band

Transfers of qualifying property, on death, into a trust for the benefit of one or more direct descendants, will qualify for the RNRB, where available, provided one of the following types of trust is used:

- Bare Trust
- Bereaved Minors' Trust
- Disabled Trust
- Immediate Post-Death Interest
- 18 to 25 Trust

Lifetime Transfers

Lifetime transfers to disabled trusts or bare trusts are PETs. Otherwise, as we saw in Section 4.2, most lifetime transfers into trust are chargeable lifetime transfers. This includes transfers to a charitable trust after 25th November 2025 (such transfers were previously exempt).

8.4 CHARITABLE TRUSTS

A trust set up for charitable purposes does not fall into the relevant property regime and is exempt from the charges detailed in Sections 8.14 to 8.16.

For deaths before 6th April 2026, and lifetime transfers before 26th November 2025, transfers into the trust were also exempt, although this no longer applies (but see Section 8.13 for transfers from an interest in possession trust). It does, however, remain possible to set up a charitable trust via a deed of variation (Section 17.1) and benefit from the exemption, where the deceased has died within the last two years (but before 6th April 2026).

To qualify as a charitable trust, property in the trust must be held exclusively for qualifying charitable purposes, or for the benefit of CASCs.

8.5 BARE TRUSTS

Assets that are simply held in someone else's name are held on bare trust, sometimes also known as an absolute trust. A bare trust only exists where the beneficiary has full beneficial ownership of the trust assets and has an immediate and absolute right to both capital and income.

Most commonly, a bare trust exists when an adult holds property on behalf of a minor who will become absolutely entitled to the asset on reaching the age of 18 (sometimes 16 in Scotland). Bare trusts for minors occur frequently because persons under the age of 18 cannot take legal title to property in England or Wales. The position in Scotland is slightly different and legal title is sometimes possible at 16. Bare trusts may sometimes continue beyond this point until the beneficiary calls for the trust assets to be transferred to them.

Assets held on bare trust are not settled property, or settlements, for IHT purposes, and are simply treated as belonging to the beneficiary. We will see some useful consequences of this in the next chapter.

8.6 BEREAVED MINORS' TRUSTS

The 'trust for a bereaved minor', to give it its proper name, is a very restrictive class of trust. Where the appropriate rules are met, trust property will be exempt from IHT and there will be no charges if a beneficiary dies or assets are transferred out of the trust. The basic conditions are:

i) The beneficiary must be under 18 years of age
ii) At least one of the beneficiary's parents is dead
iii) The trust was set up under:
    a. Intestacy,
    b. The criminal injuries compensation scheme, or
    c. The Will of a deceased parent
iv) The beneficiary must be absolutely entitled to the trust assets by the age of 18 at the latest
v) Trust assets may only be applied for the benefit of the minor until he or she reaches the age of 18
vi) Trust income may either be applied for the benefit of the minor or given directly to them. (The minor may have an interest in possession, if the settlor so desires.)

For the purposes of these rules, a parent includes a natural parent, a step-parent, an adopted parent and any other person with parental responsibility (e.g. a legal guardian).

Small payments that do not qualify under points (v) or (vi) are permitted. These are limited to the lower of £3,000, or 3% of the value of settled property in the trust, each year.

A trust may still qualify with two or more beneficiaries, as long as each of them obtains absolute entitlement to their share of the trust assets at the age of 18.

The major problem with this type of trust is the beneficiary must gain absolute possession at the age of 18. Many people are horrified at the prospect of the entire family fortune suddenly being at the whim of someone so young. The risk of them frittering everything away before they have the wisdom to look out for their own future is all too obvious.

Thankfully, these concerns were at least partly recognised when the concept of the '18 to 25 Trust' was introduced. We will come on to these trusts in Section 8.11, but it is worth noting that a bereaved minor's trust can be converted to an 18 to 25 trust without charge.

8.7 OLD INTEREST IN POSSESSION TRUSTS

Interests in possession already in existence on 21st March 2006 continue to be treated as if the beneficiary owns the asset. Subject to certain exceptions, the termination of the beneficiary's interest, on death or otherwise, represents a transfer of the underlying assets for IHT purposes.

The old rules apply to settled property transferred into trust before 22nd March 2006. Any new transfers into an existing trust will constitute new settled property and will be subject to the current rules.

Where the terms of a pre-22/3/2006 interest in possession trust are altered, including a change to the period of the interest, this will result in the settled property subject to that interest in possession becoming relevant property. The trust would then be subject to the IHT charges explained in Sections 8.15 and 8.16. However, where there is no change to the actual beneficiary, there would not be a chargeable lifetime transfer and hence no entry charge. (See Section 8.10 for exceptions where the terms of an old trust were altered before 6th October 2008.)

Spouses and Civil Partners
Where a pre-22/3/2006 interest in possession comes to an end on the beneficiary's death and a new interest in possession in favour of the deceased's spouse comes into being, this new interest will be a transitional serial interest (Section 8.10). The spouse exemption will apply to the settled property that falls into the deceased's estate under these circumstances.

8.8 DISABLED TRUSTS

Assets within a trust for the benefit of a qualifying disabled person are exempt from the relevant property provisions and are instead treated as part of the beneficiary's estate.

Self-settlement by a person with a condition expected to lead to a qualifying disability is permitted. This extension only applies to self-settlements; other settlors must wait until the beneficiary's condition deteriorates enough for them to qualify under the general rules.

A disabled trust may be either a discretionary trust or an interest in possession trust. Further rules apply to the use of funds held by a discretionary trust.

The rules on disabled trusts are mainly designed to cover beneficiaries with a mental disability, but will often also cover a person with a terminal illness. This provides the opportunity for the settlor to put property into trust during their illness. While this will not save any IHT, it will enable the trustees to manage all or part of the estate following the settlor's death without having to wait for the grant of probate or confirmation.

8.9 IMMEDIATE POST-DEATH INTERESTS

An interest in possession created immediately on death, either by Will or intestacy, is termed an immediate post-death interest and forms part of the beneficiary's estate for IHT purposes.

The settled property subject to the immediate post-death interest will therefore be included in the beneficiary's own IHT calculation if they should die while still entitled to the interest in possession or within seven years of the termination of that interest.

Most importantly, this means the spouse exemption is available on the creation of an immediate post-death interest. This provides tremendous additional potential for tax planning using the spouse exemption and we will explore this further in Section 9.6.

Furthermore, where an immediate post-death interest ends during the beneficiary's lifetime and property passes to a bereaved minor's trust under the terms of the original settlor's Will, this will be a PET. Combining this with the spouse exemption provides a potential opportunity to pass assets tax free to minor children. We will explore this in Section 9.7.

An immediate post-death interest may also be set up so that the settled property transfers to a bereaved minor's trust or 18 to 25 trust for the benefit of the original testator's children on the death of the original beneficiary (IHT is payable on the original beneficiary's death in the normal way).

When a testator adds new settled property to an existing interest in possession trust this will also be treated as an immediate post-death interest.

A TNRB may be set against the value of an immediate post-death interest brought into the spouse's estate on their death.

8.10 TRANSITIONAL SERIAL INTERESTS

As explained in Section 8.7, a transitional serial interest comes into existence when an old interest in possession comes to an end on the beneficiary's death and is replaced by an interest in possession in favour of their spouse.

A transitional serial interest also arises where an interest in possession in a settlement made before 22nd March 2006 was replaced by a new interest in possession in the same property within the same trust before 6th October 2008. Where the terms of a pre-22/3/2006 interest in possession trust were altered before 6th October 2008, including a change to the period of the interest, this will also constitute a transitional serial interest.

In each case, the replacement interest forms part of the beneficiary's estate for IHT purposes.

When a transitional serial interest comes to an end and is replaced by a new interest in possession, the new interest will be relevant property and will be taxed as set out in Sections 8.14 to 8.16. The spouse exemption does not apply under these circumstances

Where changes are made to the terms of a transitional serial interest, including the period of the interest, this will again result in the property subject to the interest becoming relevant property.

8.11 18 TO 25 TRUSTS

To meet concerns raised by many bodies in the wake of the original Budget 2006 announcements, this further category of trust was created. An 18 to 25 trust is essentially the same as a bereaved minors' trust (Section 8.6) except the beneficiary must become absolutely entitled to the trust property by the age of 25 at the latest, rather than by 18.

Between the ages of 18 and 25, the beneficiary must either be entitled to an interest in possession or else the trust funds must be accumulated for their benefit (subject to the exception for small non-qualifying payments described in Section 8.6).

An 18 to 25 trust only retains its IHT exempt status until the beneficiary is 18. Thereafter, the trust assets effectively become relevant property. There is no IHT charge when the trust assets become relevant property on the beneficiary's 18th birthday, but the exit charges explained in Section 8.16 will then apply as if the trust had been set up on this date. This means there will be a maximum exit charge of 4.2% if the trust assets pass to the beneficiary at the age of 25 (in addition to the IHT already paid on the parent's death: making a total charge of up to 44.2%!)

More details of the exit charges applying to 18 to 25 Trusts are given in Section 8.16. Exit charges also apply in the same way if the beneficiary of an 18 to 25 trust dies after the age of 18. Vultures!

An 18 to 25 trust cannot arise if an immediate post-death interest is created instead, as this takes precedence under the trust hierarchy. An immediate post-death interest will often be preferable, as this avoids the exit charge applying to an 18 to 25 trust.

8.12 RELEVANT PROPERTY TRUSTS

Any trust not falling under another category in the trust hierarchy is subject to the relevant property regime. This includes most lifetime settlements, even those conferring interests in possession on the settlor themselves (known as self-settlements), or on their spouse, as well as revert to settlor trusts (Section 8.2).

Discretionary trusts generally fall within the relevant property regime, unless they qualify under another category, as set out in Section 8.2.

When settled property falls within the relevant property regime, IHT charges may arise when the settlement is made, when assets come out of the trust, and every ten years in between (so it's 'in, out, and, every ten years, we shake it all about').

Remember, as explained previously, this may apply to any settlement, not just a separately constituted trust. There is, however, a partial exception for life policies held in trust and we will return to this in Section 11.8.

Transfers on Death

Most interests in possession created on death will qualify as immediate post-death interests, as explained in Section 8.9, and should therefore escape the relevant property regime. Dangers arise, however, where the interest in possession does not arise immediately on death. In particular, a new interest in possession that replaces an immediate post-death interest may fall within the relevant property regime (unless, as always, it qualifies under a higher category in the hierarchy).

8.13 END OF TRUST INTERESTS WITHIN BENEFICIARY'S ESTATE

As we saw in Section 8.2, there are five types of trust that are regarded as forming part of the beneficiary's estate. Property within these trusts is subject to IHT at 40% if the beneficiary's interest comes to an end by reason of their death (subject to the exemptions in Chapter 3, including the spouse exemption, and other exemptions explained below).

Under certain circumstances, property within a pre-22/3/2006 interest in possession trust may be eligible to pass into an immediate post-death interest trust, a bereaved minor's trust or an 18 to 25 trust on the original beneficiary's death.

Interests Ending During the Life of the Beneficiary

If the beneficiary becomes absolutely entitled to the trust property, this will be a non-event for IHT, as the property remains within the same estate. If the original settlor or the beneficiary's spouse becomes absolutely entitled to the property, or it goes to charity, or a CASC, the transfer is exempt.

In other cases, when the beneficiary's interest ends during their lifetime, a PET will take place if:

- One or more individuals become absolutely entitled to the trust property
- Property transfers to a bare trust
- Property transfers to a disabled trust
- Property subject to an immediate post-death interest transfers to a bereaved minors' trust

All other transfers on termination of a beneficiary's interest during their lifetime will be chargeable lifetime transfers and the transferred property will fall into the relevant property regime (except as noted below).

If the original beneficiary retains an interest in former trust property, this may constitute a gift with reservation. See Section 4.8 for further details.

Revert to Settlor Trusts

When property reverts to the original settlor on the termination of a pre-22/3/2006 interest in possession trust, the resultant transfer of value is exempt from IHT. This exemption only applies when the property passes back to the settlor absolutely.

Property Passing to Charitable Trust

Where an interest in possession that came into effect before 26th November 2025, and was treated as part of the beneficiary's estate, comes to an end on their death after 5th April 2026, or on any other occasion falling after 25th November 2025, a transfer to a charitable trust (Section 8.4) will be exempt provided the transferred property is subsequently given to charity, or CASCs, within two years.

8.14 THE RELEVANT PROPERTY REGIME

For the rest of this guide, I will refer to any trust that falls into the relevant property regime as a relevant property trust. A relevant property trust is treated as a separate person in its own right for IHT purposes. This has the following consequences:

- Lifetime transfers into a relevant property trust are chargeable transfers, ***not*** PETs
- Transfers into a relevant property trust are generally ineligible for the spouse exemption
- Assets within a relevant property trust are not generally included in a beneficiary's estate for IHT purposes
- No charges arise on the death of a beneficiary or termination of their interest in the trust's assets, but
- A charge may arise when assets leave the trust (Section 8.16)
- There is no revert to settlor exemption (Section 8.13)
- Ten-year anniversary charges apply (Section 8.15)

In essence, IHT may arise when assets go into a relevant property trust, when they come out of it, and every ten years while they're in it. Nevertheless, a relevant property trust's separate life gives rise to some useful tax-planning opportunities, which we will consider further in Chapters 9 and 13.

BPR or APR may apply to reduce or eliminate exit and anniversary charges payable by relevant property trusts. We'll take a closer look at this, and some of the planning opportunities arising, in Section 9.8. For the rest of this chapter, however, we will assume these reliefs do not apply.

Death of Settlor

When a settlor dies, PETs made within the last seven years of their life become chargeable lifetime transfers. This will often lead to an increase in exit and anniversary charges where the relevant property trust was set up within the same seven-year period, and we will see examples of the impact of this in Sections 8.15 and 8.16. In some cases, we may even see a retrospective increase in exit charges as a result of the settlor's death.

8.15 TEN-YEAR ANNIVERSARY CHARGES

Unfortunately, to counter the advantages of a relevant property trust's separate life, these trusts are subject to an IHT charge on every tenth anniversary of their creation. We will now examine how this charge is calculated. It gets rather complex, but we will work through a practical example at the end to illustrate the main points.

The anniversary charge is calculated as follows:

i) Take the value of relevant property in the trust on the anniversary date.
ii) Add other settlements (into other trusts) made by the same settlor on the same day as any settlements into this trust (see Note 1).
iii) Calculate the amount of IHT payable on a hypothetical chargeable lifetime transfer of a sum equal to the total of (i) and (ii) on the anniversary date, taking account of:
    a. The NRB, but not any other exemptions (see Note 2), and
    b. Any chargeable transfers made by the settlor in the seven years prior to setting up this trust (including any PETs becoming chargeable on the settlor's death).
iv) Using the amount derived at step (iii), the effective rate of IHT on the hypothetical lifetime transfer is calculated.

v) The effective rate is multiplied by 3/10ths and then applied to any amounts in (i) derived from assets held by the trust throughout the ten-year period.
vi) For amounts in (i) derived from assets held for less than ten years, the charge is reduced by one fortieth for every complete calendar quarter those assets were not held as relevant assets of the trust.
vii) The rate applying to charges under (vi) may be increased to take account of further chargeable lifetime transfers made by the settlor (other than to the trust itself), including any PETs becoming chargeable on the settlor's death.

Note 1: Under step (ii), we can exclude settlements:

- Into a charitable trust (Section 8.4),
- Into an immediate post-death interest trust for the settlor's spouse,
- Made before 10th December 2014, and not on the day this trust was set up, or
- Made at any time other than the day this trust was set up, where this trust was set up on the death of a testator before 6th April 2017, under a Will executed before 10th December 2014

Note 2: BPR and APR may be claimed where relevant (see Section 9.8). Technically, these are reliefs not exemptions.

Example *(Exemptions/reliefs other than the NRB are ignored for the sake of simplicity): On 1st April 2017, Mel set up the Spice Discretionary Trust for her granddaughters, Emma and Melanie. She immediately transferred assets worth £80,000 into the trust. No IHT was payable at that time as the transfer amount was below the NRB.*

On the same day, Mel transferred £50,000 into an interest in possession trust for her niece, Victoria. Previously, on 30th November 2016, Mel had given her sister Geri £135,000. Sadly, Mel passed away in January 2023 but, fortunately, the NRB covered her lifetime transfers.

On 1st April 2027, the assets in the Spice Discretionary Trust are worth £330,000. The anniversary charge is calculated as follows:

Value of relevant property on anniversary date:	*£330,000*
Other settlement made the same day:	*£50,000*
Previous chargeable transfers:	*£135,000*
(transfer to Geri becoming chargeable on Mel's death)	
Cumulative total for hypothetical transfer:	***£515,000***
Less NRB	*£325,000*
Gives:	*£190,000*
IHT at lifetime rate (20%)	***£38,000***

Effective rate on the hypothetical transfer:	
(£38,000 divided by £330,000 PLUS £50,000)	*10%*
Rate for anniversary charge: 3/10ths of 10%	*3%*
IHT Payable: 3% x £330,000	***£9,900***

The result of this rather tortuous calculation is that IHT of only £9,900 is payable on the assets in the Spice Discretionary Trust. Remember, had these assets been in Mel's estate at the time of her death, up to £132,000 would have been payable.

The calculation of the anniversary charge is sometimes so complex that some trustees simply elect to pay the hypothetical maximum charge of 6% in order to save time. You may therefore wish to check the trustees are calculating the charge correctly or, if not, at least reducing their fees accordingly.

The position in our example would have been better if Mel had waited until the next day to make the gift into Victoria's trust. The ten-year anniversary charge applying to the Spice Discretionary Trust would then have been just £8,400.

As explained above, the effective rate applying to each trust is increased as a consequence of both chargeable transfers in the previous seven years and other settlements made on the same day. Naturally, it is easy to avoid making a lifetime settlement on the same day as a settlement into another trust, but it is difficult to avoid this happening where settlements are made on death. This was the reason for the changes introduced in 2014 that have effectively blocked a well-known planning strategy known as pilot trusts. In short, pilot trusts no longer work!

Undistributed Versus Accumulated Income

Trust income that has simply not yet been distributed to beneficiaries at the anniversary date is not included in relevant property for the purposes of the ten-year anniversary charge. (Nor for any exit charges: Section 8.16.) However, once the trustees have accumulated that income, it becomes part of the relevant property of the trust. Broadly, it is then treated like a new settlement made on the date of the accumulation (although there is no chargeable lifetime transfer).

Where the trustees have a duty to accumulate the trust income, it is treated as being accumulated as soon as it is received. Where the trustees have no power to accumulate income (e.g. in the case of an interest in possession trust) it will not usually be treated as accumulated at any time (but see further below).

In other cases (e.g. most discretionary trusts), the general rule is income is accumulated when the trustees decide not to distribute it to beneficiaries. Any income that has not been distributed or formally accumulated after five years is deemed to have been accumulated for IHT purposes.

8.16 EXIT CHARGES

Transfers of assets out of a relevant property trust may also give rise to IHT charges. These exit charges are based on broadly similar principles to the ten-year anniversary charge. The effective rate arrived at in each case is multiplied by three-tenths, and then also multiplied by one-fortieth for every complete calendar quarter expiring since the most recent ten-year anniversary, or since the creation of the trust in the case of transfers taking place within the first ten years. For an exit charge arising in the first ten-year period, the hypothetical lifetime transfer used to derive the effective rate is based on the value of the assets in the trust at its commencement, plus any further settlements made into the trust between then and the date of the transfer.

Example: *Let's assume the same facts as the example in Section 8.15, except that in 2022, Mel transferred another £30,000 into the Spice Discretionary Trust and, on 29th June 2026, the trustees gave £20,000 to Emma out of capital. The exit charge on Emma's gift is calculated as follows:*

Value of property settled on 1st April 2017:	*£80,000*
Other settlement made the same day:	*£50,000*
Previous chargeable transfers:	*£135,000*
Value of property settled in 2022:	*£30,000*
Cumulative total for hypothetical transfer:	***£295,000***
Nil rate band	*£325,000*
IHT Payable:	***NIL***

As this example demonstrates, IHT can often be avoided when the trust's assets are distributed to beneficiaries before the first ten-year anniversary. We will look at the opportunities this provides in Chapter 9. To continue our look at exit charges, however, let's slightly revise our example.

Example Revised: *Let's now assume the gift to Geri becoming chargeable on Mel's death was actually £235,000. This increases the cumulative total for the hypothetical lifetime transfer to £395,000. What does this do to Emma's exit charge?*

Cumulative total for hypothetical transfer:	*£395,000*
Deducting the NRB of £325,000 leaves:	*£70,000*
IHT at lifetime rate (20%)	*£14,000*
Effective rate on the hypothetical transfer:	
£14,000 divided by £160,000	
(£80,000 + £50,000 + £30,000)	*8.75%*
Rate for exit charge:	
8.75% x 3/10 x 36/40	*2.3625%*
IHT Payable: 2.3625% x £20,000	***£473***

Points to Note

i) If Emma bears the tax, the exit charge will be £473, as above. If the trust were to bear the tax, grossing up would apply. The grossing up rate in this case would be 2.3625/97.6375 (100 – 2.3625), giving rise to a grossed-up charge of £484.

ii) Only 36 calendar quarters are counted here. The 37th quarter does not end until 30th June 2026. As the transfer to Emma took place before then, this quarter had not yet expired. If the transfer had been made two days later, we would have had to include the 37th quarter.

iii) Under this revised scenario, IHT liabilities would arise on Mel's chargeable lifetime transfers to both the Spice Discretionary Trust and Victoria's interest in possession trust, as a result of her death within seven years of the gift to Geri (see Section 8.15). I have assumed these liabilities were settled directly by the trusts, thus avoiding any grossing up of those earlier transfers.

Later exit charges are based on the effective rate applying at the previous ten-year anniversary, as adjusted for any further settlements into the trust since then.

Distributions of trust income do not give rise to exit charges. Care must be taken, however, that the income is not allowed to accumulate first.

Exit Charges on 18 to 25 Trusts

The exit charge applying to an 18 to 25 trust (Section 8.11) is based on the number of complete calendar quarters that have expired since the later of the date of the settlor's death, and the beneficiary's 18th birthday.

If the beneficiary's 18th birthday is the later date, exit charges can be kept slightly lower by allowing beneficiaries to become absolutely entitled to their inheritance two days before one of their birthdays (somewhere between their 19th and 25thbirthday, as desired). By following this technique, the maximum charge of 4.2% should never arise!

Penal Exit Charges

Bereaved minors' trusts and 18 to 25 Trusts are subject to a penal exit charge regime which, broadly speaking, will apply if trust assets are not distributed to the beneficiary by the age of 18 or 25 respectively. The maximum potential charge under this regime is 21%. The charge does not apply to distributions of assets due to the death of the beneficiary before attaining the relevant age, or to the conversion of a bereaved minors' trust to an 18 to 25 trust (or vice versa).

8.17 INCOME TAX FOR TRUSTS

As I said in Section 8.2, interest in possession trusts generally have a better Income Tax position than discretionary trusts. Discretionary trusts pay Income Tax at the trust rate (currently 45%) on all trust income in excess of a small basic rate band of just £1,000 (except for dividend income, which has its own dividend trust rate, currently 39.35%).

In other words, after the first £1,000 of trust income, a discretionary trust is taxed as if it were an additional rate taxpayer.

Some of the Income Tax paid by the trust can be recovered by the beneficiaries when income is paid out. However, at best, there remains a significant cashflow disadvantage and, at worst, the trust's Income Tax burden effectively becomes permanent when income is retained in the trust.

An interest in possession trust, on the other hand, is generally taxed at basic rate only. The beneficiary entitled to the income then includes that income in their own tax calculation and pays any higher rate Income Tax due (or reclaims any tax overpaid, as the case may be).

Looked at another way, an interest in possession trust is given the benefit of the doubt and taxed at basic rate, with any extra tax due paid by the beneficiary. A discretionary trust is treated as a worst-case scenario and, apart from the first £1,000, taxed as if it were a wealthy individual, with the resultant excess tax then being reclaimed by the beneficiary.

There is an exception for trusts for vulnerable individuals, under which a discretionary trust can be taxed as if its income belonged directly to the vulnerable beneficiary. This generally only applies to disabled trusts, trusts for bereaved minors, and a few other cases where the beneficiary is under 18. (See Section 11.10 regarding lifetime settlements made for the benefit of your own minor children.)

Charitable trusts are generally exempt from Income Tax unless they undertake trading activities.

Forthcoming Increases

From 2027/28 onwards, discretionary trusts will pay Income Tax at 47% on property or savings income (unless it is covered by their £1,000 basic rate band). Interest in possession trusts will be subject to Income Tax at 22% on property or savings income. These are the same rates that will then apply to additional and basic rate taxpayers respectively.

8.18 STAMP TAXES FOR TRUSTS

Trusts pay Stamp Duty on purchases of shares, and SDLT on purchases of non-residential property, in the same way, and at the same rates, as other purchasers. For purchases of residential property by a trust, these are treated as if they were a purchase by the beneficiary for SDLT purposes if:

- Purchased by a bare trust,
- The beneficiary will have the right to live in the property for life, or
- The beneficiary will have an interest in possession in the income from the property (see Section 8.2)

Broadly speaking, this means the horrendous 5% SDLT surcharge will not apply if: the beneficiary has no other interest in residential property; the new property is replacing the beneficiary's previous main residence; or the property is purchased from the beneficiary's spouse. The trust remains liable for SDLT at normal rates.

All other residential property purchases made by trusts will be subject to the 5% SDLT surcharge unless they fall within one of the general exemptions applicable to all purchasers.

As explained in Section 1.4, different taxes apply to purchases of property in Scotland or Wales. While many of the principles are much the same, there are some important differences, so local professional advice is essential. For further details regarding Stamp Taxes on property anywhere in the UK, see the Taxcafe guide *How to Save Property Tax.*

Chapter 9

More Advanced Planning With Trusts

9.1 THE RELEVANT PROPERTY TRUST SHELTER

Because relevant property trusts are effectively treated as separate persons for IHT purposes, they provide an opportunity to shelter assets in a vehicle that exists outside any individual's estate. (Subject, of course, to the anniversary and exit charges explained in Chapter 8.)

In Section 8.12, we saw that relevant property trusts may be created through most lifetime transfers into trust (but see Section 9.2). To create a relevant property trust on death will usually require a discretionary trust.

In effect, and subject to any other transfers you may be making, there is the opportunity to transfer assets equal in value to the NRB into relevant property trusts free from IHT every seven years.

In fact, taking into account the annual exemption and the fact the NRB will hopefully increase again one day, it should be possible to accumulate a considerable amount of value within the relevant property trust. Let's look at an example with a wealthy couple starting their IHT planning next year. Throughout this example, we will follow the assumptions in Section 3.2 regarding the future projected level of the NRB ***BUT*** please note, these are only forecast projections used for the sake of illustration.

Example: *Salvatore and Cherilyn are a wealthy couple. Neither of them has made any transfer of value prior to 6th April 2027. On that date they set up the Caesar & Cleo Family Trust with their children as beneficiaries and each transfer £331,000 into it. The first £6,000 of each person's transfer is covered by their annual exemptions for 2027/28 and 2026/27 (see Section 5.2) and the remaining £325,000 by their NRB. Hence, while there is a chargeable lifetime transfer, no IHT is payable at this stage. A total of £662,000 is now sheltered in the trust.*

On 6th April each year from 2028 to 2030, Salvatore and Cherilyn are able to put a further £3,000 into the trust each, covered by their annual exemptions. By 6th April 2030, a total of £680,000 has been transferred to the trust free from IHT.

From 2031/32 onwards, the Government ***finally*** *starts to increase the NRB again, starting with an increase to £334,000 for the 2031/32 tax year. On 6th April 2031, Salvatore and Cherilyn are therefore each able to put a further £12,000 into the trust. £3,000 of each transfer is covered by the annual exemption, leaving a chargeable lifetime transfer of £9,000. This brings each person's cumulative chargeable transfers up to £334,000 (£325,000 plus £9,000), which is covered by the NRB for 2031/32. A total of £704,000 has now been transferred to the trust free from IHT.*

The couple follow the same principle for the next two years, bringing the total cumulative amount transferred into the trust free from IHT as at 6th April 2033 up to £752,000.

After 6th April 2034, the first transfers made on 6th April 2027 will not need to be counted in calculating the couple's cumulative chargeable transfers. On 7th April 2034, Salvatore and Cherilyn will therefore each be able to transfer £337,000 into the Caesar & Cleo Family Trust free from IHT.

This is because, at this point, each person's cumulative chargeable lifetime transfers in the last seven years are just £27,000. The projected NRB at this point is £361,000, meaning each of them can make a new chargeable transfer of £334,000 without giving rise to any IHT. Adding the annual exemption gives a total tax-free transfer of £337,000 each. These latest transfers bring the total value transferred into the trust to date up to £1.426m.

Following the same principles, each individual is able to transfer a further £26,000 into the trust over the next two years meaning that, by 7th April 2037, a total of £1.478m has been sheltered.

However, on 6th April 2037, our shelter springs a leak: the ten-year anniversary charge. To calculate this charge, let's assume all the trust's income has been distributed to the beneficiaries each year, but the assets in the trust have grown at the rate of 7.5% per annum (compound). This produces a total value for the trust assets at 6th April 2037 of £2.395m.

The transfers made by each of the settlors will be treated separately, so each has their own NRB (which is now £391,000 per our projections). The effective rate is derived by taking 20% of the value of trust assets in excess of two NRBs as a percentage of the value of those assets. In this case, the effective rate is 13.47% (£2.395m – 2 x £391,000 = £1.613m x 20% = £322,600, which, divided by £2.395m, produces a rate of 13.47%).

This rate is multiplied by 3/10ths and then one-fortieth of this result is deducted for each calendar quarter the relevant assets were not in the trust. The assets in the trust from the outset are therefore subject to a charge of 4.041%. The assets that have been in the trust for nine years suffer a charge of 3.637%, those held for eight years suffer 3.233%, and so on.

In total, the anniversary charge amounts to £68,805. This represents just 2.87% of the value of the assets in the trust. If Salvatore and Cherilyn still held those assets personally, they would be exposed to potential IHT charges of 40%, or £958,000. The potential saving is huge.

You don't need to be in a couple to use this technique, nor the more sophisticated version we will look at below. Both work just as well for an individual: you just have to halve all the numbers.

I have made a fairly conservative assumption regarding future increases to the NRB: namely that it will merely rise in line with the CPI after the 22-year freeze to 5th April 2031. However, it is possible the NRB may be subject to more significant increases at some stage in the future. If so, the value of this planning technique will be substantially enhanced.

Using Serial Trusts

There is one major drawback to the method used by Salvatore and Cherilyn. By using just one trust, they had access to just one extra NRB each. It would be better to set up a new trust every seven years and thus continually increase the number of NRBs available.

What Salvatore and Cherilyn should have done is to set up the Caesar and Cleo No. 2 Family Trust on 7th April 2034 and make their next seven years' worth of transfers into that trust. Then, on 8th April 2041, they could set up the Caesar and Cleo No. 3 Family Trust, and so on, for as long as they are able. For a start, this more sophisticated approach would have reduced the charge arising on 6th April 2037 to £41,433.

The longer-term calculations for this planning technique get quite horrendous but, if Salvatore and Cherilyn survive until 8th April 2047 then, using our projection methodology above, they would have the following assets in trust:

Caesar and Cleo Family Trust:	£2.887m
Caesar and Cleo No. 2 Family Trust:	£2.083m
Caesar and Cleo No. 3 Family Trust:	£1.500m
Total:	£6.470m

These figures take account of anniversary charges of £41,433 in 2037, £46,760 in 2044 and £119,542 in 2047. The total IHT paid so far is thus £207,735. This compares with potential IHT of almost £2.6m had these assets still been held by Salvatore and Cherilyn personally.

You may wonder whether using relevant property trusts to shelter assets is really effective in view of the anniversary and exit charges. It is worth bearing in mind, however, that the tenth anniversary charges arising under the method set out above work out at less than 3%.

Twentieth anniversary charges (if the assets are still in trust) will tend to be higher, say around 4%, and, if you get to a thirtieth anniversary, we can expect charges approaching 5%. These are all based on our projected growth rate explained above. More growth would mean higher charges, but the overall saving compared with leaving the assets in the individuals' estates would also be greater. However high the growth, anniversary charges will always be less than 6%, as this is the hypothetical maximum.

In general, the anniversary charges within the trusts are likely to work out at less than 0.5% per annum on average. Even if there were no growth in value within the trusts, this means you would need to survive more than eighty years after starting the plan before the anniversary charges exceeded the IHT saved on your death.

However, in fact, because of the dynamic nature of the plan and the anticipated growth in value of the assets within the trusts, the ultimate savings will continue to grow year on year for as long as you live. Following the method (and assumptions) set out above (and using serial trusts), I have calculated the projected IHT savings for a couple based on the number of years they survive after starting the plan:

Years Survived	***Total Net Assets in Trust £000s***	***Total Net Assets in Estate £000s***	***Saving £000s***
1	*£717*	*£691*	*£26*
2	*£776*	*£726*	*£50*
3	*£838*	*£765*	*£73*
5	*£1,013*	*£888*	*£125*
7	*£1,862*	*£1,418*	*£444*
10	*£2,377*	*£1,766*	*£611*
15	*£4,317*	*£3,021*	*£1,296*
20	*£6,430*	*£4,446*	*£1,984*
25	*£10,358*	*£7,058*	*£3,300*
30	*£15,885*	*£10,809*	*£5,076*

Notes

i) In compiling the above figures, it is assumed the trusts are wound up at the time of the couple's death. This does not necessarily need to happen, but I have done so here to make the comparison fair. 'Total Net Assets in Trust' are the remaining funds distributed to beneficiaries less the IHT charges suffered at this time.

ii) 'Total Net Assets in Estate' is the total net sum left in the estate after IHT from the same assets if these had been retained personally. To create a fair like with like comparison, it is assumed the deceased's NRB is used against these assets.

iii) Saving is, broadly speaking, the overall net tax saving. To be more accurate though, it is actually the additional net sum left to beneficiaries after IHT.

iv) It is assumed neither member of the couple makes any other transfers of value outside the relevant property trust plan.

v) The above table takes the simplistic view that both members of the couple die at the same time. In reality this is unlikely to be the case, but the table still serves as a fair illustration of the savings that might be achieved.

vi) A single individual following the same technique would produce savings equal to half of those shown above.

vii) As explained above, the savings could be far greater if there are more substantial increases in the NRB at some point in the future.

It is interesting to note the projected savings start almost immediately, with £26,000 saved even if the couple die after just one year. This arises because, once the assets are in the trust, any capital growth is immediately safeguarded from inclusion in your estate.

The savings steadily increase over time but there are significant additional increments in the total saving at each seventh anniversary, as a new NRB effectively becomes available.

This table is a perfect illustration of the benefit of starting IHT planning as early as possible. The table is not given in tax terms due to the cashflow impact of ten-year anniversary charges, which render a direct tax paid comparison slightly unfair after the first ten years. Nevertheless, it does ably demonstrate that an excessive concern over anniversary and exit charges is generally unwarranted!

9.2 HOW USEFUL IS THE RELEVANT PROPERTY TRUST SHELTER?

As we have seen, using relevant property trusts can save millions of pounds when the planning is started early enough. In the case of straightforward cash settlements into the trust, a relevant property trust can even be used to give money to your own minor children tax efficiently, allowing parents to start their IHT planning early. We will look at using trusts to benefit minor children in more detail in Section 11.10.

Practical Advantages

As we know from Chapter 4, assets can be passed directly to other individuals as PETs and all that is required is to survive seven years to ensure no IHT is payable. In the right circumstances, this is naturally a much simpler way to save IHT.

However, using a relevant property trust will often have significant practical advantages over giving assets directly to your ultimate beneficiaries, including:

- Control: although you cannot benefit from the gifted assets (see below), you will be able to retain control over them.
- Assets in the relevant property trust are outside any person's estate. This will avoid the danger of unexpected IHT liabilities arising if your beneficiaries should pre-decease you.
- Relevant property trusts can be used as a vehicle to skip a generation (or even two) and pass family wealth directly to grandchildren or great-grandchildren, while still providing the settlor's children with income during their lifetime.
- The income from, or enjoyment of, assets can be given to your beneficiaries at an early age without exposing them to the risk of losing the underlying capital due to their own inexperience, a bad marriage, or some other misfortune.

On top of these practical issues there is also the fact that assets can often be transferred into a relevant property trust free from CGT, and we will look at this in Section 9.4.

However, relevant property trust shelters are subject to some limitations and it is important to be aware of these when undertaking this type of planning.

Lifetime Charges: Any transfer of value into the trust in excess of the transferor's available NRB and any other lifetime exemptions available will give rise to an immediate IHT charge at 20% on the excess (25% if the settlor pays the tax: see Section 4.2).

Settlor Must Not Benefit: Unless the settlor is completely excluded from benefit, in theory and in practice, the assets held within a trust will be subject to the gifts with reservation rules (Section 4.8), thus rendering the trust ineffective for IHT planning purposes. Worse still, while the trust assets would be subject to the gifts with reservation rules, the trust would still be subject to the anniversary and exit charges covered in Sections 8.15 and 8.16 and the initial transfer into the trust will remain a chargeable lifetime transfer.

Strictly speaking, a benefit derived by the settlor's spouse does not necessarily give rise to a gift with reservation, but there is often a danger the settlor may share such a benefit. Hence, in practice, it is usually wise to ensure the settlor's spouse is also excluded from benefit.

9.3 HOW TO AVOID ANNIVERSARY AND EXIT CHARGES

Anniversary and exit charges can easily be avoided by:

a) Distributing all trust assets to the beneficiaries before the tenth anniversary of the trust's creation, and
b) Ensuring the cumulative value of relevant transfers does not exceed the NRB when the assets are distributed

Remember, the value of relevant transfers for this purpose includes:

i) All transfers of relevant property into the trust
ii) Accumulated income within the trust (see Section 8.15)
iii) Chargeable transfers made in the seven years before setting up the trust (including PETs becoming chargeable on death)
iv) Other settlements made on the same day as any settlements into this trust (subject to the exclusions noted in Section 8.15)

We will see a simple example of how anniversary and exit charges may be avoided in Section 9.4. Even when following this strategy, up to ten years of capital growth in the value of trust assets can be accumulated free from IHT. However, in order to achieve the significant longer-term benefits we saw in Section 9.1, or to maintain some of the practical advantages discussed in Section 9.2, it may actually be preferable, in the long run, to suffer anniversary charges.

9.4 HOW TO AVOID INHERITANCE TAX *AND* CAPITAL GAINS TAX AT THE SAME TIME

As explained in Section 4.9, the transfer of assets other than cash will generally be treated as a sale at market value for CGT purposes. However, because a transfer to a relevant property trust is a chargeable transfer for IHT purposes, the transferor is given the ability to hold over any capital gains arising on the assets transferred.

This means no CGT is payable on the transfer and the trust is treated, for CGT purposes, as having acquired the asset at the same price as that originally paid by the transferor.

Furthermore, when, at a later date, the trust then transfers the asset to the ultimate beneficiary, the trustees and the beneficiary may, once again, claim that the capital gain should be held over. Hence, by this method, appreciating assets may be passed on free of both IHT and CGT.

Example: *Eric has an investment property worth £325,000, which he wishes to pass to his adult daughter, Patty. Eric is concerned he will have a substantial CGT bill if he gives the property directly to Patty.*

Instead, Eric sets up the Slowhand Trust with Patty as the beneficiary. He then transfers the property to the trust and elects to hold over the capital gain arising. Eric has made no previous transfers of value, so his chargeable transfer of £325,000 is covered by his NRB.

A couple of years later, the trust transfers the property, now worth £375,000, to Patty. Patty and the trustees jointly elect to hold over the capital gain arising, so Patty is deemed to have acquired the property for the price Eric originally paid.

There is no exit charge on the transfer to Patty as the NRB covers the £325,000 that the property was worth when Eric put it into the trust. The fact the property is now worth £375,000 is irrelevant.

As we can see from the example, where the original transfer was covered by the settlor's NRB, increases in the value of trust assets will not give rise to additional charges as long as those assets are distributed to beneficiaries within ten years of the trust's formation.

Only the transferor needs to elect to hold over the gain going into the trust, whereas the trustees and the beneficiary must jointly elect to hold over the gain when the asset is transferred out of the trust.

A simple interest in possession trust will usually suffice for the purpose of this technique, which is extremely useful for passing on investment property and other appreciating assets to adult children or other beneficiaries, and we will explore its benefits further in Section 9.5. However, it is subject to a few restrictions.

Settlor-Interested Trusts: In Section 9.2, we saw that a trust is ineffective for IHT planning purposes if the settlor themselves is able to benefit from that trust. However, the definition of a settlor-interested trust for CGT purposes goes much further.

Where the settlor, their spouse, or a dependent minor child of the settlor, can benefit in any way from a trust, that trust is a settlor-interested trust. Holdover relief is not available for transfers into a settlor-interested trust. Gifts of land and buildings, or other appreciating assets, to such trusts may thus give rise to an immediate CGT charge. Additionally, if a trust becomes settlor-interested at any time within six years after the end of the tax year in which holdover relief was previously claimed, the relief is withdrawn and a CGT charge will arise.

Private Residence Relief: Where gains have been held over on the transfer of residential property, neither the trust nor the beneficiary will be entitled to any private residence relief on the property for CGT purposes.

Charge Required: Gains cannot be held over when assets leave the trust within three months of the initial settlement or within three months of an anniversary charge. This is because the hold over relief is only available where an IHT charge arises, so there must be a technical liability for an exit charge; although there is no problem if this works out at nil.

9.5 INVESTMENT PROPERTY TRUSTS

The technique described in the previous section, which allows assets to be passed on free from both IHT and CGT, is well suited to an investment property business. The restriction on private residence relief will often be irrelevant in the case of investment properties. In addition to adult children, the technique works just as well when the trust is used to pass property to an unmarried partner, grandchild, nephew, niece, other relative, or friend. It is not generally possible to use it to pass existing investment property to your own minor children however, as CGT holdover relief would not be available.

Where two settlors jointly transfer property into the trust, two NRBs will be available. A couple could therefore use this technique to transfer up to £650,000 worth of rental property to their adult child free of both CGT and IHT. All they need to do is survive the requisite seven years.

After seven years, the couple will each have a new NRB available and could therefore do it all over again. A couple with a life expectancy of over 21 years could conservatively expect to be able to pass over £3m worth of rental property to their adult children free from tax!

Selling Property to the Trust

The technique can be refined to pass on more valuable property by selling the property to the trust for a low value. The sale price can then be left outstanding as a loan, or possibly a charge against the property.

For IHT purposes, this represents a sale at undervalue and, as we saw in Section 2.1, this means the transfer of value arising is the difference between the sale price and the property's market value. This provides a useful mechanism to tweak the transfer value to ensure it is covered by the settlor's NRB and other available exemptions.

For CGT purposes, it remains possible to hold over the part of the gain that exceeds the actual sale price. Hence, no CGT will arise if the sale price is set low enough. See Section 12.4 for more on partial holdover claims.

However, the main fly in the ointment will be SDLT. Subject to the exceptions set out in Section 8.18, charges will generally arise on residential property transfers where the sale price is £40,000 or more. For non-residential property, charges will apply to any sale price in excess of £150,000.

Example: *Paul and Linda jointly own a residential investment property worth £800,000 and wish to pass it to their adult daughter, Stella. They bought the property for just £200,000 some years ago.*

A direct transfer of the property to Stella would give Paul and Linda a total CGT bill of up to £144,000 (£600,000 x 24%). Fortunately, neither Paul nor Linda has made any other transfers in the last seven years. The couple therefore decide to transfer the property into an interest in possession trust for Stella's benefit in June 2026 and to elect to hold over the gain arising for CGT purposes. However, a straightforward gift would give rise to an immediate IHT charge of £27,600: i.e. 20% on the excess value over £662,000 (see Section 9.1).

Hence, instead of a simple gift, Paul and Linda sell the property to the trust for £138,000, and take a charge over the property for this amount. This reduces the transfer of value to £662,000 (£800,000 – £138,000), meaning no IHT arises on the transfer.

For CGT purposes, the transfer is still deemed to take place at market value but, as the actual consideration received is less than the property's original cost, Paul and Linda can still hold over the gain arising, leaving them with no CGT to pay.

The sale price of £138,000 will give rise to an SDLT charge of £7,160 (see the Taxcafe guide How to Save Property Tax *for details of SDLT rates).*

Two years later (let's say in June 2028), the trust transfers the property to Stella, subject to the outstanding charge for £138,000 due to Paul and Linda. Stella and the trustees jointly elect to hold over the gain arising.

Most of the original transfer of value (£662,000) is covered by Paul and Linda's NRBs, leaving just £12,000 exposed to an exit charge at 1.2% (two years represents eight calendar quarters so the charge works out at 20% x 3/10 x 8/40 = 1.2%). Stella therefore pays an exit charge of £144.

Stella will have to pay a further £7,160 in SDLT, due to the outstanding charge, which is deemed to represent purchase consideration for SDLT purposes. This brings the total tax cost of the exercise up to £14,464 (£7,160 x 2 + £144).

I have assumed Stella already owns another residential property, so the additional 5% SDLT charge applies on both property transfers (see Section 8.18). If not, the exercise would be considerably cheaper, as the SDLT charge on each transfer would be just £260.

The charge over the property can be dealt with in a number of ways. Perhaps, for example, Paul and Linda might waive it at some later stage. This would represent a PET and would escape IHT as long as the couple both survived a further seven years.

Despite the drawback of SDLT, the example demonstrates the huge tax-saving potential of using trusts to pass investment property to adult children or other beneficiaries. In this case, the couple faced an unpleasant choice between an immediate CGT charge of £144,000 and an eventual IHT bill of at least £320,000. By using a trust, they were able to pass a valuable investment property to their daughter almost tax free. In many cases, the same result can be achieved completely tax free.

Existing Mortgages

When undertaking this planning technique, it is important to take any outstanding loans or mortgages already secured against the property into account. Where there is an existing mortgage over a property, it may be difficult to transfer it into the trust subject to that mortgage. It may be necessary for the trust to take out a new mortgage for the requisite amount and use those funds to buy the property. The beneficiary would then either take over that mortgage or, once again, take out a new mortgage to cover the same amount.

Where it is possible for either the trust or, at a later stage, the beneficiary, to take over an existing mortgage, the outstanding balance will represent deemed purchase consideration for tax purposes.

Whatever method is used, the balance on the existing mortgage will have the same effects for tax purposes as the low sale price we looked at in the example: namely, it will reduce the transfer of value for IHT purposes, and will represent deemed consideration for SDLT purposes. As far as CGT is concerned, the gain can still be held over as long as the mortgage balance does not exceed the original cost of the property. In other cases, a partial holdover remains possible, but some CGT liability may arise.

9.6 PASSING ASSETS TAX-FREE TO ADULT CHILDREN AND OTHER BENEFICIARIES

As we saw in Section 8.9, it is possible to leave assets to an immediate post-death interest trust in favour of your spouse free from IHT. This has the tremendous advantage that you can benefit from the spouse exemption and yet still be certain your assets will eventually pass to your children (or other intended beneficiaries). As explained in Section 8.2, this is achieved by bequeathing the remainder to your ultimate intended beneficiaries.

In many cases, you may want the immediate post-death interest to persist for the remainder of your spouse's life. This means IHT will arise on their death. Alternatively, if the immediate post-death interest is terminated during the spouse's lifetime, the assets can be passed to the ultimate beneficiaries as a PET that will become fully exempt seven years later, as long as the spouse survives to the end of this period.

This is a useful variation on the technique explained in Section 6.12, as it provides certainty the assets will pass to your intended beneficiaries. It is important to retain the assets in the trust for at least two years and a day after your death. In fact, it may be wise to keep them in the trust a little longer than this (say three years) as HMRC frequently challenges life interests of only just over two years under the associated operations rules (see Section 11.11).

Generally, it is preferable to avoid any fixed arrangements for the trust's early termination and leave it to your widow/widower to give up their interest voluntarily. This may not always be desirable, however, and we will look at some alternative options in Section 9.7 (plus another below).

Assets must pass to adult children or other beneficiaries absolutely in order to be a PET. Unlike the technique described in Section 9.7 (for minor children), it is not possible to use an 18 to 25 trust to pass assets to young adult children tax-free, as the transfer from the immediate post-death interest would be a chargeable lifetime transfer.

For example, the deceased might leave an interest in possession to their surviving spouse, which terminates on their child's 21st birthday, when the assets pass absolutely to the child. As long as the deceased's spouse survives until the child's 28th birthday (i.e. seven years later), the whole process should take place free from IHT. As this is a more common-sense approach than passing assets to a minor, there is much less risk of an attack under the associated operations rules.

9.7 PASSING ASSETS TAX-FREE TO MINOR CHILDREN

In many cases, where someone dies leaving both a spouse and minor children, they will be content for their assets to remain in their widow/widower's hands until the children reach adulthood. For guidance on how to get those assets into the children's hands tax-free after they reach the age of 18, see Sections 6.7, 6.12 and 9.6.

In some cases, however, the deceased may prefer their assets to pass to their children sooner, particularly if their spouse is unlikely to survive until the children are over 25 (i.e. more than seven years after the children reach adulthood), if they are separated from their spouse, or if their spouse is not their children's other parent.

As explained in Section 8.9, where an immediate post-death interest ends during the beneficiary's lifetime and property passes to a bereaved minor's trust under the terms of the settlor's Will, this will be a PET. This provides the opportunity to pass assets tax-free to minor children.

Example: *James wishes to leave his estate to his five-year-old daughter, Beatrice. If he left the estate directly to Beatrice or a trust for her benefit, the IHT arising would be colossal. Instead, therefore, James leaves just £325,000 (his NRB) to a bereaved minor's trust for Beatrice and everything else to an immediate post-death interest trust in favour of his estranged wife, Heather. Heather's immediate post-death interest lasts for a fixed period of three years, after which the estate passes into Beatrice's bereaved minor's trust.*

The bulk of James's estate initially passes into Heather's immediate post-death interest tax free under the spouse exemption and, three years later it passes into the trust for Beatrice as a PET. As long as Heather outlives James by at least ten years, his entire estate can pass to Beatrice tax free.

Technically, taking the strict letter of the legislation, Heather's interest would only need to last two years and a day, but I made it three years in the example since, as explained in Section 9.6, a shorter period could lead to a risk of challenge under the associated operations rules (see Section 11.11). The legacy to Heather could then be ignored and James's entire estate (except his NRB) could be subject to IHT.

Whether three years is even long enough is not clear, as any fixed period for Heather's interest may make the transfer to Beatrice's trust too much of a certainty for HMRC's liking. Clearly though, the longer Heather's interest lasts, the more robust the arrangement will be (but bear in mind the transfer to Beatrice's trust needs to take place before she is 18: after that, the assets would need to pass to her absolutely, as explained in Section 9.6).

Nonetheless, the associated operations rules are usually only used in blatant cases of tax avoidance, so a more subtle version of this approach is more likely to work, especially where the couple are still living together immediately before the transferor's death.

Immediate post-death interest trusts in favour of a surviving spouse that terminate on their remarriage are commonplace and would not generally be challenged. Other conditions that might terminate the spouse's interest, such as emigration or bankruptcy, might also be acceptable.

The difficulty in a case like James's is he will want some certainty that the estate will pass to the child reasonably soon. A clause terminating the surviving spouse's interest when the child reaches a certain age might be subtle enough for the scheme to work (again, this needs to be before the child reaches 18 if you wish to use a bereaved minor's trust; otherwise the method described in Section 9.6 should be used instead).

Whatever method is used to trigger the termination of the spouse's interest, it must last at least two years and a day, and there will often need to be a risk that it could last a few years more for this strategy to be effective. This could mean the loss of several years' income for the ultimate beneficiary: although if it prevents them losing 40% of the capital, it could be worth it.

The surviving spouse may sometimes be prepared to give up their interest voluntarily. This would not create a bereaved minor's trust, but could result in a bare trust in favour of the child, with similarly beneficial results. The implications of such a voluntary transfer were discussed in Section 6.12.

Note, as the transfer from the immediate post-death interest to the bereaved minor's trust or bare trust is a PET, holdover relief is not available for CGT purposes. Hence, the method may not be entirely tax free, as CGT would arise on the increase in value of any non-cash assets in the trust since the original owner's death.

9.8 PUTTING BUSINESS PROPERTY INTO TRUST

Where a business owner holds more than £2.5m worth of qualifying business or agricultural property (£5m for a widow/widower or married couple), it may be possible to shelter some or all of the excess from IHT by putting it into a trust. For ease, I am just going refer to business property relief (BPR) for the rest of this section, but the same principles apply to assets qualifying for agricultural property relief (APR). I am also going to make the following further assumptions:

- The assets are of a type which, subject to the HPRA (Section 7.8), qualify for 100% relief, and will continue to qualify as the same type of asset throughout the trust's ownership (Sections 7.7 and 7.27). Shares in an unquoted trading company would fit the bill nicely, for example.
- There will be no increase in the NRB or the HPRA, even after 2031
- The transferor has made no previous lifetime transfers (I will ignore the annual exemption for the sake of simplicity, however)

There are, effectively, three aspects to this planning to consider: the transfer into the trust; what happens if the transferor dies within seven years; and anniversary and exit charges. We'll start with the first two.

The transfer into the trust will be a chargeable lifetime transfer. Transfers made before 30th October 2024 will, however, be fully relieved. Transfers made between 30th October 2024 and 5th April 2026 will not give rise to any immediate charge, but will use up the transferor's HPRA if the transferor dies after 5th April 2026, but within seven years of the transfer.

Transfers after 5th April 2026 will use up the transferor's HPRA immediately, with any excess using up their NRB. For example, if £3.5m worth of qualifying assets are transferred into trust, BPR will be restricted to £3m (£2.5m + £1m x 50%), leaving a chargeable lifetime transfer of £500,000. The transferor can then deduct their NRB, leaving £175,000 exposed to an immediate tax charge at the lifetime rate of 20%. There would therefore be an immediate charge of £35,000; or £43,750 if the transferor settles the tax (see Section 4.2). The higher charge could be avoided if the transferor loans the trust the necessary funds to pay the tax.

Further IHT may be payable if the transferor dies within five years. If they die within seven years, the transfer will use up their HPRA, their NRB, and all or part of any TNRB they may be entitled to.

Nonetheless, under the assumptions stipulated above, a business owner could put up to £3.15m worth of qualifying business assets into a trust without facing any immediate tax charge. A transfer worth £3.15m will use up the transferor's HPRA and NRB. A transfer worth less than £3.15m, but more than £2.5m, will use up all of their HPRA, but only some of their NRB; a transfer worth exactly £2.5m will just use up their HPRA, but leave their NRB intact; and a transfer worth less than £2.5m will use part of their HPRA, but leave their NRB intact. If the transferor survives seven years, however, both their HPRA and NRB will effectively be restored to their full value.

(As I said, I am ignoring the annual exemption, but it could potentially add up to £12,000 to all the amounts in the last paragraph.)

Anniversary and Exit Charges

Trusts holding qualifying business property have their own HPRA, which is available to reduce anniversary and exit charges. The trust's HPRA does not affect the IHT payable on the initial transfer into the trust, nor the tax arising if the settlor dies within seven years of the transfer.

Except as noted below, trusts set up after 29th October 2024, or which did not hold any qualifying business property on that date, have a 'maximum allowance cap'. That cap is £2.5m less the value of any qualifying business property previously transferred into another trust by the same settlor. Where qualifying property is transferred into two or more trusts on the same day, the maximum allowance cap is shared in proportion to the value of the property transferred.

The trust's HPRA is then the *lower* of its maximum allowance cap or the total value of qualifying business property transferred into the trust.

Hence, in most cases, the trust's HPRA will be the *lower* of £2.5m or the value of the qualifying business property transferred into it. Where less than £2.5m worth of property has been transferred into the trust, any subsequent growth in value will only attract BPR at 50%. The £2.5m maximum is also reduced by the value of any qualifying business property previously transferred into another trust by the same settlor.

Trusts already holding qualifying business property on 29th October 2024 simply have a HPRA of £2.5m. 18 to 25 trusts have a HPRA of £2.5m per beneficiary for the purpose of exit charges (see Section 8.16).

Naturally, however much HPRA a trust has, it will need to meet all the necessary conditions, including the minimum ownership period (Section 7.17) to claim BPR. Hence the trust will generally need to hold business property for at least two years before passing it to a beneficiary in order to obtain the relief.

Let's take our example of £3.5m worth of qualifying business property transferred into a trust. Let's say the property is worth £5.7m on the anniversary date. We'll also assume the transferor has not set up any other trusts, so the anniversary charge works out like this:

Value of relevant property on anniversary date:	£5,700,000
Less BPR (£2.5m + £3.2m x 50%)	£4,100,000
Cumulative total for hypothetical transfer:	**£1,600,000**
Less NRB	£325,000
Gives:	£1,275,000
IHT at lifetime rate (20%)	**£255,000**
Effective rate on the hypothetical transfer:	
(£255,000 divided by £1.6m)	15.9%*
Rate for anniversary charge: 3/10ths of 15%	4.78%*
IHT Payable: 4.78%* x £1.6m	**£76,500****

* In case you're checking my maths, these have been rounded a bit
** But this is correct

Exit charges will work similarly but will, of course, be reduced by one fortieth for each calendar quarter that has not yet elapsed since the trust was set up, or the previous anniversary charge.

For charges arising in the first ten years, these will be based on the value of the property at the date of transfer, meaning, in our example, these would work out at just £263 (£175,000 x 20% x 3/10 x 1/40) for each complete calendar quarter the assets are held in the trust. (Remember, £175,000 was the amount that was taxed on the original lifetime transfer.) For example, if the assets were transferred to a beneficiary after four years, the exit charge would be £4,200 (£175,000 x 20% x 3/10 x 16/40).

Was the Transfer Worthwhile?

To answer this question, we need to compare the outcome above with what would have happened if the transfer had not taken place. For this purpose, we'll assume the transferor also has at least another £2.5m worth of qualifying business property, and at least £325,000 of other assets. To keep things simple, we'll assume they have no TNRB entitlement. We will also assume they do not leave their estate to their spouse.

If the transferor dies within seven years, the transfer uses up their HPRA and NRB, leaving their other qualifying business property subject to IHT at an effective rate of 20% (see Section 7.8) and their other assets subject to IHT at 40%. BUT the same thing would have happened if they had *not* made the transfer.

So, the only difference is the tax on the transferred assets. Let's compare the outcomes, based on an assumed annual rate of growth for the value of the business assets of 5%. To make this a fair comparison, I will also assume the assets are transferred out of the trust at the date of the transferor's death, although this is not essential.

Death After (Years)	Value on Death	IHT if Transfer	IHT if in Estate	Saving
2	£3,858,750	£72,100	£141,750	£69,650
3	£4,051,688	£59,150	£180,338	£121,188
4	£4,254,272	£46,200	£220,854	£174,654
5	£4,466,985	£40,250	£263,397	£223,147
6	£4,690,335	£41,300	£308,067	£266,767
7	£4,924,851	£42,350	£354,970	£312,620

'IHT if transfer' includes exit charges, the tax on the original chargeable lifetime transfer and, in the case of a death after less than five years, the additional tax arising at that time. Anniversary charges will also arise if the assets remain in the trust for ten years or more (see above).

What the table *does not* include is the *further* savings of £500,000 and £130,000 respectively that will arise if the transferor survives seven years, due to their HPRA and NRB being available on the assets in their estate. Hence, the total saving after seven years in this case would be £942,620 (£312,620 + £500,000 + £130,000).

Planning for Business Owners

Using a trust, a business owner can completely shelter up to £3.15m worth of qualifying business property from IHT. Couples can shelter up to £3.15m each.

Assuming the transferor survives at least seven years, this means the total value of business property a business owner could shelter is up to £8.15m for widows/widowers, or £5.65m for other individuals. These figures apply on a 'per person' basis and take no account of the individual's NRB becoming available again after seven years, nor any TNRB that may be available.

As we saw above, a death after less than seven years may still lead to significant savings, although holding the property in the trust for more than ten years is likely to lead to anniversary charges. Having said that, in most cases, where the trust holds qualifying business property, those anniversary charges will be just 3% of any value in excess of the lower of: £3.15m; or the value of the property when it was put into the trust plus £650,000. These figures should effectively operate on a 'per settlor' basis, but this, like anything else involving trusts warrants professional advice.

Other Taxes

Holdover relief for CGT purposes (Section 12.4) will generally be available on a transfer of qualifying business property. It is, however, vital the trust is not a settlor-interested trust for CGT (see Section 9.4). Neither Stamp Duty nor SDLT should arise on a transfer to a trust, provided there is no consideration for the transfer. See also Sections 8.17 and 12.11, regarding Income Tax and CGT on trust income and gains.

9.9 DISCOUNTED GIFT TRUSTS

A useful type of trust used in IHT planning for many years is the discounted gift trust or reversionary interest trust. These trusts are usually provided by life insurance companies and different companies tend to give their trusts their own names, but the basic principles employed are broadly similar.

A discounted gift trust is actually not a single trust, but a series of mini-trusts. The transferor gives a substantial sum to the discounted gift trust, which is then divided up among the mini-trusts with the following rights:
Mini-Trust 1: income accumulated for one year, after which the original funds in the Trust are returned to the transferor.
Mini-Trust 2: income accumulated for two years, after which the original funds in the Trust are returned to the transferor.
And so on ...

The accumulated income in the trusts is held for the benefit of the transferor's eventual beneficiaries. The effect of this is the transferor continues to receive an 'income' stream from their investment, despite the fact much of it is no longer in their estate for IHT purposes. The statistical value of the reversionary interests in the mini-trusts still has to be included in the transferor's estate, but this is less than the original investment and steadily reduces over time.

Actually, what the transferor is receiving is not, strictly speaking, income at all, but a return of capital. This has the added advantage of being free from Income Tax too!

The companies providing these investments were quick to adapt to the changes made in 2006 and continue to provide discounted gift trust schemes using absolute trusts. This reduces the flexibility of the scheme but prevents a chargeable lifetime transfer on the initial investment.

Another form of discounted gift trust using relevant property trusts can also be set up but this will give rise to a chargeable lifetime transfer when the initial investment is made. Nevertheless, the structure may work satisfactorily for investments that do not exceed the NRB.

9.10 LOAN TRUSTS

Another popular scheme provided by many life insurance companies is the loan trust. In essence, the transferor does not make any transfer of value to the trust, but simply lends funds to it. As there is no transfer of value, there can be no IHT charge.

Funds invested within the trust will (one hopes) experience capital growth, but the beauty of this scheme is that the capital growth is outside the transferor's estate. All the transferor is due is a repayment of the original loan and hence this is the only value remaining in their estate.

The loan can be interest-free if desired (see Section 2.11) and the transferor may progressively withdraw their original loan capital. This capital can be spent on the transferor's living expenses, thus gradually removing its value from their estate. Alternatively, the transferor could gift the benefit of the loan to another individual as a PET (Section 4.3).

The capital growth and accumulated income within the trust belongs to the beneficiaries and is thus also kept out of the transferor's estate.

A loan trust may be set up as an absolute trust in order to avoid any danger of becoming a relevant property trust. An absolute loan trust would be exempt from anniversary or exit charges. Otherwise, as a relevant property trust, there would be some risk of anniversary and exit charges, but these could generally be avoided by ensuring the trust assets are distributed before the trust's net value exceeds the NRB (see Section 9.3 for further guidance on avoiding anniversary and exit charges).

Chapter 10

Inherited Pension Funds

10.1 PARADISE LOST

Pensions are, of course, predominantly meant to be used for retirement planning. While that is an important area of personal financial planning, and the main reason for most people to make pension contributions, what we are looking at in this chapter is *inherited* pension funds. For a detailed examination of the significant *lifetime* benefits of pensions, as well as more information regarding pensions generally, see the Taxcafe guide *Pension Magic*.

For some years prior to the October 2024 Budget, the UK pensions regime had become a steadily more attractive vehicle for IHT planning. Sadly, all that was taken away in one fell swoop (or should I say 'one foul swoop') as Labour Chancellor, Rachel Reeves, announced that, from 6th April 2027, pension funds will be subject to IHT.

But pension funds, like the family home, remain an important asset many people have, and they are still a valuable, tax-efficient form of investment. So, in this chapter, we are going to look at how they will be treated after 5th April 2027 and what can be done to prevent the Government taking up to 40% of your hard-earned pension savings in IHT.

To save some space, we are not going to cover the huge IHT saving potential of pension savings in the event of a death before 6th April 2027 in much detail. There is, however, a brief summary of how pension savings can be used for IHT planning by someone with a short life expectancy in Section 10.15. For a more detailed examination of the treatment of pension savings on a death before 6th April 2027, see the twentieth edition of this guide.

Dying after 5th April 2027 with pension savings may now represent a triple tragedy: the death itself, IHT on the pension fund, and possibly also Income Tax on the payments to beneficiaries. Yes: unbelievably, in many cases, from 6th April 2027, the Government intends to subject inherited pension funds to ***both IHT and Income Tax!***

While this guide is primarily focussed on IHT, it also has a broader remit to cover all aspects of succession planning, especially tax issues. Hence, in this chapter, we will also be covering the Income Tax treatment of inherited pensions, as this is equally vital in protecting your family or other beneficiaries from HM Treasury's greed.

In some cases, inherited pension funds can be paid out free from Income Tax, although this depends on a number of factors, including the 'lump sum and death benefit allowance' (as this is rather a mouthful, I will call it the LSDBA from now on). We will look at the factors involved in determining the Income Tax treatment of death benefits in Section 10.6 and how the LSDBA is calculated, and when it does and does not matter, in Section 10.7.

Some Terminology
In this chapter, I will use the term 'death benefits' to refer to any pension savings or other benefits payable to, or for the benefit of, a pension scheme member's beneficiaries after their death. We will take a closer look at what exactly may comprise these death benefits in Section 10.5.

Uncrystallised funds mean pension funds that remain completely untouched. A fund is typically crystallised when a member takes any benefit from it. As far as the taxation of death benefits is concerned, this is only relevant when a scheme member dies before the age of 75 and death benefits are paid as a lump sum.

In some cases, pension scheme trustees effectively fill the same role as a pension scheme administrator but, for the rest of this chapter, I will just refer to scheme administrators.

Dependants are defined in Section 10.4. Any other reference to dependants in this chapter has the same meaning.

Chapter Scope
Throughout this chapter, unless stated to the contrary, I will assume pension scheme members and their beneficiaries are UK resident. Furthermore, I will not be considering overseas pensions or transfers to or from such pensions.

Some individuals have transitional protections or enhancements, which effectively gave them a higher lifetime allowance under the old regime and may also give them a higher LSDBA under the new regime. I will not be taking such higher allowances into account in this chapter, but it is important to bear them in mind in practice where they apply.

As stated above, in this edition of the guide (except Section 10.15), unless stated to the contrary, I will only be looking at the IHT treatment of inherited pensions on a death after 5th April 2027. As far as Income Tax is concerned, we will be looking at the treatment of death benefits paid after 5th April 2024.

10.2 PENSIONS AND INHERITANCE TAX (FROM APRIL 2027)

Pension savings held by an individual dying after 5th April 2027 will fall within the scope of IHT: just like any other asset. However, this dreadful act of treachery does not mean there will be a 40% IHT charge on all pension savings, as the NRB, TNRB (where applicable), spouse exemption, and other exemptions covered in Section 3.5, will all apply, just as for any other assets.

Example Version 1: *Reg dies in May 2027. His only assets are a pension fund of £840,000, his house worth £370,000, and a holiday cottage worth £190,000. He leaves everything to his nephew, Elton, who is also his executor. Reg is a widower with a full TNRB entitlement, but cannot claim the RNRB as he has not left his house to direct descendants.*

Reg's estate totals £1.4m. Deducting his NRB/TNRB of £650,000 leaves £750,000, which is subject to IHT at 40%: £300,000.

Who Pays the Tax?

Elton has three options:

i) He can pay all the IHT arising from the general assets of the estate in his capacity as executor (this may necessitate a sale of Reg's house in this case)

ii) He can pay the proportion relating to the pension fund in his personal capacity, as beneficiary of that fund, and the remainder from the general assets of the estate

iii) He can direct the pension scheme administrator to pay the proportion relating to the pension fund (Elton will still have to pay the remainder from the general assets of the estate)

In this example, Elton is both the executor and the pension fund beneficiary. This will not always be the case, so it may sometimes be a different person paying part of the tax under option (ii).

Many people are likely to follow option (iii), as the pension fund will often be the only significant source of liquid funds available. For this purpose, the proportion of the IHT bill relating to the pension fund is calculated by allocating the NRB/TNRB between the pension fund and the general estate on a pro rata basis, as follows:

Pension fund: £650,000 x £840,000/£1.4m =	*£390,000*
General estate: £650,000 x £560,000/£1.4m =	*£260,000*

Deducting the pension fund's share of Reg's NRB/TNRB leaves £450,000 of the fund exposed to IHT at 40%. The fund's share of Reg's IHT bill is thus £180,000, leaving Elton to pay £120,000 from the general assets of Reg's estate.

In this case, after payment of the IHT, there is a net sum of £660,000 remaining in the pension fund. That sum, after payment of IHT, can be paid out to beneficiaries as a death benefit (subject to the further points below).

While the pension fund is footing part of the bill, Elton is still having to find £120,000 to pay the rest of Reg's IHT liability. In this context, it's worth reflecting that, if Reg had died before 6th April 2027, Elton generally wouldn't have had any IHT liability at all!

The only cash available is the pension fund but, if Reg died aged 75 or more, getting that cash is likely to have a considerable Income Tax cost (Sections 10.6 to 10.8). For example, if Elton already has taxable income of £60,000 per year (e.g. a salary), to get a net sum of £120,000 out of the pension fund will mean having to withdraw £221,402 (after paying Income Tax of £101,402, Elton will be left with the net sum he needs).

So, in this case, by subjecting pension savings to IHT, the Government will have wiped out £401,402 (£180,000 + £221,402), or ***almost half*** of Reg's pension fund, leaving just £438,598.

Where the deceased had more than one pension scheme, the NRB/TNRB is further divided. For instance, if Reg had one pension fund of £560,000 and another of £280,000 (instead of a single fund of £840,000), the first scheme would get £260,000 of his NRB/TNRB and the second would get £130,000.

Alternative Ways to Pay

If Elton follows either option (i) or (ii), the whole £840,000 will remain in the pension fund (at least to begin with).

The problem with this is that, if Reg died aged 75 or more, withdrawals from the pension fund will be subject to Income Tax. Fortunately, however, for deaths after 5th April 2027, there will be an exemption from Income Tax on withdrawals equal to the amount of IHT suffered on the fund where that IHT has been paid from the general assets of the estate, or by the beneficiary of the pension fund death benefit.

Hence, in our example, if Elton has paid the whole IHT bill from the general assets of the estate, or from his own pocket, the first £180,000 he withdraws from Reg's pension fund will be exempt from Income Tax.

So, whatever payment option Elton follows for IHT purposes, the amount of the fund exposed to Income Tax (assuming Reg was over 75) is always the same: in this case, £660,000. Unless stated to the contrary, it is this sum (the net sum remaining after deducting the IHT liability arising on the fund) we are talking about when we discuss the Income Tax treatment of death benefits in the rest of this chapter (except Section 10.15).

Withholding Notices

Where the deceased's personal representatives (executors, etc: see Section 2.3) have reason to believe IHT will be due on a pension fund, they can give notice of this to the pension scheme administrator. While this notice is in effect, the scheme administrator is barred from paying out more than 50% of any taxable beneficiary's entitlement to death benefits. The notice ceases to have effect on the earliest of:

- Its withdrawal by the personal representatives
- Payment of all the IHT due on the pension fund (including any interest arising)
- Fifteen months after the end of the month of the deceased's death

For this purpose, a taxable beneficiary is anyone other than the deceased's spouse, a charity, or any of the other exempt bodies listed in Section 3.5. Hence the full death benefits can be paid to a spouse, charity, etc, regardless of any withholding notice.

The Spouse Exemption and Pensions

As stated above, the spouse exemption will apply to pension funds in the same way as other assets. That's simple enough when everything is left to the spouse, but a little more complicated when only part of the estate is left to them.

Example Version 2: *Let's take the same facts as Version 1 above, except that Reg has remarried and leaves a quarter of his pension fund (£210,000) plus his holiday cottage, worth £190,000, to his spouse.*

With a total of £400,000 left to his spouse, Reg's chargeable estate is reduced to £1m, made up of the rest of his pension fund (£630,000) and his house (£370,000). His combined NRB and TNRB of £650,000 is allocated as follows:

Pension fund: £650,000 x £630,000/£1m = *£409,500*
General estate: £650,000 x £370,000/£1m = *£240,500*

Deducting the pension fund's share of Reg's NRB/TNRB leaves £220,500 (£630,000 – £409,500) of the fund exposed to IHT at 40%. If Elton follows option (iii) above, the scheme administrator will have to pay IHT of £88,200, leaving £751,800 (£840,000 – £88,200) in the fund.

Deducting the remaining £240,500 of Reg's NRB/TNRB from his general estate leaves £129,500 exposed to IHT at 40%. Elton will therefore be responsible for paying a further sum of £51,800 (if he pays this as beneficiary, rather than in his capacity as executor, this will avoid grossing up: Section 2.8).

In this version, there is £751,800 remaining in the pension fund after payment of IHT. The amount allocated to Reg's spouse will remain £210,000, with £541,800 available to pay out as death benefits to his other beneficiaries. In other words, the spouse does not suffer IHT on their share of the pension fund.

The Residence Nil Rate Band and Pensions

The RNRB cannot be allocated to a pension fund, but it may affect how much of the general estate is chargeable to IHT.

Example Version 3: *We'll go back to the same facts as Version 1, except Elton is Reg's son. This means Reg's RNRB can be deducted from the value of his house. Let's say Reg is entitled to the maximum RNRB of £350,000. This reduces his general estate to £210,000, meaning his NRB/TNRB is allocated as follows:*

Pension fund: £650,000 x £840,000/£1.05m = *£520,000*
General estate: £650,000 x £210,000/£1.05m = *£130,000*

Under option (iii), the pension scheme administrator will have to pay IHT of £128,000 (£840,000 – £520,000 = £320,000 x 40%). Elton will have to pay £32,000 (£210,000 – £130,000 = £80,000 x 40%).

If we compare this with Version 1, we can see the RNRB has saved £140,000 overall, but the benefit has not all flowed to Elton: he has only saved £88,000 while, despite not being able to claim the RNRB directly, the pension fund has saved £52,000.

This outcome could be bad news because, if Reg died aged 75 or more, part of the pension fund's saving of £52,000 will be lost in Income Tax when death benefits are paid out.

Consequences of the Nil Rate Band Allocation Method

As we have seen, the method for allocating the deceased's NRB/TNRB may have severe cashflow consequences, leading to a greater overall tax burden than we might otherwise have expected when a pension scheme member dies aged 75 or more.

If we take Example Version 1, for instance, we saw how almost half of a pension fund was absorbed in tax, simply in order to fund the IHT arising; while, in Version 3, a beneficiary missed out on £52,000 worth of relief they should have been entitled to.

One way a married person might improve their position is by changing which assets they leave to their spouse.

In Example Version 2, Elton had to pay £51,800 in IHT. If we again say his only other income is a salary of £60,000, he would need to withdraw £97,402 from the pension fund in order to pay this, and will suffer Income Tax of £45,602 in the process. That will leave just £654,398 (£751,800 – £97,402) in the fund. But let's see if Reg could have done things better.

Example Version 4: *Let's take the same facts as Version 2, except that Reg leaves his house, worth £370,000, to his spouse, plus a further sum of £30,000 charged against the cottage which, otherwise, he leaves to his nephew, Elton. Reg also leaves all his pension savings to Elton.*

As before, £400,000 has been left to his spouse, so Reg's chargeable estate is again reduced to £1m. But, this time, it is made up of his pension fund, £840,000, and a cottage worth £160,000 (net of the charge against it). His combined NRB and TNRB of £650,000 is therefore allocated as follows:

Pension fund: £650,000 x £840,000/£1m =	*£546,000*
General estate: £650,000 x £200,000/£1m =	*£104,000*

Deducting the pension fund's share of Reg's NRB/TNRB leaves £294,000 (£840,000 – £546,000) of the fund exposed to IHT at 40%. Under option (iii), the scheme administrator will therefore have to pay IHT of £117,600, leaving £722,400 (£840,000 – £117,600) in the fund.

Deducting the remaining £104,000 of Reg's NRB/TNRB from his general estate leaves £56,000 exposed to IHT at 40%. Elton will therefore be responsible for paying a further sum of just £22,400.

This time, Elton will only need to withdraw £37,333 from the pension fund to leave him with the £22,400 he needs to settle his IHT bill. He suffers Income Tax of just £14,933, a saving of £30,669 (£45,602 – £14,933). This saving is reflected in the fact there will now be £685,067 (£722,400 – £37,333) remaining in the pension fund, £30,669 more than before.

This latest version of the example shows it is possible to make significant Income Tax savings by altering how you allocate your estate between your exempt and non-exempt beneficiaries, typically your spouse and your heirs.

There will, of course, be many other factors to consider, including the fact the issue will not generally arise if you die before the age of 75 and, if you die later, the extra funds left in your pension will probably be subject to Income Tax at some point. However, taking Elton as an example, there's an extra £30,669 in the pension fund enjoying tax-free investment growth in the meantime and, if he can wait until he is a basic rate taxpayer before he takes this money out, he will only suffer £6,134 in Income Tax, leaving a permanent net saving of £24,535.

Note that, if you want your beneficiaries to enjoy this kind of saving, you will have to change your pension scheme nomination (Section 10.4) during your lifetime: this kind of planning cannot usually be done via a deed of variation after you die (your beneficiaries can change who gets your general estate, but not who gets your pension).

Paying the Tax in Instalments

In Example Version 1, Elton had to stump up £120,000 in IHT and, as there was no other cash available, he had to raid Reg's pension fund, which cost a further £101,402 in Income Tax. If Reg had died at a different time of year, Elton may have been able to spread his pension withdrawals over two tax years. That could have saved up to £3,636 in Income Tax in this scenario, so it helps a little.

Another option would be to look at paying the IHT by instalments (see Section 2.7). However, this will have a substantial interest cost and still means the beneficiary in a case like this has to make their pension scheme withdrawals in a fixed timeframe rather than being able to wait until they are paying Income Tax at a lower rate. For example, if Elton elected to pay his IHT bill of £120,000 in instalments, the total cost (at the current interest rate of 7.75%) would increase to £161,850. If Elton remains on an annual salary of £60,000 throughout this period, this will mean having to withdraw a total of £269,750 from the pension fund, suffering Income Tax of £107,900.

Taking all the costs into account, it's actually £48,348 ***worse*** than paying the IHT in one go.

A better alternative for Elton may be to sell one of Reg's properties and use the proceeds to pay the IHT. In fact, if he is not the beneficiary of Reg's pension fund, he may have no other choice. And at least there shouldn't be much CGT to worry about (see Section 12.2).

10.3 EXEMPTIONS FROM INHERITANCE TAX

Funds that can *only* be used to provide dependant's scheme pensions (see Section 10.5) will remain exempt from IHT after 5th April 2027. Trivial commutation lump sums paid from funds that could otherwise only be used to provide a dependant's scheme pension will also remain exempt.

A dependant's or nominee's annuity purchased together with a member's annuity will remain exempt from IHT.

Life policies that are part of a pension scheme package will continue to be treated separately, as they are now: see Section 11.8. This includes death benefits under an occupational pension scheme that are only payable when the member is still in employment at the time of their death.

Note that exemption from IHT does not mean exemption from Income Tax: in fact, in some cases, it is quite the reverse.

10.4 WHO INHERITS THE PENSION?

The pension scheme administrator usually has discretion over who to pay death benefits to. Nonetheless, in the vast majority of cases, the scheme administrator will follow the member's wishes: although, at present, these are not generally legally binding. This convention may change after 5th April 2027, since its current benefit of keeping the death benefits outside the member's estate for IHT purposes will no longer apply. For the time being, however, let's look at what usually happens at present.

Nominations

The scheme administrator cannot follow the member's wishes unless they have a record of them. This is done through an expression of wish form, sometimes called a letter of wishes or a nomination form. Whatever it is called, it is crucial the scheme member nominates who they would like their death benefits paid to. Nominations can be changed at any time during the scheme member's lifetime and it is important to keep them up to date. For example, you might reach a point where you would like your death benefits to go to your grandchildren instead of your children: but you will need to tell the scheme administrator!

You can nominate anyone you like to receive your death benefits, but this is where the scheme administrator might occasionally choose not to follow your wishes. For example, if a member died leaving an impoverished widow and two minor children with no other means of support, but nominated their secretary to receive their death benefits, the scheme administrator might perhaps not follow their wishes.

On the other hand, in the absence of any dependants, the scheme administrator is likely to follow your wishes, no matter who you nominate.

It is possible to nominate a charity or a trust to receive your death benefits. In these cases, the death benefit can only be paid out as a lump sum. We will look at lump sum death benefits received by trusts in Section 10.14. Death benefits paid to a UK charity will be exempt from IHT (Section 3.5).

In the absence of a valid written nomination, the scheme administrator may only be able to pay the full range of death benefits available under the scheme to your dependants. A member's dependants are usually their spouse, children under the age of 23, and disabled children of any age. Unmarried partners who were genuinely financially dependent on the member may also be classed as dependants.

The key point is that your adult children are not usually your dependants and hence, if you wish your death benefits to go to them, it is advisable to nominate them. If you have not made a valid nomination, the scheme administrator may only be able to pay death benefits to a non-dependant beneficiary as a lump sum and this could have dire Income Tax consequences (see Section 10.8).

In particular, non-dependant beneficiaries that you have not formally nominated in writing are unable to benefit from inherited drawdown (see Sections 10.5 and 10.10) if you are survived by any dependants or other nominees (some scheme administrators may not allow inherited drawdown for an unnominated beneficiary even when there are no such survivors).

As well as nominating your beneficiaries, it may also be wise to specify you would like them to have the option to take inherited drawdown (assuming the scheme allows it). Where your intended beneficiaries are adult children or other non-dependants, and you may also be survived by one or more dependants, it will also be sensible to explain (in your written expression of wish) why you do not wish your death benefits to go to your dependants (e.g. because they are already sufficiently well provided for by other means).

Finally, at the risk of labouring the point, I will repeat one last time: it is crucial to nominate your intended beneficiaries and to keep your nomination up to date throughout your lifetime. In writing!

10.5 WHAT DO THEY INHERIT?

The death benefits passing to your beneficiaries depend on what type of pension scheme you are in and on the terms of that particular scheme. Death benefits passing to your spouse will be exempt from IHT. Certain other death benefits, as noted in Section 10.3, will also remain exempt from IHT. Otherwise, unless stated to the contrary, whatever form the death benefits take, where the scheme member dies after 5th April 2027, the death benefits passing to beneficiaries will be subject to IHT.

Defined Benefit Schemes

Some occupational pension schemes are defined benefit schemes, often known as final salary schemes. Survivor's pensions may sometimes be paid to a dependant and are subject to Income Tax (see Section 10.8). These may be exempt from IHT, but this will be subject to the terms of the scheme. If paid to your surviving spouse, they will of course be exempt from IHT anyway.

Lump sums up to £30,000 paid as a 'trivial commutation' will be subject to Income Tax. These will also be subject to IHT from 6th April 2027, unless paid to your spouse or covered by the exemption in Section 10.3.

Where the pension includes life cover (generally in respect of death in service), a lump sum death benefit may be paid out. This does not fall within the pension regime for tax purposes and will generally be exempt from IHT (see Sections 10.3 and 11.8).

A pension protection lump sum may also be payable in some schemes. Lump sum death benefits are not usually subject to Income Tax but may be under some circumstances, as detailed in Section 10.6.

Defined Contribution Schemes
Most pension schemes are now defined contribution schemes, including most private pensions, self-invested personal pensions (SIPPs), and many modern occupational schemes, including those created under auto-enrolment.

What kind of death benefits may be payable depends on the terms of the scheme and on whether the member has purchased an annuity. Purchasing an annuity during your lifetime will generally limit any death benefit to continuing annuity payments for the remainder of any guarantee period, or survivor's payments where a joint life annuity has been purchased.

The greatest death benefits, of course, arise where the pension fund has either not been touched at all, or has been put into drawdown. In these circumstances, the entire fund remaining at the date of the member's death is available as a death benefit: after payment of any IHT arising!

Subject to the terms of the scheme, the member's beneficiaries may take death benefits as:

- A lump sum
- Inherited drawdown
- An annuity
- A dependant's scheme pension

It is critical to be aware that not all pension schemes allow drawdown and very few allow a dependant's scheme pension. In many cases, this leaves the beneficiary with the choice of a lump sum or an annuity. Annuities are not always suitable, especially if the beneficiary is in need of funds now. Hence, the only practical choice in some cases may be to take a lump sum. Furthermore, death benefits paid to a charity or a trust (see Section 10.14) must be paid as a lump sum, and most schemes will not permit a non-UK resident beneficiary to take inherited drawdown.

Funds that can only be used for paying dependant's scheme pensions will usually be exempt from IHT. Death benefits passing to your spouse or a UK charity will also be exempt. Otherwise, subject to the available exemptions and reliefs (see Sections 10.2 and 10.3), funds used to provide any other death benefits will suffer IHT. Whether the death benefits are subject to Income Tax depends on a number of factors we will look at in Sections 10.6 and 10.7.

10.6 DEATH BENEFITS AND INCOME TAX

In this section, we will look at which death benefits are subject to Income Tax. In Section 10.8 we will look at the consequences if they are. The good news is many of them aren't and, in this section and the next, I will refer to these as 'tax free'. Please be aware that 'tax free' in this context means not subject to Income Tax and the funds used to pay these death benefits may suffer IHT.

As explained in Section 10.2, where IHT arises on a fund, it may either be paid out of the fund, out of the general assets of the deceased's estate, or by the fund beneficiaries. In each case, only the net sum after deduction of the IHT arising is potentially subject to Income Tax. Hence, for the rest of this chapter, unless stated to the contrary, any reference to Income Tax being payable on a death benefit is only in respect of the net sum after deducting any IHT liability arising.

The Income Tax position sometimes depends on the member's available LSDBA, which will often, but not always, be £1,073,100. Those who have taken the maximum tax-free cash lump sum of £268,275 after 5th April 2020 will generally have a LSDBA of £804,825 available. But, in many cases, the position will be different, so we will take a closer look at how the LSDBA is calculated in Section 10.7.

The Income Tax status of a death benefit also often depends on a payment, designation, or other action, being made within two years. In this context, and hence for the rest of this section (unless stated to the contrary) this means within two years of when the scheme administrator became aware, or might reasonably have been expected to be aware, of the member's death.

The relevant date for the purposes of both the two-year time limit and when any critical action is deemed to have occurred is as follows:

- Lump sums: date of payment
- Inherited drawdown: designation of the drawdown fund
- Annuities: date beneficiary becomes entitled

Lump Sum Death Benefits

Lump sum death benefits are subject to Income Tax in the hands of individual beneficiaries where the scheme member died aged 75 or more, or the death benefit is paid out after more than two years.

Where the scheme member died before age 75, a lump sum death benefit is generally tax free provided it is paid within two years and is covered by the member's available LSDBA (Section 10.7).

Where lump sum death benefits paid within two years of the death of a scheme member under age 75 exceed the member's available LSDBA, the excess is subject to Income Tax in the hands of the beneficiaries. This does not apply to: lump sum death benefits taken from a fund crystallised before 6th April 2024; winding up lump sum payments of no more than £18,000; or small pot lump sum payments of no more than £10,000. In these cases, any lump sum death benefit paid within two years of the death of a scheme member under the age of 75 is tax free.

Trivial commutation lump sum death benefits are generally subject to Income Tax and sit outside the LSDBA system (see Sections 10.5 and 10.7). Other lump sum death benefits payable under a defined benefit scheme on the death of a scheme member under the age of 75 will generally represent uncrystallised funds subject to the LSDBA. In these cases, any excess can sometimes be used to pay a survivor's pension to a dependant instead.

Charity lump sum death benefits are usually tax free, regardless of how old the scheme member was. However, there are some detailed rules that need to be observed and the member generally needs to have nominated the charity and have no surviving dependants. For the treatment of lump sum death benefits paid to a trust, see Section 10.14.

Inherited Drawdown

Where inherited drawdown is available, it may be available on both the original scheme member's death and again on the subsequent death of any later owner of the fund. We will look into the potential benefits of this in succession planning in Section 10.10.

Drawdown payments are subject to Income Tax when: the previous owner of the fund died aged 75 or more; uncrystallised funds are designated for drawdown after more than two years; or payments commenced before 6th April 2015.

Subject to the above points, drawdown payments are generally tax free where the previous owner of the fund died before age 75. The LSDBA does not apply to inherited drawdown, meaning unlimited funds could potentially be passed to beneficiaries tax free in the event of an early death: we will take a closer look at the benefits of this in Section 10.10.

An important point to note is that the Income Tax status of the funds can change, as it usually depends on the age of the previous owner. For example, a scheme member might die aged 80, leaving their son with an inherited drawdown that will be subject to Income Tax. However, the son might later die aged 74 and leave the inherited drawdown to his daughter, who can then receive payments tax free.

Annuities and Dependant's Scheme Pensions

Annuities paid to beneficiaries as death benefits are subject to broadly the same rules for Income Tax purposes as payments from an inherited drawdown (except in the case of a dependant's scheme pension). Once again, the LSDBA does not apply. As noted above, the critical date for tax purposes is the date the beneficiary first becomes entitled to the annuity.

Dependant's scheme pensions are rare but are subject to Income Tax, even when the original scheme member died under the age of 75.

10.7 THE LUMP SUM AND DEATH BENEFIT ALLOWANCE

Before you wade through all the technical gobbledegook in this section, it's worth remembering the LSDBA is only relevant where *lump sum* death benefits are paid on the death of a scheme member before age 75.

Furthermore, the LSDBA does not apply to death benefits paid out of funds crystallised before 6th April 2024. Hence, if you have just one pension scheme, had already taken your tax-free lump sum before 6th April 2024, have not made, and do not intend to make, any further pension contributions, you can safely ignore the rest of this section. You can also safely ignore the rest of this section if you are already over 75.

You can probably safely ignore the rest of this section if your scheme allows inherited drawdown AND all your beneficiaries are UK resident individuals who you have validly nominated, and you've kept your nominations up to date (Section 10.4). However, there does remain the risk that a lump sum death benefit might have to be paid, such as if one of your beneficiaries becomes non-UK resident, or your beneficiaries change before you have chance to change your nomination (e.g. in the tragic event that one of your children pre-deceases you shortly before your own death and your grandchildren become your beneficiaries in their place).

The Basic Idea

The basic idea is that, on death, each individual's LSDBA is £1,073,100 ***less*** any tax-free lump sums they have taken from their pension savings during their lifetime. In many cases, it will be as simple as that. In fact, it is safe to say if you've never touched your pension savings in any way and you have no lifetime allowance protections or enhancements, your LSDBA is £1,073,100 and you can safely ignore the rest of this section.

(By the way, if you recognise that bizarre amount of £1,073,100, yes, it's the same amount as the old lifetime allowance. However, while it's the same amount, the LSDBA does not work the same way!)

But the Government couldn't keep things simple if you paid them. Wait a minute, we *do* pay them! (They still can't keep things simple though.)

In practice, it is first necessary to calculate your LSDBA at the commencement of the new regime on 6th April 2024. Most tax-free lump sums paid during the rest of your lifetime after 5th April 2024 will then be deducted from your LSDBA at commencement, although there are a few exceptions, which we will look at later. Once all relevant lifetime tax-free lump sums have been deducted, what is left will be the LSDBA available to cover lump sum death benefits paid in the event of death before the age of 75. Once you reach 75, the LSDBA becomes irrelevant.

The Standard Calculation

The standard calculation is that your LSDBA at the commencement of the new pensions regime on 6th April 2024 is £1,073,100 less 25% times the percentage of your lifetime allowance you have used up to that point times £1,073,100.

A tax-free lump sum taken between 6th April 2006 and 5th April 2024 generally used up a proportion of the lifetime allowance equal to four times the amount of the tax-free lump sum.

Example Version 1: *In 2022, Ed took a tax-free lump sum of £160,965 out of his pension scheme. This used £643,860 (£160,965 x 4), or 60% of his lifetime allowance (which was £1,073,100 at the time). His LSDBA is therefore reduced by: £1,073,100 x 60% x 25% = £160,965.*

This leaves Ed with a LSDBA of £912,135 (£1,073,100 – £160,965) at commencement. His LSDBA will generally be further reduced by any other tax-free lumps sums he takes later (e.g. from a different pension scheme).

As we can readily see, in Ed's case, the reduction in his LSDBA is equal to the tax-free lump sum he has taken. It will remain this simple for many people. However, there are some important exceptions, including individuals who took tax-free lump sums out of their pension savings before 6th April 2020. For those who took tax-free lump sums before 6th April 2016, this may produce a more beneficial result, but for those who took tax-free lump sums between 6th April 2016 and 5th April 2020, the standard calculation produces an unfair result.

Example Version 2: *Ed took a tax-free lump sum of £160,965 in 2013 when the lifetime allowance was £1.5m. This used £643,860 (£160,965 x 4) of his lifetime allowance, but this only amounted to 42.924%. His LSDBA is therefore reduced by: £1,073,100 x 42.924% x 25% = £115,154. This leaves Ed with a LSDBA of £957,946 (£1,073,100 – £115,154) at commencement.*

While this is an odd result, it's good news for Ed's family, as his LSDBA at commencement is £45,811 more than under Version 1 above. This could save his family £18,324 (at 40%) or more in Income Tax if lump sum death benefits are paid.

Example Version 3: *Ed took a tax-free lump sum of £160,965 in 2017 when the lifetime allowance was £1m. This used £643,860 (£160,965 x 4) of his lifetime allowance, which amounted to 64.386%. His LSDBA is therefore reduced by: £1,073,100 x 64.386% x 25% = £172,732. This leaves Ed with a LSDBA of £900,368 (£1,073,100 – £172,732) at commencement.*

This could be bad news for Ed's family, as his LSDBA at commencement has unfairly been reduced by £11,767 more than the tax-free cash he actually took. This could cost his family £4,707 (at 40%) or more in extra Income Tax if lump sum death benefits are paid on his death before the age of 75. Fortunately, an alternative method is available to establish the LSDBA in a case like this.

The Alternative Calculation

Where the standard calculation produces an unfair result, the individual (or their personal representatives) can apply for a transitional tax-free amount certificate (we'll call it a TTFAC from now on).

The TTFAC resets the LSDBA at commencement in line with the basic idea discussed above: namely £1,073,100 less any tax-free lump sums the individual has taken. A TTFAC can be obtained by applying to the scheme administrator of any registered pension scheme the individual is a member of. The application must be made before any tax-free cash or lump sum death benefits have been taken after 5th April 2024 from any pension schemes the individual is a member of (subject to a few exceptions as noted below). Once the application is made, the TTFAC is binding and supersedes the standard calculation: so it's important to be sure the TTFAC will be beneficial.

Generally speaking, a TTFAC will be beneficial for anyone who took tax-free cash out of a pension scheme between 6th April 2016 and 5th April 2020. For instance, under Version 3 of the example, Ed could restore his LSDBA to the £912,135 we saw in Version 1 by applying for a TTFAC. In practice, however, it is important to take any other pension withdrawals made earlier into account before applying for a TTFAC.

Those who took tax-free lump sums between 6th April 2006 and 5th April 2016 should *not* generally apply for a TTFAC as it would usually be disadvantageous: they will mostly be better off sticking with the standard calculation. A TTFAC will not generally make any difference to those who only took tax-free lump sums for the first time after 5th April 2020.

A TTFAC is not available to those with a pension in payment before 6th April 2006 and who did not crystallise any other pension savings at a later date but before 6th April 2024. In these cases, an amount equal to 25 times their annual pension must be deducted from the LSDBA.

Apart from those who took a tax-free lump sum between 6th April 2016 and 5th April 2020, there are a few others who may benefit from applying for a TTFAC, including those who:

- Took less tax-free cash than they were entitled to because they were in a scheme that had generous annuity rates
- Were in a defined benefit scheme but did not commute pension for their full tax-free entitlement
- Took benefits from a scheme subject to pension sharing (e.g. divorcees)
- Took a serious ill-health lump sum before 6th April 2024

Exceptions

Some lump sums are not deducted from the LSDBA, and nor do they prevent a subsequent application for a TTFAC being made. The main exceptions to be aware of are: lump sum death benefits taken from a fund crystallised before 6th April 2024; charity lump sum death benefits (where there are no dependants and the member had nominated the charity); trivial commutation lump sums; winding up lump sum payments of up to £18,000; and small pot lump sum payments of up to £10,000. See Section 10.6 regarding the Income Tax treatment of these lump sums when taken as a death benefit.

10.8 PAYMENTS SUBJECT TO INCOME TAX

In this section, we are going to look at *Income Tax* arising on death benefits paid to beneficiaries; we are not looking at IHT. We'll look at the combined impact of both taxes later, in Section 10.9. Remember, however, where the scheme member dies after 5th April 2027, it is only the net death benefits after deduction of the IHT liability arising that are subject to Income Tax (see Section 10.2).

Payments subject to Income Tax are taxed at the recipient's normal Income Tax rates. In effect, the taxable death benefit is added to their other taxable income for the year and suffers Income Tax at the rates given below.

Marginal Income Tax Rates 2023/24 to 2030/31

First £12,570	0%	(Personal allowance)
£12,570 to £50,270	20%	(Basic rate taxpayer)
£50,270 to £100,000	40%	(Higher rate taxpayer)
£100,000 to £125,140	60%	(see below)
Over £125,140	45%	(Additional rate taxpayer)

While the Income Tax rates on savings and property income are increasing by 2% from 2027/28 onwards, this does not directly affect the Income Tax rates on pension death benefits: pension income is not classed as savings income for tax purposes. In some instances, however, the recipient may suffer a higher overall effective rate when they have taxable property, savings, or dividend income, but little or no other income. We'll look at a few examples later in this section.

The 60% rate is the effective rate created in most cases by the withdrawal of the personal allowance from individuals with taxable income over £100,000 (again, there are a few exceptions, as noted above).

Example 1: *When Marty dies aged 78, his daughter Kim receives a taxable lump sum death benefit of £60,000 from his pension scheme. She has an existing salary of £33,270 and no other taxable income. The first £17,000 of the death benefit is taxed at 20%, and the remaining £43,000 is taxed at 40%.*

The total cost to Kim is £20,600, leaving her with just £39,400. If she has young children, she may also be subject to the Child Benefit Charge. For example, with three children, this would cost her a further £3,268 (at 2026/27 rates), effectively leaving her with a net £36,132.

If Kim had been able to place the funds in inherited drawdown, she would have been able to take her inheritance over a few years, keep her child benefit, and only suffer Income Tax at 20%. Taking a lump sum death benefit has cost her an extra £11,868. And, in some cases, it could be much worse.

Example 2: *Nina dies aged 85 with a pension fund worth £240,000. The scheme does not allow inherited drawdown and Nina's nominated beneficiary, her daughter Simone, does not wish to buy an annuity. Simone therefore takes the death benefit as a lump sum. She has other taxable income for the year of £80,000 and thus suffers Income Tax on the lump sum as follows:*

First £20,000 @ 40%	*£8,000*
Next £25,140 @ 60%	*£15,084*
Next £194,860 @ 45%	*£87,687*
Total	*£110,771*

In this case, Income Tax has eaten up over 46% of Simone's net inheritance: and that's after any IHT that has also been suffered!

What these examples go to show is how important it is to nominate your beneficiaries (Section 10.4) and make sure your savings are in a scheme that allows inherited drawdown, to give them the flexibility they need to make the most tax efficient use of your funds.

Exceptions

Different Income Tax rates apply to:

- Scottish taxpayers (higher rates apply to income over £29,526 in 2026/27)
- The highest earner in a household where child benefit is being claimed and that individual has taxable income between £60,000 and £80,000

- Dividend income (which is subject to different rates and is also treated as the top part of an individual's taxable income for the year)
- Property and savings income (Income Tax rates on these types of income will be increased by 2% from 2027/28 onwards)

From 2027/28 onwards, income will be taxed in a strict order, as follows:

i) Employment income, self-employment trading income, and pensions
ii) Property income
iii) Savings income
iv) Dividends

Taxable pension death benefits will fall under heading (i) and will continue to be taxed at the rates set out above. However, receiving the death benefit may cause additional costs for individuals with income under headings (ii) to (iv).

Example 3: *Janet is a landlord with no other source of income. In 2027/28, she has taxable rental profits of £40,000. On its own, this would give rise to an Income Tax bill of £6,035 (deducting her personal allowance of £12,570 leaves £27,430 taxed at 22%). However, Janet also receives a taxable lump sum death benefit of £20,000. The pension income must be taxed first, before her property income, so her Income Tax bill is now as follows:*

Death Benefit	
First £12,570 @ 0%	*£0*
Remaining £7,430 @ 20%	*£1,486*
Rental Profits	
First £30,270 @ 22%	*£6,659*
Remaining £9,730 @ 42%	*£4,087*
Total	*£12,232*

The tax cost on the death benefit is thus £6,197 in this case (£12,232 – £6,035) and not the £5,946 we might have expected from the table of marginal Income Tax rates above. The £251 increase is caused by the fact that Janet's personal allowance is now used up by the pension death benefit and is not available to set against her rental income. The personal allowance saves tax at just 20% instead of 22%, so there is a 2% increase in the effective marginal tax rate applying to the first £12,570 of taxable death benefit.

This effect will be seen (to at least some extent), where an individual landlord receives a taxable death benefit and does not have at least £12,570 of employment, trading, or other pension income.

Example 4: *In 2027/28, Jermaine has pension income of his own of £13,175 and savings income of £4,000. As things stand, his savings income is covered by his starting rate band, leaving him just £121 to pay in Income Tax on his pension. However, he receives a taxable death benefit of £10,000. This, itself, will be taxed at 20%, but it will also mean Jermaine's starting rate band is not available. He will still benefit from a personal savings allowance of £1,000, but £3,000 of his savings income will be subject to Income Tax at 22%, costing a further £660.*

This effect will be seen (to at least some extent), where an individual with savings income receives a taxable death benefit and does not have at least £17,570 of other income, excluding dividends.

Individuals with savings income may also suffer other Income Tax costs when receiving a taxable death benefit. If the death benefit pushes their total taxable income for the year over £50,270, their personal savings allowance will be halved, if their taxable income goes over £125,140, their personal savings allowance will be taken away altogether. Furthermore, the potential cost of up to £251 we saw in Example 3 (a landlord), where an individual does not have at least £12,570 of employment, trading, or other pension income, applies equally to savings income.

All in all, an individual with savings income could suffer up to £8,728 in additional Income Tax on that income, on top of the Income Tax on the death benefit itself (although the maximum additional cost for those with at least £17,570 of employment, trading, or other pension income is only £470).

Example 5: *La Toya is the owner and director of a small trading company. In 2027/28, she pays herself a salary of £12,570 and dividends of £60,000. She also receives a taxable death benefit of £30,000. The death benefit falls into La Toya's basic rate band and is taxed at 20%. However, it also causes £30,000 of her dividend income to be taxed at 35.75% instead of 10.75%, an increase of 25%. Hence, the overall effective tax rate on the death benefit is 45% and La Toya will face a total tax cost of £13,500 as a result of receiving this benefit.*

This effect will be seen (to at least some extent), where an individual with dividend income receives a taxable death benefit, does not have at least £50,270 of other income, and is a higher or additional rate taxpayer (after including the death benefit). See Section 10.13 for full details of the Income Tax rates on dividends.

We'll take a closer look at the impact of some of the other exceptions listed above in Section 10.12. A taxable death benefit could also lead to an increase in the rate of CGT paid by a beneficiary disposing of an asset in the same tax year. More information on all these issues is contained in our other Taxcafe guides.

10.9 SUCCESSION PLANNING WITH PENSIONS

As we know, from 6th April 2027, most pension funds will be subject to IHT in broadly the same way as other investments. Many, but not all, death benefits will also be subject to Income Tax.

But pension contributions also attract Income Tax relief, thus increasing the value of the original investment. And, the higher your Income Tax rate, the greater the increase. Plus, most other investments (certainly the low risk ones) are also subject to IHT. So where does all this leave us? Let's start by looking at the continuing benefits of the UK pension regime:

- Your pension savings can grow in a tax-free environment, free of Income Tax, CGT, and any IHT charges during your lifetime (all of which may be suffered by trusts), thus further enhancing the value of your beneficiaries' inheritance
- Where inherited drawdown is available, pensions can be passed down through multiple generations, while continuing to grow in a tax-free environment (apart from IHT)
- If it turns out you need to access your pension savings during your lifetime, from age 55 (57 from 2028) you can drawdown up to the lesser of £268,275, or 25% of your savings, tax free, and the rest as taxable income. In other words, if you are using a pension for succession planning purposes, there is no need to lock the money away where you can't touch it (as is necessary when using trusts and most other forms of succession planning, although AIM shares and some of the syndicates we looked at in Section 7.34 also provide this flexibility)
- On top of all this, pension contributions generally attract Income Tax relief, making them one of the few succession planning vehicles where you can also make tax savings when you implement your planning (unlike most others, which either have a tax cost to set up or are at best tax neutral at that point)

Bringing it all Together

In addition to IHT, there is also a strong chance your beneficiaries will be subject to Income Tax on your pension savings. Subject to the further detailed points in Section 10.6, the basic rule in most cases is that your beneficiaries will ultimately suffer Income Tax on your pension savings if you survive to at least the age of 75.

According to the ONS, men currently aged between 40 and 74 can expect to live to between 84 and 87. Women in the same age bracket can expect to live to between 87 and 89. In short, while there is a chance your beneficiaries could receive your net pension savings (after IHT) tax free, it is more likely they will suffer Income Tax.

This, in turn, means a lump sum death benefit could attract a significant amount of Income Tax and we saw the consequences of this in Section 10.8. But this may not have told the full story, as we did not factor in either the Income Tax relief obtained by the scheme member during their lifetime, or the IHT arising on their death.

To look at the overall picture combining Income Tax relief on pension contributions, IHT on the scheme member's death, and Income Tax payable by the beneficiaries, we'll start by assuming the individual already has sufficient pension savings and other assets to fully utilise their NRB and any other applicable reliefs. In other words, any further pension savings will be subject to IHT at 40%, but equally any sums retained personally, or invested elsewhere, will also be subject to IHT at 40%.

For a basic rate taxpayer, Income Tax relief is all given at source: for example, a cash pension contribution of £8,000 made by an individual is grossed up to £10,000 (the Government puts in the additional £2,000). Higher rate taxpayers receive additional tax relief through a reduction in their tax bill. The overall effect is that they receive total tax relief at their effective marginal rate of Income Tax: the same effective marginal tax rates as per the table in Section 10.8.

So, for example, if you're a higher rate taxpayer paying Income Tax at 40% and you make a cash pension contribution of £8,000, you get £2,000 of tax relief at source (the Government contribution to your pension fund) and a £2,000 reduction in your tax bill. This means it cost you just £6,000 to put £10,000 in your pension.

In Table A below we're going to look at what happens when an individual can afford a net cost of £10,000 to put money into a pension, after tax relief. For a basic rate taxpayer, that simply means a cash contribution of £10,000, which the Government will gross up to £12,500; for a higher rate taxpayer paying Income Tax at 40%, that means a cash contribution of £13,333, which the Government will gross up to £16,666 and also allow a reduction of £3,333 in the individual's tax bill: so it's the same net cost overall.

We'll ignore investment growth in this table, although we'll look at this issue further in Section 10.11.

The percentages given on the left of the table represent the individual's effective marginal Income Tax rate (see Section 10.8); the percentages across the top of the table represent the marginal Income Tax rate of the beneficiary receiving the lump sum death benefit; and the sums in the body of the table represent the net sum inherited by the beneficiary after both IHT at 40% *and* Income Tax.

Table A: Net Amount Received from £10,000 Investment

Individual's	**Beneficiary's Income Tax Rate**				
Tax Rate	**0%**	**20%**	**40%**	**60%**	**45%**
20%	£7,500	£6,000	£4,500	£3,000	£4,125
40%	£10,000	£8,000	£6,000	£4,000	£5,500
60%	£15,000	£12,000	£9,000	£6,000	£8,250
45%	£10,909	£8,727	£6,545	£4,364	£6,000

Is it a Good Outcome?

The first thing to bear in mind is, if that same £10,000 had still been in the individual's estate at the date of death (again ignoring investment growth), it would have suffered IHT at 40%. Hence, the beneficiary's net inheritance would be just £6,000. That means any amount in the table greater than £6,000 is better than could be achieved by, for example, investing the money in an ISA until the individual's death. Where it is £6,000, the outcome is equal to investing in an ISA; where's it's less than £6,000, an ISA may have been a better investment.

Looked at another way, a pension contribution will yield a better net, after-tax inheritance than most other investments where the beneficiary's Income Tax rate when they receive the death benefit is less than the individual's Income Tax rate when they made the contribution.

Of course, if the £10,000 invested by the individual was surplus wealth, another alternative would have been to simply give the money away as a PET. But there are several reasons the pension contribution might be a better route:

- As we can see from the table, there are a few instances where your beneficiary may receive more than your original £10,000 investment, even after both IHT and Income Tax are taken into account
- If you should die before age 75, your beneficiaries will generally be able to receive your death benefits free from Income Tax: unless they exceed your available LSDBA (Section 10.7). Even then, it is only the excess that suffers Income Tax, only if paid as a lump sum, and funds crystallised before 6th April 2024 are exempt. Hence, in most cases, your beneficiaries will effectively receive the amounts shown in the 0% column of the table which, provided you are a higher rate taxpayer, will be equal to your cash investment, or greater
- Income Tax savings on pension contributions are immediate; it takes a PET seven years to escape IHT
- Subject to Income Tax, you can get your money back if you need it (from age 55 or 57). In fact, if you *need* it, your income may well have dropped into a lower tax bracket, meaning you'll get more back than you put in
- Your pension savings will grow in a tax-free environment during your lifetime
- We haven't taken all the potential advantages of pension savings into account yet

Sadly, however, the more likely outcome in the case of a large lump sum death benefit is that at least some of the amount paid to the beneficiary will be taxed at 45% or 60%, meaning, unless you obtained tax relief at the same rate, or more, there will be an overall Income Tax cost. Yet again, this emphasises the importance of making sure your beneficiaries will be able to take inherited drawdown.

Gifting Your Tax-Free Cash

From age 55 (or 57), you are able to withdraw a tax-free lump sum of 25% from your pension (limited to a maximum of £268,275). However, this ability is not available to your beneficiaries after your death, and if you are then aged 75 or more, the whole of your death benefit will be subject to Income Tax.

But, if you take your 25% tax-free lump sum, and you are confident you will not need the funds yourself, you could give it your beneficiaries. They will not pay any Income Tax on this sum either (as it's a gift) and IHT will be avoided when you have survived seven years. If you do this before the age of 68, you can be certain this element of your pension savings will not suffer both IHT and Income Tax and, if you survive seven years, it will not suffer either.

Assuming you do this and subsequently die aged 75 or more, the overall total net sum received by your beneficiaries will be as per Table B below.

Table B: Total Received from £10,000 Investment

Individual's	Beneficiary's Income Tax Rate				
Tax Rate	0%	20%	40%	60%	45%
20%	£8,750	£7,625	£6,500	£5,375	£6,219
40%	£11,667	£10,167	£8,667	£7,167	£8,292
60%	£17,500	£15,250	£13,000	£10,750	£12,438
45%	£12,727	£11,091	£9,455	£7,818	£9,045

As usual, these figures ignore investment growth, which we will look at in Section 10.11. Nonetheless, we can see that by using this strategy, your beneficiaries will nearly always end up with more than the £6,000 they would have ended up with if you had invested your initial £10,000 somewhere else and kept it there until you died: sometimes considerably more!

Furthermore, even without factoring in investment growth, this strategy will yield more than your original investment whenever:

- You are a higher or additional rate taxpayer and your beneficiary is a basic rate or non-taxpayer, or
- You are suffering Income Tax at a marginal rate of 60%

Even the tax-free investment growth can be reinstated if your beneficiaries put the money they receive into an ISA, or perhaps even better, into their own pension (subject to the limitations discussed in Section 10.12).

The strategy has the drawback that you have to survive seven years to get the full benefit. But, if you should die sooner then, provided you made your gift before the age of 68, the 75% of your savings still held in the pension will be free from Income Tax for your beneficiaries. Hence, regardless of their Income Tax rate, they will benefit by the amounts in the 0% column in Table A above.

For a widow/widower, that means nothing will have been lost. The same can generally be said for a married couple where one of them already has a TNRB. In other cases, the potential impact on the surviving spouse's TNRB may need to be considered.

In principle, there is nothing to stop you giving your tax-free lump sum to any beneficiary you choose. However, in the case of your own minor children, there are a number of other issues to be considered. Having said that, if you wait until you are nearly 68 then, in most cases, your children will probably be over 18. For older parents, the relevant issues are examined in Section 11.10.

Another figure worth comparing with the results in both Tables A and B is the £8,000 your beneficiaries would end up with if you had invested your money in AIM shares (Section 7.26): and that's assuming the shares hold their value!

Gifting More

Taking more than your tax-free lump sum out of your pension will lead to an immediate Income Tax charge. This might be worth considering if you are a basic rate taxpayer and can afford to give the cash away, but if you then die before the age of 75, Income Tax will have been suffered unnecessarily and, if that's within seven years, you won't have avoided IHT either. Alternatively, if you wait until you are 75, the chances of you surviving seven years and avoiding IHT on the gift will be reduced (although the ONS tells us this is still likely). Nonetheless, this tactic may still be beneficial in some cases.

Example Revisited: *In Example 1, Section 10.8, we saw that Marty left a lump sum death benefit of £60,000 to his daughter Kim but, after Income Tax, she only received a net sum of £36,132. Let's say instead he takes £100,000 out of his pension fund over a few years, always making sure he only suffers basic rate Income Tax. This yields a net £80,000 which he can give to Kim. If he survives seven years, Kim gets to keep the whole £80,000, if he dies sooner, there will be an IHT cost of £32,000, leaving a net sum of £48,000.*

It may not be Kim who suffers the IHT in the event of Marty's death within seven years, it could fall on another beneficiary, even his spouse's eventual beneficiaries if he is married. But it will fall on someone.

In this example, I am making the simplistic assumption that the £100,000 Marty takes out of his pension fund would have been reduced to the same £60,000 lump sum death benefit Kim originally received after IHT. In practice, it will not be this simple because of the way the NRB is allocated (Section 10.2). Nonetheless, taking £100,000 out of the fund, giving it away (net of the Income Tax suffered), and surviving seven years, will lead to a £40,000 IHT saving overall, however the NRB is allocated: so the comparison is fair.

Even if Marty dies within seven years, there is still a net IHT saving of £8,000 (effectively the IHT saved by paying £20,000 in Income Tax). On top of this there is an Income Tax saving of £3,868, making a total saving of £11,868 in this case, even in the event of a death within seven years.

So, there are three elements to the savings that could potentially be generated by making taxable pension withdrawals during your lifetime, only one of which requires you to survive seven years:

i) If the Income Tax you suffer on the withdrawal is lower than the Income Tax your beneficiaries will suffer on the death benefit, there will be an Income Tax saving (£3,868 in the example).
ii) The Income Tax you suffer will reduce your estate, thus leading to an IHT saving. By contrast, Income Tax suffered by your beneficiaries does not save any IHT.
iii) If you survive seven years, you will avoid IHT on the sum gifted to your beneficiaries.

Whether there is any saving on the first element depends on how much taxable income your beneficiaries have after your death, although as long as you are a basic rate taxpayer when you make the pension withdrawals, there is at least a reasonable chance of a saving arising: especially where the beneficiaries take lump sum death benefits.

Remember though, we are not comparing 'like with like' here. Your lifetime withdrawals suffer Income Tax *before* any IHT arising (Marty suffered Income

Tax on £100,000 in the example), whereas your beneficiaries suffer Income Tax on a death benefit on the net sum remaining *after* IHT (£60,000 in the example). Despite this, there was still an overall Income Tax saving of £3,868 in the example, but this will not always be the case.

The second element is almost guaranteed to save IHT: assuming there is some IHT payable on your estate.

The third element, if you survive long enough, is effectively the 'icing on the cake'. If Marty survives seven years in our example, Kim will be £43,868 better off.

Admittedly, however, Kim could have had a net £48,000 with inherited drawdown in any case, so she may actually only be £32,000 better off.

To benefit from this strategy to this degree requires a fairly odd set of circumstances: the pension scheme member needs to be a basic rate taxpayer, yet still have cash to spare and a potential IHT liability (hence total assets of at least £325,000, even after making the gift, and that excludes any amount covered by the RNRB).

Theoretically, a higher rate taxpayer might still benefit from this strategy. For example, in Marty's case, he might be able to give Kim £60,000 and, if he survives seven years, this will leave her £12,000 better off than with inherited drawdown. But, if he dies within seven years, there will be an IHT cost of £24,000, meaning his beneficiaries are £12,000 *worse off* overall. If that's before age 75, his beneficiaries may even be £24,000 worse off.

And let's not forget, Marty has given up the tax-free investment growth on £100,000, although Kim might be able to restore some or all of that by investing her gift in her own pension and/or ISA.

The strategy might be more attractive if your beneficiaries are likely to be higher rate taxpayers for the rest of their lives, although inherited drawdown will often provide enough flexibility to enable your pension to suffer Income Tax at no more than 20% if your beneficiaries are patient.

Exceptions

The same exceptions we looked at in Section 10.8 may affect both the individual's tax relief when making their pension contributions and the Income Tax burden on beneficiaries receiving death benefits. We'll look at some of these exceptions a little further in Section 10.12.

10.10 THE ADDED BENEFITS OF INHERITED DRAWDOWN

The first benefit worth noting is that the LSDBA does not apply to inherited drawdown and hence, in the event of death before the age of 75, unlimited amounts of pension savings could potentially be passed to your beneficiaries free from Income Tax.

Example: *Ritchie dies in May 2027, aged 72, with pension savings of £1,573,100 (after payment of IHT). He nominated his daughter Donna to receive his death* *benefits. He has never accessed his pension funds, so his LSDBA is £1,073,100. If Donna takes the death benefit as a lump sum, £500,000 will be exposed to Income Tax, costing her between £211,203 and £229,022, depending on how much other taxable income she has for the year, and what type.*

Alternatively, if Donna is able to take inherited drawdown, the entire fund will be free from Income Tax while she holds it.

The real beauty of this is that, not only has Donna saved over £200,000 in Income Tax, she could take all of the funds in the drawdown account almost immediately and still not suffer any Income Tax. In other words, the practical upshot of using inherited drawdown is that an unlimited Income Tax-free lump sum could effectively be taken by the beneficiaries in the event of the scheme member dying under the age of 75. (Albeit that the payment is officially termed a 'drawdown' and not a 'lump sum'.)

Whether taking all of Ritchie's pension fund in a single drawdown payment is a good idea is another story. Nonetheless, the fact remains that over £1.5m has passed from father to daughter free from Income Tax.

Further Benefits

In Section 10.9, we saw that, even when death benefits are subject to Income Tax, there are many instances where pension savings are more tax-efficient overall than other investments you still hold when you die.

Nonetheless, it must be recognised that, after you have reached the age of 75, the Income Tax burden on your beneficiaries, combined with the IHT paid by the scheme administrator, can eat up a fair amount of your pension fund. In fact, a higher rate taxpayer beneficiary could lose up to 64% of the fund. That rises to 67% if the beneficiary is an additional rate taxpayer, or even 76% if they are suffering Income Tax at 60%.

Once again, this is where inherited drawdown is a far better option than lump sum death benefits, as it will allow your beneficiaries to either draw down income when it will be taxed at a more palatable rate or, if they don't need the income themselves, pass on the funds to the next generation.

Passing funds on to the next generation does, however, mean they will be exposed to IHT again. But that may not be a problem in some families. For example, if you have a fund worth £1.2m (after IHT) which you leave to four children, they will inherit £300,000 each, which may be covered by their NRB and/or a TNRB when they die.

Alternatively, if your children are financially comfortable, it may be better for you to leave your pension savings to your grandchildren, or even great-grandchildren. Not only is this good IHT planning but, with inherited drawdown, it could also produce Income Tax savings (we'll look at these a little later).

Inherited drawdown can be taken at any age and does not trigger the money purchase annual allowance. It may, however, lead to a tapered annual allowance if the recipient's total income exceeds the relevant thresholds as a result. (See Section 10.12 for details.)

The funds held in inherited drawdown can also be used to purchase an annuity at any time if the beneficiary ever gets to the stage where they would prefer the certainty of a lifelong income. The Income Tax position on the annuity will be the same as the drawdown payments, but if the beneficiary is a basic rate taxpayer by this stage, the tax cost, where it applies, is only 20% (some may even be covered by their personal allowance).

Let's return to Example 2 in Section 10.8 to see how inherited drawdown may have helped. We'll also take this opportunity to factor in the Income Tax relief obtained when the pension contributions were originally made. We will, however, continue to ignore investment growth for the time being (we'll look at that in Section 10.11).

I've also ignored the annual exemption: we'll assume Nina is already using it on other gifts. We'll also assume her estate will exceed the NRB and any other available exemptions. For ease of illustration, I'll ignore any NRB allocated to her pension fund: or we could say there's another amount in the fund that will use it up.

Example Revisited: *Nina worked until she was 70, earning between £90,000 and £100,000 every year. She had more money than she needed, so she was able to make net pension contributions totalling £320,000, to which the Government added £80,000 in basic rate tax relief. The contributions all attracted higher rate tax relief too, saving Nina a further £80,000 in Income Tax, so they only cost her £240,000.*

She could have given that same £240,000 to her daughter, Simone, but she was always worried she might need it herself one day or, if she died too soon, it would lead to an extra £96,000 in IHT (that was before the October 2024 Budget). So, she felt happier having £400,000 in her pension fund than possibly leaving Simone with just £144,000.

When she was 74, Nina realised that Simone would soon be exposed to Income Tax on her pension fund death benefit so (unlike the first version of this example) she transferred her pension savings to a fund that allowed inherited drawdown.

When Nina died many years later, Simone calculated that taking the death benefit of £240,000 (after payment of IHT) as a lump sum would cost her £110,771 in Income Tax (Section 10.8). This would leave her with just £129,229, i.e. £14,771 less than if Nina had simply given her a cash gift of £240,000 but died within seven years. Instead of this, however, Simone placed the funds in inherited drawdown, giving her a number of choices:

Option 1: She could draw down £20,000 per year (to take her annual taxable income up to £100,000) and suffer Income Tax at 40%, but avoid the higher rates of 45% and 60%. If she used the whole fund in this way, she would end up with a total of £144,000: the same net sum that she would have received if Nina had simply held onto her spare cash, or had gifted it to Simone within the last seven years.

Option 2: She could wait until she retired. If her income then fell below the higher rate tax threshold (currently £50,270), there would be scope to draw down funds taxed at 20%. If she used the whole fund in this way, she would end up with a total of £192,000: £48,000 more than if Nina had held onto her spare cash.

Option 3: She could leave the funds in inherited drawdown and pass them on to her own intended beneficiaries. Those beneficiaries might be able to obtain the funds free of Income Tax (if Simone dies before age 75) or, more likely, might be able to draw them down and suffer Income Tax at only 20% if their income is below the higher rate tax threshold. BUT the funds will most likely suffer IHT (again!), perhaps leaving as little as £144,000 for Simone's beneficiaries, even before Income Tax is taken into account.

Of course, it doesn't have to be one option only for Simone, she could apply a mixture of all three. A further option for Simone might be to purchase an annuity. As discussed above, some people might prefer the certainty of a lifelong income and it will often only suffer Income Tax at 20% if they wait until they are a basic rate taxpayer. However, the drawback is the funds used to buy the annuity could effectively be lost to the family, as many annuities cease when the original purchaser dies.

In this example, it is arguable that Nina could have made regular cash gifts to Simone (instead of her pension contributions) and, if these had come out of surplus net income, they might have been immediately exempt from IHT as normal expenditure out of income (Section 5.5). However, that exemption may not have applied in this case, or there may have been some doubts over whether the gifts would be covered.

Making pension contributions provided Nina with the flexibility that she would be able to access the funds herself if she needed to. At the time, there was also the chance she might die before age 75 and thus be able to leave her pension savings to Simone free from Income Tax. Furthermore, until October 2024, she expected them to be exempt from IHT!

But when Nina moved her pension funds when she was 74, she could perhaps have also taken her tax-free lump sum of £100,000 (25% of her fund) and given it to Simone. This would have escaped IHT as, in this particular case, Nina survived more than seven years. If Simone subsequently followed Option 2 above, the total net sum she received would be increased to £244,000, slightly more than Nina's original investment.

Passing Pensions to Children and Young Adults

Inherited drawdown arrangements can be made for minor children (the funds are typically paid to the child's parent who is under an obligation to apply the funds for the child's benefit). Both minors and young adults in full time education generally tend to have little or no taxable income, so they can often receive up to £12,570 per year free from Income Tax.

For example, let's say Simone doesn't really need Nina's money, and neither do her children. So, Nina nominates Simone's five grandchildren to receive her death benefits. Each grandchild is in full time education with no taxable income for four tax years so they can each draw down £12,000 per year for four years with no tax payable and the entire £240,000 has been passed on completely free of Income Tax.

10.11 INVESTMENT GROWTH

Pension funds are typically invested in a range of investments, including quoted shares, gilts, bonds, and commercial property. The aim is usually to produce good steady growth at an acceptable risk level. If you have your own SIPP, this opens up more possibilities, but residential property usually remains off the table. The key point is, throughout your lifetime, the investments grow in a tax-free environment, with no Income Tax or CGT, and no anniversary or exit charges like those suffered by trusts.

So, broadly speaking, investment growth is usually going to make pension savings even more attractive. Hence, in all our tables and examples in previous sections, the actual position in practice is generally going to be better. The only other way to get the same tax-free investment growth is to put money in an ISA.

Let's go back to Example 2 (from Sections 10.8 and 10.10) by way of illustration, but let's now say that Nina only had £120,000 available (over the course of a few years). Her tax relief allowed her to use this money to fund net pension contributions totalling £160,000, grossed up to £200,000 by the Government. Over the years from then until her death, her pension savings doubled in value to the £400,000 we saw in the example which, in turn, after both IHT and Income Tax, left Simone with somewhere between £129,229 and £192,000 (assuming Nina never took her tax-free lump sum).

Now let's say instead that Nina put £120,000 into an ISA (over the course of a few years) and it experiences the same tax-free investment growth as the pension. Hence, by the time of Nina's death it is worth £240,000. After IHT, this leaves £144,000. That's the same net sum Simone would end up with if she took inherited drawdown while she's a higher rate taxpayer, but it's much less than she receives if she waits until she's a basic rate taxpayer, or if Nina gifted her tax-free lump sum to her.

The alternative, of course, is that Nina could have given Simone £120,000 in cash, which Simone then invested in her own ISA (over a few years), so that it doubled in value by the time of Nina's death, leaving Simone with £240,000. But that simply reinforces what we saw in Table A in Section 10.9: a PET will generally be better than a pension contribution if you survive seven years.

Remember what we saw in Table B, though: a pension contribution can beat a PET if you're a higher rate taxpayer when you make the contribution, you take your tax-free lump sum, give it away and survive seven years, and your beneficiaries are basic rate or non-taxpayers when they receive your death benefits. Investment growth won't alter any of that. (If you're not sure, take the figures in Table B and double them, then compare them with £20,000 instead of £10,000.)

And a pension contribution still carries many advantages, including the fact there is no need to survive seven years, the death benefits might turn out to be free from Income Tax, the contributor has access to their pension during their lifetime, and, of course, all the benefits of inherited drawdown.

Generally speaking, the only ways your money might see better investment growth than it would get in a pension are investing in residential property, your own business, or something risky that happens to pay off. Your own trading business or shares in an unquoted trading company will generally be exempt from IHT, or suffer at an effective rate of just 20% (see Chapter 7). As far as residential property is concerned, this is where many of the other IHT planning strategies in this guide come into play!

10.12 TACTICS AND LIMITATIONS

While it is possible to make pension contributions in excess of the limits discussed in this section, these will not generally attract Income Tax relief, so they are far less beneficial and we will ignore them for the purposes of this guide. Hence, when I say something is not possible, what I actually mean is it will not attract Income Tax relief: whether it is possible is another matter.

Unless stated to the contrary, the limits given in this section refer to gross pension contributions, including basic rate tax relief given at source. Hence, for example, a limit of £60,000 means the net cash contribution is limited to £48,000.

Early Deaths

If a higher rate taxpayer knew they were going to die before the age of 75, pension savings would be hard to beat for succession planning. As we saw in the '0%' column of Table A, Section 10.9, every £10,000 a higher rate taxpayer invests in pension savings (net of tax relief) could leave their beneficiaries with between £10,000 and £15,000, *even after IHT*. Compare that with the £6,000 your beneficiaries could end up with if you die within seven years of making a cash gift.

Even if you survive seven years, but not to age 75, the pension savings are still providing an Income Tax benefit that, for a higher rate taxpayer, will at least compensate for the IHT you will suffer and, in some cases, actually increases the value of your beneficiary's inheritance. The same is true where the savings could have been covered by other lifetime exemptions, like the annual exemption.

If it turns out the relevant funds are exempt from IHT when you die under age 75 (e.g. if covered by the NRB or the TNRB), an Income Tax benefit will usually remain whatever rate of tax relief you got when you made your pension contributions.

In short, in the event of an early death, pension savings can benefit your family even after taking account of IHT. This makes pension savings very useful for higher rate taxpayers who have a strong probability of dying before the age of 75.

Gifting Your Tax-Free Lump Sum

As we saw in Section 10.9, for the majority of people who live to at least the age of 75, the overall net benefit produced by your pension savings will generally be increased if you take your 25% tax-free lump sum and, if you can afford to, give it to your beneficiaries. Remember, the whole of your death benefits will be subject to Income Tax if you survive to 75: there is no tax-free lump sum after death.

Until now, this carried the risk that the gifted funds were exposed to IHT if you should die within seven years of making the gift. Now there is really only a risk if you die before 6th April 2027 since, after that, your pension savings will be exposed to IHT in any case. Furthermore, making the gift before your 68th birthday ensures the gifted funds cannot suffer both IHT and Income Tax. If you survive seven years, the gift will escape both taxes.

Married people whose spouse has a longer life expectancy could improve the chances their gift will escape IHT by first gifting the money to their spouse, who may subsequently choose to give the funds to the ultimate beneficiaries (but see Section 6.7 for some potential issues to be aware of).

Currently, you can take your tax-free lump sum any time from the age of 55 (increasing to 57 from 6th April 2028) and many people will do this for other reasons unconnected with IHT planning. From a succession planning perspective, however, some people may prefer to wait until shortly before their 68th birthday: although there are pros and cons to this delay.

On the one hand, quite obviously, your chances of surviving seven years are generally better when you're 55 than when you're 68. On the other hand, a lot can happen in the intervening years and you may have a better idea of whether you will need the tax-free lump sum for something else, including supporting you or your spouse in old age. But if you gave it away when you were 55, you won't have those options and may have to take taxable income from your pension savings.

Sadly, some 55-year-olds won't even make it to 68. Some of those that do will have found out they are unlikely to live to 75. In these cases, the pension savings may be best left where they are (from a tax point of view) as they are unlikely to escape IHT whatever you do, but will enjoy more tax-free investment growth before being passed to your beneficiaries, probably free from Income Tax. For a higher rate taxpayer in this position, it may even be worth maximising your pension contributions for your remaining lifetime.

But, if you're in normal health at the age of 68, you now have a stronger chance of reaching 75 than you did when you were 55. In other words, the position is a bit more certain. Statistics can't tell us what is going to happen to each individual but, according to the ONS, the chances of a 68-year-old reaching 75 are about 91% for women, or 87% for men.

As well as the pension scheme member themselves, those intervening years will have made a big difference to their beneficiaries too. Their children, or other heirs will be more mature, meaning the scheme member may feel more comfortable about giving them a large cash gift. Some beneficiaries may have been the scheme member's minor children when the member was 55, but the member's children will usually be adults by the time the member is 68, meaning the issues covered in Section 11.10 will not arise.

Alternatively, the scheme member may wish to choose different beneficiaries at 68 than they would have at 55. Their children might now be financially secure enough that they wish to pass their wealth directly to their grandchildren, or a trust for their benefit (see Chapters 8 and 9).

It will sometimes also be worth keeping the funds in the pension until the age of 68 in order to enjoy an extra thirteen years of tax-free investment growth, although this does depend on what your beneficiaries intend, and are able, to do with the gifted funds. In this context, it is worth pointing out you can stagger your tax-free drawdown over a number of years so your beneficiaries can invest the funds in an ISA, or their own pension, within the relevant limits (if they are not already fully utilising them). Arguably, if your beneficiaries are able to put the cash in their own pension, passing the funds to them as soon as possible may be most beneficial.

Another reason it may make sense to pass the funds to your beneficiaries sooner rather than later is the danger of further changes in legislation beyond what we already know, although what shape those will take is hard to predict.

There are many factors to consider when deciding whether to take your tax-free lump sum and pass it to your beneficiaries as soon as possible; to wait until just before your 68th birthday; or to leave the funds where they are.

Taking the lump sum after the age of 68 may pay off for some people, and we can see this in some of the examples in this chapter. But this inevitably means there will be some period when your family could still suffer IHT on the 25% you have given away while also suffering both IHT and Income Tax on the 75% left in your pension.

Furthermore, if you wait until after you are 75 before you take your tax-free lump sum, you run the risk that your entire pension savings could suffer both IHT and Income Tax. Nonetheless, even at this stage, you can still avoid Income Tax on the lump sum: something your beneficiaries cannot do; and there's always a chance of avoiding IHT on it too.

Finally, remember there is a statutory maximum to the tax-free lump sum, which is £268,275 in most cases. I generally haven't factored this into my analysis in the rest of this section (or Section 10.13) but in practice you will need to bear it in mind if your pension savings exceed £1,073,100.

The Annual Allowance

The annual allowance is the maximum amount of pension contributions you can make each year, although any unused allowance can effectively be carried forward for up to three tax years (provided you were a member of a qualifying pension scheme in the relevant year). The annual allowance has been £60,000 since 2023/24, so the maximum possible contribution in 2026/27 is £240,000.

Not everyone is entitled to the full annual allowance. If you have withdrawn more than your 25% tax-free lump sum, you can only make maximum annual contributions of £10,000 (known as the money purchase annual allowance).

Those with total taxable income, after deducting pension contributions, of more than £200,000 *and* 'adjusted income' of more than £260,000, are subject to a tapered annual allowance, reducing it to somewhere between £10,000 and £60,000, depending on the level of their income. Adjusted income for this purpose is total taxable income *before* deducting pension contributions *plus* any contributions made on the individual's behalf by their employer.

Earnings

As well as the limitations of the annual allowance, it is only possible to make pension contributions up to the greater of £3,600 or your earnings for the relevant tax year. Not all taxable income counts as earnings, as it is limited to employment income and self-employed trading income (sole traders or business partners).

One group who are severely restricted when it comes to pension contributions are full-time landlords with no other income. Without qualifying earnings, landlords are restricted to contributions of just £3,600 per year. The only way to improve the position is to use a company (see Section 10.13).

The Rate of Tax Relief

So, let's say you have your full annual allowance of £60,000 available and you have enough earnings to cover it. The next thing you need to think about is what rate of tax relief you're going to get for your pension contributions.

Remember, if you live to at least 75, your beneficiaries will be subject to Income Tax on your death benefits. That means there is only going to be an overall Income Tax saving on your death benefits if your beneficiaries pay Income Tax at a lower marginal rate than you, and there could be an overall Income Tax cost if they have a higher marginal rate.

However, in the majority of cases, there will be the opportunity to take the 25% tax-free lump sum from your pension and, if you give this to your beneficiaries, this will enhance the overall saving available, especially if you survive seven years (or it is exempt from IHT in some other way): see Table B, Section 10.9.

So, whether there will be an overall Income Tax saving on your pension savings as a whole, including the 25% tax-free lump sum, is slightly different. In fact, if we operate on the most likely assumption that you will live to at least 75 and will have time to withdraw your tax-free lump sum, give it to your beneficiaries, and survive seven years, the ***overall*** rate of Income Tax they will suffer on your pension savings will be as follows:

Basic rate taxpayers	15%	(20% less 25% tax free)
Higher rate taxpayers	30%	(40% less 25% tax free)
Additional rate taxpayers	33.75%	(45% less 25% tax free)

A potential overall rate of 45% applies to any beneficiary foolish, or unlucky, enough to have taxable death benefits falling into the £100,000 to £125,140 income bracket.

In most cases, due to the statutory maximum of £268,275 for the tax-free lump sum, these overall rates usually apply to the first £1,073,100 of your pension savings, with the beneficiary's full marginal tax rate effectively applying to any excess.

What all this means is there will usually be an overall Income Tax saving whenever you and your beneficiaries have the same marginal tax rate, and a greater saving where your marginal tax rate is higher than theirs. Where there is an overall Income Tax saving, this means pension contributions are still better for succession planning purposes than most other investments you still hold in the last seven years of your life, despite the fact pension savings will soon be subject to IHT.

Nonetheless, it remains a fact that there could be an overall Income Tax cost if your beneficiaries' marginal tax rates are higher than yours. For example, if you are a basic rate taxpayer when you make your pension contributions, and your beneficiaries are higher rate taxpayers when they receive your death benefits, there remains an overall Income Tax cost equal to 10% of the gross contributions: even factoring in the 25% tax-free lump sum. That means a simple lifetime gift would have left your beneficiaries better off.

In fact, if we also factor in IHT, the overall tax burden suffered by your beneficiaries on your pension savings if you die aged 75 or more, once your NRB and any other available reliefs are exhausted, is as follows:

Non-taxpayers	30%
Basic rate taxpayers	39%
Higher rate taxpayers	48%
Additional rate taxpayers	50.25%

(And, for a beneficiary suffering Income Tax at 60%, it's 57%.)

These rates are again based on the assumption that you take your 25% tax-free lump sum, gift it to your beneficiaries, and survive seven years. These rates also generally only apply to the first £1,073,100 of your pension savings.

What all this means is that, unless you obtain Income Tax relief at a greater rate than the percentages shown above, a simple cash gift will leave your beneficiaries better off than a pension contribution. That, in turn, generally means you need to be a higher or additional rate taxpayer and your beneficiaries need to be basic rate or non-taxpayers.

It is, of course, easy enough to know what rate of Income Tax you're paying now, but the rate suffered by your beneficiaries in the future is hard to predict. Nonetheless, if you ensure your beneficiaries can take inherited drawdown, it will often be possible for them to time their withdrawals so they only suffer basic rate Income Tax, or even none at all (as we saw at the end of Section 10.10).

If we assume your beneficiaries will be able to do this, a pension contribution can remain better for succession planning than a simple cash gift: but you will need to be a higher or additional rate taxpayer when you make that contribution to give your beneficiaries a fighting chance of coming out on top in the end.

In summary, for it to be both possible and worthwhile to make the maximum contributions of £60,000 per year, you will need earnings of at least £60,000; adjusted income of no more than £260,000 (see above); and usually also total taxable income of at least £110,270.

Have You Got the Cash?

In addition to earnings and taxable income, you will also need to have the cash available to make your pension contributions. However, you will only need to fund 80% of the gross contribution and the cash itself could come from anywhere. For example, an individual on a salary of £80,270 might not usually have any spare cash to fund pension contributions. But if one of their parents dies before the age of 75 and leaves them a lump sum death benefit of £24,000, they could use this to fund a gross pension contribution of £30,000 (they have enough earnings and they will get higher rate tax relief).

How Much Time Have You Got?

When I was in practice, most people who came to me for IHT advice were at least 60, generally older. So, the question is, how many years are left for them to make pension contributions and get tax relief at a minimum of 40%?

In other words, how much longer will they keep earning in excess of £50,270? Plus, even if they want to keep going until they drop, their contributions will have to stop at age 75 anyway: it is not possible to make further pension contributions after the age of 75.

For the reasons explained in Section 10.11, I have again ignored investment growth in the examples below. In Example 2, I have also ignored any NRB allocated to Chrissie's pension fund for the sake of illustration.

Example 1: *Darius is aged 60. He is already a member of a pension scheme and has sufficient savings for his own needs, but he is now starting to look at his pension savings as a form of succession planning and wants to put as much in there as he can while attracting higher rate tax relief.*

He has an annual salary of £90,270 so, meeting his own criteria, he is able to make a gross contribution of £40,000 each year. He keeps working until he is 68, so he is able to build up additional pension savings of £320,000.

Example 2: *Chrissie is a partner in a large law firm. Her annual profit share is usually around £200,000, but she has a good year in 2026/27 and it increases to £260,000. She is now aged 60 and has substantial private wealth. She has been a member of a pension scheme for several years, but has only contributed a small, nominal sum so far, as she has no need for retirement planning. Now realising the potential succession planning benefits of her pension, she makes a gross contribution of £200,000 in 2026/27 and then contributes a further £60,000 (gross) each year* *until the age of 74 (I would like to say she is still working at this point, but all that is actually required is that she is still receiving a partnership profit share, which is perhaps not quite the same thing).*

When Chrissie retires at age 75, she has managed to build up an additional £1.04m in her pension fund, while also obtaining tax relief worth a total of £469,771 (mostly at 45%), so the net cost is only £570,229. But what matters is how much better off her beneficiaries are. In this context, the key comparatives are:

£570,229: the amount her beneficiaries could have received if Chrissie had made cash gifts and survived seven years, or
£342,137: the net amount her beneficiaries would have received after IHT at 40% if Chrissie had done no succession planning

Having used the pension, the final net amount received by her beneficiaries (after IHT) depends on the rate of Income Tax they pay, as follows:

Non-taxpayers: £624,000 (£281,863 more than with no planning)
Basic rate taxpayers: £499,200 (£157,863 more than with no planning)
Higher rate taxpayers: £374,400 (£32,263 more than with no planning)
Additional rate taxpayers: £343,200 (£1,063 more than with no planning)

In practice, there will often be a mix of different tax rates for the beneficiaries, but we can see that, with few exceptions (see below) whatever rate of tax they pay, there is an overall benefit to the family compared with the position where Chrissie did no succession planning.

However, in most cases, simple cash gifts would have been better for the beneficiaries (assuming Chrissie survived seven years): although there are many reasons why Chrissie might not have wanted to do this, especially if her ultimate beneficiaries were very young at the time.

As we saw in Section 10.9, it is possible to adopt a compromise solution, and increase the overall saving, by taking the 25% tax-free lump sum (up to the statutory maximum of £268,275), giving it to the beneficiaries, and surviving seven years. If Chrissie were able to implement this strategy successfully, this would increase the final net amount received by her beneficiaries as follows:

Basic rate taxpayers: £634,400 (£292,263 more than with no planning)
Higher rate taxpayers: £540,800 (£198,663 more than with no planning)
Additional rate taxpayers: £517,400 (£175,263 more than with no planning)

In this particular example, Chrissie would need to live to at least 82 to achieve these savings, so she would need to weigh up the risks involved. A good solution might be to take as much tax-free lump sum as she is able at age 68, give that to her beneficiaries, but leave the rest of her pension savings where they are: but that's her decision and there are pros and cons to both approaches.

Simple cash gifts would still have been better if Chrissie's beneficiaries are higher or additional rate taxpayers, but the compromise method brings the outcome a lot closer, and may suit Chrissie's wishes better in other ways.

I have assumed in this example that, despite her substantial private wealth, Chrissie manages to arrange her affairs so she is never subject to a tapered annual allowance (see above).

There would be nothing to stop Chrissie also carrying out other succession planning, such as setting up a trust, making other lifetime gifts, or using a family investment company for her property investments (see Chapter 14).

In theory, if she was only 40 when she started this planning, she could put over £2.2m in her pension this way. But there's a snowball's chance in Hell of the UK pensions regime not being subjected to further changes before she turned 75 in 2061!

As an alternative strategy, a healthy, wealthy 40-year-old should have time to shelter around £2m in a trust, although the funds will not enjoy the same tax-free environment and will face anniversary and exit charges (see Chapters 8 and 9). Still, as I said, there is nothing to stop them doing both if they are wealthy enough.

Using Pensions to Pass on Wealth

As I said in Section 10.1, pensions are not really meant for succession planning and the fact they will soon be subject to IHT reinforces this.

Nonetheless, unless you buy an annuity, if you want your pension to last through the whole of your retirement, you are bound to leave some death benefits to your beneficiaries. Hence, it will often not be so much a case of using pensions to pass on wealth as a deliberate strategy, but more a case of trying to ensure as much of your remaining pension savings as possible will pass to your beneficiaries rather than being snatched by the Government.

And pensions have other advantages too, which means they may be a safer place to put any surplus cash than other investments, or in the hands of beneficiaries not yet mature enough to look out for their own future.

Even from a purely mathematical point of view, pension savings can still leave your beneficiaries better off than many other succession planning strategies under some circumstances.

Firstly, as we saw at the beginning of this section, any higher or additional rate taxpayer might potentially benefit from using pensions to pass on wealth in the event of an early death. For the majority who live to at least the age of 75, using pensions for succession planning may still be beneficial for higher or additional rate taxpayers who can be reasonably certain their beneficiaries will be basic rate or non-taxpayers, at least at some point in their lives.

In addition to being at least a higher rate taxpayer though, the greatest benefits are only available to those with significant earnings. This makes pensions of most benefit to those who have taxable income well in excess of the higher rate tax threshold (£50,270) and are either employed earners, particularly those with six figure salaries (or more); or partners in a trading business or professional firm.

I include business partners because they are likely to retire at some point and also to have private assets outside the partnership. However, in the case of a family partnership, the position from a succession planning perspective is more like a sole trader.

For sole traders, where their only asset is the business, this will often be free from IHT, or at least enjoy a significant amount of relief (see Chapter 7). However, if they are likely to retire without either passing on the business to their children (or other heirs), or forming a company then, again, a pension could be a good way to pass on some of their accumulated wealth.

I haven't included company owners here because their position is usually different to everyone else's: we will look at them in Section 10.13.

Individual landlords with no other source of income have little scope to use pensions. In fact, with a maximum annual contribution of £3,600, it would take 40 years to put just £144,000 into a pension. That might be worth doing in some cases, but it's hardly going to resolve all their succession planning issues.

Exceptions

So far in this section, we've considered both pension scheme members and beneficiaries with marginal Income Tax rates up to 45% (the additional rate). However, there are many people with a marginal Income Tax rate higher than this, including:

- Scottish additional rate taxpayers, who pay 48%
- Those with taxable income between £100,000 and £125,140, who suffer an effective marginal rate of 60%, or 67.5% if they are a Scottish taxpayer
- The highest earner in a household where child benefit is being claimed, who will suffer an effective Income Tax rate of at least 47% on income between £60,000 and £80,000 at 2026/27 rates (4.65% more for each additional child eligible for child benefit after the first)

If you fall into one of these categories, using a pension could lead to even greater savings. For example, if you have income of £125,140, you may be able to put £25,140 into a pension at a net cost of just £10,056 (£8,171 if you're a Scottish taxpayer). It could be well worth making pension contributions if your income falls into the £100,000 to £125,140 bracket!

Conversely, if your beneficiaries fall into one of these categories, using a pension is unlikely to be beneficial unless these excessive tax rates can be avoided by using inherited drawdown. The last thing a beneficiary should do is draw down funds that fall into the £100,000 to £125,140 income bracket!

Other, less extreme, exceptions to be aware of are that Scottish taxpayers are subject to higher rate tax at 42% on income between £43,662 and £75,000, and advanced rate tax at 45% on income between £75,000 and £100,000. This means, if you are a Scottish higher or advanced rate taxpayer with beneficiaries living elsewhere in the UK, a pension will be more beneficial ***but***, if your beneficiaries live in Scotland, a pension is unlikely to be beneficial unless you can be reasonably certain they will have income of less than £43,662 at some stage, or you are suffering Income Tax at 60%.

Lastly, remember the additional costs we looked at in Section 10.9 where beneficiaries receiving taxable death benefits have property, savings, or dividend income, and little or no taxable income from other sources.

10.13 PENSIONS FOR COMPANY OWNERS

Most small company owner/directors have very little earnings to cover pension contributions because they usually only take a small salary and take the rest of their income as dividends. However, the company can generally make pension contributions up to the annual allowance on their behalf and, provided the payment is justified as part of the director's remuneration package (i.e. by the work the director does for the company), it will attract CT relief. There is no Income Tax relief because the director has not made the contribution personally.

Note that the company pension contribution needs to be included in the director's adjusted income for the purposes of the tapered annual allowance (see Section 10.12) so, if the director is taking total salary and dividends in excess of £200,000, the full annual allowance will not generally be available.

This all makes sense when the director is planning for their own retirement but, in this guide, we are only looking at succession planning.

If the company is a trading company and the current owner intends to pass it on to their children (or other heirs), pension contributions may not make sense for succession planning purposes, as the value of the company may be covered by BPR, or at least attract a significant amount of relief (see Chapter 7). However, there could be a greater IHT exposure if the company has significant amounts of surplus cash that may be treated as an excepted asset (Section 7.11).

The value of a non-trading company, such as a property investment company, will be fully exposed to IHT, so making pension contributions could be an effective succession planning strategy.

So, pension contributions may be beneficial where they either reduce the value of a non-trading company, or remove excepted assets from a trading company.

Example: *Dean's only asset is his property company, Mamot Ltd. He is already taking enough dividends out of the company to meet his own needs and this has made him a higher rate taxpayer. He is now considering making a company pension contribution as a succession planning strategy.*

The company makes a contribution of £60,000. This provides CT relief at an effective rate of 26.5% (see below), saving £15,900, so the net cost is £44,100.

If, alternatively, the company had used the same sum of £44,100 to pay an extra dividend to Dean, he would suffer at least £15,766 in Income Tax (at 35.75%: see below), leaving him with just £28,334. He could then give this to his beneficiaries and, if he survived seven years, it would be free of IHT.

However, as with everything, what really matters is how much better off Dean's beneficiaries are in the end and, assuming Dean lives to at least the age of 75, that will depend on those beneficiary's marginal Income Tax rates. The target to beat is the £28,334 cash gift Dean could have made.

With a pension fund of £60,000, Dean could take his 25% tax-free lump sum, £15,000, give it to his beneficiaries and, if he survives seven years, it will escape both IHT and Income Tax. The remaining £45,000 will be reduced to £27,000 after IHT (ignoring any part of the NRB allocated to his pension). To be better off than with the initial cash gift, the beneficiary needs to be left with more than £13,334 (£28,334 – £15,000) out of this £27,000. That means most beneficiaries will be better off under the pension route using this strategy, as it would take a marginal Income Tax rate of more than 50.6% before they were worse off.

See Sections 10.9 and 10.12 for a detailed look at the pros, cons, and limitations, of the strategy referred to in the last paragraph. See the exceptions given at the end of Section 10.12 for cases where marginal tax rates in excess of 50.6% may arise: plus how to prevent them arising on death benefits by using inherited drawdown.

The pension contribution is clearly a good strategy for Dean in our example and he is probably fairly typical of a small company owner. But there are, alas, a huge number of potential combinations of tax rates to consider in this scenario. Companies generally suffer Corporation Tax at the following rates:

Annual Profit	**Marginal Tax Rate**	
Up to £50,000	19%	(Small Profits Rate)
£50,000 to £250,000	26.5%	(Marginal Rate)
Over £250,000	25%	(Main Rate)

These rates can be affected by a number of factors, including the existence of associated companies, group companies, and investments held by the company (other than properties rented to unconnected third parties). For further details, see the Taxcafe guide *Putting it Through the Company*.

On top of this, we have to consider the Income Tax the owner/director would suffer on extra dividends paid to fund a cash gift. From 6th April 2026, the Income Tax rates suffered on dividend income are:

Basic rate	10.75%
Higher rate	35.75%
Additional rate	39.35%

Dividend income falling into the £100,000 to £125,140 income bracket will suffer an effective Income Tax rate between 53.625% and 58.25%, depending on how the recipient's other income is made up. It would be foolish to pay dividends falling into this income bracket in order to fund cash gifts, so we'll ignore these extreme rates in the rest of our analysis.

Dividends paid to the highest earner in a household where child benefit is being claimed, and falling into the £60,000 to £80,000 income bracket, will also lead to higher effective Income Tax rates and should, again, generally not be used to fund cash gifts.

So, combining our three CT rates with our three main dividend tax rates, let's see how much of a cash gift a company owner can fund when they have a spare £10,000 of profit before tax available in the company.

Table C: Cash Gift Funded from £10,000 Profit

Dividend	Corporation Tax Rate		
Tax Rate	**19%**	**26.5%**	**25%**
10.75%	£7,229	£6,560	£6,694
35.75%	£5,204	£4,722	£4,819
39.35%	£4,913	£4,458	£4,549

We then need to compare this with the net sum the director's beneficiaries would end up with when the same £10,000 is used to fund a pension contribution. For this purpose, we'll assume the director takes their 25% tax-free lump sum by the age of 68, gives it to their beneficiaries, and survives seven years (see Section 10.9). We'll also assume they are unaffected by the statutory maximum for the tax-free lump sum (see Section 10.12).

On this basis, the beneficiaries end up with a total net sum, after both IHT and Income Tax, as follows:

Non-taxpayers	£7,000
Basic rate taxpayers	£6,100
Higher rate taxpayers	£5,200
Additional rate taxpayers	£4,975

What this comparison tells us is that a company pension contribution will always be better than a cash gift if the company owner is an additional rate taxpayer, or the company owner is a higher rate taxpayer and the company's marginal CT rate is 25% or 26.5%.

Where the company pays CT at just 19%, a pension contribution may be beneficial where the owner/director is a higher rate taxpayer and can be reasonably certain their beneficiaries will be basic rate or non-taxpayers. A company pension contribution will *not* generally be beneficial for succession planning purposes if the company owner is a basic rate taxpayer.

As usual, the exceptions listed at the end of Section 10.12 need to be borne in mind. The position may also be different if the director's pension savings exceed £1,073,100.

Couples Can Double Up

Many small companies are owned by couples. If a couple own and manage a company together, it may be possible to put up to £120,000 per year into pensions on their behalf. Each director will also have their own separate limit for tax-free lump sums, so that up to £536,500 (in total) could often be taken and passed to the couple's children (or other beneficiaries).

Other Options

In this section, we have only compared the benefits of pension contributions against using the available cash to fund gifts. Small company owners with an exposure to IHT have other options to consider, such as passing on shares as lifetime gifts (Sections 4.5, 7.30, and 12.10), or passing on shares via a trust (the method described in Section 9.4 works equally well for shares). Married company owners can also use a family debt scheme to get the value of shares out of their estate (Sections 6.13 and 7.31).

10.14 BYPASS TRUSTS

Pension scheme members sometimes nominate a trust to receive death benefits, allowing them to direct not only who receives the income derived from the trust funds after their death, but also who benefits from the trust funds later, after the original beneficiary's death. Typically, a scheme member might do this if they are survived by a spouse or partner (the original beneficiary) and children from another, earlier relationship, who they perhaps want the bulk of the funds to go to eventually.

But bypass trusts of this nature carry some disadvantages. Firstly, the funds become relevant property, subject to anniversary and exit charges (see Chapter 8). While the lump sum paid to the trust only becomes relevant property at the date of the scheme member's death, the trust anniversary dates may be based on the date the trust arrangement was first set up or, in some cases, the date the pension was set up.

The bigger problem, however, is that the lump sum death benefit paid to the trust (and remember it has to be a lump sum) on the death of a scheme member at age 75 or more, is subject to an immediate Lump Sum Death Benefit Charge of 45%. Some or all of that charge can be recovered as trust funds are paid out to beneficiaries, but this may take many years, especially if the scheme member wishes the bulk of the funds to be passed on after the original beneficiary's death.

And, for deaths after 5th April 2027, all of this is after IHT, which will be payable before the remaining funds can be passed to the trust. It is possible that IHT may be avoided at this stage if the original trust beneficiary is the scheme member's spouse, however.

Example: *Paula dies aged 76 with a pension fund of £1m remaining after IHT. She nominated the Yates Family Trust to receive her death benefit so the scheme administrator pays £550,000 to the trust and £450,000 to HMRC (on top of the IHT they have already paid). In accordance with Paula's instructions, the trustees pay £22,000 to her partner, Michael, each year. This payment is treated for Income Tax purposes as a gross payment of £40,000, with a tax credit of £18,000 (45% of the gross).*

Michael has other taxable income of £22,270, so £28,000 of his grossed-up trust income is taxed at 20%, and £12,000 at 40%. That totals £10,400, so Michael will receive an Income Tax repayment of £7,600 (£18,000 – £10,400).

It may work out the same as inherited drawdown in the long run but, from a cashflow point of view, it's a disaster. And, this time, investment growth will make a big difference!

The Lump Sum Death Benefit Charge also applies when death benefits are paid into a trust more than two years after the scheme member's death.

Where a scheme member dies before the age of 75 and a lump sum death benefit is paid into a trust within two years, any amount covered by the LSDBA (or not subject to the LSDBA: see Section 10.6) remains tax free (for Income Tax purposes). However, amounts in excess of the member's available LSDBA (where it applies) are subject to Income Tax at 45%.

The 45% tax charge suffered under these circumstances is *not* the same as the Lump Sum Death Benefit Charge, and can only be recovered where future income arising in the trust is paid out to beneficiaries. It cannot be recovered where capital payments derived from the original lump sum death benefit are made. Hence, this tax may again take a long time to be recovered.

10.15 DEATHS BEFORE 6TH APRIL 2027

Provided the scheme administrator has discretion over who to pay death benefits to, pension savings held by an individual dying before 6th April 2027 will usually be exempt from IHT. For details of the few exceptions where IHT is currently due on pension scheme death benefits, see the twentieth edition of this guide. For the rest of this section, I will assume those exceptions do not apply and look at the position for pension scheme members dying before 6th April 2027, including some of the planning opportunities that may be available to those with a short life expectancy, as well as some pitfalls to avoid.

Taxable Transfers of Value

Because most death benefits currently fall outside a pension scheme member's estate, any payments into a scheme, as well as certain other actions, are potentially transfers of value (Section 2.1). However, HMRC takes the view there is no transfer of value unless the member is in ill health at the time of the payment or other action. HMRC will usually assume the member was in normal health if they survive two years. The result of all this is that paying pension contributions or transferring funds to a pension scheme with better death benefits within two years of a death before 6th April 2027 could result in IHT costs.

However, the member must have been in ill health so if, for example, they died in an accident, while HMRC may look at the position, there should not be any transfer of value. There must also have been a gratuitous intent. Hence, if the member was unaware that they had a life-threatening illness, there is again no transfer of value.

If there is a transfer of value, other exemptions may be available. For example, continuing to pay an established, regular pension contribution should be covered by the normal expenditure out of income exemption (Section 5.5). However, the spouse exemption is not available to cover these transfers of value, as they do not go directly to the spouse.

Where the transfer of value is taxable, it is treated as a lifetime transfer made within seven years of death in the same way as the gifts we looked at in Section 4.5. In some cases, it may be covered by the NRB but consequent additional

IHT may then fall on the beneficiaries of the member's estate. Calculating the amount of the transfer of value arising under these circumstances is a complex matter requiring specialist advice.

Paying the Deceased's Liabilities: A Risk Area

Since, in most cases, pension fund death benefits arising on a death before 6th April 2027 fall outside the deceased's estate, they should not be used to settle the deceased's liabilities, as this would mean those liabilities cannot be deducted from the value of the estate for IHT purposes. See Section 2.10 for further guidance.

Deathbed Planning

As stated above, pension contributions made within two years of death by someone in poor health could give rise to an IHT charge. But there are many reasons why it could still be worth making those contributions:

- Even if no IHT is saved, there will still be Income Tax savings if you die before age 75
- The resultant transfer of value might be covered by your NRB or other exemptions
- The transfer of value could work out at less than the amount you have removed from your estate, thus still producing an IHT saving
- While there is a transfer of value, the contributions will generally lie outside your estate at death. If your estate is in the £2m to £2.7m bracket, this could increase the amount of RNRB available (Section 3.4), thus providing an IHT saving at an effective rate of 20%

In particular, as discussed above, continuing an existing regular pension contribution is likely to be exempt from IHT and is thus probably worthwhile.

Existing Pension Savings

From a tax planning perspective, those with a short life expectancy, such that a death before 6th April 2027 is likely, should generally avoid or minimise pension fund withdrawals wherever possible, as any sums withdrawn and not spent during your lifetime will be subject to IHT.

Married Persons

Most people want to be sure their widow/widower will be comfortable after they've gone so, in practical terms, it often makes sense to nominate them to receive your pension death benefits.

From an IHT point of view, however, this is currently a waste, as your death benefits will generally escape IHT if you die before 6th April 2027. Hence, where practical, it currently makes more sense to leave other assets to your spouse and nominate other beneficiaries (e.g. your children) to receive your pension death benefits. If you survive to 6th April 2027, you could then change your nomination and your Will: but see also Section 10.2 in that event.

Lastly, if leaving your pension fund death benefits to your spouse, beware that a transfer of value (see above) could actually *increase* your IHT burden under some circumstances.

Chapter 11

Practical Aspects of IHT Planning

11.1 THE BIGGER PICTURE

No-one should do IHT planning; they should do estate preservation planning. What is important is not just saving IHT, but preserving family wealth for the benefit of the next generation. Saving IHT is just one part of preserving wealth and it is important never to lose sight of this bigger picture.

When we come to the bigger issue of estate preservation, there are many other factors to be taken into account. In this chapter we will look at some of these other factors, as well as some practical aspects of IHT planning itself.

From early in my career, I was taught 'never let the tax tail wag the commercial dog'. In other words, it is usually more important to get the commercial aspects right before letting tax planning dictate your actions.

For example, putting all your savings into a share of *'Dave's Dodgy Autos'* might be a great way to save IHT, but what's the use of that if Dave runs off to South America with all your money? When all is said and done, Keir Starmer and Rachel Reeves will only take 40%, so they are (just slightly) better than Dodgy Dave.

On the other hand, saving 40% may still be beneficial overall, even in some slightly uncommercial situations. It's a question of getting the right balance and is best expressed as follows:

Bayley's Law: *"The truly wise taxpayer does not seek merely to minimise the amount of tax paid but rather to maximise the amount of wealth remaining after all taxes have been accounted for."*

After commercial issues, the next important issue to watch out for is other taxes. When undertaking tax planning, it is essential to consider all taxes, not just the one you're trying to save. We saw this in action in Chapter 10 with pension savings, where the Income Tax benefits and costs are just as critical as IHT itself.

In other cases, IHT planning often involves transferring assets and this can have important implications for Income Tax, CT, Stamp Duty (on shares and securities), or SDLT (on land and buildings). But the tax that interacts most frequently with IHT is CGT, and we will look at that particular 'clash of the titans' in Chapter 12.

While lifetime transfers of assets can often trigger other taxes, transfers on death usually escape them, with such transfers being exempt from Stamp Duty, SDLT, and CGT. These exemptions generally only apply to a direct transfer from the deceased's estate to the beneficiary, however, so more complex transactions may lead to tax liabilities.

In particular, where property is to be passed to a beneficiary subject to a mortgage, it will generally be better for the beneficiary to take on the existing debt, as this will be exempt from SDLT, rather than buy the property from the estate, or take out a new mortgage. As long as there is an arm's length commercial mortgage provider involved, the original debt should still be deductible from the deceased's estate (see Section 2.10).

As far as Income Tax is concerned, the deceased's personal representatives will generally need to submit a tax return for the period from the beginning of the tax year in which the deceased died up to the date of death. The deceased is entitled to a full year's worth of personal allowance, basic rate band, etc, for this period, so there is often a tax repayment due if they were paying tax under PAYE on a salary or private pension. Sadly, while such a repayment is welcome, it then falls into the deceased's estate and is subject to IHT.

The personal representatives will also have to submit further tax returns on behalf of the estate for the remainder of the tax year in which the deceased died and subsequent tax years until the estate has finally been wound up. The estate is taxed on any income or capital gains it receives during this period: although the uplift on death (see Section 12.2) usually ensures there is very little CGT to pay.

11.2 RELATED PROPERTY

When valuing assets for IHT purposes, an individual's assets are treated as if they are part of a larger holding made up of all the assets held by the individual and their spouse; plus any assets held by a charity or similar exempt body at any time within the last five years that were originally transferred to that body by the individual or their spouse.

Example: *Christine and John are an unmarried couple. Christine owns 3,000 of the 10,000 issued shares in Fleetwood Ltd; John owns 2,200. It has been established that shareholdings of 10% or more (but less than 25%) can be valued at £2,000 per share; holdings of 25% or more (but less than 50%) can be valued at £5,000 per share; and holdings of over 50% are worth £10,000 per share. Hence, at present, the couple's shareholdings are valued as follows:*

Christine: 3,000 x £5,000 = £15m
John: 2,200 x £2,000 = £4.4m

Christine and John have a son, Lindsay, and eventually intend to leave their shares to him. As things stand, this would give rise to transfers of value totalling £19.4m.

Christine and John decide to get married. The related property provisions mean their shares must now be valued as a combined shareholding of 5,200 shares worth £52m (5,200 x £10,000). Leaving their shares to Lindsay will now give rise to transfers of value totalling £52m, or £32.6m more than before they married, thus potentially costing up to £13.04m in extra IHT (£32.6m x 40%). Even if the shares qualify for BPR, the extra cost could be £6.52m (£32.6m x 20%: see Section 7.8).

Christine and John will, of course, have gained the benefit of the spouse exemption and that may be worth more to them. Nonetheless, while marriage is nearly always beneficial for IHT purposes, the example shows there are exceptions.

Practical Problems and Solutions

These related property provisions can cause unexpected problems, with small gifts sometimes being given large hypothetical values for IHT purposes. However, the impact of the related property rules can be reduced if transfers are timed carefully. This is particularly relevant to unquoted shareholdings held by married couples.

Example: *Jack and Diane are a married couple and both own shares in Mellencamp Ltd, an unquoted investment company not qualifying for BPR. Jack owns 2% of the company and his shares are worth just £2,000. Diane owns 49% of the company and her shares are worth £245,000. Under the related property rules, however, their shares must be valued as part of a combined shareholding of 51%. This shareholding, being enough to provide control of the company, is worth £510,000.*

The couple now wish to give their son, John a 25% share in the company. Jack transfers his 2% stake to John first. This represents a transfer of value of £20,000 (2/51 x £510,000). Diane then transfers a further 23% to John. This represents a transfer of value of £115,000 (23/49 x £245,000), bringing the total to £135,000.

If Diane had made her transfer first, this would have been a transfer of value of £230,000 (23/51 x £510,000). Jack's subsequent transfer would then have been a transfer of value equal to 2/28ths of the value of a 28% shareholding, let's say £10,000 for the sake of argument.

By making the smaller transfer first, the couple have reduced the effective transfer of value by £105,000, providing a potential IHT saving of up to £42,000 (at 40%).

Post-Death Relief

Where an inherited asset that was valued under the related property rules is sold within three years of the previous owner's death, it can be re-valued at the date of death (for IHT purposes), without taking account of the related property. The sale must be made on arm's length terms, must not be to a connected person (Appendix A), and must not be made in conjunction with other related property sales.

11.3 JOINTLY HELD PROPERTY

Any form of property can be held jointly, including bank accounts, shares and securities, or land and buildings. The key point to note about jointly held property is that, on a joint owner's death, their share may sometimes pass by survivorship and not by intestacy or under the deceased's Will. This has major implications for IHT planning, as you may not be free to transfer your share of jointly held property in the most tax-efficient way.

After the joint bank account, the next most common form of jointly held property in the UK is land and buildings, sometimes referred to as real property. In fact, most couples in the UK now own their home jointly.

In England and Wales, there are two different legal forms for jointly held property: Joint Tenants or Tenants in Common.

Joint Tenants
In a joint tenancy, each joint owner has an equal share (e.g. 50/50 for two joint owners) and each share passes automatically to the other joint owner/owners on death. This is what is meant by survivorship. Furthermore, joint owners are normally unable to sell their share of the property without the consent of the other joint owner(s).

This may restrict the scope for IHT planning with the property and joint tenancies are therefore generally less desirable than tenancies in common from a tax planning perspective. However, the security provided by the right of survivorship is often considered of more value by many couples.

Tenants in Common
Under a tenancy in common, the joint owners are generally free to do as they wish with their share of the property and there is no right of survivorship. The joint owners' shares in the property need not be equal. A tenancy in common therefore opens up a wide range of IHT planning opportunities that may not always be available under a joint tenancy.

Practical Implications
As explained above, each person's share in a joint tenancy will usually pass to the other joint owner by survivorship. In the case of the family home, the surviving joint owner will usually be the widow/widower of the deceased. Following the introduction of the TNRB (see Chapter 6), this will usually be the best result anyway.

Nevertheless, for the reasons explained in Section 6.8, this may sometimes still be bad IHT planning. It is, however, possible to break a joint tenancy via a deed of variation (Section 17.1) within two years after a joint owner dies. Alternatively, it may be preferable to sever the joint tenancy during both owners' lifetimes, as this provides more certainty. It is not always wise to rely on a deed of variation to rectify the situation!

Once a joint tenancy has been severed or broken, whether during the owner's lifetime or via a deed of variation, it becomes a tenancy in common.

A share in property held under a tenancy in common may be passed to anyone, under the terms of the deceased's Will, or possibly via a deed of variation, as explained in Section 17.1. Hence, whenever undertaking any IHT planning on the family home in England or Wales that involves passing a share of the property to anyone other than the surviving spouse, it may be wise to first ensure the property is held under a tenancy in common.

Breaking a joint tenancy to create a tenancy in common can be achieved at a reasonably modest cost and should, in itself, be tax free, as it is not treated as a disposal for CGT purposes, nor an acquisition for SDLT purposes. If you change your property to a tenancy in common and then draw up your Wills to put the appropriate IHT planning measures in place, remember to make sure you also buy any new property as tenants in common if you move!

Scotland
In Scotland, joint ownership of real property mainly comes in a form known as Pro Indivisio, which operates in a broadly similar manner to a tenancy in common. A form of beneficial joint tenancy is also available in Scotland using a survivorship destination. This cannot be severed unilaterally, which can lead to practical difficulties if one joint owner decides they wish to pass their share to someone other than their co-owner. A survivorship destination can, however, be broken by a deed of variation where the surviving joint owner is prepared to co-operate.

Nonetheless, relying on using a deed of variation when the time comes may not always be wise so it may make sense to break the survivorship destination during both owners' lifetimes to better facilitate any IHT planning that involves passing a share of the property to someone other than the surviving joint owner. And be careful when you move house too!

Valuing Jointly Held Property
A useful benefit of jointly held property is the fact a discount often applies to the value of a joint owner's share of the property.

Example: *Two sisters, Mel and Kim, live together in Appleby Manor, which they own jointly. Sadly, Kim dies in September 2026, when Appleby Manor is worth £1.5m. Kim's half share is not valued at £750,000, as one might expect, but at a discount of 15%, i.e. £637,500. This discount produces an effective IHT saving of £45,000.*

The discount applies to reflect the practical difficulty in selling a joint owner's part share of a property. The discount also reflects the fact that the other joint owner has a right to occupy the property and is therefore akin to a sitting tenant, thus further reducing the value of a joint share in the property.

The 15% discount used above was established by an IHT case back in 1982. In a more recent case, it was suggested a discount of 10% might now be more appropriate, especially where the surviving joint owner is not likely to remain in occupation of the property. Nevertheless, conventional wisdom seems to be that a 15% discount is still appropriate in the case of residential property occupied by the surviving joint owner. A lower discount rate may be appropriate in other cases but it is certainly still worth claiming.

HMRC takes the view that the related property rules (Section 11.2) prevent any discount applying where a property is held jointly by spouses. Furthermore, due to the different nature of joint property titles in Scotland, the usual discount does not generally apply to property there.

Other Jointly Held Assets
A jointly held bank or building society account in England or Wales passes in its entirety to the surviving joint account holder on the other account holder's death. In Scotland, a joint account holder's share of a joint account usually falls

into their general estate to be dealt with according to the terms of their Will or the laws of intestacy (Section 11.7).

In either case, the deceased's share of the joint account is included in their estate for IHT purposes (although it will usually be exempt if it passes to their spouse). The deceased's share will generally be taken to be half the account balance and no discount can apply.

Other jointly held property, such as paintings, antiques and personal effects may be subject to a substantial discount due to the fact that a joint owner is generally unable to sell such property. Unmarried couples can therefore save substantial amounts of IHT by jointly holding tangible moveable property (e.g. antiques) and separately passing each joint share to their intended beneficiaries (but not each other).

11.4 MORTGAGES

It is important to be aware that any transfer of property subject to a mortgage will require the lender's consent. If the transferee takes over the mortgage, the outstanding borrowings will be deemed to constitute purchase consideration and may give rise to a SDLT charge if they are £40,000 or more; or more than £150,000 in the case of commercial property.

Transfers to spouses are not subject to the extra 5% SDLT surcharge. Hence a spouse can take over a mortgage (or share of a mortgage) on a residential property with a balance up to £125,000 without any SDLT cost.

Mortgages are deducted from the value of the property they are secured against for the purposes of the RNRB, unless they must be deducted from the value of another asset under the rules in Sections 2.10 or 15.6.

11.5 RESIDENTIAL CARE FEES

While IHT is a major worry, many people are more concerned about losing their property to the local authority in order to pay nursing home or residential care fees in their old age. In some cases, the local authority may even be able to force a sale of a property that has previously been given away if they can show this was done to avoid payment of the fees.

In some instances, it has been accepted that, where a property has been given away for IHT planning purposes, the local authority were unable to claim the taxpayer's motive was to avoid care fees. Nevertheless, this approach is not entirely reliable, as many families have found to their cost (see Section 12.8).

A better approach is often to take out long-term care insurance or even emergency care assurance. The latter approach generally requires the payment of a single lump sum premium in exchange for an annuity covering the residential care fees. The amount of the premium is generally equal to around two to three years' worth of care fees.

Emergency care assurance is a useful strategy employed by many families who wish to have certainty about the cost of looking after their elderly relative. If necessary, the premium can be funded by way of a loan secured against the relative's former home, thus enabling the family to keep the property and perhaps even benefit from the CGT uplift on death (Section 12.2).

11.6 LEGAL DOMICILE

Generally speaking, for deaths, or other transfers of value after 5th April 2025, an individual's legal domicile is no longer directly relevant for IHT purposes. However, legal domicile can still affect other issues covered in this guide. Hence, it is worth us taking a brief look at it.

In essence, your legal domicile is the country you regard as your permanent home. Technically, you cannot have legal domicile in the UK, but only in England and Wales, Scotland, or Northern Ireland. This can be important for a number of reasons: see Sections 2.13 and 11.7, for example.

At birth, each individual acquires the same legal domicile as the parent on whom they are legally dependent, usually their father. This is known as their domicile of origin. In most (but not all) cases, an individual's domicile of origin will therefore be the country in which their father was born. Most people retain their domicile of origin for the rest of their life, although a new legal domicile (a domicile of choice) can be acquired when an individual makes a permanent home in a different country. For further details, see the nineteenth edition of this guide.

Double Tax Treaties

The following countries have Double Tax Treaties with the UK covering IHT: France, India, Irish Republic, Italy, Netherlands, Pakistan, South Africa, Sweden, Switzerland, and the USA. These may affect your IHT position if you have, or acquire, legal domicile in one of these countries.

11.7 WILLS, INTESTACY, AND STATUTORY RIGHTS

Most people are pretty relaxed about dying intestate (without a valid Will) until they realise what would actually happen. Most of us know we should make a Will, but a great many of us put it off until it's too late.

Quite apart from IHT planning, a Will is sensible as, without a valid Will, your assets will be divided up according to the ancient laws of intestacy and this may be very different to what you would have liked. More importantly, a Will is essential for nominating the future guardians of your children if, as Oscar Wilde would have put it, they are careless enough to lose both parents.

In the tables that follow, 'issue' generally means your children but, if your children pre-decease you, their children will take their place. For example, if you have three children and one of them pre-deceases you, leaving two children of their own, the share going to your children will be divided so that one third of that share goes to each of your surviving children and one sixth goes to each of your grandchildren by your deceased child.

Under these rules, children include natural children (whether 'legitimate' or not) and adopted children. Unlike some aspects of IHT law, step-children and foster children are not included (unless legally adopted).

Dying Without a Will: England and Wales

If you have legal domicile in England and Wales, and die without a valid Will, your spouse must survive you by at least 28 days to be entitled to any assets in your estate. If your spouse does not survive for this period, you will be treated as if you were not married. Subject to this, your estate will be divided as follows:

1. If you leave a spouse and issue: The first £322,000 and all personal possessions go to your spouse. 50% of the balance is divided equally between your children. The remaining 50% is held on trust, with your spouse having a life interest and the remainder going to your children.

2. If you leave a spouse but no issue: Your entire estate goes to your surviving spouse.

3. If you leave issue but no spouse: Your estate is divided equally between your children.

4. If you leave no spouse or issue: Your estate goes to the nearest relatives to survive you, using the following order of precedence: your parents; full siblings, or their issue (i.e. your nieces and nephews); half siblings, or their issue; grandparents; aunts and uncles, or their issue (your first cousins).

5. If no near-relatives survive you: Your entire estate goes to the Crown!

Dying Without a Will: Scotland

If you have legal domicile in Scotland and die without a valid Will, your estate will be divided as follows:

1. If you leave a spouse and issue: Your spouse gets: your interest in any dwelling (the family home) up to a value of £473,000 or, if the family home's value exceeds this amount, the right to receive the sum of £473,000; personal possessions up to the value of £29,000; the first £50,000 of the remaining estate; and one third of any other moveable property (i.e. anything other than land and buildings). Your children then get the remainder of your estate.

2. If you leave a spouse but no issue: Your entire estate goes to your surviving spouse. (This rule came into force in March 2024 and represents a significant change from the previous rules.)

3. If you leave issue but no spouse: Your estate is divided equally between your children.

4. If you leave no spouse or issue: If you are survived by at least one parent and at least one sibling (or their issue), 50% of your estate goes to your parents and 50% to your siblings or their issue. In any other case, your estate goes to the nearest relatives to survive you, based on the following order of precedence: siblings; parents; aunts and uncles; grandparents; grandparents' siblings; great-grandparents, etc. Any claimant's children or remoter issue may take the place of a claimant who pre-deceased you, except where the deceased claimant was your parent. Half siblings only count as siblings for these purposes if you have no surviving full siblings or their issue. If your entire clan has been wiped out and you have no surviving relatives: yes, you've guessed it, everything goes to the Crown (who, in centuries past, often did the wiping out!)

So, as you can see, whether you live in Swansea, Manchester, or Aberdeen (and probably Belfast too, although I don't have those rules to hand), you really shouldn't be relaxed about dying without a Will. This is especially true if you are separated because, as far as the laws of intestacy are concerned, a spouse is still a spouse until you get divorced.

It is not unknown for widows or widowers to be forced to sell the family home due to the operation of the above rules and, without proper provision, children could end up being taken into care.

The statutory intestacy rules take no account of common-law partners, step-children, or many other important personal relationships. A remote cousin could get everything in priority to a fondly loved step-child. The Crown could even get your house in priority to a common-law partner you've lived with for decades. And you thought IHT was bad enough!

Will Limitations

A Will is rendered void by marriage, unless written in contemplation of that marriage. Furthermore, your Will can only determine what happens to assets falling into your estate and which you are free to dispose of as you wish. Jointly held property may be subject to survivorship (see Section 11.3), and most pension fund death benefits and life insurance proceeds need to be dealt with separately (see Sections 10.4 and 11.8).

Apart from these points, in England, Wales, or Northern Ireland, you may generally distribute your estate as you wish under the terms of your Will. Surviving spouses may, however, apply to the courts for an increased share of the estate where the amount provided in the Will does not represent adequate financial provision for their care and maintenance. In essence, this is something akin to posthumous divorce proceedings. Similar applications may be made on behalf of dependant minor children of the deceased.

A different system operates in Scotland where legal rights take priority over the terms of the deceased's Will unless waived by the beneficiaries concerned. Legal rights for beneficiaries of a deceased with legal domicile in Scotland are:

Surviving spouse: Where there are no issue of the deceased, one half of the deceased's moveable property, otherwise one third.
Surviving issue: Where there is no surviving spouse of the deceased, one half of the deceased's moveable property, otherwise one third.

The question of whether you have legal domicile in Scotland is the same as any other legal domicile issue (Section 11.6). Hence, you may have lived in England or Wales for decades but, if you or your parents were born in Scotland, you could still have legal domicile in Scotland, and your spouse and children will have legal rights as set out above.

11.8 LIFE INSURANCE

One simple way to prevent your estate being excessively inflated on your death is to ensure all forms of life insurance cover you have are written in favour of other family members. Such a policy effectively constitutes a bare trust (Section 8.5) and means the proceeds will never fall into your estate but will go, instead, to your intended beneficiaries free of IHT. This may extend to some death benefits under occupational pension schemes: see Section 10.5.

Ideally, if they can afford to do without it, your spouse should not be the beneficiary under any of your life policies. In practice, this suggestion may sometimes be somewhat impractical, especially when you have a young family, but it is worth reviewing the position as you get older.

Payments of regular insurance premiums will usually be covered by the annual exemption or the exemption for normal expenditure out of income (Section 5.5), so these do not usually present a problem.

Depending on the exact circumstances, and for the reasons outlined in Section 4.4, a large lump-sum premium paid on a policy written in favour of another individual may represent a PET, a chargeable lifetime transfer, or a mixture of both.

Life Policies Written in Trust

By writing a life policy into trust, you will be using a form of interest in possession trust. This retains the advantage of keeping the proceeds of the policy out of your estate, but also means you can vary the intended beneficiaries over the course of your lifetime. Furthermore, this also ensures no IHT arises if any of your beneficiaries pre-decease you. For these reasons, it generally made sense to write life policies into trust before March 2006.

For many policies written into trust before March 2006, it is business as usual and their beneficial treatment continues. HMRC has even confirmed that paying a regular premium on a policy already held before 22nd March 2006 will generally continue to be classed as a PET, if not already exempted under another provision.

One change of beneficiary before 6th October 2008 will have turned the trust into a transitional serial interest (Section 8.10) and it will effectively retain its beneficial treatment. Any other changes of beneficiary, however, will bring it into the relevant property trust regime (Sections 8.14 to 8.16).

Life policies written into trust after March 2006 will generally fall into the relevant property trust regime. This also applies where changes are made to existing policies and those changes were not permitted under the terms of the policy as at 22nd March 2006.

Where a life policy falls into the relevant property trust regime, it may potentially be subject to entry, exit, and anniversary charges. Payments of regular premiums will usually be covered by the annual exemption or the exemption for normal expenditure out of income (Section 5.5), so these do not usually present a problem in themselves. Any large, lump-sum premium payments, however, will be chargeable lifetime transfers and will give rise to immediate IHT liabilities where the policyholder's NRB has been exhausted.

Ten-yearly anniversary charges will be applied to the policy (Section 8.15). Generally, the policy's value for this purpose will be taken to be the cumulative amount of premiums paid to date, although in cases where the policyholder is in poor health at the anniversary date, it is feared HMRC may argue a greater value should be used to reflect the likelihood of the policy's imminent maturity. (An image of a vulture has jumped into my mind!)

Worst of all, of course, an exit charge of up to 6% (Section 8.16) will apply when the policyholder dies. That's still a lot better than 40% though!

Insuring for Inheritance Tax Liabilities

Much of the IHT planning discussed elsewhere in this guide depends on the transferor surviving a certain period after a transfer, or some other transaction, has been made. Often the period concerned will be seven years, but survival to other anniversaries can also be critical. When death occurs before the expiry of the critical period, unexpected tax bills can arrive as a nasty surprise. It is often a good idea, therefore, to take out some term life insurance on the transferor to guard against this possibility. It is important to make sure the transferor is not the beneficiary of the term insurance as this will inflate the value of their estate and lead to an effective grossing up of IHT liabilities.

11.9 LOTTERY SYNDICATES

Lottery, pools, and other gambling syndicates are breeding grounds for potential IHT problems. Just imagine this:

Example: *Donny wins £125m on the National Lottery. It's in all the media, so you can bet HMRC knows about it. He gives £25m to each of his brothers, Wayne, Merrill, Jay, and Jimmy. Tragically, just a few weeks later, Donny is killed water skiing in Utah.*

HMRC demands almost £50m in IHT from Donny's family as the transfers to his brothers were made only weeks before his death. "But we were in a syndicate," protest the brothers. "Prove it!" replies HMRC.

The simple answer to this problem is to make sure you have documentary evidence of any syndicate arrangements.

11.10 MINOR PROBLEMS

You may have noticed I tend to base a lot of my examples around gifts to adult children. This is because transfers of value to minor children carry a few extra complications.

Gifts to Minors by Parents

Any gift from a parent to, or for the benefit of, their own minor child is subject to the Income Tax settlements legislation. This means the parent is subject to tax on any income derived from the gifted assets (subject to a general exemption for income not exceeding £100 per annum and the further exemptions for Child Trust Funds and Junior ISAs below). The Income Tax burden can often be reduced by making sure the parent with the lower level of income makes the gift.

The child has their own annual exemption and basic rate band for CGT purposes, so some savings can be generated on capital gains, such as where funds are invested in a stock market portfolio on behalf of the child.

Assets gifted to a child, or purchased with gifted funds, are usually held on bare trust, with one parent acting as trustee. Bare trusts are treated as if the child owned the assets directly for IHT purposes (Section 8.5); although it is important not to fall foul of the gifts with reservation rules (Section 4.8).

The best way for a parent to make large IHT effective gifts to minor children is generally to use relevant property trusts (Section 9.1). Such trusts will be settlor-interested trusts for CGT purposes (Section 9.4). Hence, given the inability to hold over capital gains, it will generally make sense to make cash settlements into the trust; although other assets might sometimes be suitable where there would be little or no CGT liability arising on the transfer.

When using a settlor-interested trust, it is essential to ensure the parent making the settlement cannot benefit. If both parents are making a settlement into the trust then neither can benefit. Even when there is only one settlor, it is generally wise to ensure their spouse cannot benefit. If a settlor can or, in practice, does benefit from a trust, the assets and funds within the trust will be treated as gifts with reservation (Section 4.8) and the trust will be rendered ineffective for IHT planning purposes.

This makes it vital that any income, or other funds, derived from the relevant property trust is effectively ring-fenced and cannot be used in any way to benefit the settlor. This requires some careful management, as using trust income, or other funds, to settle any expenses or obligations that would normally fall on the settlor, as the beneficiary's parent, could render the trust ineffective for IHT purposes.

For smaller gifts, either a Child Trust Fund or Junior ISA may be the best vehicle to use (see further below).

Grandparents, Aunts, Uncles, Etc

Other family members may generally make gifts to minor children without the problems set out above. Hence, you could make gifts to your grandchildren or your nephews and nieces, and these will usually be PETs; or you could transfer assets into trust for these children and holdover any capital gains arising. Similarly, your parents or your siblings could make gifts to your children or into a trust for their benefit, with the same results. Be careful to avoid any kind of reciprocal arrangements as these might trigger the associated operations rules (Section 11.11). Also, don't forget the gifts with reservation rules (Section 4.8) can apply to a gift to any person or any trust where you are not excluded from benefitting.

Will Trusts for Minors

HMRC appears to take the view that a minor cannot have an immediate post-death interest (Section 8.9), as trust law would make such a trust discretionary in nature. Anyone intending to leave assets in trust for the benefit of a minor should therefore consider using a bereaved minor's trust, an 18 to 25 trust, or even just a bare trust.

A bare trust carries some advantages for Income Tax and CGT purposes, as the minor's own allowances could be set against income and capital gains. A similar result may be obtained via the trusts for vulnerable individuals exception (see Section 8.17), but this carries a few limitations that will not always be desirable.

Child Trust Funds and Junior ISAs

Minor children born in the UK before 3rd January 2011 should have a Child Trust Fund. Junior ISAs are available to UK resident minors who were not eligible for a Child Trust Fund.

Parents, family, and friends of minor children may put up to £9,000 in total into the child's Junior ISA or Child Trust Fund each tax year. Monies grow free from Income Tax or CGT, like a normal ISA. On maturity, funds within a Child Trust Fund may be transferred to an ISA in the child's name. Junior ISAs automatically convert to a normal ISA when the child reaches 18. No withdrawals are permitted before this time.

Payments into Child Trust Funds or Junior ISAs are PETs unless covered by an exemption, such as the annual exemption or the exemption for normal expenditure out of income.

Funds within a Child Trust Fund or Junior ISA form part of the child's estate and, crucially, ***not*** their parent's. They remain subject to IHT, however, in the tragic event that the child should die before the age of 18. (Yes, if a child's estate exceeds the NRB, they are subject to IHT like anyone else. Vultures!)

11.11 ANTI-AVOIDANCE MEASURES

There is a great deal of targeted anti-avoidance legislation aimed at blocking specific areas, or types, of IHT planning (e.g. the rules on deduction of liabilities: Section 2.10). In this section, it is worth looking at some of the more general anti-avoidance measures at HMRC's disposal.

Where there are two or more transfers of the same property, or two or more transactions that affect the same property, HMRC may invoke the associated operations rules. Broadly speaking, where these rules are applied, the transfers or transactions are treated as if just one transfer from the original transferor to the ultimate recipient had taken place, thus undoing any tax planning the intermediate steps aimed to achieve.

HMRC's powers under the associated operations rules are extremely wide-ranging and, as we have seen several times, there are many IHT planning techniques that might potentially be caught. Nevertheless, where there are sufficiently good non-tax reasons for carrying out the transactions, the application of the associated operations rules may still be avoided.

Time is a good defence against the associated operations rules: the longer the gap between one transaction and the next, the less likely the planning measures are to be attacked. Uncertainty is also important. Where subsequent transfers are uncertain of being carried out at the time of an earlier transfer, they are far less likely to be deemed associated operations.

It is also worth noting, as a general principle, death itself is not regarded as an associated operation or a step in a tax avoidance scheme (perhaps because, while the event itself is certain, the timing is not). This saves many planning techniques from being caught by the associated operations rules.

The general anti-abuse rule (GAAR) is targeted at 'artificial' and 'abusive' or 'aggressive' tax avoidance schemes that go beyond the scope of normal tax planning and use loopholes in tax legislation in a way not intended by Parliament. Where the GAAR applies, any tax advantage gained through the use of the 'abusive' scheme will be reversed.

We are told normal tax planning should not be affected and, to date, HMRC have not applied the GAAR to any of the IHT planning strategies in this guide. It also seems unlikely the GAAR could affect any techniques not already at risk of attack under the associated operations rules. Nonetheless, there is a risk some more advanced IHT planning techniques might one day be challenged under the GAAR.

There is a legal obligation to disclose certain types of IHT planning techniques under the 'DOTAS' (disclosure of tax avoidance schemes) regime. In other words, the taxpayer using the technique must advise HMRC they have done so. Disclosure does not necessarily mean the scheme doesn't work, but it may lead to greater scrutiny from HMRC. Only more advanced techniques are affected, specifically those which:

- Reduce or eliminate the entry, anniversary, or exit charges where assets or funds are placed in a relevant property trust (see Chapter 8)
- Reduce or eliminate charges on company participators (not referred to in this guide, but potentially an issue for family investment companies: see Chapter 14)
- Avoid the gifts with reservation rules (Section 4.8), without leading to a pre-owned assets charge (Section 11.12)
- Reduce the value of a person's estate without creating a chargeable lifetime transfer or PET

The arrangements must also involve one or more 'contrived or abnormal' steps to require disclosure. Writing a Will is never regarded as abnormal, so anything put in place purely through a Will need not be disclosed.

By and large it is only commercial products, such as those covered in Sections 7.26, 9.9, and 9.10, or complex arrangements, such as those in Chapter 14, or Sections 15.1 and 15.2, that may need to be disclosed. These generally require professional advice, so ***my*** advice is: whenever an IHT planning technique is complex enough to require professional advice, seek advice regarding whether the scheme needs to be reported under DOTAS at the same time.

11.12 THE PRE-OWNED ASSETS CHARGE

An Income Tax charge may be levied on the former owner of an asset who continues to benefit from that asset, or on a donor who benefits from the use of assets purchased with funds they had previously gifted. While this is an Income Tax charge, its purpose is to deter IHT planning. Hence there is a general exemption for assets already caught under the gifts with reservation rules (Section 4.8) or that are otherwise still included in the donor's estate.

Assets subject to the charge are known as 'pre-owned assets' and, broadly, the charge taxes the annual value of these assets as a benefit-in-kind. For land and buildings, the annual value is the property's open-market rental value. For most other assets it is based on a fixed sum of 5% of their capital value. The initial values to be used are those prevailing on the date the asset first falls within the provisions. These values can be used for five years before the asset must be revalued.

Any amounts the former owner is paying for the use of the asset may be deducted from the annual value in arriving at the taxable benefit. These payments must be made under a legal obligation so, in the case of property, a formal lease is required.

The charge is designed to hit back at a number of IHT planning schemes but, technically, could also catch many unintended, innocent victims, as there is no motive test. Furthermore, there is no exemption for an unexpected change of circumstances in the same way as for gifts with reservation (Section 4.8).

HMRC have been accused of 'institutional disinterest' in the pre-owned assets charge as it is really designed to deter IHT planning and they seem to have very little interest in actually collecting it. Nonetheless, where the charge is technically due, it remains the taxpayer's duty to report it.

One of the greatest risk areas is gifts between unmarried partners. For example, if an individual gives their partner some money to help purchase a property they then live in together, that property is caught by the charge. Furthermore, the charge still applies if the couple subsequently get married. Such problems can usually be avoided by either purchasing the property in joint names or by marrying before the gift is made: although these simple strategies will not be available in every case.

There are a few exemptions from the charge, including:

i) Gifts to your spouse; or to a former spouse under the terms of a court order (including gifts to a trust for their benefit: although the exemption ceases to apply if their interest comes to an end before their death)
ii) Gifts for maintenance of family (Section 5.4)
iii) Gifts wholly covered by the annual or small gifts exemption
iv) Sales of your entire interest in an asset made on commercial, arm's length terms (even if made to a connected party)
v) Sales of a part interest in an asset made on normal, commercial, arm's length terms to an unconnected party, or for consideration not in the form of money, or assets readily convertible into money (see Appendix A for a list of connected persons)
vi) The donor's total annual taxable benefits ***before*** deducting contributions paid by the donor do not exceed £5,000. This is an 'all or nothing' exemption so, if total taxable benefits exceed this amount, the ***whole*** sum (less donor contributions) is taxed
vii) The asset was acquired with funds derived from an outright gift of money seven years or more before the donor enjoyed any benefit
viii) The donor has retained a suitable interest in the gifted asset, such as a parent who has given a joint share in a property to an adult child who lives there with them

Furthermore, the charge does not apply to non-UK residents, or to assets that would not be chargeable to IHT, such as foreign assets formerly held by, or purchased with funds donated by, an individual who is not subject to IHT on their worldwide estate (see Section 2.2).

The charge does not apply where the donor's enjoyment of an asset is minor and incidental, such as social visits to the current occupier of a property. The charge can only apply to property if the donor is in occupation (see Section 4.8 for further guidance: the same principles apply here).

Finally, there is a *'Get Out Of Jail: But Not Free'* card, in the shape of an option to elect out of the pre-owned assets charge by allowing the relevant asset to be included in the donor's estate for IHT purposes. The asset is then treated as a gift with reservation (Section 4.8) and effectively remains in the donor's estate for as long as they continue to enjoy a benefit. The election should be made by 31st January following the tax year in which the charge would have first arisen, although HMRC generally accept late elections. Once made, the election is irrevocable.

The most likely application of the pre-owned assets charge is in the case of the family home. It should not generally arise under any of the planning methods described in Chapter 13, but the following points are worth noting:

- If the former home is sold after being given away, a charge could arise if the transferor benefits from an asset purchased with the proceeds.
- Methods that involve realising cash and giving it away could give rise to a charge if the donor benefits from the use of an asset purchased with the proceeds within seven years after making their gifts.
- Methods that involve passing the deceased's share of the property to a trust or to someone other than their surviving spouse could pose a risk if the surviving spouse had originally given a share in the property to the deceased, or had given them the funds with which to purchase their share, and had done so before they were married.

11.13 FOREIGN ISSUES

As explained in Section 2.2, IHT applies to overseas assets held by long-term UK residents (and some former long-term UK residents). However, it is important to understand some form of succession or inheritance tax may also apply to overseas assets in the country in which they are located. Furthermore, foreign succession law may also apply to those assets. You may also be subject to some form of succession or inheritance tax in any country where you are a national, a citizen, or a resident; or have been at some time in the past.

Lastly, it is worth noting some countries tax the beneficiary of a gift or inheritance. Hence, if you are leaving assets, or funds, to a beneficiary resident, or with legal domicile, overseas, this could create a foreign tax liability, and this may even end up falling on your estate.

As with all foreign tax issues, it is wise to take local advice if there is a chance you may be affected.

Chapter 12

Interaction with CGT

12.1 A QUICK CAPITAL GAINS TAX UPDATE

Before we look at that 'clash of the titans' created by the interaction between CGT and IHT, I will provide a quick update on the current CGT regime.

Individuals currently pay CGT at two main rates: 18% and 24%. The lower, 18% rate, applies to the extent of any basic rate band remaining available. A reduced CGT rate applies where business asset disposal relief (BADR) or investor's relief (IVR) is available (and is claimed): see Section 12.5 for details.

Generally speaking, however, once your combined taxable income and gains for the year exceed the higher-rate tax threshold of £50,270, you must pay CGT at 24% on any further gains arising in the same tax year.

Example: *Beyoncé has taxable income of £38,270 for 2026/27. After deducting her personal allowance of £12,570, she is liable for Income Tax on £25,700. This means £12,000 of her £37,700 basic rate band remains available. In February 2027, she makes a capital gain of £38,000 on an investment property. After deducting her annual CGT exemption of £3,000, she is left with a taxable gain of £35,000. The first £12,000 of her taxable gain is taxed at 18% and the remaining £23,000 is taxed at 24%.*

Anyone with taxable income in excess of the higher-rate tax threshold simply pays CGT at 24% on all their capital gains after deducting the annual CGT exemption (unless BADR or IVR is available and is claimed).

Disposals of UK residential property giving rise to any taxable gain must be reported to HMRC within 60 days of completion. This includes gifts to another individual (other than your spouse), transfers into trusts or companies, and any other disposal of UK residential property, even when the gain arising is held over. Any CGT arising must also be paid by the same deadline. Non-UK resident individuals must report *all* disposals of UK property, and pay the related CGT, by the same deadline.

As the annual CGT exemption has been reduced to a pathetic £3,000, I am simply going to ignore it throughout the rest of this guide. In practice, however, it will often produce small additional savings. For further details of the current CGT regime, including the application of the reliefs mentioned in this chapter to property, see the Taxcafe guide *How to Save Property Tax.*

12.2 THE UPLIFT ON DEATH

Do you remember my opening comments in Section 4.5: "For CGT purposes, death is often a good tax-planning strategy." The reason for this rather dark-humoured remark is one simple fact: on death, the CGT base cost of the deceased's assets is uplifted to their market value at that date.

Example: *In 1985, Jerry set up Killer Ltd with an investment of just £10,000. By July 2026, his controlling interest in Killer Promotions PLC (the same company) is worth £100m. Jerry's CGT bill on a sale of these shares would be almost £24m.*

Sadly, Jerry dies in August 2026, and leaves his entire Killer Promotions PLC shareholding to his son, Lee. Lee sells the shares for £102m in March 2027. His CGT bill will be just £480,000 at most.

Lee is treated as if he acquired the shares in August 2026 for a price of £100m. We call this the CGT 'uplift on death'. His taxable gain on the sale in March 2027 is therefore just £2m.

12.3 THE CAPITAL GAINS TAX vs INHERITANCE TAX DILEMMA

While death is very good CGT planning, lifetime transfers generally pose a problem. As explained in Section 4.9, a lifetime transfer of anything other than cash will give rise to a CGT disposal, which is deemed to take place at market value. Hence, in the example in Section 12.2, if Jerry had given the Killer Promotions PLC shares to Lee before he died, he may have given himself a £24m CGT bill!

This creates a bit of a dilemma: the best way to save IHT is often to make lifetime transfers, whereas the best way to save CGT is to hold on to assets until death. What we really want to do is minimise the overall tax burden or, to be more precise, follow ***Bayley's Law*** (Section 11.1). To do this, we need to start by considering what reliefs the assets will qualify for, both under the IHT regime and under the CGT regime.

The three major areas to consider are: business assets; transfers to spouses; and the family home. We will look at each of these areas in turn. Assets that do not fall under any of these headings are dealt with in Sections 12.9 and 12.10. Remember always, as we proceed through this analysis, that lifetime transfers are generally only fully effective if the transferor survives seven years. Nonetheless, we will see instances where there is still some benefit, even if the transferor dies sooner.

Another point to factor in is that paying CGT in your lifetime will inevitably reduce your estate on death. So, in most cases, when we are looking at IHT planning, a £10,000 CGT bill will ultimately only cost your family £6,000. But that's cold comfort when you're having to pay £10,000 on a lifetime transfer now, usually without any sale proceeds to fund it!

12.4 GIFTS OF BUSINESS ASSETS

Where a qualifying business asset is transferred by way of gift, the capital gain arising may be held over. This provides an effective CGT deferral, but means the uplift on death will be lost.

Example: *Kurt set up Nevermind Ltd in 2011 with a share capital of just 100 £1 ordinary shares. The shares currently qualify for both holdover relief and BADR (see Section 12.5). In December 2026, Kurt gives 25 shares to his unmarried partner, Courtney, and they elect to hold over the capital gain arising. In effect, this means Courtney is treated as if she acquired the shares for £1 each: the price Kurt paid.*

Kurt dies in March 2027 and, fearing a drop in value, Courtney decides to sell her Nevermind Ltd shares at their current value of £5,000 per share, £125,000 in total. Courtney's base cost for her shares is just £25, so she ends up with a capital gain of £124,975. Her CGT bill, at 24%, is therefore £29,994 (assuming she is a higher-rate taxpayer).

Sadly, despite its name, holdover relief on gifts of business assets does not actually apply to assets used in a 'business', but generally only to assets used in a trade. What will qualify as a trade can be difficult to define, but it certainly does not include a property investment or property letting business (it used to include furnished holiday lets, but that finished in April 2025).

Broadly, the assets that qualify for holdover relief are:

- Assets used in a qualifying trade (including goodwill)
- Unquoted shares in a trading company (this time, 'unquoted' does not include shares traded on AIM or other stock markets classed as 'unlisted')
- A holding of at least 5% of a quoted trading company

To be a trading company for the purposes of both holdover relief and BADR, the underlying business must not include any substantial element of non-trading activities. HMRC generally accepts non-trading activities are not substantial where neither non-trading income nor non-trading assets exceed 20% of the totals for the company as a whole. However, this test is only a yardstick and is not conclusive. In a recent case, it was held that non-trading activities would only be regarded as substantial where they were of material or real importance in the context of the company's activities as a whole.

Nonetheless, to avoid any argument over the issue, it is wise to keep both non-trading income and non-trading assets below 20% in order to safely preserve the company's trading status wherever possible.

Anything that qualifies for APR (Section 7.27) also qualifies for CGT holdover relief. However, many modern farms include elements HMRC would regard as investment activities, such as letting cottages, letting land out for solar energy or wind farms, or wayleave (right of access) payments for electricity pylons and mobile phone masts. Where these elements are significant (under the criteria discussed above), holdover relief may not be available.

Holdover relief on gifts of business assets is not available for a transfer of shares or securities to a company, or any transfer to a settlor-interested trust (Section 9.4). A claim for holdover relief requires a joint election by the transferor and transferee (the transferor alone where the transferee is a trust).

Partial Holdover Relief Claims

Where assets qualifying for holdover relief are not gifted, but instead sold at undervalue, it is possible to hold over the artificial gain (the amount by which market value exceeds actual consideration) and effectively pay CGT based on the actual sales price. This may be a useful strategy for business owners wishing to retire, but who cannot afford to simply give the business away.

It can also be used as a means to limit the taxable gain to the amount covered by BADR (Section 12.5). Capital gains of up to £1m can often be triggered subject to CGT at just 18%, while reducing the amount of gain taxed at 24% in the hands of the transferee in the future.

There is the drawback that SDLT will be payable on any properties transferred but, in the case of a sale to another individual, this will be based on the actual price paid. Residential property will seldom qualify for holdover relief, so we will generally be looking at the non-residential SDLT rates:

Up to £150,000	0%
£150,000 to £250,000	2%
Over £250,000	5%

These rates apply to non-residential or mixed-use property, including many farms. See the Taxcafe guide *How to Save Property Tax* for further details.

In the case of a sale of shares, Stamp Duty is just 0.5%, and this is perhaps where the best opportunities to use a partial holdover relief claim arise, especially where the shares qualify for BADR.

Example: *Harry has built his trading company up from scratch, so his base cost is negligible. The company is now worth £2m, but he sells it to his son, Zane in 2026/27, for £1m. Harry makes a partial holdover relief claim and pays CGT of just £180,000. Zane pays Stamp Duty of £5,000, giving him a base cost of £1.005m.*

After running the company for a few years, Zane sells it for £3m, giving him a taxable gain of £1.995m and a CGT bill of £418,800 (£1m x 18% + £995,000 x 24%). If Harry had simply given him the shares, his CGT bill would have been £660,000.

While Harry lives, there is an overall saving of £56,200 (£660,000 – 418,800 – £180,000 – £5,000). Assuming the company would have been sold during Harry's lifetime anyway (or the shares do not qualify for BPR), and he survives at least seven years, there is also an IHT saving of up to £872,000 (£3m – £1m + £180,000 = £2.18m x 40%).

But, if the transferee intends to keep the business, at least until after the transferor's death, and it qualifies for BPR, the position is different. Assuming Harry survives seven years, a gift would have avoided IHT altogether; the sale for £1m leaves a potential IHT bill of £328,000; or if Harry had held onto his shares until death, the IHT bill would have been just £100,000 (based on a value of £3m) and CGT could have been avoided altogether.

In short, while it may have practical benefits, from a tax perspective, the sale at undervalue technique is only worth considering if the business either doesn't qualify for BPR or is likely to be sold during the current owner's lifetime.

12.5 BUSINESS PROPERTY RELIEF (BPR) AND BUSINESS ASSET DISPOSAL RELIEF (BADR)

As we have already seen, the uplift on death provides enormous potential to save CGT. Whether that saving is achieved at an IHT cost, however, is highly dependent on whether BPR or APR is available. Another important factor for business assets is the question of whether BADR is available.

Where a disposal of business assets qualifies for BADR the rate of CGT applying is reduced. Each individual may only claim BADR on a maximum cumulative lifetime total of £1m of capital gains (£10m for disposals before 11th March 2020). Thereafter, the CGT rate reverts to the main rates set out in Section 12.1.

The CGT rate where BADR is claimed is currently 18%, the same as the rate paid on gains covered by the individual's basic rate band.

The qualifying rules for BADR are different to the rules for BPR or holdover relief, so it is essential to consider each relief separately in every case. Broadly speaking, BADR is available on the disposal of: the whole or part of a qualifying business; assets formerly used in a qualifying business that has ceased or been disposed of; or shares and securities in a 'personal company'.

A qualifying business for this purpose is generally a trade or profession. A part of a business can only be counted for these purposes if it is capable of operating as a going concern in its own right and HMRC interprets this point very strictly. However, an interest in a business, such as a partnership share, may qualify. A disposal of assets formerly used in a qualifying business must take place within three years after the cessation or disposal of the business.

In all cases, the individual making the disposal must have owned the qualifying business for at least two years prior to its disposal, or cessation, as the case may be.

Personal Company

The definition of a personal company for the purposes of BADR is broadly as follows:

i) The individual holds at least 5% of the ordinary share capital
ii) The holding under (i) provides at least 5% of the voting rights
iii) The company is a trading company (based on the same criteria we looked at in Section 12.4)
iv) The individual is an officer or employee of the company (an officer includes a working director, non-executive director, or company secretary)
v) The individual's shareholding gives them at least a 5% interest in both the distributable profits and net assets of the company, OR
On a disposal of all the company's ordinary shares, the individual would be entitled to at least 5% of the proceeds

Each of these rules must be satisfied for at least two years prior to the disposal in question or, if earlier, the cessation of the business. In the latter case, the disposal must again take place within three years after cessation.

Associated Disposals

BADR may sometimes extend to assets owned personally but used in the trade of a personal company, or a partnership in which the owner is a partner. A number of restrictions apply to these associated disposals, however. Broadly, the relief is only available where the owner is also disposing of at least a 5%

stake in the company or partnership, or is disposing of their entire remaining stake, having held at least a 5% stake at some time in the past.

The assets must have been used in the company or partnership's business for at least the two-year period immediately prior to the sale of the business stake or, if earlier, cessation of the business. In the latter case, the disposal must again take place within three years after cessation. The asset needs to have been owned for at least three years at the date of disposal.

The relief is restricted where the asset has not been used in the business throughout the seller's ownership or where any payment has been received for the use of the asset after 5th April 2008.

Investor's Relief (IVR)
IVR is available to investors subscribing for new issues of ordinary shares in unlisted trading companies after 16th March 2016. Shares must be held for at least three years and the investor must ***not*** be an officer or employee of the company. Shares qualifying for IVR are subject to the same reduced CGT rate as assets qualifying for BADR (see above). IVR is subject to a lifetime limit of £1m of capital gains (£10m for disposals before 30th October 2024): this is a separate allowance to the limit applying to BADR.

Where an individual holds shares qualifying for IVR, the implications for IHT planning discussed in this guide will be the same as in the case of shares qualifying for BADR.

Critical Interactions
The interaction between BPR and either BADR or IVR has enormous consequences for estate preservation planning. There are three possible combinations we need to consider, so let's examine each in turn.

BPR & Either BADR or IVR Available: The First £2,500,000
The first £2.5m worth of these assets can be passed on free from IHT and it will therefore often make sense for the transferor to hang on to these and transfer them on death to obtain the CGT uplift with no IHT cost.

If it is not possible to hang on to the original assets until death, the same result can sometimes be achieved by exchanging these assets for replacement assets, as explained in Section 7.18. To avoid any CGT liabilities on the exchange, the replacement assets generally need to be one of the following:

i) Shares issued in exchange for shares in the transferor's own company (e.g. a 'takeover')
ii) Shares issued in exchange for the transfer of an unincorporated business into a company
iii) Business property acquired within the three-year period following the disposal of the original assets. (E.g. buying business premises to replace previous premises used in the same business or the acquisition of property for use in a new qualifying business.)

Assets qualifying for holdover relief on gifts of business assets (Section 12.4) can generally be transferred during the transferor's lifetime without any CGT liability. However, while this avoids CGT on the transfer, it also denies the transferee the benefit of the uplift on death.

On the other hand, a transfer of assets qualifying for BADR or IVR will often be subject to a reduced CGT rate on the first £1m of gain arising. In some cases, it may make sense **NOT** to claim holdover relief on the transfer, so the transferee may benefit from an increased CGT base cost. This is particularly relevant where the transferee is considering a sale of the asset in the near future (although the potential impact of such a sale when the transferor dies within seven years needs to be considered: see Section 7.19).

BPR & Either BADR or IVR Available: Excess Over £2,500,000

For any excess value over £2.5m, only 50% BPR will be available, giving rise to an effective IHT rate of 20%. We then need to consider whether, and to what extent, we are comparing this with the reduced CGT rate under either BADR or IVR: while these reliefs are subject to limits of £1m, these limits apply to lifetime gains, not total value. So, lifetime transfers of part of the qualifying assets could lead to savings, but it will mean the uplift on death will be lost.

Example: *Julian owns an unquoted trading company, currently worth £5m. He inherited the company from his father when it was worth £3m and intends to pass it on to his children.*

Let's say Julian hangs on to all his company shares and eventually leaves them to his children in eight years' time when the company is worth £7.5m. He will be eligible for BPR of £5m, leaving £2.5m exposed to IHT, resulting in a liability of £1m (assuming his NRB and other reliefs are used on other assets).

Alternatively, let's say Julian gifts half his shares to his children now, giving rise to a gain of £1m. He is eligible for BADR on the gain, so chooses not to claim holdover relief and pays CGT at 18%, i.e. £180,000. When he dies, he will hold £3.75m worth of shares and will be eligible for BPR of £3.125m, leaving just £625,000 exposed to IHT and costing £250,000 in IHT. His estate will also be reduced by the CGT he has paid, leading to a further IHT saving of £72,000.

(For the sake of illustration, I have assumed a 50% shareholding is worth 50% of the value of the company: but see Section 7.11 for a closer examination of this issue.)

In this scenario, Julian has saved £642,000 by making a lifetime transfer of half his shares (£1m – £250,000 – £180,000 + £72,000).

If Julian had died within seven years of the gift, however, the transfer would have used up his HPRA (Section 7.8), thus restricting the BPR available on his death to 50% and giving rise to an IHT bill of £750,000 on his remaining company shares. His total tax costs would then be £858,000 (£750,000 + £180,000 – £72,000), reducing the saving yielded by the lifetime transfer to just £142,000.

We also need to consider his children's CGT position. On the one hand, if they intend selling the shares after Julian's death, the transfer will mean their base cost is £1.25m less than it might have been, thus costing them between £225,000 and £300,000 extra CGT, depending on whether they qualify for BADR. That still leaves an overall saving of between £342,000 and £417,000 under our original scenario though.

On the other hand, if the children have no intention of selling the shares, it may have been better for Julian to claim holdover relief and avoid an unnecessary CGT bill, thus increasing the saving to £750,000 in our original scenario. But, if the children do subsequently sell their shares, the transfer will then cost them between £405,000 and £540,000 in extra CGT. So, there is much for the family to discuss!

Once the £1m lifetime limit for either BADR or IVR has been exhausted, the position for any further lifetime transfers will be the same as if these reliefs were not available, as discussed below.

BPR but Not BADR or IVR: The First £2,500,000

The first £2.5m worth of these assets can be passed on free from IHT but would attract an immediate CGT charge of up to 24% on a lifetime transfer. It will therefore generally make sense to hang on to the assets and transfer them on death. CGT uplift will be obtained and both IHT and CGT can be avoided if the transferee sells the assets shortly afterwards. At the very least, there should be a substantial reduction in CGT.

Again, it may be possible to achieve the same results when the assets are exchanged for replacement assets before death. The opportunity to avoid CGT on such an exchange is more limited, however, and item (iii) outlined above may no longer apply in some cases.

Lifetime transfers of these assets will often give rise to immediate CGT liabilities, as holdover relief on gifts of business assets (Section 12.4) may not be available. Even where it is available, the uplift on death will be lost and the transferee will most likely suffer CGT at up to 24% on the held over gain when they ultimately sell the asset (although there will be a few instances where the transferee is eligible for BADR and thus pays CGT at a reduced rate).

BPR but Not BADR or IVR: Excess Over £2,500,000

For any excess value over £2.5m, only 50% BPR will be available, giving rise to an effective IHT rate of 20%. Any lifetime transfers will suffer CGT at 24% unless the gain is held over. Even if it is held over, the transferees will be left with a low base cost and may face the same CGT bill on an ultimate sale. But it isn't simply a case of comparing the relevant percentages because 24% of the gain now could still be less than 20% of the value when the owner dies. Plus, paying CGT in your lifetime reduces your estate and saves IHT, so lifetime tax at 24% ultimately only costs your family 14.4%.

Among others, this situation may face those who have already used up their £1m lifetime limit for either BADR or IVR.

Example Revisited: *A year after gifting half his shares, Julian's remaining 50% shareholding is now worth £2.75m and is continuing to increase in value. He decides to give a further 10% stake to his children, giving rise to a capital gain of £250,000 (£2.75m x 10/50 – £3m x 10%). Unlike the previous year, he holds over this gain, so his children's base cost in these shares is just £300,000.*

When Julian dies more than seven years later, his 40% shareholding is worth £3m (£7.5m x 40%) and attracts BPR of £2.75m, leaving an IHT bill on his remaining shares of just £100,000. (I have again made the simplistic assumption that each shareholding is worth the appropriate proportion of the value of the company.)

Compared with the first version of this example, Julian has saved a further £150,000 in IHT. But at what cost? His children have missed out on the uplift on death, thus further increasing their CGT bill on an ultimate sale by between £81,000 and £108,000, depending on whether they qualify for BADR (the uplift on death on this 10% shareholding would increase its base cost by £450,000).

Alternatively, if Julian had chosen not to hold over his gain, he would have paid CGT of £60,000 (£250,000 x 24%) and the impact of losing the uplift on death for his children would be extra CGT of between £36,000 and £48,000 (they would lose an uplift of £200,000 on these shares in this case). Julian's CGT bill also leads to a further IHT saving of £24,000.

Taking everything into account, the transfer would ultimately leave Julian's children somewhere between £42,000 and £69,000 better off if he held over his gain: or between £66,000 and £78,000 better off if he did not hold over the gain.

In absolute terms, it will be better if the transferor does not hold over their gain under this scenario (in some cases, they may not have the option anyway), although there is, of course, the cashflow impact to consider.

As usual, the IHT savings will be greatly reduced if the transferor dies within seven years. Some saving will remain if the assets have grown in value (or are worth more than £2.5m plus twice the transferor's NRB/TNRB, and the transferor survives at least three years). Nonetheless, the family are likely to be worse off unless the transferor held over the gain and the beneficiaries never sell the transferred assets.

For example, if Julian died within seven years of both his transfers, having not held over either of his gains, a total of £3.05m (£2.5m + £550,000) would be brought back into his estate, using up his HPRA and £275,000 of his NRB, leading to increased IHT costs totalling £610,000. He would, however, have an IHT saving of £96,000 as a result of paying CGT totalling £240,000. So, the total net tax cost is £754,000 (£610,000 + £240,000 – £96,000). Add in the impact of the lost uplift on death for the children and we're looking at between £1.015m and £1.102m.

If those same shares had still been in Julian's estate when he died, they would have been worth £4.5m, leading to increased IHT costs of £900,000 (at an effective rate of 20%). So, the transfer has cost the family between £115,000 and £202,000 overall.

Alternatively, if holdover relief is available and the children have no intention of selling the assets, any IHT saving is worthwhile, as it can be achieved at no CGT cost. (Although there is always a risk that a sale will occur at some stage.) For example, if Julian held over the gains on both his transfers, his total IHT saving would amount to £900,000 if he survived seven years and would still be £290,000, even if he died sooner.

BADR but Not BPR *(Shares qualifying for IVR will always qualify for BPR)*
This scenario could apply where a qualifying business has ceased within the last three years or an individual has shares or securities in a quoted company qualifying as their personal company for the purposes of BADR.

In these cases, we face a dilemma. A lifetime transfer will often give rise to a CGT charge of just 18% on the first £1m of gain, but the opportunity to achieve the CGT uplift on death will be lost and the transferee may face a charge of up to 24% on future growth in the asset's value. On the other hand, if the assets are still held at the time of death, IHT will be fully chargeable.

Furthermore, in some cases, the assets may not be eligible for holdover relief on gifts of business assets (Section 12.4). Even where this relief is available, it only provides a CGT deferral: the uplift on death will be lost.

In practice, it may be difficult to establish the best course of action, but an early transfer will often produce an overall saving.

Example: *Sanjeev has a large estate well in excess of the NRB, including a 5% shareholding in a quoted trading company that qualifies for BADR. Sanjeev's base cost in these shares for CGT purposes is £2m. In February 2027, Sanjeev transfers his shares to his daughter Meera when they are worth £3m. He decides not to claim holdover relief in order to secure the benefit of BADR. His resultant CGT bill is £180,000. In March 2034, Sanjeev dies when the shares are worth £5m. As the transfer to Meera took place more than seven years previously, no IHT is due. If Sanjeev had still held the shares at this time, the IHT arising would have been £2m.*

Meera now sells the shares, giving rise to a capital gain of £2m and a CGT bill, at 24%, of £480,000 (she is a higher-rate taxpayer and is not eligible for BADR).

Hence, while father and daughter between them have paid £660,000 in CGT, the overall net tax saving for the family is £1.34m. In fact, if we take account of the additional IHT saved due to the reduction in the value of Sanjeev's estate when he paid his CGT bill, the overall net saving is actually £1.412m.

Clearly, in this example, it was worth incurring a relatively low CGT cost, as the asset was successfully removed from Sanjeev's estate by way of a PET more than seven years before his death. On the other hand, if Sanjeev had died immediately after his transfer to Meera, there would have been no IHT saving (other than the £72,000 saved due to Sanjeev's CGT bill). The CGT liability would have been incurred needlessly when Meera could have had a CGT uplift on her father's death. Furthermore, if Sanjeev had left a surviving spouse, the transfer to Meera would have used up his NRB, leaving no TNRB to be used against the spouse's estate.

Between these two extremes lie an almost infinite variety of possible outcomes. As a general guide, I have produced the table below (Version 1). It follows broadly the same lines as the example, but with a few minor modifications based on the following assumptions:

i) There is an existing gain of £1m giving rise to a CGT liability of £180,000
ii) The asset is currently worth £3m and its future value will increase at a rate of 7.5% per annum (compound)
iii) The transferee will sell the asset immediately after the transferor's death and will not be entitled to BADR
iv) The transferee is a higher-rate taxpayer
v) The transferor will not hold over the gain arising on the transfer
vi) The NRB and any TNRB to which they are entitled would have been fully utilised against other property within the transferor's estate if the transfer had not taken place
vii) The transferor survives just beyond the relevant anniversary
viii) The NRB in future years is as per our forecast in Section 3.2

Transferor Dies After	Value on Death	IHT on Transfer*	CGT on Final Sale	IHT if Still in Estate	Net Saving or (Cost)**
< 1 year	£3,000,000	£1,200,000	£0	£1,200,000	(£108,000)
1 year	£3,225,000	£1,200,000	£54,000	£1,290,000	(£72,000)
2 years	£3,466,875	£1,200,000	£112,050	£1,386,750	(£33,300)
3 years	£3,726,891	£986,000	£174,454	£1,490,756	£222,303
4 years	£4,006,407	£772,000	£241,538	£1,602,563	£481,025
5 years	£4,306,888	£560,160	£313,653	£1,722,755	£740,942
6 years	£4,629,905	£349,760	£391,177	£1,851,962	£1,003,025
7 years	£4,977,147	£0	£474,515	£1,990,859	£1,408,344
10 years	£6,183,095	£0	£763,943	£2,473,238	£1,601,295

* Includes additional tax on estate arising as a result of the transfer (due to the transfer using up the deceased's NRB in the event of their death within seven years). For this purpose, it is assumed no TNRB is available to the deceased.
** Net saving/(cost) takes account of the CGT paid on the original transfer less the IHT saving arising as a result of this cost.

As we can see, under this scenario, the transferor only needs to survive three years to make the transfer worthwhile. The above savings are based on the assumption the transferor's NRB (and any available TNRB) would be used up on other assets within their estate. This will not be the case if they would otherwise have left everything to their spouse and the points to be considered in this situation are covered in Chapter 6.

Transferees Eligible for Business Asset Disposal Relief
A lifetime transfer becomes even more attractive where the transferee will also be eligible for BADR on the transferred asset. This might apply above if the company Sanjeev held shares in became Meera's personal company after the

transfer. This could generally be achieved by ensuring at least 5% of the ordinary shares are transferred and the transferee is or becomes an officer or employee. The following table (Version 2) shows the same scenario as before except the transferee now qualifies for BADR on the transferred asset.

Transferor Dies After	Value on Death	IHT on Transfer	CGT on Final Sale	IHT if Still in Estate	Net Saving or (Cost)
< 1 year	£3,000,000	£1,200,000	£0	£1,200,000	(£108,000)
1 year	£3,225,000	£1,200,000	*£84,038	£1,290,000	(£102,038)
2 years	£3,466,875	£1,200,000	£84,038	£1,386,750	(£5,288)
3 years	£3,726,891	£986,000	£130,840	£1,490,756	£265,916
4 years	£4,006,407	£772,000	£181,538	£1,602,563	£541,025
5 years	£4,306,888	£560,160	£253,653	£1,722,755	£800,942
6 years	£4,629,905	£349,760	£331,177	£1,851,962	£1,063,025
7 years	£4,977,147	£0	£414,515	£1,990,859	£1,468,344
10 years	£6,183,095	£0	£703,943	£2,473,238	£1,661,295

* It is assumed in the case of the transferor's death after one year that the transferee keeps the shares for another year to qualify for BADR.

Remember the £1m cumulative lifetime limit for BADR applies to each individual. Hence, a transferor and transferee may be able to obtain relief on up to £2m between them. In this scenario, the transferee is paying CGT at 18% on the first £1m of the shares' growth in value after the transfer and at 24% on any excess. Nonetheless, the transferor again needs to survive three years to make the transfer worthwhile.

12.6 TRANSFERS TO SPOUSES OR CIVIL PARTNERS

As we know, transfers to your spouse are usually exempt from IHT. Furthermore, subject to the further points below, transfers to your spouse are also usually exempt from CGT. However, only transfers on death will benefit from the CGT uplift explained in Section 12.2. It therefore makes sense to hold on to assets that are subject to CGT, and which you ultimately intend to leave to your spouse, so they can benefit from the uplift on death.

Alternatively, a lifetime transfer of assets to your spouse could be used to get a CGT uplift on their death. You need to be pretty sure the assets are going to come back to you though!

Separation and Divorce

Unlike the IHT exemption, the CGT exemption for transfers between spouses does not always apply to transfers between separated spouses. The general CGT exemption only extends to transfers made on or before the earlier of:

a) The last day of the third tax year after the tax year in which the couple separate; or
b) The date on which their divorce is finalised, their marriage or civil partnership is annulled or dissolved, or they are formally, legally separated under a separation order or judicial separation

Hence, for example, where a couple separate in June 2026, and none of the events under (b) have occurred, the exemption ends on 5th April 2030.

However, in addition to the general exemption, transfers between spouses made under a formal legal divorce or separation agreement are also exempt.

Another useful provision is that transfers of the former marital home to *anyone* as part of a divorce or separation agreement may be exempt from CGT. The exemption applies to a transfer of the whole or a part share in an individual's former main residence where their separated spouse still resides in the property (as their main residence) and the transferor has not elected any other property to be treated as their main residence in the interim.

As we saw in Section 6.6, transfers made as part of a formal, legal divorce or separation agreement are generally exempt for IHT purposes. Hence, it may be possible for an estranged spouse to transfer the whole or a part share in the former marital home to their children, or a trust for their benefit, free from both CGT and IHT.

12.7 CAPITAL GAINS TAX AND THE FAMILY HOME

I could write an entire chapter on this subject alone. In fact, I have, but that chapter already appears in the Taxcafe guide *How to Save Property Tax*. To put it simply, your home is exempt from CGT for as long as you live in it as your only or main residence, and for at least nine months thereafter. Full exemption will generally apply as long as you moved into the property within two years of acquisition and did not use it for anything else in the interim. Other periods of absence may result in a partial loss of your exemption, although additional reliefs are often available.

Each married couple or single individual may have just one main residence for CGT purposes at any given time.

Hence, as far as CGT is concerned, a lifetime transfer of your qualifying main residence while you are still living there, or within the next nine months thereafter, will usually be exempt.

So, what's the problem? Well, apart from the IHT problems we will look at in the next chapter, there are two major CGT problems with giving away your main residence: the transferees lose the ability to benefit from the CGT uplift on death and, unless they move into the property, the transferees also lose any main residence exemption. In essence, the transferees will be treated for CGT purposes as having acquired the property at its market value on the date of transfer and will be exposed to CGT on any growth in value thereafter.

Practical Implications

A sale of the parent's home within nine months of them ceasing to occupy it as their main residence would generally be fully exempt from CGT if they were still the owner at that time. This additional nine-month period is extended to three years if the owner is disabled or resident in a care home. Furthermore, if the parent retained the property until death, it would be subject to the uplift on death, giving the children complete exemption from any gain arising during the parent's lifetime, even if the parent had been absent from the property for a longer period.

Conversely, if a child owns their parent's current or former home, but does not occupy it as their main residence, it is effectively treated like an investment property and is fully exposed to CGT on a subsequent sale.

The capital gain in such cases will be based on the property's increase in value since the time the child acquired it, not since the time of the parent's death. The relevant transfer may have been several years earlier, when the property's value was considerably less, thus leading to a much larger taxable gain.

The interplay between CGT and IHT can produce one of three results:

i) The IHT saving may outweigh the CGT exposure that has been created. This is fine and means the planning is still worthwhile
ii) The IHT saving comes at the price of a similar level of potential CGT liability. Such instances may still be worthwhile, as they may still produce a significant cashflow saving by deferring the tax arising. (This will often be the case where the beneficiaries have no intention of selling the property, or at least not for some considerable time)
iii) The IHT saving results in a significantly greater amount of potential CGT. This, clearly, would be foolhardy if the beneficiaries are contemplating any sale of the property in the foreseeable future

The introduction of the RNRB (Section 3.4) has significantly altered the potential outcomes of this interplay in many cases. Far more cases now fall into the third category, meaning that retaining the property in the parent's ownership until death will often be the most sensible thing to do.

In many cases where a married couple, widow or widower, intends to leave the family home to the children, there will be little point trying to avoid IHT on it, as properties worth up to £1m can sometimes be covered by the available exemptions. But there are many exceptions to this, and we will look at these in the next chapter.

Where the parent still resides in the property, a simple transfer will usually be a gift with reservation. As we will see in the next section, it is generally wise to refrain from making any transfer that would be a gift with reservation, as there would be no IHT advantage but all the CGT disadvantages would remain. We will look at ways to resolve this in the next chapter.

12.8 CAPITAL GAINS TAX AND GIFTS WITH RESERVATION

As explained in Section 4.8, when a transfer falls foul of the gifts with reservation rules, it will be ineffective for IHT purposes until such time as the relevant reservation comes to an end.

This has absolutely no impact on the CGT treatment of the asset. The transfer that was subject to a gift with reservation may still give rise to CGT based on the market value of the asset transferred, and the new legal owner of the transferred asset will lose the benefit of any reliefs the transferor may have been entitled to, including main residence relief on the transferor's home. Generally, with few exceptions, this situation should be avoided as it usually creates CGT problems without saving any IHT.

Example: *Tina is an elderly divorcee. In 2006 she gave her house to her son, Robert, but continued to live there until April 2024, when she moved into a nursing home. The house was worth £275,000 in 2006 but £725,000 by 2024.*

Tragically, Tina dies in March 2027, leaving only a few small possessions with no material value and just enough cash to pay her last month's nursing home fees and funeral expenses. However, as she only moved out of her house in 2024, its value at that date must be brought back into her estate, resulting in an IHT bill of £160,000.

To help pay the IHT, Robert sells the house in August 2027. Let's assume the house is still worth £725,000. For CGT purposes, he is treated as having acquired the house for just £275,000, thus giving rise to a CGT bill of £108,000 on top of the IHT bill (he is a higher-rate taxpayer, so his capital gain of £450,000 is all taxed at 24%).

I have seen this type of situation many times and it's an absolute tragedy. Had Tina simply held on to the house, the RNRB would have been available, and Robert's IHT bill would have been reduced to £90,000. He would also have paid little or no CGT on a sale of the property shortly after Tina's death. The transfer in 2006 has cost Robert £178,000 in unnecessary extra tax.

Many families have attempted this type of planning to their cost. To make it worse, many of these transfers were done to avoid paying residential care fees (see Section 11.5) but, as a result of a number of rule changes and successful cases taken by local authorities, this part of the plan has often failed as well.

We will return to gifts with reservation of the family home in Section 13.11, although the above example has already demonstrated that, in the vast majority of cases, gifts with reservation should be avoided like the plague!

12.9 EXEMPT TRANSFERS

There are a few classes of assets other than cash that are exempt from CGT. For IHT planning purposes, these assets can often be regarded much like cash, since a lifetime transfer will not give rise to any CGT liability, but could save IHT if the transferor survives seven years (even just three in some cases). The following assets may be exempt from CGT:

- Enterprise Investment Scheme shares (only the shares themselves, not any gain held over and only if certain qualifying conditions are met, including a minimum holding period of at least three years)
- Tangible movable assets worth no more than £6,000 (also known as chattels). This includes items like paintings, antiques, and silverware
- Government securities (also known as gilts)
- Foreign currency held by an individual (but not cryptoassets)
- Motor cars
- Other tangible wasting assets with an expected life of less than 50 years (vans, motorbikes, machinery, computers, household equipment, etc.) This exemption does not generally apply where assets are used in a business
- Medals and certain other awards when still held by the original recipient or their heirs (these are usually exempt from IHT anyway)

Exemption from CGT does not necessarily provide exemption from other taxes. Anyone trading in any of these items would be classed as a dealer and subject to Income Tax and National Insurance on their profits.

As far as chattels are concerned, a lifetime transfer means foregoing the CGT uplift on death, so it might lead to increased CGT liabilities at a later date for the transferee where the assets are later worth over £6,000. The transfer is likely to remain advantageous overall if an IHT saving is achieved though.

Married persons must bear in mind these transfers could lead to a reduction in their spouse's TNRB if the transferor does not survive seven years. The pros and cons were discussed in Chapter 6. Items like cars and other wasting assets will generally reduce in value, meaning the loss of TNRB will be greater than the eventual reduction in the transferor's estate, leaving the family worse off on a death within seven years.

Other ways to make lifetime transfers free from CGT include:

- Transferring assets while you are non-UK resident: you must be non-resident for at least five years, this doesn't work for land and buildings in the UK, and foreign tax implications must be considered.
- Cashing in an ISA and passing over the proceeds

As always, it remains important to remember the loss of the CGT uplift on death and, for married persons, the potential impact on your spouse's TNRB.

12.10 OTHER ASSETS

What about other assets, that don't qualify as business assets or main residences, which aren't exempt, and which you don't plan to give your spouse? Here we're considering assets that do not qualify for BPR, BADR, IVR, or holdover relief on a gift. This makes a lifetime transfer less attractive from a CGT perspective. But the chance to save IHT via early transfer remains.

Let's return to the scenario in Version 1 of our table in Section 12.5, except for one change: BADR is ***not*** available to the transferor. The position arising is as follows (Version 3):

Transferor Dies After	Value on Death	IHT on Transfer	CGT on Final Sale	IHT if Still in Estate	Net Saving or (Cost)*
< 1 year	£3,000,000	£1,200,000	£0	£1,200,000	(£144,000)
1 year	£3,225,000	£1,200,000	£54,000	£1,290,000	(£108,000)
2 years	£3,466,875	£1,200,000	£112,050	£1,386,750	(£69,300)
3 years	£3,726,891	£986,000	£174,454	£1,490,756	£186,303
4 years	£4,006,407	£772,000	£241,538	£1,602,563	£445,025
5 years	£4,306,888	£560,160	£313,653	£1,722,755	£704,942
6 years	£4,629,905	£349,760	£391,177	£1,851,962	£967,025
7 years	£4,977,147	£0	£474,515	£1,990,859	£1,372,344
10 years	£6,183,095	£0	£763,943	£2,473,238	£1,565,295

* Net saving/(cost) takes account of £240,000 CGT paid on the original transfer less the resultant IHT saving arising due to the reduction in the value of the transferor's estate.

Apart from BADR being unavailable, all notes and assumptions made for Version 1 of this table in Section 12.5 apply. I also assume the transferor is a higher-rate taxpayer. In this scenario, such a transfer remains beneficial if the transferor survives at least three years.

The position would be different if the asset is a residential property qualifying for main residence relief in the hands of either the transferor or the transferee. The situation for a main residence was examined in Sections 12.7 and 12.8, and will also be the focus of Chapter 13.

In conclusion, the tables in this section and Section 12.5 tell us early transfers of assets that are appreciating in value will often lead to significant overall tax savings in the end. However, married persons must remember the tables take no account of the impact of the transfers on the spouse's TNRB: see Chapter 6 for a thorough examination of this issue.

12.11 CAPITAL GAINS TAX AND TRUSTS

A trust for a vulnerable individual may elect to be taxed as if any capital gains arising belong directly to the beneficiary (except that any capital losses made by the individual cannot be set against the trust's gains). However, as explained in Section 8.17, this will generally only apply to disabled trusts, trusts for bereaved minors, and other trusts where the beneficiary is under 18.

Most other trusts (apart from bare trusts and charitable trusts) are subject to CGT at 24% and generally have an annual CGT exemption equal to half that applying to individuals (Section 12.1). This is further reduced where the settlor has set up more than one trust.

In Chapter 8, we considered the various different types of trust and saw some of them had their own separate life for IHT purposes and some did not. With the exception of bare trusts, however, trusts are treated as a separate legal entity for CGT purposes. This effectively means, subject to any available exemptions or reliefs, that both transfers into, and out of, a trust are treated as disposals at market value.

In the case of a bare trust, it is only the transfer to the trust that represents a disposal for CGT purposes. Thereafter, the assets of the trust are generally treated as belonging to the beneficiary for both IHT and CGT purposes.

The Capital Gains Tax Uplift on Death

Assets subject to an interest in possession that fall into a beneficiary's estate for IHT purposes (see Chapter 8) will generally qualify for the same CGT uplift on the death of the beneficiary as assets held absolutely. However, the uplift does not apply where property reverts to the original settlor absolutely on the beneficiary's death (but does if the settlor only obtains an interest in possession). The CGT uplift on death also generally applies to assets in a bereaved minor's trust, or an 18 to 25 trust, on the death of a beneficiary under the age of 18.

Held Over Gains
When an interest in possession that is not within the relevant property trust regime (Chapter 8) ends on the death of the beneficiary and a capital gain was held over when the same assets entered the trust (see Sections 9.4 and 12.4), that held over gain becomes chargeable. The held over gain can usually be held over again provided IHT is chargeable on the beneficiary's death, or the assets qualify as business assets for hold over relief purposes (Section 12.4).

Hold Over Relief on Absolute Entitlement
CGT hold over relief is generally available when the beneficiary of a relevant property trust, a bereaved minor's trust, or an 18 to 25 trust becomes absolutely entitled to trust assets. There is no restriction on holdover relief when assets are *leaving* a settlor-interested relevant property trust.

In some cases, it may be worth changing the terms of a pre-22/3/2006 interest in possession trust so that it becomes a relevant property trust (see Chapter 8). Although this will expose the trust to anniversary and exit charges, the ability to hold over capital gains when assets leave the trust may produce greater CGT savings than any resultant IHT cost.

Chapter 13

The Family Home

13.1 WHEN OUR MAIN ASSET BECOMES OUR MAIN LIABILITY

For most of us, the family home is our major asset. It has often also been the main cause of IHT liabilities. For a few years, with both the TNRB (Section 6.2) and RNRB (Section 3.4) available in many cases, for many people the family home was no longer a problem from an IHT standpoint. Now, however, the tide has turned again, with other assets competing for, and even taking away part of the main exemptions.

In Chapter 7, we saw how many farmers and other business owners may have an exposure to IHT, meaning, in some cases, their business assets will be competing for their NRB/TNRB. In Section 10.2, we saw how pension savings will soon be taking up part of an individual's NRB/TNRB, and even reducing the benefit of the RNRB.

So, the protection family homes have been enjoying for the last few years is being eroded away. And that means IHT planning for the family home is moving back up the agenda.

If you don't have a business or farm worth more than £2.5m, and you don't have any pension savings, you could have exemptions totalling £1m available to cover the family home, made up as follows:

Nil rate band	£325,000
Transferable NRB	£325,000
Residence NRB	£175,000
Transferable RNRB	£175,000
Total exemption available:	£1,000,000

This means some married couples, widows, or widowers, intending to leave their home to their children have no need to worry about IHT on the family home and would do better to focus on other assets. But, throw in a business worth over £2.5m, or ***any*** pension savings, and these reliefs are whittled away.

For example, let's say you're a widow with a full entitlement to all these reliefs and all you own is a house worth £750,000 and pension savings of £500,000. If you leave your house to one of your children, you can deduct £350,000 (the RNRB), leaving £400,000. But, if you die after 5th April 2027, your pension savings will absorb £361,111 of your NRB/TNRB leaving just £288,889 (see Section 10.2). That means there is £111,111 of the value of your house exposed to IHT at 40%, and a bill of £44,444.

So, that £1m of protection George Osborne disingenuously claimed to have delivered in 2015 has gone, and IHT planning for the family home is back!

And, even before Rachel Reeves' treacherous raid on pensions, farms, and businesses, we had to remember not everyone fits neatly into the Government's 1950s-style vision of a world where everyone gets married, raises a family, and lives happily ever after: until the time comes to hand 40% of everything over to them!

There are many people who never enjoyed the £1m of exemption Osborne promised back in 2007, including:

- Single, divorced, or unmarried people. You have to become a widow/widower in order to benefit from the TNRB or transferable RNRB. This does not apply to everyone! Those who never become a widow/widower will only be able to enjoy maximum total exemptions of £500,000 (at current rates)
- Widows/widowers whose former spouse used some or all of their NRB or RNRB. In some cases, they may also be unable to claim some or all of their former spouse's RNRB (see Chapter 6 and Section 3.4)
- Those with total estates worth over £2m: remember this includes businesses, farms, and, from 6th April 2027, pension savings too!
- Those who do not intend to leave their family home to direct descendants. Not everyone has children, and not everyone who does intends to leave their home to those children. If you do not leave your home (or its sale proceeds) to direct descendants (see Section 3.4), or the right kind of trust for their benefit (Section 8.3), you will not be entitled to the RNRB.

As we can see, there are many people who need to take action to protect the family home from IHT.

As already mentioned in Section 4.8, the major stumbling block to effective IHT planning with the family home is the gifts with reservation provisions. Another issue to consider is the pre-owned assets charge, although this will rarely apply in practice: the potential risks posed to the planning techniques in this chapter were summarised in Section 11.12.

It is also important to remember giving your home away may mean you are unable to benefit from the RNRB. We will look at this issue further in Section 13.11. Selling your home will have a different effect, however, and we will return to this subject in Section 13.10.

Despite these drawbacks, there are still a number of methods for saving IHT on the family home. Many of the methods described in this chapter will also have CGT implications for the transferee. These are discussed in more detail in Section 12.7. For more information on CGT, SDLT, or any related reliefs on residential property, see the Taxcafe guide *How to Save Property Tax*.

The methods described in Sections 13.5 to 13.7 are only beneficial for married couples where one or both spouses already have a TNRB available (see Section 6.8). Any methods that involve mortgages, loans, or other borrowings will only work if those liabilities are repaid out of the assets of the deceased's estate, or if there is a valid commercial reason for non-repayment (see Section 2.10 for further details).

See also Sections 6.6 and 12.6 regarding the potential opportunity for married couples who are separating or divorcing to pass on the whole or a part share in the family home free of both IHT and CGT. Where the family home is a farmhouse, this is covered in more detail in Section 7.28.

13.2 MOVE OUT THEN GIVE IT AWAY

If you can afford to, and are willing to do it, you can simply move out of the property then give it away. The gift is a PET that will escape IHT as long as you survive seven years. Furthermore, as long as you make the gift within nine months of the date you move out of the property, it will also be exempt from CGT under private residence relief. If you are prepared to do this, you could then move into rented accommodation, or buy a more modest property.

No gift with reservation should arise as long as you never move back into the property, or only do so under unforeseen circumstances meeting the requirements detailed in Section 4.8.

13.3 SELL UP OR RE-MORTGAGE

If you can't quite afford to follow the strategy in Section 13.2, you could, instead, sell your current home, buy a smaller one, and give away the surplus left-over cash. All you need to do then is survive another seven years. If you're feeling really brave, you could even give away all the sale proceeds and move into rented property. While this is good IHT planning, it doesn't leave you with much security in your old age and it might cause some problems with the local authority if you ever need to go into a residential care home.

Alternatively, if you would prefer to stay in your current home, another way to get most of its value out of your estate is to re-mortgage the property then give away or spend the borrowed funds.

The outstanding mortgage balance will be deducted from your estate (subject to the rules explained in Section 2.10) and this will reduce your IHT bill as long as you have either given away the borrowed funds and survived seven years, or spent the borrowed funds before you die.

The major drawback to this method is the need to service the mortgage from your retirement income. Hence, a sensible refinement may be to buy an annuity with some or all of the mortgage proceeds. This will enable you to service the debt and give away or spend any surplus. The problem then, of course, is that in the event of a premature death shortly after purchasing the annuity, a lot of your home's value will have been lost: not to His Majesty's Treasury, but to the annuity provider.

A better approach might be to release equity in your property, either by selling or re-mortgaging it, and invest the proceeds in a discounted gift trust (Section 9.9) or loan trust (Section 9.10). These investments provide an effective income stream, but also carry the advantage that your wealth is not lost in the event of a premature death.

Alternatively, you could sell your property and invest the proceeds in qualifying syndicate arrangements (Section 7.34). You would need to limit your investment to the amount you can genuinely afford, as any subsequent borrowings, including any mortgage on a new property, would be deemed to have indirectly funded the purchase. Hence, while qualifying syndicate arrangements may provide complete shelters from IHT (after two years and only up to £2.5m), they are probably only suitable where you sell the family home, buy something smaller, and just invest the surplus.

13.4 SALE AT MARKET VALUE

If you sell your property to your children, or other beneficiaries, at full market value, no transfer of value will take place and hence the property will immediately be excluded from your estate for IHT purposes. However, whether the sale proceeds are paid in cash or left outstanding as a loan, they will remain in your estate. Your beneficiaries will also have to pay SDLT. The rates can be quite prohibitive for a more valuable property and they will have to pay the 5% surcharge on top if they have other residential property.

Any prior arrangement to give any part of the sale proceeds back to the purchaser, or waive any loan balance, will render this planning void, since the sale would not have taken place on arm's length terms, as required, and a transfer of value will have taken place.

Furthermore, there must not be any obligation on the purchaser to allow you to continue to occupy the property. This means you may subsequently only be able to live in the property under an informal licence to occupy, which is totally at the purchaser's whim. This will not suit everyone!

If the purchaser pays you in cash, perhaps in instalments, you will be free to spend the proceeds, perhaps to support yourself in your retirement. Any future growth in the property's value is also safely excluded from your estate.

As you spend the proceeds and the property grows in value, the reduction in your taxable estate starts to accumulate. These savings also start immediately after the sale and it is not necessary to survive for any period to benefit. Alternatively, you could invest the proceeds in one of the IHT shelters suggested in Section 13.3.

On the other hand, as time passes there is a danger that the adverse CGT considerations discussed in Section 12.7 could outweigh any IHT savings. Combining these with the SDLT cost of putting the plan into place may sometimes render this technique too costly to be worthwhile.

13.5 THE WIDOW'S LOAN SCHEME & THE FAMILY HOME

The method described in Section 6.11 generally works just as well for the family home as for any other assets. Probably better, in fact, as there is an asset on which to secure the loan and thus give it the necessary commercial substance. As explained in Chapter 6, however, this method is now only worth exploring where one or both spouses already have a TNRB available.

Example: *Oscar and Freddie are registered civil partners and equal joint tenants in common of a house worth £1.3m. Each of them already has a full TNRB available from the death of a previous spouse. Freddie dies in December 2026 and leaves an* *amount equivalent to twice the NRB, £650,000, to a discretionary trust. He leaves everything else to Oscar.*

No IHT is payable on Freddie's death, since the legacy to the discretionary trust is covered by his NRB/TNRB and the rest of his estate is covered by the spouse exemption. The trust takes a charge for £650,000 over the couple's house and then passes the title to Freddie's share over to Oscar. Oscar survives Freddie by just over two years and passes away in January 2029 when the house is worth £1.4m.

The value of the house in Oscar's estate is reduced to £750,000 by the £650,000 charge taken by Freddie's discretionary trust (provided the charge meets the conditions explained in Sections 2.10 and 6.11). After deducting the NRB of £325,000 and Oscar's TNRB from his previous marriage, just £100,000 of the house's value is subject to IHT at 40%, giving a charge of £40,000.

Without the widow's loan scheme, the whole value of the house would have been subject to IHT on Oscar's death. After deducting his NRB/TNRB, £750,000 would have been subject to IHT at 40%, giving a charge of £300,000. The widow's loan scheme has thus produced a saving of £260,000.

Further details of how to implement the widow's loan scheme and some of the pitfalls to be avoided are given in Section 6.11.

13.6 LEAVE A SHARE TO THE CHILDREN

Another method worth considering where one or both of a married couple are already entitled to a TNRB is to simply leave a share in the property to your children, who will then, after your death, own it jointly with your surviving spouse. See Section 6.8 for guidance on the value this share should ideally have in order to optimise the overall IHT position. Any RNRB to which you are entitled should also be taken into account. Remember, as explained in Section 11.3, a joint share in a property held as tenants in common may be any proportion and need not be an equal share.

If your surviving spouse and children sell the property immediately after your death, there should be no CGT liability: the children will benefit from the CGT uplift on death (Section 12.2) and the surviving spouse should be covered by the main residence exemption.

Opinions differ, however, on the more common situation that arises when the property is retained and the surviving spouse continues to occupy it.

The surviving spouse's joint share gives them a continuing right of occupation. Some experts think this means the survivor can remain in the property without paying any rent and the children's share does not need to be included in their estate. Hence, as planned, when the surviving spouse dies, their estate would only include their share of the property.

Other experts, however, believe the surviving spouse's continuing occupation amounts to an interest in possession and the children's share of the property would therefore fall into their estate unless they pay rent for their occupation of that share. Still others consider a relevant property trust would come into being in respect of the children's share of the property. The consequences of this are explored below.

Unfortunately, at present, it is not yet clear which set of experts is correct and HMRC has refused to comment. Personally, I've always favoured the view of the first set of experts, which means the IHT planning will work as intended, although it must be admitted the position is far from certain.

If the method does work as intended, it still has the drawback that the children are exposed to CGT on the growth in value of their share of the property after the first parent's death. However, the resultant CGT liability arising will often be considerably less than the IHT saving. Furthermore, if the family intend to retain the property in the long term, CGT is less of a concern.

Another issue to consider is the fact this simple route relies on your children, and, more particularly, ***their*** spouses or partners, getting along OK with your spouse after you're gone. In practice, this is not always the case, and families in this situation have been known to come to blows (both metaphorically and physically). The joint owners have even been known to force the surviving spouse into selling the former family home against their wishes.

The best way around these practical problems is for the children to set up a trust with the surviving spouse as both trustee and beneficiary. After inheriting a share in the property, the children transfer this into the trust. The provisions of the trust are that the property reverts to the children, as settlors, on the death of the surviving spouse.

The drawback is that the trust set up by the children will be a relevant property trust (see Chapter 8). The transfer into the trust will be a chargeable lifetime transfer, and the trust will be subject to anniversary and exit charges. Nevertheless, these charges may well be substantially less than the amount saved by keeping part of the property out of the surviving spouse's estate. In many cases, where each individual child's share of the property is worth less than the NRB, the structure may, in practice, still avoid IHT altogether.

The children will be unable to benefit from any CGT uplift (in respect of the trust's share of the property) on the surviving spouse's death. However, if the trust were then to sell its share of the property, the main residence exemption should be available as the property had been the main residence of the trust beneficiary (the surviving spouse). The trust could then pass the sale proceeds to the children.

Hence, while this technique may be slightly flawed in theory, it will often work reasonably well in practice.

The children may be subject to a gift with reservation if they have any use or enjoyment of the property during the life interest of the surviving spouse. As the property is ultimately intended to pass to the children, this will not generally pose much of a problem, although there is the risk one of the children might pre-decease the surviving spouse. Minor, incidental use of the property, e.g. limited social visits, should not cause any difficulty, however.

13.7 LEAVE A SHARE TO A DISCRETIONARY TRUST

In Section 6.10, we looked at the drawbacks to using a discretionary Will Trust and the possible problem of it being treated as an immediate post-death interest and thus falling into the surviving spouse's estate. As explained in Chapter 6, this is now only a problem for certain 'second time around' married couples.

A possible solution to this problem, where it still exists, is to leave an appropriate share in the family home (see Section 6.8 for what is appropriate) to a discretionary trust in which the surviving spouse is ***not*** a beneficiary.

As explained in Section 13.6, as a joint owner, the surviving spouse already has a right to occupy the property, so the fact they are not a beneficiary of the discretionary trust does not make any practical difference to them.

After an interval of at least two years and a day, the discretionary trust can be changed into an interest in possession trust in favour of the surviving spouse. This will be a relevant property trust and hence will not fall into the surviving spouse's estate. Anniversary and exit charges may apply but these may be avoided if the trust's share of the property is not worth more than the NRB.

This technique is a fairly new idea and, as such, it is currently untested. Even the experts are still debating whether it actually works in practice!

13.8 THE FULL CONSIDERATION METHOD

The gifts with reservation rules can be bypassed if, after giving the property to your children, you pay them a full commercial rent for continuing to live in it. Payment of the rent would also further reduce your estate for IHT purposes.

It is ***essential*** rental payments are made under an enforceable legal obligation, rather than a mere casual arrangement. Hence, a formal lease will generally be required and the rent should be subject to a regular review, in line with normal commercial practice. The pre-owned assets rules (Section 11.12) require a review every five years, but a more frequent review may be required to prevent a gift with reservation.

The major drawbacks to this method are the fact your children have to account for Income Tax on the rent they receive and are also fully exposed to CGT on the future growth in value of the property.

13.9 CO-OWNERSHIP

This method is popular with widows, widowers and other single parents with adult children. Quite simply, you put the property into joint ownership with one or more of your adult children then live together with them there.

The transfer of one or more shares in the property is a PET as long as the child or children are living there. It is the children's occupation of the property that prevents the transfer being a gift with reservation.

However, if one or more of the donee children should subsequently move out of the property while the parent is still in occupation, the gift with reservation rules will come into play: unless the parent pays a full market rent for their use of the child's share; or the child rents their share to another occupier.

It is important each party bears their share of the household running costs. If any child were to pay the full household running costs, or even just part of the parent's share, a gift with reservation would have taken place and the IHT planning will be undone.

While in practice this method works best when the children remain single, there is nothing in principle to prevent it from continuing to work when they marry, or even have children of their own. It just gets crowded!

13.10 DOWNSIZING

The RNRB may be claimed against other assets or cash left to direct descendants, or certain types of trust for their benefit (see Section 8.3), to the extent these assets are covered by the sale proceeds of a former qualifying private residence sold after 8th July 2015 (see Section 3.4 for details of direct descendants and qualifying private residences).

Such a claim under the 'downsizing' provisions may be made when an individual dies with no qualifying private residence, or an individual had a more valuable qualifying residence at some time after 8th July 2015.

To be more precise, the downsizing provisions actually apply when you previously had a more valuable residence ***as a proportion*** of the RNRB applying, or deemed to apply, at that time. As the RNRB has increased significantly since it was first introduced, this is not the same thing as a more valuable residence in absolute terms. In fact, a ***less*** valuable residence sold before 6th April 2020 may sometimes allow you to increase your RNRB claim using the downsizing provisions.

The RNRB applying, or deemed to apply, at the time of the property's sale for the purpose of these provisions is:

Sales completed	**Residence Nil Rate Band**
9th July 2015 to 5th April 2018	£100,000
6th April 2018 to 5th April 2019	£125,000
6th April 2019 to 5th April 2020	£150,000
After 5th April 2020	£175,000

There is no need to actually trace the sale proceeds of the former qualifying private residence; it is simply a case of using the amount of those proceeds to derive the available exemption. Nonetheless, the relief may only be claimed against amounts, or the value of assets, which actually do go to qualifying beneficiaries or trusts. Furthermore, only actual sale proceeds (not deemed proceeds) may be used in the calculation of the relief available.

A widow/widower may include any RNRB transferred from their deceased spouse in their downsizing claim. The maximum claim is derived as follows:

i) Calculate the proportion of the individual's maximum available RNRB actually used against qualifying property on their death
ii) Calculate the proportion of the individual's maximum available RNRB that could have been used if the individual had died immediately before selling the former qualifying residence, based on the assumption the actual sale proceeds received for the property represented its open market value
iii) Deduct the proportion derived under step (i) from the proportion derived under step (ii)
iv) The maximum relief available under the downsizing provisions is derived by multiplying the individual's maximum available RNRB by the proportion derived under step (iii)

The amount of RNRB used for the purposes of the calculation at step (ii) is dependent on the date of sale of the former residence, as detailed above. To this we add any RNRB transferred from the individual's deceased spouse: BUT the transferred RNRB is not the amount available at the time of the property's sale, it is the amount available at the time of the widow/widower's death.

Example 1: *Billie has been divorced for many years. In March 2017, she sold her house for £80,000 and moved into a care home. When she dies in March 2027, she does not own any qualifying property and leaves her entire estate to her son, Duke. The sale proceeds for Billie's house amount to 80% of the RNRB deemed to have been available to her at that time (£100,000). The maximum amount of RNRB to which she would be entitled on her death is £175,000. Hence, she may claim an exemption of £140,000 (£175,000 x 80%) under the downsizing provisions.*

Example 2: *Chip is a widower whose wife died in 2014 with a very modest estate. In August 2018, he sold his home for £225,000 and moved into a small bungalow. When Chip dies in January 2027, he leaves his entire estate to his son, Chesney, including the bungalow, which is then worth £105,000.*

If Chip had died in August 2018, he would have been entitled to a RNRB of £125,000. To this we must add a full RNRB entitlement transferred from his late wife, but we count this as £175,000, the amount applying at the time of Chip's death. This produces a total of £300,000, so the sale proceeds of £225,000 for Chip's former home are deemed to represent 75% of his maximum entitlement (£225,000/£300,000 = 75%).

When Chip dies, his maximum RNRB entitlement is £350,000 (2 x £175,000). He therefore uses only 30% of his entitlement (£105,000/£350,000 = 30%). He is thus able to claim 45% (75% less 30%) of his maximum RNRB entitlement under the downsizing provisions. Hence, £157,500 (£350,000 x 45%) of other assets left to Chesney can be exempted under the RNRB, in addition to Chip's bungalow.

Where an individual dies owning a qualifying private residence, but does not leave that property to a direct descendent, or a qualifying trust for their benefit, any RNRB available is reduced by the value of that qualifying private residence. For example, if Chip had left his bungalow to his brother, the RNRB available to exempt the assets left to Chesney would have remained £157,500, but there would be no exemption on the bungalow itself.

Making the Most of the Residence Nil Rate Band

Thanks to the downsizing provisions, many married couples, widows, and widowers will be able to get the maximum benefit from the RNRB by ensuring they own a private residence worth at least £350,000 at some stage. To get the maximum relief, they will also need to ensure they:

- Have equity of at least this amount in the property (after deducting any mortgage against it),
- Sell the property for actual proceeds (rather than give it away, etc), or keep it until they die
- Leave at least one of any qualifying properties they own at the time of their death to their direct descendants, or a suitable trust for their benefit (Section 8.3), and
- Leave sufficient further sums to qualifying beneficiaries or trusts in order to fully utilise the relief available under the downsizing provisions

The third and fourth steps can take place on the second death. The third step becomes unnecessary where no qualifying properties are held at the time of death.

The maximum potential RNRB may also be available as a result of an earlier sale of a qualifying property for at least the following amounts (net of any mortgage over the property):

Sales between 9th July 2015 and 5th April 2018: £275,000
Sales during 2018/19: £300,000
Sales during 2019/20: £325,000

Similar principles apply to single or divorced people, and unmarried couples, but each individual will need to own a share in a property, net of any mortgage, worth at least £175,000 at some stage after 8th July 2015, or to have sold a share in a property for at least the following amounts (again, net of their share of any mortgage):

Sales between 9th July 2015 and 5th April 2018: £100,000
Sales during 2018/19: £125,000
Sales during 2019/20: £150,000

For an unmarried couple, the third and fourth steps described above will need to take place on ***each*** death.

13.11 THE RESIDENCE NIL RATE BAND AND GIFTS WITH RESERVATION

Many of the planning techniques described in this chapter involve a lifetime transfer of the family home and are designed to avoid a gift with reservation. Sadly, if the planning is not carried out correctly, a gift with reservation may still arise (e.g. failing to pay full market rent under the full consideration method in Section 13.8). A gift with reservation will also arise on a simple gift of the property while the original owner is still in occupation. We looked at the CGT implications of a gift with reservation of the family home in Section 12.8, but what happens to the RNRB in these situations?

Example Part 1: *Marilyn has been a widow since her husband, Jack died in 2018. Jack left his entire estate, worth £1m, to Marilyn, including their family home, at 63 Fitzgerald Gardens. In May 2026, Marilyn gives Fitzgerald Gardens to her son, Curtis, when the house is worth £425,000, but continues to live there on her own.*

The gift of Fitzgerald Gardens represents a gift with reservation. Hence, if Marilyn should die while still residing in the property, its value will be included in her estate. As she gave the property to a direct descendant, she will be able to claim the RNRB against it. Including the RNRB transferred from Jack, she can claim up to £350,000 at current rates (see Section 3.4).

However, as we saw in Section 4.8, if Marilyn dies within seven years of making the transfer, we must also prepare a second calculation, on the basis that the transfer ***did*** take place. While this second calculation will be based on the property's value at the date of transfer, the RNRB will not be available as the transfer has not taken place on death.

Example Part 2: *In June 2029, Marilyn is taken seriously ill. Things are touch and go for a while, it is not clear if she will recover. Her advisers, Miller & Co., prepare some deathbed planning options for her. At the same time, they carry out a preliminary assessment of her IHT position if she should die. Under the first calculation, Fitzgerald Gardens, now worth £535,000 is included in her estate but she is able to set off her RNRB entitlement of £350,000, leaving £185,000 exposed to IHT and resulting in a charge of £74,000 on the house (at 40%).*

In the second calculation, the gift of Fitzgerald Gardens in 2026 becomes a chargeable lifetime transfer. While the gift is covered by Marilyn's NRB/TNRB, it still results in an extra £425,000 of her remaining estate being exposed to IHT, increasing her IHT bill by £170,000. As this calculation produces the greater tax, this is the one used if Marilyn were to die. The gift of Fitzgerald Gardens would thus cost Marilyn's family an extra £96,000.

Once more than seven years have elapsed since the gift with reservation, the second calculation is no longer required. The property remains in the transferor's estate for IHT purposes and, where it has been gifted to a direct descendant, the RNRB continues to be available. As far as IHT is concerned, it is really as if the transfer had never taken place.

However, while the gift with reservation is ineffective for IHT purposes, it can be disastrous for CGT (Section 12.8). On the other hand, where tax is not a concern, there is the practical advantage that title to the property has already passed without the need to wait for probate. It might also avoid a few family squabbles in some cases.

The IHT position changes again when the reservation comes to an end. Surprisingly, in many cases, this may actually make matters worse!

Example Part 3: *Thankfully, Marilyn makes a full recovery and continues to live in Fitzgerald Gardens for several more years until, in June 2034, she decides she is tired of living alone and moves in with her sister, Jane. This means the reservation* *over Fitzgerald Gardens comes to an end, and Marilyn is treated as making a PET. By this time, Fitzgerald Gardens is worth £760,000.*

If Marilyn dies with the next seven years, the deemed PET in 2034 will become a chargeable lifetime transfer of £760,000 and the RNRB will ***not*** be available. This means her NRB/TNRB will be used against Fitzgerald Gardens, costing her family an additional £304,000 in IHT on her death (see Note 2).

Example Part 4: *Sadly, Marilyn passes away in June 2036 when Fitzgerald Gardens is worth £875,000. If the reservation had still applied, the property would be treated as part of her estate, but the RNRB, which is £205,000 by this time, would have been available. With Jack's transferred RNRB, this would have given Marilyn a total exemption of £410,000, leaving only £465,000 of Fitzgerald Gardens' value exposed to IHT, giving rise to a charge of £186,000. Ending the reservation has therefore cost Marilyn's family an additional £118,000 (£304,000 – £186,000) in IHT.*

Where a property eligible for the RNRB is subject to a gift with reservation, ***ending*** the reservation within seven years prior to the original owner's death could lead to additional IHT of up to £140,000 at current rates, possibly more in future. In many cases, it may be unlikely the original owner will survive for seven years after ending the reservation. It may therefore be better to keep the reservation going. This could be difficult if the original owner's health begins to fail and they need to be taken into care. Nonetheless, with up to £140,000 at stake, it may be worth the additional cost of having them cared for at home.

A potential alternative strategy in this scenario might be to rent the property out and ensure the rental income goes to the original owner, or is applied for their benefit: perhaps to pay nursing home fees. Better still: avoid the gift with reservation in the first place!

Notes to the Example

1. I assumed throughout the example that Marilyn's estate will not exceed the threshold for tapering of the RNRB (currently £2m: see Section 3.4), but will include sufficient other assets to fully utilise her NRB/TNRB.
2. Future values for the NRB and RNRB are based on our projections in Section 3.2. Based on those projections, on a death after 5th April 2036, Fitzgerald Gardens would use up £760,000 of Marilyn's NRB/TNRB, leading to the cost of £304,000 in the example. On an earlier death, Fitzgerald Gardens would completely use up Marilyn's NRB/TNRB with the excess exposed to IHT. As this would be less than three years after the deemed PET, there would be no taper relief. Hence the overall cost would again be £304,000.
3. See Section 12.8 regarding the CGT implications of a gift with reservation of the family home, which again apply in this example.

The position on a gift with reservation, where the RNRB is available on the gifted property, can be summarised in most cases as follows (assuming the property is increasing in value):

Death within seven years of gift; reservation still in effect: IHT is charged on the greater of the property's value at the date of death ***less*** the amount of RNRB available; **or** the property's value at the date of the gift. This leaves the family worse off than if the gift had never taken place: unless the property increases in value between the date of gift and the date of death by more than the amount of RNRB available; in which case it leaves the family no better or worse off for IHT purposes.

Death more than seven years after gift; reservation still in effect: IHT is charged on the property's value at the date of death ***less*** the available RNRB. This leaves the family no better or worse off for IHT purposes.

Death within seven years after the reservation has ceased: IHT is charged on the property's value at the date the reservation ceased. This leaves the family worse off than if the gift had never taken place: unless the property increases in value between the date the reservation ceases and the date of death by more than the amount of RNRB available.

Death more than seven years after the reservation has ceased: the property escapes IHT. This obviously leaves the family better off for IHT purposes, but, like all the other scenarios, the CGT position also needs to be taken into account (see Section 12.8).

In summary, there are two seven-year periods (the first and third scenarios) when the gift with reservation is likely to leave the family worse off. Although these periods may overlap, this still means up to fourteen years of increased exposure to IHT. Where there is a gap between these periods (second scenario) the family is no better off during the interval. Only the fourth scenario produces an IHT saving: and even then there is likely to be a CGT cost.

Valuable Properties or Estates

The position may differ where the value of the property at either the time of the gift, or the time the reservation ceases, was more than the amount of the NRB, plus any available TNRB, at the time of the transferor's death. In the case of the transferor's death more than three, but less than seven, years after the original gift, this will reduce the IHT arising under the second calculation. However, where the reservation still applies, this can, at best, still only leave the family no better or worse off than if the gift had never taken place.

Once the reservation ceases, the position will remain the same as described above for the first three years thereafter. It is only when the transferor dies more than three years after the reservation ceases that transfers of these more valuable properties may begin to produce additional IHT savings, although detailed calculations are required to fully assess the position where the transferor does not survive the full seven years.

I have also assumed throughout this section that the RNRB is available, and will not be eliminated by the tapering provisions (Section 3.4). If the RNRB was not available, there would generally be IHT savings on a death any time after the reservation ceases, although the CGT costs would remain.

Chapter 14

Family Investment Companies

14.1 INTRODUCTION TO FAMILY INVESTMENT COMPANIES

A 'family investment company' is a broad term used to describe companies set up to hold investments, including rental property, and also used to pass wealth to, or share it with, adult children or other family members.

In addition to the IHT planning benefits we will explore in this chapter, holding investment or rental property through a company can also produce substantial tax savings on income and capital gains during your lifetime. These are explored in the Taxcafe guide *Using a Property Company to Save Tax*, as well as tax issues around transferring property to a company, including CGT, SDLT, and the reliefs applying under both taxes, as referred to in this chapter. One important relief in this context is the ability to pay non-residential SDLT rates (see Section 12.4) on a transfer of six or more residential dwellings.

Family investment companies come in a number of forms, with a variety of share structures, loan accounts, etc. In this chapter, we will explore some of the most popular structures.

14.2 SHELL COMPANIES AND LOAN ACCOUNTS

A simple method to create a family investment company is to start by setting up a new, 'shell' company with a small nominal value, say £100. New companies can easily be set up via an online service at a very modest cost (less than £50 in many cases, but more if you require a complex share structure).

The next step is to transfer the shares to your adult children or other intended beneficiaries. It is important to do this while the company is still an empty shell as this means the transfer of value is very small, just the value of the nominal share capital and in most cases, covered by your annual exemption.

You now transfer your investments, rental property, etc, to the company in exchange for an interest-free loan account, repayable on demand. The loan account means you have received full consideration for the transfer: hence no transfer of value has taken place and no IHT charges can arise.

Example: *Joe and Katherine are a married couple with ten adult children and wish them all to benefit equally from their substantial residential rental property portfolio, worth £4m. They also have cash and other investments of £1m and a home of their own worth £800,000. At present, they have no other income apart from their rental property and a small amount of savings and investment income. In future, they will each receive a modest state pension, but they have made no other pension provision.*

They set up a family investment company (FIC), Gary Investments Ltd, with a nominal share capital of £100 and then give 10% of the shares to each of their children. These transfers are covered by their annual exemptions and are thus immediately exempt from IHT and cannot be subject to the pre-owned assets charge.

They now transfer their entire property portfolio to the company in exchange for an interest-free loan account of £4m. Unfortunately, while this is free from IHT (as no transfer of value has taken place) it must be treated as a sale at market value for the purposes of both CGT and SDLT (we'll assume there are at least six properties).

Let us suppose the portfolio was originally purchased for a total cost of £1.5m. This means the couple have capital gains of £2.5m, giving rise to CGT of £600,000 (at 24%: I have assumed they are both higher rate taxpayers). Additionally, the company has a SDLT bill of £189,500. Joe and Katherine lend this sum to the company to enable it to pay the SDLT. They also lend the company a further £10,500 to give it some working capital, thus taking their loan account balance to a total of £4.2m.

The property portfolio yields an annual profit before tax of £275,000. After paying CT at 25% and setting aside a small reserve, the company is able to repay £200,000 to Joe and Katherine each year, giving them sufficient money to live on. While this is effectively an income stream, it is tax free, as it is a loan repayment and therefore not subject to Income Tax.

Ten years later, the loan account balance has reduced to £2.2m; the rental property portfolio is worth £7.5m; Joe and Katherine's home is worth £1.5m; and the NRB and RNRB have increased to £391,000 and £211,000 respectively. Let's take a look at the couple's IHT exposure at this stage:

		With FIC	**Without FIC**
Property portfolio		-	*£7.5m*
Home		*£1.5m*	*£1.5m*
Loan account		*£2.2m*	-
*Cash and investments**		*£0.2m***	*£1m*
Total assets		*£3.9m*	*£10m*
Less:	*NRBs*	*£0.782m*	*£0.782m*
	*RNRBs****	*£0.422m*	-
Chargeable estate		*£2.696m*	*£9.218m*
IHT exposure at 40%		*£1.078m*	*£3.687m*

** Assumed no growth as after-tax income and capital gains used to pay living costs*
*** Reduced by payment of CGT, SDLT, and loan of further £10,500 to the company*
**** Using the company, the couple's estates now amount to less than £2m each, so they should be able to benefit from their RNRBs if they plan carefully. Without the company the tapering provisions (Section 3.4) will mean no RNRBs are available*

After ten years, the family investment company has reduced Joe and Katherine's IHT exposure by over £2.6m. However, this has come at a significant cost, with a total of £789,500 in tax paid at the outset. Nonetheless, there is still an overall net saving, after ten years, of over £1.8m.

You might wonder if Joe and Katherine could have achieved greater savings by simply giving properties directly to the children. Let's say they gave all their properties to their children, so their total CGT bills would be the same. This would avoid the SDLT charges but, as the gifts to the children would be PETs, the value of the properties would remain in their estates, still exposed to IHT, for the next seven years. Furthermore, it would be impractical to treat the children fairly, as Joe and Katherine wish. But the biggest problem with these direct gifts is they would be left with almost nothing to live on in retirement!

To summarise, a family investment company has the following advantages:

- No transfer of value, hence IHT savings start to accumulate immediately
- There are no immediate IHT charges on transfers in excess of the NRB
- The loan account provides a tax-free income stream
- Profits arising within the company are subject to CT at 25% at most, instead of Income Tax at up to 47% (even more in some cases)
- Children or other beneficiaries can benefit equally, or in whatever proportions you wish (difficult to achieve with direct transfers or bequests)

There is a slight disadvantage in that capital gains arising within the company are likely to be taxed at 25% instead of the 24% paid by higher rate taxpayers such as Joe and Katherine. However, CT will only be payable on future capital growth, and an appropriate proportion of the SDLT suffered at the outset will also be deductible from the company's capital gains (around 4.74% of each property's value at the date of transfer in the example above).

To further illustrate the benefits of a family investment company, the table below shows the overall saving achieved under the scenario set out in the example above, with the following additional assumptions:

i) The transfer to the company is on 6th April 2027 (you don't have to wait until the start of a new tax year, but it makes the number crunching easier!)
ii) Property values grow at a compound rate of 7.5% per year
iii) The first parent to die leaves their entire estate to the surviving spouse
iv) Joe and Katherine spend all the cash they receive from the company, from pensions, and from their investments
v) Rental profits from the property portfolio remain at the same level
vi) Income Tax rates and thresholds remain at 2027/28 levels: see below (they are currently expected to remain at these levels until at least 2030/31)
vii) The CT rate for companies with annual profits in excess of £250,000 remains 25%

Second Death After (Years)	Estate without FIC	Estate using FIC	IHT Saved	Overall Net Saving/(Cost)*
1	£6,160,000	£5,060,000	£440,000	(£316,594)
2	£6,547,000	£4,924,500	£649,000	(£74,688)
3	£6,963,025	£4,793,838	£867,675	£176,893
5	£7,891,021	£4,548,503	£1,337,007	£712,037
7	£8,963,436	£4,327,239	£1,854,479	£1,295,321
10	£10,892,951	£4,048,825	£2,737,650	£2,277,210
15	£15,202,611	£3,767,102	£4,574,204	£4,278,294
20	£21,389,685	£3,798,281	£7,036,562	£6,905,182

* After accounting for up-front tax charges of £789,500; but also including annual tax savings on rental profits from the property portfolio of £32,906 each year. This saving increases to £46,703 per year after the first death, although this potential increase is not accounted for in the table.

The annual tax savings on rental profits are increasing from 2027/28 onwards due to the forthcoming 2% 'across the board' increase in Income Tax rates on property income. From 2027/28 onwards, the effective rates applying to taxable rental profits received by full-time landlords like Joe and Katherine will be:

Taxable Rental Profit (Each)	**Effective Tax Rate**
First £12,570	0%
£12,570 to £50,270	22%
£50,270 to £100,000	42%
£100,000 to £125,140	63%
Over £125,140	47%

Using a family investment company provides the added benefit of avoiding this tax increase. Taking the Income Tax savings into account, we can see it takes just three years before the family investment company starts to produce an overall saving. As this is based on the date of the second death, this means most couples have a good chance of benefitting from this method.

Unlike the example above, the table ignores any further savings that may be yielded if the RNRB becomes available. This will require some additional planning after the first death, but could lead to a further saving of up to £140,000 (at current rates).

Problems and Limitations

The major problem with this strategy is the up-front tax cost. The couple need to have sufficient liquid resources (cash and short-term investments) to cover this cost. As a very broad rule of thumb, if we say the value of your rental properties has roughly doubled since purchase, the up-front tax cost is likely to be around 17% of the value of your portfolio (it was almost 20% for Joe and Katherine as their portfolio had more than doubled in value).

If you do not have enough liquid resources, you will need to sell some properties which will lead to more CGT. Selling a former home can be helpful as some or all of the gain will usually be exempt from CGT, and an arm's length sale will usually preserve your RNRB entitlement (see Section 13.10).

Alternatively, a former home may be a suitable property to transfer to the company at a lower CGT cost, although this might jeopardise your RNRB. See the Taxcafe guide *How to Save Property Tax* for further details on the CGT exemption for a former home.

In our example, I have also assumed the properties were debt-free. It may be difficult to transfer properties subject to a mortgage.

The loan account in the example will run out after twenty-one years, hopefully long enough for Joe and Katherine. Getting the duration of the loan account right is a matter of luck, or perhaps good timing, but the closer the second death is to the date the loan account is exhausted, the better.

If one or both parents survive for longer, they will need to use other resources to fund living expenses. It is important the children/company owners do not support them, as this could lead to problems under the gifts with reservation rules (Section 4.8), effectively bringing the value of the company shares back into their estate. In a case like Joe and Katherine, this might be the time to sell the family home and downsize (Section 13.10), perhaps putting some surplus funds into a suitable IHT shelter, as explained in Section 13.3.

Another potential problem in some families is the practical issue of running the company. Sibling rivalry may render this impossible and there may also be the worry of outside influences, such as the children's partners. Some of the children may also be less mature than others, which may be a cause for concern. In the next section we will look at some possible solutions.

Not Limited
An unmarried couple could use a family investment company in a similar way, except that IHT charges would arise on the first death. The loan accounts would need to be kept separate and it would be important to ensure both of the couple's NRBs (and RNRBs if available) were fully utilised on their deaths. Similarly, a single or divorced parent could use a family investment company, but would only benefit from a single NRB.

A family investment company could be used to pass investment assets to other beneficiaries, such as nieces, nephews, siblings, or friends. The only difference to the figures given in the example above is that no RNRB would be available on the deceased's home where this is not left to direct descendants.

14.3 OPTIONAL EXTRAS

There are a number of potential refinements and improvements to the strategy discussed in the previous section.

Golden Shares: The parents may be concerned their children will not be able to manage the company together. To combat this, the parents can hold a 'golden share' that carries no rights to dividends, is non-transferable, and will be redeemed and cancelled on the second death. As such, the golden share will have little or no value in its own right. However, the share will carry the power to appoint or remove directors and to block any resolution to remove a director appointed by the golden shareholders. Hence, the golden share allows parents to intervene, if necessary, and thus ensure the smooth running of the company (often the mere threat of intervention will be enough!)

Shares in Trust: The family investment company's shares can be gifted to a trust rather than directly to children. This could be used to keep control of shares allocated to a less mature (but adult) child until parents feel they are ready to participate directly in the company's management.

Alternatively, shares can be placed in a discretionary trust to benefit grandchildren or other family members (but not the donor's own minor children). Furthermore, if each parent sets up a separate discretionary trust to hold shares, the widow/widower could, if desired, be included as a beneficiary of the other parent's trust after the first death.

Provided the shares are held in the trust for less than ten years, no IHT charges should arise. Alternatively, it may be worth paying some anniversary or exit charges to secure longer-term benefits (both practical and financial).

Avoiding the SDLT Cost: It might be possible to avoid SDLT on the transfer by initially going into partnership with your children for a few years before forming the company. This will mean delaying the formation of the company. It will also mean you need to retain some shares (although, with careful planning, your shareholding may be kept small). For more see the Taxcafe guide *Using a Property Company to Save Tax.*

Accelerating the IHT Savings: If the parents reach the point where they have sufficient personal resources outside the company to sustain them for the rest of their lives, they can gift the benefit of some or all of the remaining loan account to the children. This will be a PET and the gifted amount will escape IHT if the donor survives seven years. Note, however, there may be CGT consequences for the donee on a subsequent repayment of the debt.

14.4 GROWTH SHARES

By creating a different share structure, incorporating growth shares, a family investment company can be used to pass on some or all of the future growth in value of your investments or rental property free from IHT. In many cases, the company can be set up with no up-front tax costs, or at least much less than using the technique in Section 14.2.

Example: *James and Mary, a married couple, run a residential rental property business in partnership. They each spend an average of more than twenty hours per week working in the business. The portfolio comprises ten houses purchased over several decades at a total cost of £1.5m and currently worth £6m. Their only other significant asset is their home, worth £1.2m. They now wish to start passing on some of their wealth to their adult sons, Paul and Michael, but the cost of using the method in Section 14.2 would be almost £1.4m (£1.08m in CGT and £289,500 in SDLT), which they simply cannot afford.*

Instead, they transfer their property business to a new company, Walton Investments Ltd, in exchange for Class A Ordinary Shares. This transfer qualifies for incorporation relief for CGT purposes, meaning their capital gains of £4.5m can be held over against the value of their shares and no CGT liability arises at this point. The transfer of partnership property to a company controlled by the same individuals is also exempt from SDLT. Hence, there is no up-front cost of forming the company.

The company issues Class B Ordinary Shares to Paul and Michael. These carry the right to any growth in value in the company in future, but the first £6m of the company's assets belongs to the Class A shareholders. In effect, the Class B shares are currently worthless, there is no transfer of value, and no IHT can arise.

While the current value of the Class A shares, £6m, remains in James and Mary's estates, the future growth in the property portfolio's value will now effectively belong to Paul and Michael. Furthermore, if James and Mary are able to limit the dividends they withdraw from the company, any surplus after tax profits can either be paid to their sons, or accumulated within the company for their benefit.

Notes to the Example

i) The transfer was only exempt from SDLT because James and Mary were operating as a partnership. In other cases, including joint ownership, SDLT will arise, and it would be necessary to operate as a partnership for a few years in order to obtain exemption.

ii) CGT incorporation relief is usually available where the business owners spend an average of at least twenty hours per week working in the business. In other cases, it will depend on the circumstances. The whole business must be transferred in exchange for shares in order to obtain this relief.

iii) Whether the Class B growth shares have any voting rights is entirely up to you. If you wish to retain control over the company, the Class B shares can be non-voting.

iv) Similarly, it is up to you whether the growth shares carry rights to dividends. My recommendation would be that they do, but this is at the discretion of the Class A shareholders (this is important to ensure the B shares have no value at the date of issue).

Next Steps

At this stage, James and Mary still hold £6m worth of shares. However, to date, they have not made any transfers of value. They could therefore transfer £650,000 worth of Class A shares into a trust for Paul and Michael's benefit and hold over the capital gains arising, using the method described in Section 9.4 (which works just as well for shares).

To transfer any significant further amount of shares to their sons within the next seven years, the couple face a choice of either paying CGT on a direct transfer, or IHT at the lifetime rate if they pass on shares via the trust. Since CGT only applies to the gain (not the full value), this will be the cheaper option in this case.

If we suppose there are 10,000 Class A shares, the capital gain arising on the transfer of each individual share will be £450 (£4.5m/10,000), giving rise to CGT, at 24%, of £108 (if James and Mary are higher rate taxpayers).

Funding that cost would entail taking additional dividends out of the company, on top of what James and Mary already need for living expenses. Hence, there would also be an Income Tax cost. For a higher rate taxpayer to take an extra £108 out of their company, they need to take a dividend of £168 (after paying Income Tax at 35.75% they are left with the net £108 they need: see Section 10.13 for dividend tax rates).

This means the total tax cost of passing each share worth £600 (£6m/10,000) to one of their sons is £168, or 28%; and it will be more if the couple's total taxable income goes over £100,000 (each). For an IHT saving of £240 (£600 x 40%), which will take seven years to achieve, many might not consider this to be worthwhile.

Alternatively, it might be possible to pass small parcels of shares into a series of trusts over many years, with significant extra additions every seven years, using the method described in Section 9.1. As the Class A shares will not increase in value, anniversary and exit charges will be negligible. Based on our assumptions regarding the NRB, if James and Mary start this strategy in 2027/28, they could have sheltered a further £3.418m worth of shares from IHT by 2048/49 (including the initial £650,000 described above). If the couple are both, say, 60 now, it is not unreasonable to suppose they will survive long enough to achieve this. (Arguably, one might say they have only sheltered £2.378m, as their projected NRBs of £520,000 each by this time have been fully utilised.)

A third alternative is to pursue a mix of direct transfers, with their consequent CGT and Income Tax costs, and transfers via trust, utilising the available exemptions, over many years.

Whichever method is used, there are some limiting factors to be aware of. As the parents' shareholding reduces, the amount of income they are able to take from the company will reduce. Hence, they cannot take this past the point where they have insufficient income to live on. Furthermore, if they wish to retain control of the company, they will need to keep more than 50% of the Class A shares in either their personal ownership or within the trusts (and not allow the B shares any voting rights).

14.5 PICK AND MIX

The method described in Section 14.2 produces the greater IHT savings, but comes at a significant up-front tax cost. The method in Section 14.4 can be implemented with no up-front tax cost in many cases, but only achieves IHT savings on future growth in value of rental property or other investments (unless further steps are taken). It is possible to have a compromise solution, combining some of the benefits of both methods.

Example Revisited: *Let's go back to the same opening position we had for James and Mary at the start of the example in Section 14.4. However, let's now assume they have cash and short-term investments of at least £360,000 available to fund any up-front tax costs.*

As before, they transfer their rental property business to Walton Investments Ltd in exchange for Class A shares but, this time, there is also cash consideration of £2m in the form of an interest-free loan account repayable on demand. This means the value of their Class A shares is £4m (£6m – £2m).

Their incorporation relief is restricted to the part of the gain attributable to their shares, £3m (£4.5m x £4m/£6m), so £1.5m of their gain is exposed to CGT at 24%, giving them a CGT bill of £360,000, which they fund from their savings.

The Class B shares can then be issued to Paul and Michael in the same way as before (except it is now the first £4m of the company's net assets that belongs to the Class A shareholders, rather than £6m).

Instead of taking taxable dividends, James and Mary can now take tax-free loan repayments that will reduce their loan account, thus producing significant additional IHT savings, similar to those we saw in Section 14.2, as well as significant annual Income Tax savings.

Class A shares can subsequently be passed to Paul and Michael using the methods described in Section 14.4. The costs of direct transfers will be considerably less as James and Mary may only be basic rate taxpayers if they are funding their living costs wholly or mainly through tax free loan repayments, thus reducing some of the CGT to 18% (see Section 12.1). This reduced CGT bill can also be funded through further loan repayments rather than taxable dividends.

14.6 MORE OPTIONAL EXTRAS

Once again, there are some potential refinements or improvements to the strategies discussed in Sections 14.4 and 14.5.

Parent/Directors' Ongoing Income: The method described in Section 14.4 will leave the parents with no income from their rental portfolio, so they will probably need to take dividends out of the company to fund living expenses. Provided the parents continue to play an active role in the business, they will first be able to take small annual salaries, which will provide CT relief at up to 26.5% (see Section 10.13). Where the parents have no taxable income from outside the company, salaries of £12,570 each will be covered by their personal allowances and thus be free from Income Tax. In the case of a family investment company like Walton Investments Ltd, the salaries will usually also be free from National Insurance thanks to the employment allowance. Hence, in many cases, paying these salaries will provide an annual CT saving of up to £6,662 at no tax cost to the parents themselves.

Under the hybrid method explained in Section 14.5, the parents have a loan account and can thus take tax free loan repayments. However, taking the same level of salary described above will both provide the same annual CT saving and prolong the life of the loan account.

For example, taking the same facts as the revised version of the example in Section 14.5, if James and Mary need total net income of £150,000 per year, they could increase the life of their loan account from thirteen years to sixteen, while producing CT savings totalling up to £106,594 over the same period, by taking annual salaries of £12,570 each.

Going further, if the couple have no other sources of income from outside the company and are concerned the loan account may be exhausted too soon, it may be worth them also taking dividends of £37,700 each year (assuming the company is making sufficient profits to fund these). The total combined Income Tax cost would be just £7,998, giving the couple total annual after-tax income of £92,542 before they even need to consider loan repayments.

Based on the same assumptions as before, this would extend the life of James and Mary's loan account to over thirty-five years. But, let's not forget, the purpose of the family investment company was to save IHT, so extending the life of the loan account too far may be counter-productive!

A better solution may be to take the tax efficient salaries, the low tax dividends, and as much further money by way of loan repayments as the company can afford each year. The amount that is surplus to the parents' requirements can be invested in an IHT shelter, such as a loan trust, gift trust, qualifying investment syndicates (Section 7.34), or perhaps even gilts if the parents intend to emigrate some day (see Section 15.6).

If the parents begin to receive any taxable income from outside the company, including the state pension, they will need to revise their plans from then onwards, as the same level of salary and dividends will no longer be tax efficient. In fact, for directors over state pension age, a larger salary can often be more beneficial overall, but the dividends would need to be reduced to make sure they didn't become higher rate taxpayers. For a detailed examination see the Taxcafe guide *Salary versus Dividends*.

Lastly, it is important to point out that if and when the parents fully retire from the business, they should no longer be paid a salary, as this will not attract CT relief and will represent a gift with reservation, thus undermining the IHT savings achieved. However, if they remain active as directors, attending board meetings, reviewing company accounts, etc, those duties alone should continue to justify a small salary, certainly at least £12,570 each.

Pension Contributions: Where the parents continue to run the business after the transfer, it may be possible for the company to make pension contributions of up to £60,000 per parent per year. These will attract CT relief and, while they will no longer provide an effective IHT shelter, they could have other benefits: see Section 10.13. As with salary payments, it is vital the parents do sufficient work in the business to justify the pension contributions made on their behalf, otherwise CT relief may be denied and a gift with reservation may arise.

Golden Shares: If the parents may eventually wish to give 50% or more of the Class A shares to their children, they may also wish to hold a golden share (see Section 14.3) so they are able to retain control over the company. The golden share should ideally be issued at the outset before there are any concerns over values, voting rights, etc.

Shares in Trust: The Class B shares could be put in a trust rather than issued directly to the children, if desired. This could provide the same potential benefits as discussed in Section 14.3. If this is done at the outset, the shares would be virtually worthless, hence no transfer of value will have taken place, and no IHT charges can arise in the first ten years.

Accelerating the IHT Savings: If the parents have followed the method set out in Section 14.5, it may later be possible to create additional IHT savings by gifting some or all of their loan account to the children (subject, again, to the comments in Section 14.3).

Chapter 15

Other Advanced IHT Planning

15.1 BUSINESS BUY BACK

Assets qualifying for 100% BPR or APR (Chapter 7) can be transferred to a trust free from IHT. At some later stage, the transferor may decide to purchase the business back from the trust at market value. The end result would be that funds equal to the value of the business (at the time of the buy back) have been passed into the relevant property trust regime (and are thus outside any individual's estate) without incurring any entry charge on the transfer.

Example: *Sheridan and Smithy own an unlisted trading company, Two Pints Ltd, which they founded some years ago for an initial investment of £1 each; the company is now worth £2m. They transfer their shares to the Barry Family Discretionary Trust to benefit their adult children, Gavin and Stacey. The transfer qualifies for BPR so no IHT arises.*

The transfer qualifies for business asset disposal relief (Section 12.5), so Sheridan and Smithy decide not to claim holdover relief for CGT purposes. Each of them has a capital gain of £1m, on which they pay CGT of £180,000 (18%).

A few years later (more than two), Sheridan and Smithy buy the company back from the trust for its then market value of £3m. As the trust has held the company for the benefit of Gavin and Stacey for more than two years, it may also claim business asset disposal relief on its gain of £1m, so it pays CGT at 18%, i.e. £180,000. Sheridan and Smithy pay Stamp Duty of £15,000 on the purchase (£3m x 0.5%), bringing the total tax costs incurred to £555,000.

A net sum of £2.82m (£3m – £180,000) has now been placed in trust with no entry charge, leading to an eventual IHT saving of £1.128m. Taking account of the tax costs incurred by Sheridan, Smithy, and the trust, (and the consequent reduction in their estates), the overall net saving achieved is £795,000 (£1.128m – £555,000 + £555,000 x 40%).

Furthermore, this saving may be achieved after two years, not seven (i.e. once Sheridan and Smithy are eligible for BPR on the shares again) and no exit charges will apply to funds paid out to the trust beneficiaries within ten years of when the trust was set up.

By way of comparison, a couple putting a net sum of £2.82m into a relevant property trust by way of a lifetime transfer would incur immediate IHT charges of at least £434,000 (£2.82m – 2 x £325,000 = £2.17m x 20%). Exit charges of at least 0.1154% would also arise for each calendar quarter the funds were held in the trust, and it would take seven years before the funds were exempt from IHT on the couple's deaths.

There must be no fixed arrangement to buy the business back from the trust at the time of the original transfer. Even an intention to purchase the business back may be enough to require disclosure under DOTAS (Section 11.11).

The transferor must actually pay the funds required to purchase the business back from the trust. Any amount left outstanding as a loan would not be deductible from the purchaser's estate, as it would be deemed an artificially created debt (Section 2.10).

The purchaser will need to hold the business for another two years before they are eligible for BPR again. If they were to borrow to fund the purchase, those borrowings will be deducted from the value of the business for BPR purposes, and not from their general estate.

As detailed in Section 7.8, 100% BPR is now limited to the first £2.5m of value per person (the HPRA). If either Sheridan or Smithy dies within seven years of the original transfer, that transfer will use up £1m of their HPRA, so there could be an IHT cost if the company has grown further in value beyond the £3m it was worth at the time of the buy back. After seven years, the transferor's HPRA will be fully restored.

In summary, the transferor's BPR entitlement will ultimately be unaffected provided they survive at least seven years after the original transfer and at least two years after the buy back.

While the entry charge may be avoided under this technique, the trust will still be subject to anniversary and exit charges (see Chapter 8) if the funds (or assets purchased with them) remain in the trust for ten years or more after it was formed. Income accumulated within the trust (see Section 8.15) might also give rise to some exit charges, even within the first ten years, if this exceeds the NRB (or twice the NRB where there are two settlors). Such charges are likely to be modest, however.

15.2 THE DOUBLE DIP

Where full BPR or APR is available on a business owner's death (see Chapter 7), up to £2.5m worth of the relevant assets can be left to a discretionary trust free from IHT. The deceased's spouse (or unmarried partner) can then buy the relevant property from the discretionary trust for full market value. Due to the rules on deduction of liabilities (Sections 2.10 and 7.12), the purchase will need to be funded from other existing assets and not by way of borrowing.

On the survivor's death, the chargeable value of their estate will effectively be reduced twice: through BPR or APR on the qualifying property; and then again by using other chargeable assets or funds for the purchase. This provides the effective double dip, illustrated by the following example.

Example: *On his death, Damon leaves the family business to the Parklife Discretionary Trust and the remainder of his estate to his widow, Justine. Justine buys the business from the trust for £1m, its current market value, using funds inherited from Damon. On her death, her estate comprises the family business, worth £1.25m, and other assets worth £650,000. Her IHT calculation is as follows:*

Total estate value	*£1,900,000*
Less: Business property relief	*£1,250,000*
Chargeable estate	*£650,000*

Justine's chargeable estate is covered by her NRB of £325,000 plus her TNRB received from Damon, leaving her executors with no IHT to pay. If Damon had left the business to Justine rather than the trust, she would not have used £1m of other funds to purchase it. Those funds would then have been in her estate on her death, giving rise to an IHT bill of £400,000.

Hence, as we can see from the example, this technique effectively enables a surviving spouse or partner to benefit from a double deduction in respect of qualifying business or agricultural property.

The purchase of the business shortly after the original owner's death should give rise to little or no CGT due to the uplift on death (Section 12.2). The same would apply to any inherited assets sold to fund the business purchase.

However, the major drawback is the purchase of the business must be funded from other existing assets: either assets already held by the surviving spouse or partner, or other assets inherited from the deceased spouse or partner. Funding the purchase through borrowing will not be effective. This restriction severely limits the usefulness of this technique, although it will still be possible to use it in some cases. There are a few other little 'flies in the ointment' here:

- Stamp Duty or SDLT will be payable on the surviving partner's purchase of the business
- Although inherited assets will benefit from the uplift on death, the surviving spouse or partner may suffer CGT if they have to sell any of their own existing assets to fund the purchase of the business
- The discretionary trust will be subject to higher rates of Income Tax on income from the funds it holds; although the effects of this can be mitigated by paying income out to beneficiaries (see Section 8.17)
- The discretionary trust will be subject to anniversary and exit charges if it holds assets with a value in excess of the NRB for ten years or more

Having said all that, it is worth bearing in mind the technique allows funds equal to the market value of the deceased's business (up to £2.5m) to be put into a discretionary trust with no entry charge, and no exit charges during the first ten years (subject to my comments in Section 15.1), so it is a very efficient way to set up a trust.

Note that, in the example, I assumed Damon and Justine were married. This technique works almost as well for unmarried partners but, in such a case, Damon's estate would have suffered IHT on his other, non-business assets, and Justine would not have been entitled to a TNRB (unless she already had one from a previous deceased spouse).

One thing married business owners need to be aware of, however, is that leaving the business to a discretionary trust means not all of their HPRA will transfer to their widow/widower (see Section 7.8). For instance, in our example, Justine's HPRA (after Damon's death) will only be £4m, and not the full £5m it would have been otherwise (assuming she had no previous deceased spouses). This didn't matter in the example, and often won't in many other cases, but it is an important point to bear in mind.

Having said that, even if the business is worth more than the available HPRA on the widow/widower's death, the excess will only suffer IHT at an effective rate of 20%, whereas the double dip will have saved IHT at 40% on the funds used to buy the business from the trust.

15.3 MONEY BOX COMPANIES

In one case, a company with a business consisting of lending money to other, associated companies was held to be carrying on a qualifying business for BPR purposes. However, an important factor in this particular case was the fact the loans were unsecured and repayable on demand. This meant the company's business comprised a business of making loans rather than one of investing in loans: this was enough to enable the company's owner to obtain BPR. The fact the loans were made to associated companies did not affect the position.

This decision opens up interesting planning possibilities. A person with a non-qualifying company, such as a property investment company, could set up a money-lending company to make loans to the non-qualifying company. The loans would need to be unsecured and repayable on demand and the volume of activity carried on by the money-lending company would need to be enough to make it a business (Section 7.3). The money-lending company would also need to charge interest.

Under these circumstances, it would be possible to reduce the value of the non-qualifying company while the value of the money-lending company may be eligible for BPR, thus saving IHT when the owner of both companies dies.

The non-qualifying business probably needs to be in a company in order to get the necessary reduction in value that saves the IHT (see Section 15.4). Note that strategies involving multiple companies may lead to additional CT costs: see the Taxcafe guide *Putting it Through the Company*.

15.4 CORPORATE DEBT

As we saw in Section 7.14, liabilities owed by a company reduce the value of that company and hence also the value of its shares. When a person dies owning shares in a company, it is the value of those shares that is brought into their estate and there is no need to claim a separate deduction for the company's liabilities. Hence, there is also no need to meet the rules described in Section 2.10 regarding payment of liabilities out of the assets of the deceased's estate. It may therefore make sense if borrowings to finance investments not qualifying for BPR or APR are made through a company.

Example: *Phil has offered to lend his brother Don £500,000 to help him start a property investment business. The loan will be unsecured and interest-free. If Don borrowed the money personally and later died still owing this money to Phil, his executors would need to repay Phil out of the assets of Don's estate in order to claim a deduction for IHT purposes (see Section 2.10). Instead, Don sets up a company, Ever Lee Investments Ltd. He then gets Phil to lend the money to the company. The debt to Phil will now automatically reduce the value of Don's shares in Ever Lee Investments Ltd without having to worry about meeting the rules in Section 2.10.*

This technique solves the problem of having to repay a loan on the borrower's death but if such a loan was used to indirectly finance relievable property, the other rules in Section 2.10 would apply: although there may still be some benefit if that property is worth over £2.5m.

15.5 LONG-TERM UK RESIDENCE AND EMIGRATION

It is possible to avoid IHT on overseas assets, and certain UK assets (Section 15.6), if you either avoid becoming a long-term UK resident, or emigrate and become non-UK resident for long enough. Whether you are a long-term UK resident at any time depends on whether you are UK resident in 2025/26 or any later year and on your legal domicile on 30th October 2024 (see Section 11.6). Legal domicile is unaffected by any 'opt in' election (see Section 3.3).

If you ***are*** UK resident in 2025/26 or any later year, ***or*** you had legal domicile in the UK on 30th October 2024, you will be a long-term UK resident if you have been UK resident for at least ten of the previous twenty UK tax years.

If you are ***not*** UK resident in 2025/26 or any later year ***and*** you did not have legal domicile in the UK on 30th October 2024, you will be a long-term UK resident if you were UK resident for at least fifteen of the previous twenty UK tax years, including at least one of the previous three UK tax years.

Once you become a long-term UK resident, you will need to become non-UK resident for the required number of consecutive UK tax years in order to lose your long-term UK resident status and enjoy exemption from IHT on excluded property (Section 15.6). The required number of consecutive years of non-UK residence depends on how many of the last twenty years you were UK resident, up to and including your last year of UK residence.

If you were UK resident for all of the previous twenty years, you will need to be non-UK resident for ten consecutive years in order to lose your long-term UK resident status. If you were UK resident for between fourteen and nineteen of those years, the number of years you will need to be non-UK resident is ten less than the number of years (out of the last twenty) you were UK resident. If you were UK resident for between ten and thirteen of the last twenty years, you will only need to be non-UK resident for three years to lose your long-term UK resident status. Special rules apply to people aged under 20 at the end of the previous tax year.

Example: *Kylie was UK resident for eight years, from 2006/7 to 2013/14 and then another seven years from 2019/20 to 2025/26. This makes a total of fifteen of the previous twenty years, making her a long-term UK resident. In 2026/27, she emigrates and ceases to be UK resident. She will, however, remain long-term UK resident for five years (fifteen less ten), up to and including 2030/31.*

Since 2013/14, an individual's tax residence has been determined under the statutory residence test. The test is complex but a good general rule of thumb is you are UK resident if you spend more than 90 nights in the UK in a tax year. This is only a very rough generalisation of a far more complex issue: for further details see *How to Save Property Tax*.

While the long-term UK resident regime means it now generally takes far longer to avoid IHT by emigrating, it is much clearer what steps are needed (since residence is based on the statutory residence test), and is equally open to everyone, regardless of their legal domicile.

A much quicker way for emigrants to avoid IHT, however, may be to invest in gilts, as it is generally only necessary to be non-UK resident at the time of death for these to escape IHT (see Section 15.6).

Finally, remember, if you become resident or legally domiciled in another country, you will be subject to that country's tax regime. Believe it or not, some of them are worse than us! Hence, it is essential to take local advice in your destination country before you go.

15.6 EXCLUDED PROPERTY

Certain assets are excluded from charge to IHT. From 6th April 2025, for assets held by an individual, this exclusion is based purely on the residence status of that individual (for the position before 6th April 2025, see the twentieth edition of this guide).

Individuals Not Long-Term UK Residents (Section 15.5)

Individuals who are not long-term UK residents are not subject to IHT on foreign assets. They are also exempt from IHT on holdings in authorised unit trusts or open-ended investment companies. However, indirect holdings of UK residential property or, from 6th April 2026, UK agricultural property (e.g. through a company, partnership, trust, or more complex structure) generally remain subject to IHT. The proceeds of sale of UK residential or agricultural property is also subject to IHT for a further two years. APR may be available on UK agricultural property under the usual rules (Section 7.27).

Foreign Currency Bank Accounts

Foreign currency bank accounts held by an individual who is neither UK resident nor long-term UK resident at the time of their death are generally exempt from IHT, even when held with a UK bank or the Post Office. UK bank/Post Office accounts covered by this exemption are not technically excluded property, as this is a separate exemption.

Government Securities (Gilts)

Gilts acquired after 5th April 2013 and held by a non-UK resident individual are generally exempt from IHT. This provides tremendous scope to make IHT savings, as it is far quicker to achieve non-UK resident status than to lose long-term UK resident status. Remarkably, UK government securities may be exempt from IHT far sooner than foreign assets. Hence, an investment in gilts may be a good strategy for anyone looking to retire abroad, or even just spend a few years away from the UK.

It is important to ensure you are beneficially entitled to the gilts at the time of death, or the exemption does not apply. HMRC are on the look-out for last-minute purchases where the buyer may not yet have obtained beneficial ownership.

Not all gilts carry the same advantages, however. In the case of FOTRA (free of tax to residents abroad) securities issued before 29th April 1996; or 3½% War Loan issued at any time; it is necessary to be both non-ordinarily resident in the UK and non-UK domiciled. For other gilts issued between 29th April 1996 and 5th April 2013, and earlier issues of gilts that did not originally have FOTRA status, it is necessary to be non-ordinarily resident in the UK. Becoming non-ordinarily resident will generally mean being non-UK resident for at least three years, although this is subject to the details of each individual case.

Liabilities Incurred to Acquire Excluded Property

Liabilities incurred, directly or indirectly, to finance the acquisition, enhancement, or maintenance of excluded property, must be taken to reduce the value attributed to that property. In effect, this means such liabilities are non-deductible for IHT purposes. HMRC takes a very broad view of the scope of 'indirectly' for these purposes (see Section 7.12 for an example: similar principles apply here).

Excluded Property Trusts

In the past, non-UK domiciled individuals have sometimes been able to exclude non-UK assets held in a trust for their benefit, even after they acquired actual or deemed UK domicile (see the nineteenth edition of this guide for details). The status of these trusts after 5th April 2025 is subject to complex new legislation: professional advice is essential.

Chapter 16

The Inheritance Tax Planning Timetable

16.1 IT'S NEVER TOO EARLY TO START

Most tax advisers will tell you it's never too early to start IHT planning, but when you're struggling to pay a mortgage and make some headway at the beginning of your career, IHT will probably be the last thing on your mind.

Nevertheless, as we saw in Section 9.1, the earlier you start, the more effective your planning will be, and if you are lucky enough to have the wealth to follow the kind of planning in that section, long term planning will help to pass on more family wealth to the next generation, or even the one after that. Even if you have little wealth, your first step should be to ensure life policies are written in favour of other family members.

16.2 MARRIAGE

First of all, marriage is a good time to remind the family to do ***their*** IHT planning by making the exempt gifts set out in Section 5.3. This is also a good time to put money into trust for your children, even before they're born!

Next, remember to make a new Will. An existing Will is rendered void on marriage unless it was made in contemplation of your union. Once you are married, it may be worth taking steps to ensure your NRB is fully available to transfer to your spouse on your death. As we saw in Chapter 6, this may not always be the best course of action but is certainly something you should at least consider.

16.3 BECOMING A PARENT

This is the one that focuses the mind and gets most people thinking about IHT planning. It's time to step up the ante and begin thinking about tax efficient trust structures for your children (see Section 11.10). Get your parents to give money directly to your children instead of you (if you can afford to).

It's time to re-write your Will again as well; you will need to think about how to provide for your children if you die prematurely. Consider what kind of structure you would like to put in place from the choices available (see Chapter 8). Don't forget to appoint a guardian too!

Now you're a parent, the RNRB comes into play and you should start to factor it into your planning (see Sections 3.4, 13.10, and 13.11).

16.4 ADULT CHILDREN

You can now start giving assets directly to the children without the need for trust structures. Making use of the annual exemption may make sense, although most of us seem to have little choice anyway!

Normal expenditure out of income can be established to pass on substantial sums to the children and, when they marry, you can use the exemptions in Section 5.3. You may want to consider putting a family debt scheme in place (Sections 6.13 and 7.31), or using a family investment company (Chapter 14).

16.5 YOUR FIRST GRANDCHILD

Time to start looking at trust structures again; as we saw in Section 11.10, gifts to grandchildren are much more tax effective. Bare trusts for grandchildren are useful and avoid the problems you get with your own minor children.

You may want to re-write your Will again. Think about skipping a generation. What's the point of leaving money to the children if they're already well established? It might be better left to the grandchildren, so IHT doesn't come up again for another two generations.

16.6 GRANDCHILD'S EIGHTH BIRTHDAY

Your grandchild's eighth birthday is a key date. From the next day onwards, you will be able to put money into a relevant property trust for their benefit and pass it to them absolutely within less than ten years, i.e. before any anniversary charges can arise (Section 8.15). This opens up additional planning opportunities, as we have seen in previous chapters.

16.7 MIDDLE AGE

I'm not sure exactly when middle age is. A client of mine once said it was always ten years older than he was and, the older I get, the more I like that definition. For the purposes of this guide though, it is perhaps better defined as still working, but financially comfortable. This is when it may be worth considering maximising pension contributions, not so much for your own retirement planning, but for succession planning: see Chapter 10 for details.

If your pension savings are more than you are likely to need for your own retirement, it is worth considering taking your tax-free lump sum and giving it to your beneficiaries somewhere between the age of 55 and 68. As explained in Chapter 10, this will generally enhance the overall tax-saving potential of your pension savings.

16.8 RETIREMENT

As pensions or other savings income starts to come in, you may now be able to afford to pass on income-producing assets, perhaps by using a trust (Section 9.4). Alternatively, a family investment company may be a good vehicle to allow you to retire and still enjoy a tax-free income stream.

If you decide to downsize your home, you may be able to benefit from some of the planning strategies considered in Section 13.3, while still preserving your RNRB entitlement (Section 13.10).

If you have assets qualifying for BPR or APR (Chapter 7), consider how to preserve the relief after you retire (see Sections 7.20 and 7.28). Consider also whether it is better to pass these on now or hold on to them so your children (or other beneficiaries) can obtain a tax-free uplift on death for CGT purposes when you pass away.

If you take the tax-free lump sum from your pension at this point, consider whether to gift the funds to your children, as discussed in Chapter 10.

16.9 LOSING A PARENT

If one of your parents dies intestate or with a Will that isn't tax efficient, a deed of variation (Section 17.1) can be used to put IHT planning into place retrospectively. When your first parent dies, consider whether it is better for them to use their NRB on assets that might be appreciating in value (see Section 6.7) or for it to transfer to your surviving parent (if they are married).

If you don't need the money, get your legacies transferred to your children (or even grandchildren) instead. Gifts to charity may also reduce the IHT bill (see Sections 3.5, 3.6, and 17.1).

16.10 STILL TOGETHER AFTER ALL THESE YEARS

Elderly married couples face a dilemma. As you're both getting older, it may make sense to start giving away surplus wealth. However, if you die within seven years of making a PET or chargeable lifetime transfer, this will restrict the proportion of your NRB that transfers to your spouse. As we saw in Chapter 6, this may have adverse consequences, although there are also times when such transfers will be advantageous, especially when assets appreciating in value are gifted.

You need to weigh up these conflicting factors before making any lifetime transfers that are not immediately exempt. While such transfers may sometimes be beneficial for elderly married people, any potential impact on your surviving spouse's TNRB should also be considered. If you do decide to make lifetime transfers that are not immediately exempt, it will often make sense for these to be made by the spouse with the longer life expectancy.

16.11 LOSING A SPOUSE

You have two years to put a deed of variation into place to make sure your late spouse's estate is dealt with tax efficiently. The key point is to maximise the benefit of their NRB, either by having it transfer to you, or by using it to pass on appreciating assets free from IHT (see Section 6.7).

If your spouse leaves property qualifying for BPR or APR, it may make sense to pass this directly to the children (or other beneficiaries), in case the relief is later lost. This is often particularly important in the case of a family farm where the surviving spouse may no longer be able to run it. Alternatively, you may want to put a 'double dip' in place (Section 15.2).

Generally, your spouse's RNRB will transfer to you and should form part of your own subsequent planning. However, there will be some instances where it will be better to utilise your spouse's RNRB at this stage, if you can (e.g. if their estate was less than £2m, but you now expect yours to significantly exceed this level).

This is also a good time to assess your own financial needs and start making plans to give away any surplus. Consider your own life expectancy and review the appropriate actions set out in Sections 16.13 to 16.15.

16.12 REMARRIAGE

Remarriage provides another opportunity to make some of the exempt gifts outlined in Section 5.3. On this occasion, the ability to make tax-exempt transfers into trust for the benefit of your children may be particularly useful.

If either or both of you are a widow/widower, you may have an existing TNRB entitlement. If so, you should now consider taking steps to maximise the benefit of your existing TNRB. The methods discussed in Sections 6.9 to 6.11 and 13.5 to 13.7 are available to save your family up to £260,000.

This is also a good time to consider your new combined estate and decide whether there are surplus assets that can be given away. If your spouse already has an existing full TNRB entitlement, you will be able to make lifetime transfers without risking any loss of relief. If they have an existing partial TNRB entitlement, some lifetime transfers may still be made without risk.

Once again, you should re-write your Will, as any previous Will not made in contemplation of your new marriage will be rendered void.

16.13 LIFE EXPECTANCY OVER SEVEN YEARS (Per the ONS: men under 83, women under 85)

There's still time to make PETs that should hopefully have time to become fully exempt. Ending the reservation on a gift with reservation will give it time to become exempt also (but beware of the potential risks arising in the case of the family home: see Section 13.11).

Remember, if you are single and survive at least three years, some savings may still be made. If you are still married, however, some caution may be required (see Section 16.10, but also Section 16.12 if this is not your or your spouse's first marriage).

Longer-term planning strategies, such as family investment companies (Chapter 14) may still be viable but, after this, it's probably too late. Having said that, they would still have worked for Captain Sir Tom Moore; Vera Lynn; Glynis Johns; Joan Graham; the Queen Mother; Jean Steer; David Attenborough; and many others! I had hoped to add Prince Phillip to this list of British centenarians, but sadly he didn't quite make it. Nonetheless, he deserves a mention, if only for the fact he once said, "All money nowadays seems to be produced with a natural homing instinct for the Treasury."

16.14 LIFE EXPECTANCY THREE TO SEVEN YEARS (Men aged 83 to 92 and women aged 85 to 94)

Transfers made now should still benefit from tapering (see Section 4.5), so some tax may be saved if you are single. Transfers by married people at this stage carry a strong risk of having an adverse impact on your spouse's TNRB unless they are immediately exempt (see Section 16.10 but also Section 16.12 if this is not your or your spouse's first marriage).

Whether you're married or not, it's time to really start making the most of the annual exemption, the small gifts exemption, and normal expenditure out of income (these are all immediately exempt). A loan trust or discounted gift trust may make sense at this point, and possibly also gifts of appreciating assets (but see Chapter 12 regarding the CGT implications).

16.15 LIFE EXPECTANCY TWO TO THREE YEARS (Men aged 92 to 96 and women aged 94 to 98)

Now's the time to think about AIM shares or qualifying investment syndicates (but never forget 'Dodgy Dave': Section 11.1). Anything that gets your money into qualifying business property (Chapter 7) may still save IHT if you can survive two years. Rights issues or transfers of assets into a company under your control could provide immediate savings.

Loan trusts and discounted gift trusts may still save you money even now, as well as other transfers of appreciating property (but watch the CGT position). You may still have time to become non-UK resident, so investing in gilts and emigrating abroad could save substantial amounts of IHT (see Section 15.6).

16.16 LOSS OF CAPACITY

If you expect to lose the ability to take care of your own affairs in the near future, it may make sense to appoint a power of attorney. A power of attorney, or next of kin, can apply to the Court of Protection to make a Statutory Will on your behalf. The Court of Protection can also authorise your attorney to make lifetime gifts on your behalf, but this is generally limited to modest birthday and Christmas presents. The attorney is not usually entitled to make the more substantial gifts needed for IHT planning purposes. Where you have already set up a standing order to use your annual exemption, or make your normal expenditure out of income (Section 5.5), it is possible the attorney may be able to allow this to continue, but this point is not clear and may be challenged by HMRC.

In view of these problems, it is sensible to put as much IHT planning as possible in place before you lose capacity: everything becomes considerably more difficult once an attorney has been appointed. Write a new Will, make appropriate gifts, and consider the actions set out in the next section. A disabled trust may also be a good idea at this stage (Section 8.8). Do as much as you can before it's too late!

16.17 DEATHBED PLANNING

So, if you've really left it far too late, what can still be done? Some of this may seem a little flippant and, as I said in Section 1.1, I have no wish to cause any offence to anyone. Tax planning may be the farthest thing from your mind at this stage, and who could blame you. Nevertheless, here are some of the things you could think about if time is running out:

Deathbed Marriage: The biggest deathbed planning point, if you're still single at this stage, is to marry your partner. No point trying to hang on to your freedom now, just get on with it. That's exactly what one of HMRC's most famous adversaries, Sir Ken Dodd, did two days before his death.

It will almost always be worth marrying at this stage, even if you have very few assets, as any unused proportion of your NRB, RNRB, and HPRA will transfer to your spouse.

Last Gasp Gifts: If you haven't used your annual exemption (Section 5.2) for this, or the previous, tax year, get gifting. If you've made no previous gifts, one simple £6,000 payment to one of your nearest and dearest will save your family £2,400. For the rest of your family and friends, there's the small gifts exemption (Section 5.2). Every person you can find to give £250 will save your estate £100 in IHT. Remember, however, as explained in Section 4.7, if made by cheque, these gifts will not be effective unless the cheque clears before you pass away. Online banking may be better if you feel up to it.

What about the House? Although your family may be able to sort things out with a deed of variation (Section 17.1), it could make things easier for them if you change the title to a tenancy in common now.

Make Pension Contributions: If you're aged under 75 and still have earnings for this tax year, you may be able to make pension contributions. These probably won't escape IHT at this stage but, as explained in Section 10.15, they could still yield significant savings.

Maximising the Residence Nil Rate Band: As explained in Section 3.4, some or all of the RNRB is withdrawn if your estate is worth more than £2m at the time of your death. Hence, while PETs and chargeable lifetime transfers made at this stage will not usually save IHT, it may be possible to use them to reduce the value of your estate and thus prevent your RNRB being withdrawn.

Example: *It is March 2027 and Nelson, a widower, is dying. His late wife Sheena died some years earlier, leaving her modest estate to him. Nelson's estate is worth £2.7m, including his home, worth £1m, which he plans to leave to his children, and various cash and savings totalling £700,000. As things stand, Nelson's RNRB will be completely withdrawn by tapering and the IHT on his estate will total £820,000 (£2.7m – £650,000 = £2.05m x 40%).*

Instead, Nelson gives his cash and savings to his children before he dies. These transfers become chargeable on his death, so IHT of £20,000 (£700,000 – £650,000 = £50,000 x 40%) will be payable. However, the gifts reduce the value of his estate to £2m, meaning he will be entitled to a RNRB of £350,000. IHT of £660,000 (£2m – £350,000 = £1.65m x 40%) will then be payable on his estate. The lifetime gifts have therefore led to a saving of £140,000 (£820,000 – £660,000 – £20,000).

A married person could easily reduce the value of their estate to £2m by giving the excess to their spouse shortly before they died. This would generally be an exempt transfer and would have no impact on the TNRB; but it would mean the deceased's RNRB was available to transfer to their widow/widower.

Where assets other than cash are transferred, the CGT consequences will need to be considered. We looked at these in Chapter 12. However, in some cases, it may be worth taking a CGT hit to save more in IHT.

Example Revisited: *The facts are exactly as before, except Nelson transfers various assets worth £700,000 to his children, rather than cash. The transferred assets stand at an overall capital gain of £400,000, so CGT of £96,000 arises on the transfer. Nelson's CGT liability is deducted from his estate, so this increases the total*

IHT saving to £178,400 (£140,000 + £96,000 x 40%). Overall, the family remains £82,400 better off (£178,400 – £96,000).

For transfers to a spouse, there would generally be no immediate CGT cost but the uplift on death (Section 12.2) would be lost and this may eventually lead to a higher CGT cost that should be taken into account.

Transfers of assets qualifying for BPR or APR may also help to reduce your estate, as these are still counted for the purposes of the RNRB tapering rules (Section 3.4). Where CGT holdover relief also applies (Section 12.4), the transfer can be made free of CGT. However, once again, the uplift on death will be lost and you need to consider whether this may be more valuable to your heirs in the end.

If you are married, it is important to remember most transfers to anyone other than your spouse that are not immediately exempt will affect your spouse's TNRB. Transfers that are covered by 100% BPR or APR will not affect your spouse's TNRB, but may affect their HPRA.

Remember Your Normal Gifts: The exemption for normal expenditure out of income applies to lifetime gifts only. To get that final year's exemption, you need to make sure you've made that expenditure before you go.

Consider Setting up a Disabled Trust: As explained in Section 8.8, it may make sense to set up a disabled trust during your terminal illness. This may make things easier for your beneficiaries.

Spend! 'There are no pockets in shrouds,' they say, so why not spend it before HM Treasury gets hold of it. Any money you spend that qualifies as maintenance of family (Section 5.4) will escape IHT. For example, you could spend £3,000 buying clothes for your teenage daughter instead of leaving her a legacy of £3,000 that produces an IHT charge of up to £2,000.

You could also think about buying depreciating assets. "How will that help my family?" you may ask, but think about this:

Example: *Ian knows he has only a few months to live and wants to give his friend Chas a last gift. What Chas would really like is a new car and the model he has his eye on, a Rhythm Stick Blockhead, costs £75,000 new.*

Ian buys a Rhythm Stick Blockhead but doesn't give it to Chas straight away. Instead, he leaves the car to Chas in his Will. When Ian dies a few months later, the car, now second-hand, is worth only £45,000 and this is the value to be used for IHT purposes. If Ian had simply given the car to Chas brand new, a sum of £75,000 would have been included in his estate. Hence, by leaving the car in his Will instead, Ian has saved up to £12,000 in IHT.

Contractual Obligations: The liabilities under any contractual obligations existing at the date of your death will be deductible from your estate provided they meet the rules set out in Section 2.10. Hence, if your beneficiaries would like something done to an asset that is about to pass to them under the terms of your Will, why not contract for the work to be done at your expense?

Review (or Make) Your Will: While you're still of sound mind, there is still time to change (or make) your Will. Maximising the value of your NRB should be top of the list if you are married (see Chapter 6) and you should consider the RNRB if you have children or grandchildren.

As we shall see in Section 17.1, your beneficiaries can enter a deed of variation within the next two years as long as all affected parties agree. What you might need to consider at this stage, however, is whether any beneficiaries in your current Will are likely to stand in the way of IHT saving measures by refusing to agree to a deed of variation. Furthermore, as we shall see in Section 17.1, deeds of variation have some significant drawbacks that can be avoided by making the relevant provisions in your Will instead.

The easiest way to save IHT at this stage is to change your Will to leave some or all of your estate to charity (Section 3.5). Your existing beneficiaries may not be happy, but it's your decision (mostly: see Section 11.7).

If you wish to benefit from the additional relief for charitable legacies we examined in Section 3.6, you may wish to include the relevant provision in your Will as, again, one of your beneficiaries might not agree to the necessary deed of variation. Furthermore, as explained in Section 3.6, there have been some doubts over whether deeds of variation can be used for this purpose. There are also a few technical hurdles to be overcome.

All in all, while deeds of variation are an extremely useful IHT planning tool, it will generally make sense to put as much of your IHT planning in place via your Will as you can.

Maximise Your Business Property: While, as explained in Section 7.17, the business property itself generally needs to have been held for at least two years to qualify for BPR, you can enhance the value of existing business property at any time. This might, for example, include:

- Paying business debts from private resources
- Paying off liabilities incurred to finance the acquisition, enhancement, or maintenance of business property (again from private resources)
- Buying additional assets for use in your business (as long as these are funded from existing private resources, not from borrowing): for example, could you buy the business premises you currently rent?
- Rights issues of shares by a qualifying private company
- Transferring assets into a qualifying private company (Section 7.21): such transfers may have CGT or SDLT consequences, which should be considered, and may not save IHT if your company is already worth at least £2.5m (£5m if you are a widow/widower)

Remember, if you have disposed of qualifying business property within the last three years, you can restore BPR by buying replacement property (Section 7.18), including qualifying AIM shares (although these now only provide 50% relief).

Deathbed CGT Planning: What you should ***not*** generally do at this stage is make disposals that give rise to CGT liabilities. (Although there are exceptions, as we have seen.) If you sell assets before you die, your estate will be liable for the CGT arising based on your original base costs for those assets. Subject to this liability, the net proceeds of the sale will remain in your estate and will be subject to IHT.

If you hang on to those assets, the IHT may be a little greater (as there is no CGT liability to deduct) but, as we saw in Chapter 12, your personal representatives or beneficiaries will be able to sell them later with little or no CGT liability. Conversely, therefore, the best deathbed planning for CGT purposes might be to accumulate more assets: especially, as we saw in Section 12.6, from your spouse!

Chapter 17

Planning after Death

17.1 DEEDS OF VARIATION

Perhaps the last resort in IHT planning is the deed of variation. This is an essential planning tool where a family finds the terms of the deceased's Will (or intestacy) have an undesired effect. Where all affected beneficiaries are in agreement, it is possible to vary the Will in order to create a better result.

As the deed of variation is a legally binding document, it is wise to consult a lawyer when completing it. Strictly speaking, the IHT rules only require the document to be a written instrument, although a formal deed is generally recommended.

Conditions: The required variations must be recorded in writing within two years of the death (this is the deed); all existing beneficiaries affected by the variations should sign the deed (new beneficiaries do not need to sign, although this does no harm); the deed should include a statement that the signatories intend the deed to have effect for IHT purposes; where the deed results in additional IHT being payable on the deceased's death, a copy must be sent to HMRC within six months, HMRC must also be notified of the amount of additional tax due at the same time; the variation must not be made for any consideration in money or money's worth, except in the case of compensatory variations to the deceased's Will or intestacy.

It is also common practice for the deceased's personal representatives to sign the deed, although this is not required by law.

Variations made by such a deed are treated for IHT purposes as if they had been made by the deceased. This treatment extends to the pre-owned assets regime (Section 11.12). This means a beneficiary who becomes a party to a deed of variation and, as a result, gives up a right to all or part of their inheritance, is not regarded as having made any transfer of value.

Deeds of variation may be used to create any type of trust or implement many of the other planning techniques described throughout this guide.

Deed of Variation Drawbacks

Variations made under a deed of variation effectively rewrite history and are treated as if they had been made by the deceased: *but not for Income Tax purposes!*

For Income Tax purposes, the original beneficiary (under the deceased's Will or laws of intestacy) is regarded as having made a transfer to the new beneficiary, or to any trust that receives property under the deed of variation. This could result in the settlements legislation applying where the new beneficiary is a minor child of the original beneficiary (see Section 11.10).

Where a deed of variation is used to make, or increase, charitable legacies, there are a few additional formalities that need to be observed. It is essential the charity (or trustees of a charitable trust in the case of a death before 6th April 2026) is notified of the existence of the deed. HMRC will look for evidence that the charity (or trustees) are aware assets or funds are being redirected to them under the deed. Copies of an exchange of letters between the parties involved should be sufficient for this purpose.

As explained in Section 3.6, there have been doubts over whether it is possible to use a deed of variation to increase charitable legacies in order to benefit from the reduced IHT rate. This may no longer be the case, so it will certainly be worth a try, but it is better to make the appropriate provisions in a Will.

Where property is passed to a new beneficiary under either a deed of variation, or a transfer out of a relevant property trust within two years of the settlor's death (Section 17.3), and the new beneficiary makes a PET of that same property shortly afterwards, there is a strong chance HMRC will apply the associated operations rules (Section 11.11). This would mean the deceased is treated as having left the property directly to the ultimate recipient which, in most cases, is likely to make it chargeable to IHT.

17.2 DISCLAIMERS

Under a simpler procedure, a beneficiary can disclaim their inheritance. The disclaimer must again be recorded in writing within two years of the death (preferably by way of deed) and must not be made for any consideration in money or money's worth. The disclaimed inheritance will generally fall into the residue of the estate and be dealt with accordingly. This procedure may be particularly useful where NRB legacies have been included in older Wills and the family decide it would be more sensible for the surviving spouse, as the residuary beneficiary, to receive the entire estate.

In addition to its simplicity, a disclaimer has the advantage that the disclaimed legacy is treated as passing directly from the deceased to the new beneficiary for Income Tax purposes. This is therefore a much better way to pass a legacy directly to the original beneficiary's minor child.

A disclaimer is not possible where the original beneficiary has received any benefit from their legacy since the deceased's death (e.g. by living in an inherited property). However, it will often remain possible to use a deed of variation to achieve the same result: for IHT purposes at least!

17.3 TRANSFERS OUT OF TRUSTS WITHIN TWO YEARS

Transfers of property placed into a relevant property trust on the death of the settlor that take place within two years of the settlor's death, are treated as if they were legacies made by the deceased directly. Such transfers are exempt from exit charges (Section 8.16).

Where the transferee is another trust, it will be treated as if it had been established under the deceased's Will. This provides scope to set up an immediate post-death interest, a bereaved minors' trust, or an 18 to 25 trust. In effect, this enables testators to create a discretionary trust under the terms of their Will that can be converted, as appropriate, within the two years following their death.

Once again, these provisions do not apply for Income Tax purposes. Hence, the relevant property trust will be liable for Income Tax on income received prior to the transfer. See also Section 17.1 regarding the risks of making a PET of the same property shortly after the transfer out of the trust.

Second Chances

Only one variation under the procedure in Section 17.1 is allowed in respect of any item of property. Similarly, only one transfer of any item of property can fall under the rules explained above. Nonetheless, it is possible for the same item of property to be subject to a deed of variation and later transferred out of a relevant property trust within the rules set out above (or vice versa). The variation and the transfer must both take place within two years of death to be effective for IHT purposes.

17.4 POST-MORTEM RELIEF

Where a beneficiary, or the deceased's personal representatives, sells certain types of inherited assets for less than their probate value, they may claim post-mortem relief for their effective loss. The relief decreases the value of the deceased's estate for IHT purposes and a refund of the IHT already paid may be claimed where appropriate.

The assets must not be sold to a connected person (Appendix A), and must be sold for a freely negotiated price, on arms' length terms, within a specified period after the deceased's death: twelve months for quoted shares, three years for land and buildings. Actual sale price must be used, there is no discount in respect of jointly held property.

The beneficiary must take account of all sales within the relevant period. Hence, when some inherited assets have also been sold at a profit, it is only the beneficiary's overall net loss on assets of that type that may be claimed. Furthermore, in the case of land and buildings, profits made on sales during the fourth year after the deceased's death must also be taken into account.

In effect, the values of all the inherited assets sold by the beneficiary within the specified period are adjusted to their sale price. This is to prevent 'cherry picking', i.e. only claiming for losses without taking account of profits. However, a form of cherry picking can still be achieved by leaving the relevant assets to a discretionary trust in the first instance and then appointing all loss-making assets to one beneficiary prior to sale, and within two years of the deceased's death. As explained in Section 17.3, the beneficiary is treated as if they had inherited these assets absolutely, thus enabling them to make the post-mortem relief claim.

A similar form of relief is available on assets subject to the related property rules: see Section 11.2.

Appendix A

Connected Persons

The definition of connected persons differs slightly from one area of UK tax law to another. Generally, however, an individual's connected persons include the following:

i) Their husband, wife, or civil partner
ii) The following relatives:
   - Mother, father or remoter ancestor
   - Son, daughter or remoter descendant
   - Brother or sister
iii) Relatives under (ii) above of the individual's spouse or civil partner
iv) Spouses or civil partners of the individual's relatives under (ii) above
v) Spouses or civil partners of an individual under (iii) above
vi) The individual's business partners
vii) Trusts where the individual is:
   - The settlor (the person who set up the trust or transferred property, other assets, or funds into it), or
   - A person connected (as defined in this appendix) with the settlor
viii) Companies under the control of the individual, either alone, or together with persons under (i) to (vii) above

Additionally, for the purposes of the pre-owned assets charge (Section 11.12), connected persons also include:

- Aunts and uncles
- Nephews and nieces
- Companies under the control of any of these relatives
- Trusts where any of these relatives are a beneficiary

Appendix B

Abbreviations Used in this Guide

AIM	Alternative Investment Market
APR	Agricultural Property Relief
AUV	Agricultural Use Value
BADR	Business Asset Disposal Relief
BPR	Business Property Relief
CASC	Community Amateur Sports Club
CGT	Capital Gains Tax
CPI	Consumer Prices Index
CT	Corporation Tax
DOTAS	Disclosure of Tax Avoidance Schemes
EEA	European Economic Area
FIC	Family Investment Company
FOTRA	Free of Tax to Residents Abroad
GAAR	General Anti-Abuse Rule
HMRC	HM Revenue and Customs
HP	Hire Purchase
HPRA	100% Relief Allowance
IHT	Inheritance Tax
ISA	Individual Savings Account
IVR	Investor's Relief
LLP	Limited Liability Partnership
Ltd	Limited (i.e. a limited company)
LSDBA	Lump Sum and Death Benefit Allowance
NRB	Nil Rate Band
NRB/TNRB	Total combined NRB and TNRB
ONS	Office for National Statistics
PET	Potentially Exempt Transfer
RNRB	Residence Nil Rate Band
RPI	Retail Prices Index
SDLT	Stamp Duty Land Tax
SIPP	Self-Invested Personal Pension
TNRB	Transferable Nil Rate Band
TTFAC	Transitional Tax-Free Amount Certificate
UK	United Kingdom of Great Britain and Northern Ireland

www.ingramcontent.com/pod-product-compliance
Lightning Source LLC
LaVergne TN
LVHW052044200926
848481LV00005B/1728

* 9 7 8 1 9 1 7 3 9 2 1 2 9 *